MENNO DUERKSEN'S
HISTORY OF THE
GREAT AMERICAN CLASSICS

Published by Amos Press Inc., 911 Vandemark Road, Sidney, Ohio 45365

Publisher of *Cars & Parts,*
(The Magazine Serving the Car Hobbyist)
and the *Collector Car Annual*

Introduction

Cars & Parts–March 15, 1964:

"Introducing...Mr. Menno Duerksen

Mr. Menno Duerksen is a newspaper reporter who is vitally interested in traffic, its problems, automobiles, and anything pertaining thereto. He is a former race car driver (kinda way back), and has spent much of his spare time tinkering around under the hood. He has collected many intersting facts concerning automobilia, and has agreed to write a series of articles for us. The series will follow no special format, each month the subject will differ. For his first article please turn to page 3, 'FREE WHEELING' by Menno Duerksen."

With this brief announcement, Menno Duerksen's column, "Free Wheeling," began. For the next 25 years, Menno would be a regular contributor to the magazine, bringing his unique insights, knowledge of automotive history, and a one-of-a-kind style of telling stories that would fascinate his readers.

Menno was born June 23, 1916, on a farm near Weatherford, Oklahoma. His grandparents and parents were Mennonites, and it was the custom among Mennonites to name the first born son in each family after Menno Simon, the "renegade" Catholic priest who broke away from the Catholic church to found the Mennonite religion.

It was in the spring of 1924, on a farm near Weatherford, that a Ford mechanic named Jake Kroeker was overhauling a Fordson tractor for the "man of the farm," while a red-headed eight-year-old boy dogged his footsteps. In fact, every time Jake went under that machine to fit another connecting rod, little "Red" was right under there with him. Not only watching every move with eyes big as saucers, but asking a million questions. The youngster asked so many questions, it's a wonder poor Jake didn't grab his heaviest wrench and chase his little tormentor away. But instead, Jake patiently answered every question, and by the time he had that old Fordson running, the little red-head had a pretty good picture of every part inside that Fordson engine etched in his brain.

That incident might be as good as any to "date" the time when a youngster named Menno Duerksen became interested in internal combustion engines. In fact, even before that young Menno had already built several little toy tractors, using old cast off timing gears from Model T Ford engines as "drive wheels." It was the beginning of a "love affair" with motors that would continue for more than 50 years.

At age 14, while attending high school in Weatherford, Duerksen began work as an "apprentice" in an automotive machine shop where the boss, Charlie Kendall, was one of those old-fashioned perfectionists who insisted that the word "can't" didn't belong in the English language. When Kendall told young Duerksen he wanted some parts cleaned, that meant he wanted to be able to wipe a white hankerchief over those parts without getting a smudge. The nearest Duerksen ever came to being "fired," was when he used a chisel on a stubborn rusted bolt that refused to budge for a wrench.

Duerksen's other "love affair" at this time was reading. He read as many as six books a week, and somehow from this came the dream of being a writer. For a long time, it was a toss-up and a battle going on in his mind—newspaperman or mechanic? In the end, the newspaper profession got him. In the meantime, there was a big economic depression when newspaper jobs just weren't available, especially for green country boys. It was during that time that Duerksen spent more years in machine shops, body shops, and auto repair shops. He also did a bit of dirt track racing in a Studebaker President Eight powered half mile sprint car.

In between, he cruised about the country on barnstorming trips, trying to break into the newspaper profession. He finally made it in Memphis, Tennessee, just on the eve of World War II, as jobs began to open up a bit.

As the guns of the war began booming, new opportunities and challenges appeared, at home and abroad. Duerksen wanted to see the war in Europe, but the Army turned him down because of a childhood ear infection which left him deaf in one ear. He finally managed to wangle a job with the Office of War information, the U.S. Government's official wartime propaganda service, and reached Europe just before the war ended.

As the war ended and the propaganda service cranked down, Duerksen switched to the United Nations Relief and Rehabilitation Administration in Europe on a public relations job. Part of his job was escorting visiting congressmen, senators, and VIPS around the refugee camps to show them how the world's relief money was being spent. One of those VIPs happended to be Mrs. Eleanor Roosevelt. "That woman had so much energy, she wore us out just trying to keep up with her," Duerksen remembers.

In 1946, Duerksen managed to talk his way into a job with United Press in Germany, and spent the next six years covering the news in Germany, Turkey, Palestine, Switzerland, England. "I missed the shooting part of the war in Europe, but I made up for it in Palestine. It's a wonder I ever got out of that place alive," he remembers of that experience.

Among the "big stories" he helped cover during this time was the Nuremberg War Crimes trials, a "scoop" on the execution of the convicted war criminals, writing an award winning story on the black market in Germany, covering the "Truman Doctorine" military aid program to Turkey, which helped that country stand up to Stalin, and the war of independence in Palestine which brought the creation of the State of Israel.

Meantime, Duerksen had married a German girl in Europe, and decided to come home in 1951 to start the education of a young son who turned out to be retarded. "Home" in this case was now Memphis where he started his newspaper career: he stayed on that job with the Memphis Press-Scimitar until July of 1978. He had 37 years of newspaper work to his credit.

But during all this time Duerksen had never lost his interest in motors and motor cars. In Europe, he had rescued an old worn out 1936 Open cabriolet and nursed her back to a reasonable enough state of health that he was able to drive her over the Swiss alps, through Italy, and load her aboard ship for Turkey on his assignment there. "One of the toughest trips I took in that old car was to drive her up to the Russian border on the Black Sea. I knocked a muffler off on that trip, but we got back home to Istanbul," Duerksen remembers. Once, he also drove the Opel to the Bulgarian border where he interviewed Bulgarian and Romanian refugees who had sneaked across the communist guarded borders.

It was while working for the Press-Scimitar, in the spring of 1964, that he was invited to start writing a monthly motor car column for *Cars & Parts,* then being published in Memphis. He has been with *Cars & Parts* ever since.

Menno's "Free Wheeling" column has been the single most popular editorial feature of *Cars & Parts* over the years. Menno has earned many awards as well as the respect and admiration of hundreds of thousands of readers. During his quarter century as a published automotive historian, Menno Duerksen has written numerous "classics" of his own. Eight of his personal favorites are presented in this special anniversary collector's edition of *Menno Duerksen's History of the Great American Classics.*

Contents

Introduction.. iii

Chapter I: The STUTZ... 1

Chapter II: The DUESENBERG.. 41

Chapter III: The FRANKLIN 81

Chapter IV: The KISSEL KAR 121

Chapter V: The PACKARD 139

Chapter VI: The STEARNS-KNIGHT 161

Chapter VII: The DOBLE 193

Chapter VIII: The DORRIS... 205

Index.. 213

I
STUTZ

The beginning: 1897-1911

In 1911, the first Stutz placed " . . . in the money in the gruelling 500-mile race at Indianapolis." A year later, the factory began to manufacture cars for the public.

Stutz, the car with guts! America could live with a slogan like that today. In the 1911-1920 period, when Stutz machines were earning their spurs as the "Bearcat" breed of car, it might have been slightly out of taste — especially in parlor conversation, in front of the ladies—to describe a car as "gutsy."

So Harry C. Stutz and his compatriots had to make do with something a bit more on the tame side: "The car that made good in a day."

A man could have argued that this slogan wasn't quite true. Since it was gleaned from the first performance of the first Stutz in the first of the famed Indy 500 races, in 1911, it should have signified that the Stutz won.

Actually, the car came in 11th — not even quite good enough to put it in the lineup of the 10 money winners. Why crow about that?

But Stutz and his people did crow because, they said, they had never expected it to win. They could boast because the car had barely been completed in time for the race, in a short five-week period, and had never had a chance to be thoroughly tested or have the bugs worked out. In spite of all that, it completed the 500-mile race without a single breakdown, or even a mechanical adjustment. What stops it had made, 11 of them, had been for tires and fuel. If those pesky tires had been a bit more durable, the showing would have been much better.

Such a performance, Stutz decided, had earned him the right to boast that his brand new creation had, indeed, "made good."

One thing is certain: there would be a lot of other races in the future for Stutz cars, and they would make a lot of history. As time went on, they would even earn a goodly share of that so-called "mystique" which seemed to hover over certain select makes of motor cars—the kind of allure that would make folks perk their ears when hearing the name "Stutz."

As for Indy, fate tantalized Stutz just as it had Fred Duesenberg, allowing Stutz to come close, but never quite make it to the winner's circle.

The very next year, in the second running of the big 500, a Stutz made a much better showing, with a fourth-place finish. In 1915 Gil Anderson wheeled a Stutz into third place.

Year after year they fought the good fight, clawing their way into the money finishes. In 1919 a Stutz finished second. There were times when it was clear that Stutz had the fastest and toughest cars on the track, but couldn't keep tires under them.

Some historians credited Stutz with a win at Indy, in 1923, but that was after Harry Stutz had severed his connections with the Stutz Motor Car Co., and bought himself a couple of Miller-powered racers, which he dubbed the H.C.S. Specials (H.C.S. for Harry C. Stutz). Tommy Milton wheeled one of them into the winner's circle—but you couldn't quite call it a Stutz win.

Perhaps the reason Duesenberg finally made it to the coveted winner's circle, in 1924, was because Fred Duesenberg stuck with his mania to win just a bit longer than Stutz did.

Meanwhile, Stutz cars would be winning plenty of glory on other tracks around the country. Some of them, in their day, were just about as prestigious as the Indianapolis Speedway—Elgin, the Chicago 500, and Sheepshead Bay, where a Stutz set a world speed record.

That would be the story during the years when Harry C. himself was at the helm, designing and building the cars. It's also the story of the famed Stutz Bearcat, one of the most glamorous sports cars of all time.

But the Stutz story must be divided into two eras: the Harry C. Stutz period, and the Fred Moscovics period. The Stutz was a car with one name, but two heroes—for Moscovics would do almost as much for Stutz as Harry himself, but at a later date when the cars would become the creations of the man from Hungary, but

continue to carry the Stutz name.

That would be a time when Stutz would claim the stock car championship of America, produce a throat-gripping performance at Le Mans in France, and engage in a gripping one-on-one duel with a Hispano-Suiza on the Indy track, a story that would become almost a legend and the subject of arguments for years.

There would come a time, in the early 1930s, when a magnificent straight eight engine Stutz, with double overhead cams and four valves per cylinder, would become one of the hottest hunks of machinery being made in this country, or any country—second, perhaps, only to a mighty machine called Duesenberg.

The Harry C. Stutz story is the kind of story a motor-loving man can get his teeth into, another of the all-American sagas of the country boy touched with that magic gift of mechanical genius at birth — the gift of making things, and making them go; of creating wheels, gears, pistons, and cams in shapes and designs just a bit different and a bit better.

The boy would become a man with the dream of making motor cars of his own, just a bit better, and tougher, than they had ever been made before—and darned near doing it—with those cars with guts.

Since all stories must have a start, make it Ansonia, Ohio, near Dayton, on September 12, 1876. The scene: the farm home of a Pennsylvania Dutch couple, Henry J. and Elizabeth Stutz. The event: the birth of a baby boy, to be christened Harry C. Stutz.

At the beginning, there was the familiar routine of a youngster learning the how and why of growing plants and animals. But then, so quickly, came the revelation of the great gift of understanding the wheels and gears of farm machinery. Neighbors would remember a backyard at the Stutz farm, cluttered with farm machines brought to the talented Stutz kid who knew how to fix them.

For formal education, young Harry made do with the usual grade school routine—to which, in another old time American tradition, he added correspondence school courses to improve the mechanics end of it.

Before he had completed his teen years, he went to nearby Dayton, where

The Stutz eagle-winged logo is well-known among car collectors.

he obtained jobs with the Davis Sewing Machine Co. and the National Cash Register Co. The next move was to acquire a turning lathe, the first step toward operating a repair shop of his own. Then Harry designed and began building one-cylinder pump engines, and installed one of these engines in a discarded horse buggy.

It happened in 1897, and Stutz was barely 21. He had built his first motor car only a year after Henry Ford had built his first "quadricycle." His neighbors, who flocked to gape at the new contraption, had to agree it ran quite well, despite the farm machinery origins of some of the parts.

People who knew young Harry well said he was intelligent enough to realize that that first crude machine was not good enough to put on the market—but the dream had been born.

By this time Harry was certain his future was in the infant motor car industry, then aborning. His next step was a natural, to move to Indianapolis, then rivaling Michigan as the home of the motor car industry.

Before he left Dayton, Harry went ice skating one day and met a blue-eyed 18-year-old who seemed a natural for a

twosome. Clara Deitz had entered his life. Two years later it became a threesome, with a baby named Emma Belle.

In Indianapolis Harry quickly held a succession of jobs. In truth, it was his way of acquiring an education in his chosen field—motor cars. One job was with the Lindsay Russell Axle Co., where he learned how to make axles and transmissions for early day automobiles. That's where he also cooked up the ideas for what would one day become a patented combination rear axle and transmission. At the J. & G. Tire Co., he learned about tires and wheels. The Schebler Carburetor Co., perhaps the country's top maker of practical carburetors, taught the young Stutz all about carburetor systems.

By 1905 came one of the most fateful moves of all. He now felt he was ready to design that first marketable motor car—and two men who had made their fortunes in the lumber industry, V.A. Longaker and D.S. Menasco, decided to take a flyer in the new motor car industry. Patriotic men, they decided to call it the American Motor Car Co.

When they set about to look for an engineer to design their new machine, there was brilliant young Harry Stutz, who had already built a car and had been busy learning all about motors, transmissions, axles, tires, wheels and carburetors. This lean, trim, bright-eyed young man had also picked up that philosophy of work so dear to the American heart—that a man can do anything if he tries hard enough.

Thus was born the first motor car to be designed by Harry Stutz for the marketplace. The new American would have a 4⁹⁄₁₆ x 5-inch engine, rated at 35-40 hp. Weighing 2,300 pounds, with a "King of Belgium" body, the car was advertised to be capable of 50 miles per hour. Stutz apparently went to great lengths to make sure his new creation would be as quiet as possible, for the advertising slogan used for the debut of the new machine was, "No Noise but the Wind"—stealing a march on the Rolls-Royce, perhaps.

Now one must discuss one of the most radically designed motor cars of its day, the American Underslung. In this startling design, which was later copied by several other makes of cars, the axles were mounted above—rather than below—the frame. In effect, the frame was simply turned upside down.

By using extra large wheels, one could still retain sufficient road clearance and come up with such a low center of gravity that the car would, folks said, outcorner anything on wheels. It was a design simply made for sports cars. It was the second design of cars introduced by the American Motor Car Co., near the end of 1906, and would continue in production, virtually unchanged in design, until 1920.

Most Stutz historians have credited Harry Stutz with this design, but at least one historian, Walter Seeley, of Jamestown, N.Y., who spent years of painstaking research into the history of the unique machine, had a different version. In a story published in the July-August, 1972, issue of *Antique Automobile,* Seeley wrote that the famed underslung design was the work of Fred I. Tone, the former chief engineer for the Marion Motor Car Co., who came to American in that capacity when Stutz went to Marion in 1906.

There seems to be little in the record to explain this coincidental switch: Tone from Marion to American, and Stutz from American to Marion, almost simultaneously.

In any case, according to the Seeley version of the story, it was Tone, in his new job at American, who happened to spot some new motor car frames from the A.O. Smith Co. being unloaded, upside down, at the American plant. The sight of the upside down frames clicked a switch on in Tone's brain: "Why not mount them that way on the car?" to get that low center of gravity and make possible a virtually straight driveshaft.

Seeley told this writer that he credited Tone, rather than Stutz, with the underslung design after interviewing F.F. Tone, the son of the engineer, and Ralph R. Teetor, of the once famed Teetor-Hartley engine making firm, which supplied engines for the early American cars. Teetor was closely associated with the American company at this period of its history.

"I was well aware of the fact that Stutz had been credited with this underslung design when I wrote my article," said Seeley. "When we published the Tone version, I expected a lot of static but strangely enough not a single person has challenged my version. I am convinced that Tone was responsible for this design."

Such a switch in history does not necessarily detract from the Harry Stutz story, for the real Stutz legend rests—not on the American Underslung nor on the Marion — but on the Stutz cars themselves, most especially that "gutsy" Bearcat, which has just about become a legend of its own.

Meanwhile, Stutz remained at Marion from 1906 to 1910, the longest period, to date, that he had remained on one job. He started as engineer and ended up as superintendent of the works.

One of the first changes he made at Marion was to switch from an air-cooled powerplant to a conventional water-cooled engine. The car he was credited with designing was known as the Marion Flyer. It was advertised as the car which incorporated every important engineering feature known to the industry at that time—but not an underslung frame.

It was also at Marion that Stutz designed a limited production sports car version called the Marion Bobcat — a foretaste of the Bearcat to come?

Some surviving records indicate that Stutz actually drove Marion cars of the Bobcat design in several local races. The records indicate that he wrecked a car in one race and that a mechanical failure put one out of another race.

It was also at Marion that Stutz became acquainted with a Swedish mechanic and test driver named Gil Anderson, and persuaded the big Swede to try his hand at race driving. It was another touch of fate, for it was Gil Anderson who reaped many of the top glory laurels for Stutz in years to come.

Harry Stutz was doing other things besides building motor cars. Always attracted to the "good things of life," he was interested in classical music — Hoffman's "Barcarole" was one of his favorites. He began trap shooting and became so skilled at it that folks became used to the idea of seeing Harry Stutz walk off with first place trophies in both local and national competitions. He was a fan of baseball and motor boat racing. He be-

4

Harry C. Stutz as he appeared at age 21, the year he made his first motor car. Since the year was 1897, that meant he made his first car only one year later than Henry Ford made his first "quadricycle."

came an avid hunter, going on hunting trips to places like Wyoming and Florida. It's said he also liked good food and ate heartily, but remained trim because of his "perpetual motion" level of activity.

But Stutz also had a stubborn streak—coupled, perhaps, with a bit of a temper, which occasionally got him into trouble. Getting fired from the Marion Motor Car Co. is a good example, although that might not have been such a bad thing, after all, since it launched him into making cars bearing his own name.

It was in 1910, the story goes, when that little "blow up" came. John North Willys, a fast-moving whirlwind of a motor car producer, had acquired control of Marion, and ordered that a single accounting system be installed in all plants controlled by the Willys-Overland Co.

When Willys-Overland accountants arrived at Marion to install the new system, they were told by Harry C. Stutz, manager of the works, that nobody would install a new system as long as he, Stutz, remained in charge.

Wallace T. Miller, one of the accountants involved, told the story in the

Horseless Carriage Gazette for July-August, 1970. When Miller reported back to his boss, Walter Stewart, W-O treasurer, about the impasse with Stutz, Stewart himself came to the Marion plant and repeated the orders for the new accounting system.

Stutz was quoted as saying, "I'll take my dinner pail and walk out of here before I'll let you do that."

Whereupon Stewart told Miller to hand Stutz his paycheck and let him "walk."

Stutz walked—into a destiny of his own.

It turned out to be a costly firing, Miller reported, for Stutz had been building the Marion Flyers largely without blueprints. The "prints" and designs were mostly in Stutz' head. After Stutz had taken his "walk," W-O management was forced to hire a crew of draftsmen to reduce the Marion parts to paper.

Perhaps Stutz never revealed why he was so stubborn about an accounting system ordered by the people who owned the plant, and had every right to install it. But Stutz may have been just about ready to make his next move anyway, and used the little ruckus as an excuse. It did prove that Stutz could be a stubborn cookie when he wished to be —a characteristic that could be an asset at times, like when making race cars.

There is little doubt but that the big dream in Stutz' mind, perhaps for a long time, had been to make a motor car of his own: a Stutz.

One of the men Stutz had met while at Marion was Henry Campbell, one of the financial backers of the company before the W-O takeover. He was a man of means with whom Stutz had become friends.

It was to Campbell that Stutz now turned with his plan to make a car of his own. Campbell agreed to help raise the money to finance the project. Stutz had probably acquired a bit of money of his own by this time.

But before starting on the new project, Stutz made a quick sweep through Europe, most particularly the motor car making plants of Germany, France, England, Holland and Belgium. He absorbed any usable ideas about design, metallurgy and engineering.

Back home Stutz discovered that the management of the new Indianapolis Speedway, which had been built in 1909 and which had already been the scene of several race meets, had made an announcement that was sending shock waves, of sorts, through American motor car racing circles.

Motor racing had already gotten a grip on the soaring imaginations of American motor car lovers. Races and racetracks were cropping up everywhere but, until now, most races had been relatively short, running 5, 10, or 25 miles and, occasionally, stretching to 50 miles. If someone went really wild, perhaps a 100-miler would be staged. Few cars of the day could run at top speed for longer than that.

Now came the announcement from Indy Speedway management that for May 30, 1911, Memorial Day, they would stage a 500-miler. It set off a flurry of activity in the motor racing world, and the motor car industry itself. It had already become largely axiomatic that if you wanted to sell motor cars, you had to prove they would stand up on the racetracks.

Nobody knew it then, but that 500-mile race was to become one of the great racing events of America, and the world, for many decades to come.

Harry C. Stutz was also swept up by the excitement of it all. What if he built and designed his first motor car — and then entered the very first one, the prototype, in this big race about to come off? Audacity par excellence!

How could you know that a new car, without a lot of testing and running, could make such a grueling run?

It was a gamble Harry Stutz was willing to take. As he explained to Campbell, they had nothing to lose. If they failed, they would have given their new car a road test that could not be equaled. If they succeeded, it would mean thousands of dollars of free advertising for a brand new name in the industry.

Several reputable Stutz historians have suggested that Stutz was not so bold as to believe he could win the race. The fact that several of the best race cars from Europe would be represented would virtually preclude that. It was acknowledged, if somewhat reluctantly, that Europe was a few years ahead of America at this time in the design and building of motor cars, including race cars.

Harry's plan was to build a car tough enough to run the 500 miles and perhaps finish as high as 10th place—at least that is the way Stutz has been quoted. He put the number 10 on his car to emphasize that goal, it was suggested.

The new Stutz plant was being constructed at Tenth and Capitol in Indianapolis, with equipment being installed for the production of 500 cars per year. But the plant, and the assembly line, were not even in place yet — and it was only a couple of months before that big date: May 30.

Stutz and his men got busy, virtually putting the new car together by hand. Stutz Number One was to be exactly what would come off the assembly line later.

Harry Stutz was enough of a realist to know that, for such a small operation, he could not design and build an engine of his own. On the other hand, he desperately wanted to avoid the stigma of building an "assembled car." He also had his own design of that patented combination rear axle-transmission unit, but on the engine he had little choice.

By this time he had acquired enough knowledge in the building of motor cars to know that even if he did not come up with startling innovations — like the American Underslung, for example—the fine points of chassis design made so much difference in the handling of a car. That design, with sturdy, long leafed springs, he carefully engineered himself.

As for the engine, the Wisconsin Motor Manufacturing Co. had, by this time, acquired a reputation for making some of the toughest, most reliable motor car engines of the day. Stutz worked with Wisconsin engineers for the design he wanted, a four-cylinder T-head, 4¾ x 5½, for 390 cid. A T-head would develop just about as much power as an overhead.

In five weeks' time they put the machine together. It went directly to the Indy track, where Stutz had persuaded his friend, Gil Anderson, to drive it.

After a good shake-down cruise on the track, Anderson was amazed at how well-built the machine was. "She looks like she can stay," he said, and added, "I'll make her go."

The first Stutz was ready to challenge the best.

The glory years of the Stutz racers: 1911-1915

It's tough when a pesky funnel, the kind you pour gasoline through, is blamed for the loss of a big race — especially when the race is the first Indy 500 in 1911.

And there were all those flat tires, too. Tires have been getting the blame forever, it seems. There has been hardly a car race since 1895 in which at least one of the drivers hasn't been able to claim, with a perfectly clear conscience, that if his tires had just stayed whole he would have won the race.

As for the funnels, not even Harry C. Stutz blamed them for the comparatively lousy showing of 11th place for the first Stutz ever built in the first Indy 500 ever run. Harry was busy trying to prove that the 11th place showing wasn't so bad after all— to turn it into something his ad men could brag about in promoting the new Stutz cars he was getting ready to build.

It was a reporter for The Horseless Age, covering the race, who noticed that the little Stutz seemed to be spending an ungodly amount of time in the pits. When he looked closer, he saw it was because the funnel spouts had to be offset to fit the sloping sides of the boat-tail containing the fuel tanks.

When Gil Anderson came wheeling into the pits for his tires and fuel, the reporter noticed, the pitmen almost invariably shoved the funnels in wrong. By the time they got them straightened out, the Stutz had spent a lot of time stuck in the pits, when it should have been out on the track chasing those big guys up front.

The tires involved another factor — something called "unsprung weight." That term probably hadn't been invented in 1911—but if it had, few people, including those making race cars, knew much about it or realized how vital it was when trying to keep tires under a race car.

Even before he cranked up to build Stutz motor cars, Harry C. had designed and patented what would come to be called a "transaxle," a combination transmission and differential. It was mounted, of course, on the rear axle.

It was a good design, worked well and would take a lot of beating. Several makes of cars, other than Stutz, used it for years — and the tires could handle it pretty well, until you went to the races.

Harry went to the races as soon as he had his first car finished, and he raced himself right into a horrendous run of shredded tires.

He probably didn't realize that at least part of the tire shredding was due to the extra weight the rear axle was carrying. The transmission gears which, in most cars, were mounted up front, were heavy and Stutz likely didn't realize that he would have made a better showing if he had had a lighter axle.

Harry probably knew about it before he died. The Duesenberg brothers certainly did—and Harry probably had a twinge of regret that he had been so stubbornly proud of his transaxle.

But there was another reason why Stutz couldn't win at Indy that year — the size of the cars. Every car which nailed down one of the first 10 spots had a bigger engine than the 390 cubic inch T-head Stutz. The winning car, a Marmon Wasp, had 447 cubic inches and carried only one man, plus a rear view mirror. All the other cars carried two men, one of whom could look back if he had to.

The next three top-placing cars had engines ranging from 544 to 589 inches. It was the age of the monsters, the age when race car designers believed that you won races by smashing your way to the front with sheer size and power. For a few years they got away with it, until men like the Duesenbergs, Porter (Mercer), Miller and even Stutz showed them another way to go.

In fact, the tough, gutsy little Stutz cars would reap a golden harvest of glory in years to come, transaxle or no. They would go all the way to the top as the winningest cars in America, even without a win at Indy.

Almost as soon as the thunder of motors died away after that first fateful race at Indy, Harry C. Stutz and his new plant in Indianapolis began building passen-

The famous Stutz White Squadron of racers claimed numerous race victories and speed records in the 1915 season.

ger cars for the public. All of the cars used motors and chassis virtually identical to the first stripped-down machine Harry and Gil Anderson had taken to the big race.

Stutz cars were a success from the start. Maybe it was because Stutz cars kept on going to the races, and started winning.

Between May 30, 1911, and July 7, 1913, Stutz cars were entered in at least 39 races and won 29 of them—and the real glory was still to come.

Those 39 races included the Indy races for 1912 and 1913. In 1912 a Stutz took fifth place, and another wheeled across in the seventh spot. Once again, the winning cars had much bigger engines.

In 1913 a Stutz made it all the way up to third place. The winning car, a French Peugeot, had 444 cubic inches.

Then came 1914, a year of glory for Stutz at Indy, even though the record books show that the best a Stutz could do was fifth place. To explain: when the famed Indy 500 was inaugurated in 1911, it was, for all practical purposes, an all-American show. Virtually all of the racers were big bore American cars, and the big Americans won. For 1912 the picture remained much the same. In 1913, although the French Peugeot won, most of the cars in the race were American and they took most of the top places.

By 1914, however, the picture had changed. It was no secret that the Europeans, up to this stage of the game, had been ahead of America in the development of race cars and passenger cars. As early as 1912, Peugeot had developed an overhead cam engine for its race cars, a design that would be widely copied and would dominate racing for 25 years. But an obscure race at a place called Indianapolis? On a 2½-mile oval? The Europeans liked their car racing in road race fashion. Indianapolis was just a hick, corn country race by comparison.

Word about the Indy race had trickled into Europe by 1914. Perhaps what really roused their interest was word about the big money paid to winners. "Let's go steal their bacon," the Europeans said. The foreigners began to show up in Indianapolis. The invasion was on.

The Americans knew they were in trouble — and, when it was over, the scoreboard showed it. Delage, Peugeot, Delage, Peugeot: the first four places. And then, in fifth place, was a car called Stutz, driven by none other than Barney Oldfield.

Who says it is not a good measure of glory when you've got the fastest and toughest car made in America? To put it another way, if the race had been restricted to American cars, the Stutz would have won. In fact the speed of the fifth-place Stutz, 78.5 mph, would easily have won at Indy in 1913.

Harry Stutz had been refining the old T-head concept until he was able to travel with the best of them. Fred Duesenberg had done much the same thing with his walking beam concept. But Harry Stutz was no fool, either. He could see the handwriting on the wall. It spelled "overhead cam."

Ray Harroun, the engineer who drove his own creation, the Marmon Wasp, to victory at Indy in 1911, was now the designer for the Maxwell racing team. He had gone at least part way to meeting the foreign competition by building four-cylinder, overhead cam engines. But he didn't have enough valves, and those valves were not inclined. The Maxwell cars were fast, but not quite as fast as the Europeans.

Now it was Harry C. Stutz' turn. For 1915 he had his own version of the hot Peugeot motor. He went whole hog with four cylinders and 16 valves, twin overhead cams and inclined valves for a true hemi-head, plus all the quality and durability he had been learning about so painfully over the years.

One factor that he had to take into consideration was that the American Auto Club, sponsor of the top American races, including Indy, had chopped its size limit to 300 cubic inches. The day of the big bore monsters was gone. The new Stutz, with a bore of 3.8 x 6.46 stroke, would displace 295 cubic inches, yet it would whip out 130 bhp.

With this new engine performing flawlessly, Stutz won his measure of glory at Indy: not the big win, but glory nonetheless.

It started with the qualifying rounds. To eliminate the "clunkers," Speedway officials had decreed that each car, to qualify, must run at least two consecutive laps at 80 miles per hour, or more. In one stroke, that eliminated 18 of the 40 cars.

The Maxwell team, with the improved overhead cam design, qualified at 82 to 85 mph. The Duesenbergs qualified at 82 to 90. Then came the Peugeots. Bob Burman, an American driver, shot the speed up to 92.4 mph. The great Dario Resta pushed it all the way to 98.5.

Could anybody top that? It was a new record. Barney Oldfield, with a 16-valve Sunbeam (British), tried but failed. Then came Ralph DePalma, another American great, in a Peugeot. He managed to squeeze it up to 98.6. Certainly, nobody could top that.

Stutz was still to come. Gil Anderson and Earl Cooper, the old faithfuls, came in with 96.4 and 96.7 mph — sensational, if it had not been for the Peugeots. Stutz had only one ace left up his sleeve, a new Stutz driver named Howdy Wilcox. Stutz asked Wilcox if he could make it 99. Howdy said he would try.

It was a great moment of truth. Wilcox wheeled his white Stutz out onto the track and the gutsy engine began to whine. There came a white streak and, when it was over, Wilcox had the pole. He had squeezed it to 98.8 mph.

At long last Harry C. Stutz had the fastest car at Indy. But could it win?

As the race started it was Resta, in his Peugeot, who shot to the front. By the middle of the second lap, Wilcox had passed him. It was too good to be true. Wilcox was running well in first place when a valve spring broke.

Now it was up to the old faithfuls, Cooper and Anderson — but it was tires that ruined their day. The cars clearly showed they were masters of the pack, able to stay with anything on the track, but every time they cranked the revs up high enough to pass the leaders, the tires would go. It was tires, tires, tires and pit stops galore.

To Harry C. Stutz, standing on the sidelines, it was a gut-ripping experience. Knowing he had created the cars which could win at Indy, he was being robbed of his victory by the melting tires. In the end it was the great DePalma, in a Mercedes, who took the checkered flag. Resta, with his Peugeot, took second. The speedy Stutz team had to make do with third and fourth, a remarkably good showing considering the tire problems.

As for Harry, he was so frustrated and depressed by it all that friends said he was considering retiring from the racing game. If only somebody could have told him about the unsprung weight formula, and the fact that it was his beloved transaxle that was largely responsible for his tire problem.

In the end, it was only his knowledge that he had the fastest cars he had ever built, perhaps the fastest race cars in the world, that made him keep on trying. Even in defeat, the American cars had reached a new pinnacle. The tire people were promising better shoes.

The decision not to quit was a fateful one, for it would bring to Stutz the most brilliant glory of his entire racing career — but not until after more frustration, sweat and tears.

The next scene of battle was Chicago, where a great new two-mile board track had been built. When Cooper wheeled his Stutz out onto the amazing oval for the first time, he found he was on a track the likes of which no race driver had seen before. It was so perfectly banked a driver could open a car up and hold it there, his speed limited only by the limits of his engine. When Cooper opened up the white Stutz, he started turning speeds that made the glorious runs at Indy seem slow. A new track record of 109.09 mph was set. It was going to be one of the fastest races ever run—if not the fastest.

At the beginning of the race, it truly seemed that way. Harry C., determined to win even if it cost him his car, ordered his drivers to set a blistering pace. They did, whipping around the oval at 105 to 108 mph.

But the pace was too hot. Running flat out at more than 100 mph, Wilcox blew a piston. It was one of the few times a Stutz would drop out due to a serious engine failure. For the other Stutz cars, it was tires. The old story: Stutz had to be satisfied with fourth and fifth place.

But it is amazing how much of a beating the human spirit can take, and come back for more after a few new days have dawned, easing the pain of defeat.

When the Chicago track officials, a few weeks later, announced a special 100-mile race on that "fastest track in the world," there were Stutz and his White Squadron, ready to try once more.

Once again, the result was bitter disappointment. With less than 20 miles to go, and leading the race, Cooper's right rear tire blew. Victory was so near.

But Stutz and his men would taste victory in full measure at Elgin, Illinois, home of the famed Elgin road races.

Perhaps one of the things that prompted Stutz to try once more was the

This 1914 Stutz Bearcat was on display at the AACA Fall Meet at Hershey, PA, October, 1982. The Westinghouse air shock absorbers on the front were not Stutz items, and these accessories were apparently added later.

fact that at Elgin they would be running on dirt — and smooth dirt, at that — no tire-slaughtering hard surface. The events were two 301-milers, back to back: the Chicago Auto Club Cup race on Friday, August 20, and the famed Elgin National Trophy race on Saturday.

For once Stutz had made the right decision. This time the tires held—so well, in fact, that Anderson was able to run both races without a pit stop for tires. Cooper ran both races with a single stop for tires. It was a clean sweep: Cooper-Anderson, one-two, in the Chicago Cup race and Anderson-Cooper, one-two, in the Elgin National.

Perhaps most amazing of all was that Anderson ran the last 100 miles of the Friday race on three cylinders, with a broken valve spring—but still managed to come in second.

In any case it was a golden triumph, the greatest triumph to date, for the White Squadron. Harry C. Stutz could smile once more. And there was more glory in the wind.

It had been the Indy track officials who had flung the great challenge in 1911, when they announced the first 500-mile race, at a time when 500 miles at top speed seemed impossible. But by 1915, the 500-milers had caught on.

The Twin Cities, St. Paul and Minneapolis, had teamed up to build what was billed as the greatest racetrack in the world: a giant, two-mile oval with a concrete surface instead of boards. On this track, the promoters announced, another 500-miler would be run, and a purse of $50,000 offered — big money, indeed. Perhaps the backers had visions of pulling a march on Indy. Be that as it may, with that pot of gold dangling in front of their eyes, race drivers considered September 4 a must at the Twin Cities.

At first glance the new concrete oval seemed perfect. New speed records were predicted. But only after wheeling their mounts out onto the track and revving them to speed did the drivers find that the concrete-laying engineers had done a less than perfect job. At high speed, the surface seemed to have one moon crater after another. At 100 mph, the craters were so severe they threatened to wreck the sturdiest of race cars. Some

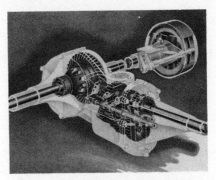

Harry C. Stutz developed and patented what would come to be called a "transaxle," a combination transmission and differential before the first Stutz was built.

drivers openly predicted that no car, or driver, could survive 500 miles on that track.

Unless, perhaps, the car happened to carry a name like Stutz, and the drivers happened to be men like Anderson and Cooper, the two faithful Stutz warriors.

The two drivers immediately reported their findings of "rough going" to their boss. But Harry, confident that his cars were as tough as anything the competition had to offer — maybe tougher —decided that if the murderous track was going to tear the cars up, he wanted to see whose cars would rip apart first. He told his men to try.

When the race started, it seemed that the drivers were trying to kill themselves. They roared around the cratered track at speeds of 100 to 110 miles per hour, with cars and drivers being jolted mercilessly.

Resta and Burman, both in Peugeots, made the early challenge, setting a blistering pace. Accepting the challenge were Cooper and Anderson, pushing hard. Then the whole thing began to unravel, for everybody except the Stutz team.

Pushed to his limit, Burman drove his Peugeot so hard it threw a rod. When the two white Stutz cars began pushing Resta, the vibration broke an engine stud and his oil pump failed. The devilish track began taking a terrible toll.

Ralph Mulford, in a Duesenberg, had to quit when his frame broke. Eddie O'Donnel, also in a Duesenberg, went out when a radius rod broke. Barney Oldfield, in a Delage, was forced out when all four of his shock absorbers were chewed to bits. Ralph DePalma, in a Mercedes, lasted 180 miles when things let go on his car.

Now, with all the major competitors out of the race, the two unshatterable Stutz machines roared on, performing flawlessly and defying the murderous track to tear them up. It couldn't.

With no competition remaining to challenge them, Stutz ordered his two drivers to cross the finish line side by side, and share the honors. They did, and some journals of the day called it a tie — but the judges must have spotted the nose of Cooper's Stutz just inches ahead of Anderson's, so the record books call it a Cooper win.

It didn't matter. The Stutz triumph was complete. The victory was made sweeter by the knowledge that the superb Stutz machines had turned out to be the toughest racing machines in the world. Perhaps most amazing of all was the fact that Cooper and Anderson had averaged better than 86 mph for the entire 500 miles on the bone-shattering track.

There would be one more day of triumph for Stutz that year. It came in the 350-mile Astor Cup race at Sheepshead Bay in New York, where the race teams found another glass-smooth board track that permitted speeds limited only by the capacity of an engine to rev. It was like the great Chicago oval, only better.

At first glance the drivers had thought this track was not quite a match for the Chicago oval, so it had to be a surprise when they tried it and the clock began showing speeds up to 110 mph.

Once again the competition was tough. All the top drivers were there, with cars like Peugeot, Delage, Mercedes and Sunbeam.

At the beginning it was Dario Resta, one of the best, who took the lead in his Peugeot. Well out in front, he had reason to believe everything was going his way until he suddenly became aware of two white ghosts creeping up on his tail. The Stutzes were howling.

Resta drove so fast to ward off the challenge that, at 58 miles, a tire went and the Anderson Stutz wheeled into the lead.

Back on the track, Resta drove his car

so mercilessly to retake the lead that he burned a rod, swiftly ending his challenge. Eddie Rickenbacker, in one of the hot new Maxwells, mounted a challenge of his own and also burned a rod.

After that it was a see-saw battle. One after another Peugeot, Delage, Mercedes made their challenges, sometimes going into the lead for a few laps. But the boiling pace was knocking them out, one by one. Near the end of the race the magnificent Bob Burman, in a Peugeot, made the final challenge. It cost him his gear box, and he was out. Cooper's Stutz broke a valve and was out. But the other two Stutz machines, one driven by a new Stutz driver named Tom Rooney, had never performed better or gone faster.

Anderson crossed the finish line with an average speed of 102.60 mph, and Rooney was right on his heels to grab second place, at 102.19 mph. Both men had broken the world record for speed at this distance. The Stutz eagle had never flown higher or screamed louder.

Out of the entire fleet of foreign cars to start that race only one, a Delage, finished. After all those years of frustration, Harry Stutz could now be proud.

At the end of the racing season, when the points were counted, including points for second and third places, it was found that Stutz cars were supreme. Earl Cooper was crowned U.S. racing champion.

It would have seemed that Harry Stutz would want to go on forever, but now, at the peak of success, he announced that the Stutz White Squadron was being retired from racing. He would build no more race cars. He sold Gil Anderson's car to Cliff Durant, who entered it in the Indy 500 for 1919 (races at Indy were suspended during the war) and placed second. Later the car showed up in New Zealand, where it won the New Zealand Motor Cup three years in a row — 1926, 1927 and 1928. Other Stutz machines, now owned by other men, continued to win races around the country for years.

But for Harry C. Stutz, the man who had produced for America its first world class thoroughbred racing car, his heart had gone out of the racing picture. Other things were happening at the Stutz Motor Car Co. that would have a fateful effect on his career.

The Bearcat era: 1911-1919

Bearcat!
Perhaps no other name in American motor car history has evoked quite the same aura of adventure, romance, excitement, and flashing speed.

There really wasn't much to the car —from the chassis up, that is. There was a hood, a dashboard, a steering wheel, a gas tank and two bucket seats. It did have fenders, but not much more.

The concept, the execution of the idea and the name itself somehow symbolized the fulfillment of an American dream. It captured that singular niche in the minds of motor car lovers to whom a car had suddenly become something more than a set of wheels. In later years, they would call them sports cars. In the 1911-1916 period, they would be called Bearcats.

It was a name, and a car, that would do much to ensure success for Harry Clayton Stutz, the country boy with the dream to make the best, the toughest, the most durable and the fastest motor car a man could make. If the Bearcat fell anything short of that dream, the public didn't know it. In creating the Bearcat, Stutz had created an American legend.

Perhaps it was inevitable that the Bearcat would be born. For when Harry C. Stutz made the first Stutz car and took it, the prototype, to the Indianapolis track to run it in the first of the famed 500-mile races, he proclaimed that it was exactly the same car he would be selling for passenger car use.

Never mind that the car had no body —just a cowl, a steering wheel and a couple of bucket seats. He assumed that the buying public would look beyond the "bare bones" car he ran at Indy and envision a touring car, a four-passenger "tonneau," or a full-fledged roadster.

When he began a few months later to assemble and sell the Stutz cars, they had bodies that included touring, tonneau and roadster designs. But the ads the company ran showed the bare bones Indy car. The concept was unavoidable.

How could anybody be surprised if sports-minded customers should show up at a new Stutz dealership, glance questioningly at the tourings, the tonneaus and the roadsters on display, and then say: "You folks said that the first Stutz car you ran at Indianapolis was exactly like the ones you would sell. Well, where is it?"

So Harry C. Stutz gave them the Bearcat.

Perhaps nobody — least of all, Harry Stutz himself— could have foreseen how much the Bearcat, a bare chassis duplicate of the racing Stutz, would contribute to the success of the Stutz enterprise.

The name itself contributed much to the image which brought success: Bearcat — symbol of the pugnacious, the impudent, the gutsy, the tough fighter.

Perhaps nobody knows for certain where the name came from. It could have been from Stutz himself: a take-off from the Marion Bobcat, a special sports and racing car made by the Marion Motor Car Co., where Stutz had been chief engineer before beginning his own enterprise.

In any case, the name and the car, through some mysterious process which nobody can explain, grabbed the imagination of sports-minded Americans. Many who could afford the price, $2,000,

bought one—if they could find one. The others, family men forced by wife and children to buy something more practical, could still look at it and sigh with desire. Even a youngster, to whom the matter of owning a motor car was only a dream, found it a romantic hunk of car to dream about.

The legend had been born.

Stutz admen certainly did not detract from the growing image when they described the Bearcat as being "designed to meet the requirements of a customer desiring a car built along the general lines of a racing car."

Stutz added fenders and headlamps. The frame was kicked up a bit to make the machine ride lower. The brake drums were enlarged from 14 to 16 inches. The "cat" was given a higher rear end gear ratio which, because of the light weight, it could handle with ease. A tiny trunk

The 1915 "6-F" Touring Car was one of two larger models added in 1915. The idea was to continue the sporting image with a bit more people-carrying capacity.

sat behind the bucket seats. Most pictures one sees of Bearcats today show that famed "monocle," the tiny, round windscreen mounted on the steering wheel post. But it was optional and, in all probability, most Bearcats were originally sold without it. Somehow it destroyed the he-man racing image buyers wanted to keep.

In looking back at it now, it seems a classical case of the tail wagging the dog. Harry Stutz had never intended it that way, but now that it had happened he couldn't be unhappy with the results. The snappy little Bearcat was providing an image that dragged the regular Stutz cars — the touring, tonneau, roadster and, later, a three-passenger coupe — along with it. All those races Stutz cars were winning across the country tantalized the public's appetite.

As for the other, more conventional cars, Stutz had announced them in June, 1911, barely a month after that run at Indy. Production and sales on the new Series A were well under way before the end of the year.

The first series ran on a 120-inch wheelbase, offering a big touring, a small four-passenger touring, and a so-called Torpedo roadster. Colors were Vermillion red, French gray and Stutz blue. The engine was the same 4¾ x 5½ Wisconsin T-head that had been used in the Indy run. With a healthy 390 cubic inches, the engine was rated at 60 horsepower at 1,500 rpm. Remember, this was 1911 and the Model T Ford was rated at 20 HP. The

T-head design allowed for larger valves, better breathing and, thus, more power.

Beyond that, a multiple disc wet clutch, a Schebler carburetor and dual ignition were used. The dual ignition was a must on quality cars of that day, and the Schebler was, in a sense, almost a must on the Stutz, in view of Harry's work with the Schebler firm in previous years.

The one major feature on the new Stutz cars to bear the true imprint of its designer, Harry C., was the combination transmission and rear axle (transaxle) which Stutz had designed and patented. Although it violated concepts of unsprung weight, as they would come to be understood in later years, it was a dependable design that would be featured on all Stutz cars, as well as some other makes of cars, for many years to come.

While the cars were, indeed, called Stutz, it was not yet the Stutz Motor Car Co. It was the Ideal Motor Car Co., formed with the backing of Henry Campbell, whom Harry had met while he was chief engineer at Marion.

There was a Stutz company, the Stutz Auto Parts Co., which was formed in 1910 primarily to make and sell the Stutz-designed transaxle. Ideal was formed to make the cars. The two companies merged, under the Stutz name, in 1913.

Regardless of name, the new car manufacturing and selling enterprise was a success from the start. Perhaps nobody will ever know how much of the early success was due to the Indy-born slogan, "The car that made good in a day," or the wins Stutz cars were scoring on tracks throughout the country. Later success may have been due to the sporty image created by the perky Bearcat.

By July of 1913 Stutz cars had been entered in 39 races and had won 29 of them. By 1915, at the peak of their racing success, Stutz cars won more important races than any other make of car. A Stutz and its driver were crowned U.S. racing champion. Stutz set at least two world speed records.

Perhaps almost as important as winning was the word going around motordom that "even when Stutz cars are not winning, they always manage to finish." Reliability and durability were as important to a prospective customer as blinding speed.

In 1912 Stutz announced the new Series B cars. In appearance they were virtually identical to the Series A. There were improvements in the cooling system, the transaxle was strengthened, a generator and battery were added, the gear shift was moved inside the car to the right of the driver and — perhaps the biggest news of all — a six-cylinder engine was added.

The trend of the time was to sixes. The competition was touting the sixes. Drivers of the heavier passenger cars liked the reduced vibration of the sixes, especially at lower speeds. The new Stutz six was similar to the four: a T-head with blocks cast in pairs. It had a bore of 4¼ inches and a stroke of 5 inches for 426 cubic inches.

After the six had been added to the line, buyers of the Bearcat were offered a choice of engines but, strangely enough, drivers reported they got virtually the same performance out of the four as the six. Besides, the four weighed a bit less. Harry C. obviously knew what he was doing, for he continued to use the fours in his race cars.

It was in 1913 that Stutz and his management pulled off a production and financial coup which, in the end, probably also contributed greatly to the Stutz success story. It was a year in which a short but sharp economic crisis hit the country. Sales of cars dropped sharply, and most makers met the crisis by slowing down production, or halting it altogether and laying off workers. At Stutz, however, management was confident the crisis wouldn't last long, and ordered production to continue, full speed ahead. Not a single worker was laid off. Thus, when business conditions did improve quickly, there was Stutz with a backlog of cars to sell, while other manufacturers were playing "catch up."

It was the sort of thing that could "snowball" for the future, especially when buyers continued to report that Stutz machines were, in toughness and reliability, not to mention speed, virtually unbeatable.

The Series E cars, offered in 1913, were again largely carbon copies of the Series B. The Roadster and Bearcat, both fours and sixes, rode on a 120-inch wheelbase, while the six-passenger touring, both in the four and the six-cylinder models, rode on a 130-inch base. The Stutz catalog showed an ornate three-passenger coupe priced at $2,600 with a four, and at $2,850 with a six. The base price on the Bearcat remained a flat $2,000 for the four, with the six running $250 more. On the big touring, the four went for $2,150, while the six carried a $2,400 price tag. Prices on the Torpedo Roadster were the same as for the Bearcat. In 1913 the six was listed with slightly smaller specs, a flat 4 x 5. An electric starter was offered as standard equipment on all models. Stutz, however, had not been satisfied with standard starters offered on the market. He created his own design and had it made by Remy.

By 1915, impressed by the spectacular success of his sport models, Stutz decided to add two new models to the line embodying the sports motif. The first was the Bulldog, a machine which shared the Bearcat chassis but carried a smaller, four-passenger "tonneau" touring body. The idea was to continue the sporty image with a bit more people-carrying capacity.

The other offering was a smaller, lighter roadster dubbed the Speedster. This machine, entirely new for Stutz, used a smaller engine, 3¾ x 5, in the conventional L-head design. It was the first time it would be used in a Stutz. The wheelbase was a short 108 inches, and the price tag was $1,475. Somehow, buyers sensed that such a machine simply could never be a Bearcat and, as the cliche goes, "stayed away in droves." Only 125 were sold and the model was dropped the next year. The Bulldog concept also failed to "catch" and was never a success. The Bearcat simply had to be a Bearcat.

It might be noted, incidentally, that when the Speedster appeared, even Harry C. may have been a bit hesitant to call it a Stutz, and the emblem simply bore his initials, H.C.S. It was, however, a nameplate that would appear again, under other circumstances.

For 1916 Stutz more or less allowed his models to continue, with only the slightest changes. After all, you couldn't argue with success. Customers were grabbing the Stutz cars as fast as the factory could turn them out, and the assembly lines were unable to catch up.

But Stutz was not standing still. He was working on a hot new engine designed to breathe new life into the Stutz picture and to keep abreast of the competition, which was now offering more sixes and V-8s, even V-12s. Strangely enough, it would be another four. Perhaps nobody but Stutz, riding so high and so fast on the Bearcat image and the fantastic success of his racing cars, could have gotten away with it. Stutz not only made that hot new engine a four but, after testing it, decided it was so good he could afford to drop his previous sixes. It was sheer audacity, and bucked every trend in the industry.

Earlier, Stutz had copied the famed French Peugeot racing engine design with double overhead cams on a four-cylinder engine. This had been the super hot Stutz engine that set new lap speed records at Indy in 1915, won some of the top races in the country, and set at least two new world speed races.

Harry probably would have liked to have plunked this engine down intact into his passenger cars, especially the beloved Bearcat. But he was a sharp enough engineer to know that manufacturing costs would be too high and the engine a bit too complicated to be trusted to the public. So, he decided, it would have to be a slightly de-tuned version of the race machine.

What he ended up with was, indeed, a 16-valve four, but of the T-head rather than the overhead cam design. It was

plenty hot for the design. With a much smaller bore, 3⅜, but a super long stroke and 360 cubic inches, the motor churned out 80 hp at 2,400 rpm. It would drive the Stutz at 85 mph, or more.

Cadillac had startled the motoring world by introducing a V-8 in 1915, but Cadillac had claimed only 70 hp. Packard had trumped that one with a mighty V-12, introduced only a few months later but even here, with 424 cubic inches, Packard claimed only 85 hp. If power and speed were what you wanted, the new Stutz four would deliver.

The new engine went into the most changed Stutzes ever, the Series R. The bodies were leaner, lower and sleeker, with more rounded contours.

Even the old "bare bones" appearance of the famed Bearcat had changed. It finally got a body that bore a resemblance to a true roadster, with windshield and side panels. A true roadster? Well, not quite.

It had side panels, yes, but no doors. The panels were cut low enough to be called "step-overs." It worked well enough for a long-legged man, but for the ladies? Well, they could always use a stepladder or a horse mounting block.

Incidentally, the Stutz factory was being expanded once more and facilities were being installed so that the hot new engine would be built by Stutz.

Talking about the enormous success of the Stutz enterprise, with the factory being expanded several times to meet demand, might lead some to visualize production in the thousands. An explanation is in order.

Success must always be measured against original expectations and capacity. Harry Stutz had never visualized his car as a mass production machine. He simply wanted it to be the best, the toughest, the most reliable. At the beginning he had planned for production measured by a few hundred cars. The factory could make no more.

Of course, when he found customers snapping up his cars faster than he could make them, he and his backers went for an expansion—and again. But when you start out with 200 or 300 cars per year and double it, or even triple it, you are still talking, essentially, only hundreds of cars.

This 1916 Stutz Bearcat is one of the many antique cars on display in the John Price Automobile Collection Museum.

Accurate production figures for Stutz in the earliest years are not available, but by 1914 several sources have given it as 649. That was a boom year. By 1915 that figure had jumped to 1,079. The factory had been enlarged. Output climbed to 1,412 in 1916.

After a second expansion, the figure went to around 2,000 cars per year for 1917 and remained there through 1919. This was largely the period of World War I, when production was more or less frozen by steel and raw material shortages. There would be a peak of 4,000 Stutz cars in the boom post-war year of 1920 (one source quotes 3,000).

After that? Well, that is another story. It was during this period, 1916-1919, when Harry C. Stutz was losing control of his "own" company. It was a classic example of success breeding disaster.

When any company has been as successful as Stutz had been, it is perhaps inevitable that someone would like to steal the goldmine. It happened when Stutz decided to expand the factory again in 1916, and needed money. Instead of raising the money as he had previously done, by going to contacts at the banks, Stutz and his backers decided to do it by going public, listing Stutz stock on the New York Exchange and selling a stock issue to raise the needed capital.

That was when the wolves—or the wolf —moved in for the kill. A Wall Street financier, Alan A. Ryan, saw gold in the glittering Stutz success story and began buying up Stutz stock. The money he paid made it possible for Stutz to build the

needed factory addition, but it also allowed Ryan to gain control of Stutz.

Ryan allowed Harry Stutz to remain as president, placing himself in the vice president's chair. For the moment, at least, Ryan needed Stutz, the man who had created the company and the cars. But Harry was no fool and he knew who was really boss.

Harry was not the outgoing, talkative type who discussed his motivations and dreams with other people. Thus, it is difficult to know exactly what was going on in Harry's mind in this period. But it is probably safe to say that he was disappointed, perhaps even bitter, about what had taken place.

As a clue to his stubborn character, we need only go back to that instance at the Marion plant. When new owners moved in and wanted to install their own accounting system, Harry walked out rather than accept the new system. His decision now, in the 1916-1919 period, may not have been as explosive, or as sudden, as that "walk-out" at Marion. It probably built up over months, years. But it came, inevitably. In 1919 Stutz called it quits—at least as far as the Stutz Motor Car Co., which he no longer controlled, was concerned.

He did it by selling what stock he still owned and walked out, leaving "his" company and the car he had so proudly nursed into life, to Ryan and his compatriots.

Harry Stutz was not finished. He had acquired a considerable fortune and would try again. But, like the famed Ransom E. Olds, who had been barred from reusing the famed Oldsmobile name he had created, Stutz was barred from using his own name when he cranked up for a new try. The new cars would bear the emblem "H.C.S"—those initials again. But the new enterprise would never be the success that Stutz had been. He would never again produce a Bearcat.

The beginning of the Moscovics era: 1920-1925

If Harry C. Stutz wanted revenge for being "robbed" of his control of the Stutz Motor Car Co., he got it. But he had to stand by and watch while others did the "gun slinging" in the "shoot-out."

Alan A. Ryan and his buddies had bought enough of the Stutz stock in 1916 to take control of the company. In 1920, they decided they wanted it all.

The story of the "shoot-out" couldn't happen today because there are too many legal controls on the operation of the stock market. To put it as simply as possible, Ryan and his pals bought virtually every share of Stutz stock, until there simply wasn't any left for trading: the classic "corner" on the market.

Their buying took place in the $100 to $134 per share price range. The Stutz stock had originally gone on the market at $55.

Ryan's plan was to loan some of his "cornered" stock to several so-called "short traders," operators who counted on the price to drop in the future. They would sell their borrowed stock at the present high prices and count on replacing the borrowed stock with new stock bought at lower prices in the future.

But Ryan's plan had a kicker in it, something that might sound like a doublecross of the men to whom he loaned the stock. He took advantage of the fact that they didn't realize he had the "corner."

Since he controlled all the stock, he could hold it off the market and make the prices go up, instead of down. If he held the stock off the market until the time came for the short traders to replace their borrowed stock—which they had already sold — he could name his price.

For a time, it worked. Within weeks, as the squeeze on the short traders began, the offers for Stutz stock rose as high as $390 per share. If Ryan had been willing to take these profits, he could have made his killing and retired a rich man.

His fatal mistake was in wanting too much. When he finally revealed his hand and named his price, it was no less than $750 per share!

The trapped short traders got together and planned a new strategy of their own. One factor Ryan had overlooked was that some of the men he had in his "trap" happened to be members of the Exchange, and they had enough friends on the Exchange to control it.

Without the present-day controls of the U.S. Securities and Exchange Commission, they could do it by simply "delisting" Stutz stock — taking it off the Exchange and halting all trading in Stutz shares. These people had found out that Ryan had borrowed several million dollars to create his monopoly. The strategy of the Exchange men was to hold the Stutz stock off the market beyond the due date on Ryan's borrowed money.

Now the squeeze was working in the opposite direction: on Ryan. When he decided to start selling, he had no place to do the selling so he tried to do a bit of dealing. He offered to sell the short traders enough stock to cover their obligations. He would be generous, and reduce his price by $200 per share. That would still leave the price at $550 — some generosity.

But now that the Stock Exchange people had Ryan in their trap, they went for the kill and taught him a lesson. In the end they forced Ryan to sell his holdings for as little as $20 per share. The one-time high roller ended up not only broke, but so badly in debt he was, as one writer put it, literally in the poor house.

Talk about revenge! Now was the time for Harry C. Stutz, standing on the sidelines and watching, to do his cheering as he saw his erstwhile conquerer being shot down.

But all the "shooting" did nothing to help Harry Stutz regain control of his beloved company. It simply meant that another crowd of speculators owned it. So Stutz was through with the Stutz Motor Car Co. of America, as it was now known. While he was still a motor car maker at heart, he would never again be able to place his name on any car he designed. But he could still use his initials, as Ransom E. Olds had done with Reo.

So, using funds he had left from the sale of his Stutz stock, and with some financial backing from friends, he was soon back in business — this time as the HCS Motor Car Co.

As the new HCS company was organized in November, 1919, it was significant that once more his old friend and financial backer was in his corner. To go with Stutz, Henry F. Campbell—who had known Stutz since his days with Marion and had helped him organize the Stutz company—gave up his jobs as chairman of the board and secretary-treasurer at Stutz. He also was fed up.

When Stutz started his new company, he announced that his aim was to produce a high quality car, modeled on the lines of the original Stutz, to sell for less than $1,000. That part of his new dream exploded very quickly.

In the first place, Harry Stutz wanted —and insisted on—too much motor car, too much quality, for it to sell under $1,000. Beyond that, the war had caused labor costs and material costs to shoot upward.

Thus, when the new HCS motor car appeared on the market in 1920 it bore a striking resemblance to the original Stutz, especially the sports roadster which looked so much like the old Bearcat. But the $1,000 price tag had exploded to $2,950 — and, when it came to performance, it simply wasn't a Bearcat.

Starting again from scratch, Stutz obviously wasn't in a position to build his own engines. He ended up with a Weidely four-cylinder with conventional overhead valves rated at 50 hp. Compare that to the hot 88 hp, 16-valve job he had been building at Stutz.

But 1920 was a post-war boom year for America, and the name of Harry C. Stutz still carried some magic. At the be-

The 16-valve, 4-cylinder had a super long stroke and 360 cubic inches, generating 80 horsepower at 2,400 rpm. The 1915 V-8 Cadillac could only claim 70 horsepower.

ginning, sales were good and some 800 cars were sold the first year. But then came 1921, which would go down in history as the year of a short but severe economic depression for the country. It was cruel enough to put dozens of car makers out of business, and it dealt harshly with the fledgling HCS enterprise, which was just barely under way.

Sales dropped sharply and, even when business conditions improved in 1922, the new HCS project failed to make a rebound. Stutz never had the time, nor the facilities, to re-create that magic image he had produced at the original Stutz company.

He stuck with his passenger and HCS sports car concept until 1923. Then, faced with a shutdown, he switched to the manufacture of something far short of his dreamboat Bearcat—taxicabs.

But by 1926, even that venture had failed. By 1927 the company was in the hands of a receiver and Harry C. Stutz was forced to call it quits once more. Stutz had not put all his eggs in one basket. He had also started the Stutz Fire Engine Co., as a builder of high quality fire engines. But that enterprise also failed in 1927. It was later reorganized and managed to survive until 1940, but under other management.

By 1930 Harry C. Stutz, the man who had created the car that "made good in a day" and the legendary Bearcat, was dead.

After the debacle of 1926-1927, he had been able to salvage enough money to "retire" to Orlando, Florida. In June, 1930, he planned a trip back to Indianapolis to consult with others on a new engineering design he had created for a four-cylinder, opposed aircraft engine.

On the eve of the trip he became ill but was told it was intestinal influenza, so he went ahead, driving all the way to Indianapolis. There, he learned that his "flu" was appendicitis, and that his appendix had burst. Emergency surgery was undertaken, but Harry C. Stutz didn't make it. On June 25 he died. The career of one of the best self-made engineers of the American motor car industry had ended.

But what about the Stutz Motor Car Co. of America, last heard of in 1920, the year of the financial "shoot-out" for control? The magic of the Stutz name continued to work. Obviously, the people who bought motor cars knew little about all the financial "finagling" going on behind the scenes. They continued to buy cars bearing the name Stutz. In fact, it was a record year, with sales near the 4,000 mark.

Actually, that was the high water mark. The Stutz enterprise was "coasting" on the momentum Harry Stutz had created, coasting on the performance of the hot 16-valve engine Harry had designed back in 1916. The company would coast on that single engine, with few changes in the chassis, all the way to 1923. The new owners were reaping the harvest from the seeds that Stutz had planted—but it could not go on forever.

One reason the coasting period could last so long was the war, World War I, when material for motor car production was rationed by the government and a seller's market reigned. A maker could sell all the cars he could make. After the war, the boom brought on by wartime shortages continued through 1920.

During that period and even beyond, Stutz continued to rely on that one engine and chassis, with virtually no changes. Wheelbases remained at 120 inches for the Bearcat and the small roadster models, and 130 for the passenger models. For unexplained reasons, Stutz even clung to the outmoded right-hand steering, which virtually all American motor car makers had long ago abandoned. Ford had set the pace on that one as early as 1909, with the introduction of the Model T. Stutz would not have left-hand drive as standard until 1923.

It must also be remembered that it was in 1915 when the great swing to V-8 engines had begun, especially for the upper price class machines. Several makers, notably Packard, had even gone to V-12s.

And here was Stutz, the car with the great name, chugging along with a four-cylinder engine and selling it for prices near that of Cadillac. True, the hot 16-valve engine could outperform most of the fours, or even sixes, on the market, but it was an engineering concept that was becoming outmoded for quality motor cars.

Even the T-head design, which had offered such impressive advantages at the beginning, was being overtaken by engineers producing cars costing much less. The T-head was expensive to make.

Perhaps still another reason why Stutz coasted so long was the change of management. When the smoke of the stock "shoot-out" cleared, the men who ended up in control were Charles M. Schwab, chairman of the board at Bethlehem Steel, one of the great steel companies of America, together with Eugene R. Thayer and Charles J. Schmidlapp, prominent investors.

These men had no background in motor car making, and knew little about automobiles. As long as the Stutz company continued to make profits, they saw little reason to change anything. But by 1922, after that sharp economic depression had cut deeply into Stutz sales and the economic recovery failed to revive Stutz, even these men could see that the time had come for change.

The first thing they needed was a new chief engineer who could create new designs, new engines, new cars. The man they chose was Charles S. Crawford.

Crawford came to Stutz with solid credentials. He had been chief engineer at the Cole Motor Car Co., where he had produced a high quality, V-8 powered motor car that challenged the Cadillac for quality and performance. Some observers said the Cole V-8 was even better than the Cadillac.

It might have been expected that, when Crawford arrived at Stutz—given his background in V-8's, and with the Stutz reputation for performance — he would have designed another V-8. However, for reasons not completely clear but

Rackish Stutz roadster of 1920 appeared at a Pebble Beach, Calif. outing in the late 1980's.

possibly reflecting the conservative philosophy of the new owners of Stutz, the engine that Crawford created for Stutz was a somewhat conventional six.

Quality-wise, the new engine may well have been worthy of the Stutz name. Crawford used a spring-loaded overhead valve design for which Stutz claimed "complete silence." The engine was carefully balanced and made from the best materials. In a test on the Indianapolis track, it ran for 16 hours at an average of 60 miles per hour and a top speed of 70.

Not bad—but it wasn't all that great when compared to the old Stutz-designed four that it was replacing. The new six had a 3⅜-inch bore by 5-inch stroke for 268 cubic inch displacement, and was rated at 66 hp (some sources said 70). But compare this to the veteran 360-inch four, rated at 88 hp, that drove the Bearcat to speeds of 80 to 90 miles per hour. If the new six could not outperform the old four, what had been gained other than a somewhat quieter and smoother operation?

Apparently, someone realized the implications of all this and, for 1924, the six was upgraded and upsized. It had a 3½-inch bore with the same 5-inch stroke, for 288 cubic inches, and a horsepower rating of 80. Perhaps the

only part of the new engine which remained to remind Stutz owners of past glories was its name—the Speedway Six. But it still was not a match for the old 16-valve four.

To remove that source of "in-house" comparison, the old standby four would simply be dropped from the roster after 1924.

It was a mixed hodge-podge of models and engines the small Stutz company offered to the public in 1924. You could still buy the old four for $2,450 for the roadster, $2,765 for the Bearcat, or $3,115 for a small, four-passenger Bulldog touring type. You could take a seven-passenger touring for $2,640 or a four-passenger coupe for $2,990.

If you wanted one of the smaller Special Six models held over from 1923, you had a choice of four body styles—roadster, touring, Tourster or sedan—for prices ranging from $1,995 to $2,550.

If you wanted one of the new Speedway Sixes, you had a choice of five models ranging in price from $2,850 to $3,800:
• A five-passenger sports touring
• A Sportbrohm (although some trade publications insisted on spelling it brougham)
• A seven-passenger touring
• A seven-passenger Suburban
• A seven-passenger Berline.

The big cars, incidentally, weighed from 3,900 pounds for the sports touring to 4,445 pounds for the Berline.

Despite all these models, sales for Stutz in 1924 dropped near the 1,000 mark and for 1925 the picture remained dismal.

What kind of market and what kind of buyer was Stutz now aiming at, with a new six priced lower than the old four, and a bigger six selling at prices in the Cadillac range (but which could not compete with a Cadillac)? The old four, which had been a sensation in its day, had been on the market since 1916 and its prices were still above the medium range.

The biggest model Buicks for that year were selling for prices ranging from $1,275 to $2,795 (for a seven-passenger town car). Fords were selling for as low as $345 for a roadster and only $695 for a four-door sedan.

Somebody certainly should have realized that Stutz could not coast on a great name and past glories forever. Perhaps Schwab and company did realize that, for when a certain glib engineer-designer-salesman-manager came knocking at the door with designs for an exciting new car under his arm, they looked and listened. His name was Frederick E. Moscovics.

Moscovics was an engineer of a different breed. Born in Europe—Hungary, to be exact — he was brought to America as a child by his parents. He grew up to be an American, but with a European flavor. He retained strong ties to Europe which would show in times to come. Growing up in a bustling new land, in an age when the motor car industry was being born, his intellectual curiosity gravitated toward the new motor cars, especially their engineering.

He first studied at the Armour Institute of Technology in Chicago. Then, in keeping with his European connections, and armed with the knowledge that Europe contained some of the finest technical schools in the world, he returned to Europe for post-graduate courses in engineering.

For a time he was employed, as an apprentice engineer, at the famed Daimler-Benz (Mercedes) plant, before returning to the U.S. Where could a budding engineer have obtained better training?

Back in America, Moscovics went to work for the Remy Electric Co., one of the country's top makers of electrical equipment, most of which was designed for motor cars. Later he worked for Marmon-Nordyke, makers of the famed Marmon motor cars, where he worked his way up to vice president.

It was at Marmon where he was involved in the design and development of the famed Marmon Model 34. It was a car that appeared on the market almost simultaneously with the famed Stutz 16-valve job, and had a nearly parallel history, remaining on the market until 1924.

It was also at Marmon where he was involved in the production of the famed Liberty aircraft engine of World War I, with the company winning awards as top producer.

But there had been a certain parallel with Stutz history at Marmon—if not in financial finagling, at least in the sense of clinging to a once-successful model too long. In 1916, when it first appeared, the high quality Marmon 34, with its advanced six-cylinder, valve-in-head engine, had been highly successful. Then, aided by the same war-imposed shortage of cars and the immediate post-war boom when buyers couldn't get enough cars, the model had stayed and stayed. As at Stutz, it remained too long.

It wasn't Moscovics' fault. Keeping abreast of engineering developments in the motor car field and bubbling over with prospects of bringing exciting new models onto the market, he encountered or conceived several new engineering ideas that could well be developed into exactly what he wanted —that exciting new model of a car.

He presented his ideas to Howard Marmon, head of the firm, but Marmon wasn't convinced. It would cost a lot for retooling. The Model 34 was still doing well. The answer was no.

To a young engineer with a head full of ideas, this was a stagnating situation. Moscovics resolved it by resigning.

For a short time he worked as sales manager at the H.H. Franklin Co., maker of the famed Franklin air-cooled motor car. Here he became involved in a dispute over company policies with stubborn Herbert H. Franklin. Beyond that, the company obviously was not a candidate for his new ideas because of its tra-

1925 Stutz Seven-passenger Suburban — Series 695.

ditional commitment to the air-cooled concept.

Somewhere in the midst of all this, Moscovics learned that the Stutz company was not doing well. He guessed, rightly, that much of the trouble stemmed from the lack of a truly imaginative new motor car that could restore the fading Stutz image.

With the plans for his exciting new model under his arm, Moscovics decided it was time to go knocking on the doors at Stutz. Was he, at last, the man who could replace Harry C. Stutz and recapture the glories of the past?

The car and the man who saved Stutz: 1925-1927

Stutz needed a new winner, a new concept for a motor car that would permit the Stutz name to once again stand tall in the industry. It had to be something that would re-create the mighty magic of the Bearcat image. Without it, Stutz was dead. The managers and owners were already considering closing the doors.

But now appeared a man who said he had the much needed winner in a new motoring concept based on the best of engineering dreams. The man was Frederick E. Moscovics, a European-born engineer who had already proved himself as a man with ideas.

He was as much a part of the engineering package as the plans and blueprints he carried under his arms. Dynamic, cosmopolitan, glib of tongue, a salesman as much as an engineer, Moscovics not only had bold concepts but could bring them to life.

In truth Moscovics would never, with a few notable exceptions, be the inventor or creator of new motoring engineering features. But he was enough of an engineer to understand what other men created, realize their potential, develop them into concepts, and turn them

into reality. Some people said his ideas and dreams, in relation to the motor car, were a generation ahead of the industry.

There was, for example, the new engine design Moscovics brought with him in the package he wanted to sell Stutz. It was a straight eight, of overhead cam design.

The design had been developed by Peugeot, of France. After it showed its brilliant potential on the racetracks, it had been adopted by the Duesenberg brothers in the U.S., by Harry Miller, and even by Harry C. Stutz—with startling, sensational success.

The Duesenberg brothers, Fred and August, had even introduced it in a limited production passenger car, their famed Model A, in 1921. But, for the most part, the industry still considered it an impractical design. It was too expensive and too prone to problems, they said.

But a very capable American engineer, Charles R. (Pop) Greuter, had been experimenting with and building, for testing purposes, engines with the overhead cam design as early as 1902. He had refined the concept over the years, until he had all the bugs worked out. Some observers have suggested that the Greu-

23

ter design had a few refinements the Peugeot type did not have.

At one point in his career, Greuter, who worked on the engineering staffs of several U.S. car makers, had sold the Excelsior Motor Manufacturing Co., of Chicago, on accepting and building one of his overhead cam designs, but Excelsior was unable to find any major American manufacturer who would accept it.

Nobody, it seems, was interested — except Moscovics. He had tried to sell the design to Marmon, in a straight eight configuration, when he had been vice president there, but Howard Marmon had turned it down. This was the engine facet of the new Moscovics concept.

The other major ingredient in the concept was a worm drive rear axle, turned upside down, which would make it possible to lower the overall height of a motor car by five inches or more. The worm drive had also been kicking around the industry for years, mostly in trucks. Where it had been used, it had been employed mostly with the worm on top, a very high design that was suitable only for trucks.

Another reason why the worm drive had never been given much attention by the motor car makers was the fact that it worked best in the low gear ratios—more suitable for trucks, again — and was known as an energy eater. It simply soaked up too much of the energy being put out by the engine. In trucks, at lower speeds, it didn't matter so much.

But while on a trip to Europe, Moscovics discovered that a new worm drive gear tooth design was available that not only eliminated the "energy eater" image, but would work at higher ratios as well. Nobody in America seemed to be aware of it — or, if they were, they were satisfied with their old ring gear and pinion design.

What made the Moscovics package — the high-performance engine, coupled with worm drive — so significant at the moment was that another type of revolution had been taking place in the motor car industry: the closed body revolution.

The closed bodies, in one form or another, had been around almost from the beginning of the motor car industry. But closed bodies had always been very expensive, almost doubling the cost of a car, while the other half of their bugaboo had been their top-heaviness. A sharp turn or a sharp curve, at almost any speed at all, was risky business.

In spite of this, by the early 1920s, as the motor car began to play its true role as an integral part of the American cultural scene, people began demanding more and more closed bodies. They were beginning to demand comfort as well as transportation.

Up to this time the open models, the so-called touring cars and roadsters, had always been the mainstays of the industry. But now, as the industry continued to find ways of making them cheaper, the sedans, the coaches and the coupes were forming the bulk of what the motorist was asking for and buying.

Beyond that, by the 1920s, engine and chassis developments had constantly made more speed and performance available, even to the average driver. The top-heaviness of the closed bodies was becoming a critical factor.

But now, into this picture was introduced a man with a new package: a high-performance engine, an axle design that would permit the lowest center of gravity in the industry, new-fangled hydraulic brakes, and even safety glass — of a sort — long before laminated glass was available. Tiny wires were imbedded in the glass.

Moscovics sold the package. Eugene Thayer, chairman of the board at Stutz, liked it. He told Charles Schwab, the chief financial backer of the company. Schwab, somewhat of a motor car enthusiast himself, also liked it. Moscovics and his package were in—and the company was reorganized with none other than the newcomer, Moscovics, as president.

When Moscovics first walked through the doors of the Stutz manufacturing and assembly plants, his engineering heart told him he was in seventh heaven. The Stutz Motor Car Co. may have been on the verge of bankruptcy, but it had one of the best equipped and most efficient assembly plants in the country.

One of the first moves Moscovics made after taking charge was to assemble one of the best engineering teams he could find — and he knew where to look. It is significant that one of the men who

In December, 1927, Lockheed hydraulic internal expanding 4-wheel brakes were adopted.

joined the team was none other than "Pop" Greuter, the man who had come up with the new and exciting design for the eight-cylinder, overhead cam engine. You couldn't do much better than that.

"The New Stutz Vertical Eight, with Safety Body" was the phrase the team chose to tack onto its new car.

The word "safety" may seem a little strange in the 1920s. There was a time, in the 1950s, when the Ford Motor Co. tried to sell safety as a motor car concept. Ford lost its shirt on the project. Safety, the company found, didn't sell cars —at least not at that particular time. The V-8 engine was coming into its own, and buyers wanted performance and speed.

But, going back to the mood of the buying public in the 1920s, Moscovics may have been right. Safety was not such a lackluster word then. The days of the Bearcat, other than the magic image, were over. People were well aware of the "tip-over" rate on the closed cars.

Actually, people who knew Moscovics also knew that he liked speed, performance and racing as well as the next man—maybe even a bit more. But what he was proposing was a subtle approach to the problem: allowing the buyer to know he might have the speed and performance he loved, with the safety of no

tip-overs with the new Stutz. He was counting on drivers finding out for themselves about the performance and, as in the days of the great Bearcat, word would get around. Such was the logic of Moscovics.

In any case this was the machine, brought from concept into reality, that Moscovics and his engineers began testing late in 1925. It was unveiled for a private showing to Stutz dealers on December 17, and to the public at the January, 1926, New York auto show.

The engine was a straight eight with single overhead cam. With a bore of 3³/₁₆ x 4½ stroke, it weighed in at 296 cubic inches and was rated at 92 brake horsepower at 3,200 rpm. This may not sound like much in later-day terms, but in 1925-1926 it was almost sensational.

All one need do is compare it to its competitors. Jesse Vincent, Packard's brilliant engineer, the creator of the famed Twin Six, had just put a very fine straight eight of his own on the market, a year earlier. Although it was a bigger engine than the new Stutz Vertical Eight, with 357 cubic inches, it was rated at a conservative 84 bhp.

Cadillac, still sticking to its time-tried V-8 design, also had more size on the engine, at 314 cubic inches, but it was rated at only 87 bhp. The very fine Lincoln engine, also a V-8, had a 358 piston displacement and was rated at 90. It was clear that Stutz, with the smallest of these engines, had the most "oomph."

When Stutz engineers began testing their new engine on the Indianapolis track, they found, after the engine was well run in, that the shaft and gear drive on the overhead cam became a bit noisy. It was one of the times when Moscovics drew on his own personal engineering ability to do a bit of designing himself.

He came up with a chain drive with two automatic tension idlers. The chain drive was also set up to drive all engine accessories. Some engineers, in taking a look at the layout of this chain drive system, said it was not a practical design. But the crazy wiggle-waggle chain worked perfectly and was one feature of the new engine that never caused trouble.

The straight eight type engine had been, up to this point, virtually unheard of as far as the general buying public was concerned. No major American manufacturer had ever put one on the market.

The Duesenberg brothers had done it with their very limited production Model A in 1922. Auburn and Jordan had also introduced straight eight engines in 1924, but both the Auburn engine (a Lycoming) and the Jordan engine (a Continental) were flatheads with five main bearings and much lower horsepower ratings. Both were also limited production machines.

It was a pioneering concept. True, the straight eight engines had been burning up the tracks in race cars, both Duesenbergs and Millers. But engineers had shied away from the design for passenger cars, largely because of the difficulty of keeping that long, whippy crankshaft under control.

Vincent, at Packard, had solved that problem in typical Packard fashion through the use of nine main bearings. The Stutz, significantly, also had nine bearings. The Packard straight eight design would remain the backbone of the Packard for 30 years, and was a magnificently reliable engine. The big reason why this was important to Stutz now was the fact that Packard — the major producer in the luxury car field — was, in placing its reputation on the line with a straight eight, affirming to a possibly doubting public that it was, indeed, a viable design. In the end, it would also help sell Stutz cars.

In the meantime, as they tested the peppy new engine, Stutz engineers were in for another surprise. In most conventional engines of the day, the torque curve dropped off rather sharply at high speed. The new Stutz engine was holding its "oomph" up to much higher rpm levels. One Stutz engineering report said that the engine turned out a healthy 198 foot-pounds of torque at 1,400 rpm, when the car was moving at approximately 27 miles per hour. The surprise came when they found that, at 65 mph, with the engine turning at 3,200 rpm, it was still whipping out 158 pounds of torque. In layman's terms: at 65 mph, there was still a lot of "go" left.

When a driver for *Motor Age* magazine took the new Stutz out for a test drive, he put it this way: "At 60 miles per hour the car shows terrific punch and can be taken up to 75 miles per hour like a racing job." There was no faint praise in that report.

Moscovics and his engineers had designed the engine so well, and balanced it so perfectly, that it did not need—and did not use—a vibration damper on the crankshaft. The crankshaft, incidentally, weighed 85 pounds.

To keep reciprocating weight down as much as possible, making possible the peppy performance of the engine, Stutz engineers made the connecting rods out of aluminum and, while the pistons were cast iron, Moscovics was able to come up with a special strut design that allowed a cast iron piston weighing little more than aluminum pistons.

Well aware of the fact that any high performance engine must be well lubricated, especially with those nine main bearings, the design called for high pressure pump lubrication to all bearings, including the overhead cam bearings.

To improve cooling, the Stutz engineers used a cast aluminum oil pan with cooling fins cast as an integral part of the pan.

To further assure absolute rigidity — remember the freedom from vibration — the engine block casting extended 2¼ inches below the center line of the

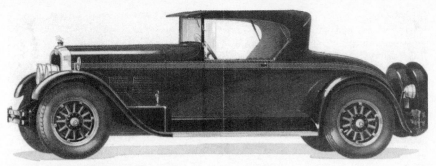

1927 Two-passenger Speedster as shown in the company sales literature.

crankshaft. No wonder a harmonic balancer was not needed.

As for the remainder of the car, there were other pioneering features, such as hydraulic brakes. Stutz called them "Hydrostatics," a unique system with the shoes divided into six parts and pushed against the drums by a circular, hydraulic tube. The steering was described as virtually shock-proof and responsive to the point of, "As you wish, Sir." A super rigid frame with seven cross members was used.

The new machine was built around the super low center of gravity which, Stutz ad men claimed, made a Stutz stick to the road as if held by a magnet. The low center worm drive rear axle made still another plus feature possible, a nearly straight drive train.

So there the new Stutz stood, on a 131-inch wheelbase and available, at first, in six body styles: the two- and four-passenger open-bodied speedsters, a five-passenger sedan, a five-passenger brougham, a four-passenger victoria coupe, and a two-passenger coupe. Later, with a 145-inch wheelbase, a seven-passenger sedan and a limousine would be added, with bodies by Brewster. Prices ran from $3,150 to $3,795.

The next year, in an effort to save weight, Moscovics worked with engineers at the Weymann body plant to produce a lightweight combination wood and fabric body. It was another pioneering effort. Wire netting was stretched over the wooden frame and built up with padding and fabric. A Weymann body of this type was 500 pounds lighter than the conventional body.

Moscovics was well aware of the advantages of slicing off several hundred pounds of weight. He knew a stripped Stutz chassis, with the new Vertical Eight engine, would do 87 mph around the Indianapolis track. In 1927, at a Stutz dealer convention, he demonstrated what that 500-pound savings in weight would do. He put a conventional Stutz sedan, with steel body, on the track and determined that its top average speed was 74 mph. A second sedan, exactly like the first except for the lighter Weymann body, was able to average 78 mph.

Was this, then, the winner Stutz needed to remain in business? The answer, for the moment at least, was a resounding yes. When the car was first shown to dealers, in December, 1927, they were so enthusiastic about what they saw that they ordered a whopping $3,000,000 worth of cars on the spot. When the car went on public display at the New York show, 236 private buyers voted their approval by placing orders.

Moscovics and his backers had hoped to be able to produce and sell 4,000 of the new machines that first year. When the year was over, the total came to 5,000. It was almost as if things were back as they had been after 1911, when Harry C. Stutz had been able to boast about "the car that made good in a day." The new Stutz Vertical Eight had just about made that true all over again.

Stutz had, indeed, been rescued.

Some critics, even latter day critics, have suggested that for such a radically different kind of car, Moscovics and his styling engineers might have come up with a bit more of the sensational, the flashy, in terms of styling.

The truth was that the new Stutz, aside from its engineering features, was as modern and handsome in appearance as just about anything on the market. Even if Stutz stylists had been able to come up with something sensationally different, men of other opinions say, it would have detracted from the one feature that Moscovics and his men desperately wanted everyone to notice: the extremely low slung chassis and body—the lowest in the industry. The safety factor was the biggest selling point Stutz had. Observed from that standpoint, the styling of the new Stutz may have been a stroke of genius.

Incidentally, another decision Moscovics made soon after taking over the Stutz presidency was to cancel production of the Speedway Six, even before the new Vertical Eight was completed and tested. Someone has suggested that it was a gamble, and production of the older model should have been continued at least until the new model could be tested and proven as a viable concept. In that respect Moscovics had, indeed, been a gambler—or at least had supreme confidence in the new design. At any rate, it was a gamble he won.

And while Moscovics had, in introducing the new machine, stressed the safety factor, it is clear that he had never forgotten the old image of Stutz: the glory years of the Stutz racers from 1911 to 1916, and the grand tradition of the Stutz Bearcat concept.

It had been said in those days that the Stutz was loud, rough and fast. The concept had appealed to a certain segment of American drivers, who had bought Stutz cars and made Stutz a success. Moscovics was well aware of the fact that nobody would ever again make a success out of the "rough and loud." But in his new car, he could boast that he had something very smooth, very quiet and, well, very fast.

Moscovics never said much about this at the beginning, as he was trying to sell his new concept. But lurking in the back of his mind all the time had been the idea that if it all turned out well and the new engine was as hot as he had hoped it would be, he might yet put the Stutz name back on the glory boards.

He would soon have the opportunity.

It came in 1927 when a motor car enthusiast, Samuel B. Stevens, offered the Stevens Trophy Cup to the maker of a

1927 Stutz AA 4-door Sedan.

standard production passenger sedan which could go around the Indianapolis Motor Speedway at top speed for 24 hours without breaking down, while turning in the fastest average time.

The idea was based on a worry that had been gnawing at Stevens' mind. He was well aware of the fact that specially prepared race cars could go very fast indeed. He was also aware of the fact that the average production passenger car was now much peppier, much faster, than had been thought possible 10 or 15 years earlier.

But he had learned from experience that every time one of those production passenger cars was pushed hard and fast for a long time, something almost inevitably happened. A valve would burn. A piston would break. A connecting rod bearing would hammer out. Something was always breaking down on the hard runs. He was looking for a standard production passenger car that could be pushed hard, and fast, and long—without a breakdown.

Moscovics was convinced that he and his engineers had just created the machine Stevens was thinking about.

He accepted the challenge.

The glory years return: 1927-1928

The scene at the Indianapolis Motor Speedway on the night of April 21, 1927, was enough to make a man shiver in his boots.

A cold wind was howling, and from the sky came a cold rain which finally turned into snow and sleet. Out there on the track three cars were roaring through the night, their drivers peering anxiously ahead, trying to keep the track in sight in the wet, cold and enveloping darkness.

Someone watching it might have suggested that it was all a bit crazy.

Crazy or not, the drivers of the three cars were on a 24-hour endurance run at top speed, trying to win the Stevens Trophy Cup offered to the strictly stock passenger sedan that could turn in the fastest average speed.

Fred Moscovics had brought a new concept in motor cars to Stutz, to rescue the company from oblivion. He was confident that he had the answer to Stevens' question about why no American auto manufacturer could build a stock passenger car that could run at sustained high speed without breaking down.

The three cars out there on the track, all examples of the new Stutz model, were trying to prove Moscovics right.

When forbidding weather had threatened, several Stutz officials suggested postponing the run until better weather. Moscovics himself said, "No, we will go ahead."

The average owner of a motor car could not always wait for good weather when he needed his car, Moscovics said. If his new cars couldn't make the run in lousy weather, they didn't deserve the trophy.

If the cars did make a success of it in bad weather, it would only add to the glory — and that was part of what it was all about. Moscovics was determined to win back for Stutz some of the past glories of racing and the Bearcat days.

Moscovics had prepared three cars for the run — not that he lacked faith in a single car, but he wanted to prove several things besides winning that trophy. One of the cars was a regular steel-bodied sedan. The second was one of the lightweight Weymann-bodied cars, with 500 pounds lopped off the total weight. The third, because of its body style (a two-passenger speedster), was not eligible for the trophy.

Moscovics wanted the two sedans to compete against each other to see how much advantage the lighter car would have. And the speedster: was it a prototype of a new machine that would be called the Black Hawk? Let's face it, Moscovics had been advertising the new Stutz car as the Safety Stutz, but he had never forgotten the old days of Stutz' racing glories. Just perhaps, if the sports type car was good enough, and fast enough, Stutz might go back to the races.

As for the trophy, Moscovics had his highest hopes set on the Weymann sedan. After the run started, it was the one to give trouble — showing the very purpose of the run. At high speeds the motor on the car was missing. It had to be wheeled into the pits several times for work on the distributor, the fuel feed, and the carburetor before it finally began to purr.

Then it did, indeed, prove to be the faster of the two sedans. It began catching up with the steel-bodied sedan, yard by yard, mile by mile. But the heavier machine had been performing so flawlessly the Weymann never caught it. When it was over, it was the heavier car that had nabbed the trophy, with a remarkable 68.44 miles per hour.

The Weymann car, despite the repeated pit stops, had come so close, with a speed of 67.17 mph. Moscovics had hoped it would average over 70 — and, indeed, it probably would have if it hadn't been for the miss problems.

In any case, Moscovics had his trophy and Stutz was back on the glory trail.

What about the speedster? Here was the machine which truly told a significant story. Its average speed was disappointing, only 71.35 mph. Moscovics had been hoping for something near 75, or even 80. But the drivers of this light machine had been forced to slow it down. It ran too fast for its own good.

Equipped with a regular sedan type rear end gear ratio, and running in a chassis which literally allowed it to run away, rpm had crept up to the incredible range of 4,300 to 4,500. The car would literally fly. This would have been wonderful, except that when the engine speed crept up beyond the 4,300 mark, the cylinder head began to overheat and the valves to warp.

This was both good and bad. Pop Greuter, the man who had designed the overhead cam engine and nursed it to "perfection" after so many years, thought he had all the bugs worked out. And he had, except that neither he nor Moscovics had ever dreamed it would rev so high. If the engine had been mated with a higher ratio rear end, the results of the run might, indeed, have lived up to Moscovics' expectations.

All of this aroused an exciting dream for Moscovics. What if they could solve the overheating problem, and match the blazing engine to a proper rear end gear ratio?

The overheating problem turned out to be a baffling one. When Moscovics and his men were unable to solve it, Moscovics fell back on his European connections. He took the blueprints of the Stutz cylinder head to none other than Ettore Bugatti, of Bugatti motor fame. Bugatti examined the blueprints, penciled in a few changes, and handed them back to his friend Moscovics.

Moscovics quickly ordered the changes made in the head. It would take a bit of time.

Next on the list was the rear end gear ratio. When Moscovics had designed the worm drive rear end, he had reckoned with normal speeds for road sedans. The ratios available were 4:75, 5:00 and 5:21 to 1. When trying to go higher, the worm design caused troubles. Moscovics huddled with engineers at Timken Axle. They said they would try.

But before any of this could bear fruit, Moscovics found himself with another challenge on his hands—one that quickly turned into a hot potato.

It was, at least partly, Moscovics' own fault. He had been so confident that he had all the bugs out of the new model Stutz car that he, together with other motor car makers, had been bugging the American Automobile Association (AAA) to stage some stock car races. The competition was tough in the price range Stutz was selling in, and everybody was trying to prove they had the best car. Racing would be one way to settle it.

The AAA, in answer to pressure from people like Moscovics, announced a stock car race, a 75-miler, on the Atlantic City mile and a half board raceway. It was set for May 7, 1927.

When Moscovics looked at the AAA rules for the race, his heart dropped. The rules specified that, while the cars must be strictly stock, they could run stripped.

In other words, fenders and windshields could be removed. The joker was that when Moscovics and his people designed their proud new Stutz, they made the windshield a fixed one. It wouldn't come off. In a race, that could mean as much as a 10-mph difference in speed.

Moscovics had only one recourse. He balked. He declared that Stutz would not run unless all cars were forced to leave the windshields on. Now the AAA people began to snort and huff. But in the end, they agreed. It had been a close one.

The race would be just as close. Moscovics sent into battle the same two sedans that had run for the Stevens Trophy at Indy, plus the same speedster. The competition was one Duesenberg Model A, two Auburn straight eight roadsters, and two Paige straight eight roadsters.

Moscovics knew that, on paper at least, he had the Auburns and Paiges outgunned but, wise in the ways of racing nuts, he suspected that the Paige and Auburn people had probably been up to a few tricks to get a bit more oomph out of their machines. There was no way of finding out, except to run the race. The Stutz roadster was now in production and thus was legal as a stock car in this race.

As the race started Tom Rooney, driving the Stutz speedster, quickly found that he could, indeed, outrun the opposition, but those opposition engineers had been up to a few tricks and his margin was not as much as he would have liked. When he slowed to keep the cylinder head from overheating, he found the Auburns and Paiges right on his tail. When he speeded up to shake them, he was in danger of burning up his engine.

Near the end of the race he found that two of his enemies—a Paige and an Auburn—had slipped into his tail draft and were using his power, that Stutz power, to stay there. And that was the way they finished: one, two, three. It was so close that only a fraction of a second separated them. Moscovics and Rooney had their win, but it was close enough to scare a man. It was bitter to know that they had the speed, but couldn't use it.

In the next AAA-sponsored race, things got a bit hairy. This race was scheduled for the July 4th weekend at the Rockingham board track near Salem, N.H. Moscovics and his men were sweating

Quoting from the 1928 Stutz catalog, "The Stutz worm-gear permits a lowered body and chassis without sacrifice of either headroom or road clearance."

like crazy to get the new cylinder head in production, and test it. They estimated they might make it by the middle of July, but not by July 4. The new Timken axle with higher ratios wasn't available yet either.

Moscovics simply backed out. He notified the AAA that he wouldn't be running at Rockingham. It was then the AAA's turn to explode. Moscovics had been demanding races, and now that the AAA had agreed, he was refusing to run.

Moscovics managed to save face, but barely, by agreeing to run a six-cylinder Mercedes roadster with America's new racing hero, driver Frank Lockhart, at the wheel. Moscovics had to agree to remove a supercharger from the Mercedes.

This time it was the Mercedes that was outclassed. Lockhart, driving with his legendary skill, was close on the tail of the winning Auburn, which set a new record of 89.17 mph. But he couldn't win. Apparently those Lycomings were not such duds after all—and their engineers were learning a few tricks, too.

The next AAA race was scheduled at Atlantic City for September 7, 1927. This time Moscovics would be ready. The new cylinder head and manifolds Bugatti had suggested were now in production. When Moscovics and his men tested an engine equipped with that set-up, their eyes popped. The 95 bhp they had been getting with the old head jumped all the way to 115. Peak rpm had jumped from

3,200 to 3,600. Best of all, the engine would rev all the way to 4,300, even 4,500 and further, with no sign of the overheating problem. There was joy in the Stutz camp.

As if that wasn't joy enough, Timken came up with an axle with all the gear ratios a man could want—all the way to 3:6 to 1.

But there was one more bug to work out. In testing the new machine with the new Challenger engine and higher gear ratios, they found they did, indeed, have a hot number on their hands. It was roaring all the way to the 100-mph mark. Now the tires began to melt. The best tires available couldn't stay with what the new engine had to dish out.

Moscovics took his problem to the Mason Tire Co., which came up with a high speed tire that seemed to stay with the car.

When the race came, it was glory all the way. Moscovics took three brand new Stutz roadsters, Black Hawks, to Atlantic City and devastated the opposition. His three cars, all painted a glittering black, blasted to a one, two, three win, with the top car posting an average speed of 96.308 mph.

On the same day a special chassis fitted with one of the new Stutz Challenger engines blasted its way to the top of Pikes Peak to win the Pikes Peak hill climb, topping all classes. A Stutz Weymann sedan won the Penroe Trophy by besting all cars in its class.

On September 27, 1927, Stutz won a stock car race at Charlotte, N.C., averaging 94.22 mph. Almost simultaneously another Stutz Black Hawk, owned by a wealthy sportsman, entered the Mexican road race, a grueling 100-mile run from Mexico City to Pueblo. The road was so terrible it was known as a car killer, and nobody expected the Stutz to win. But it did. The Stutz had proved to be not only very fast, but tough. The combination of hot engine and low slung chassis had been unbeatable.

When the smoke and dust cleared away at the end of the 1927 racing battles, Stutz was crowned undisputed U.S. champion stock car for the year. Stutz had won every race in which it entered, and every Stutz that had started a race had finished. What more could Moscovics want?

The Stutz glory flag had never flown higher. It was something to match the old Bearcat days.

The year 1928 would be different. There would be more glory for Stutz, but also bitter disappointment. There would be one shattering tragedy, and two important events in which Stutz won a considerable measure of glory, but circumstances were such that one had to dig below the surface to find it.

First, the glory.

Daytona Beach had been, almost from the beginning of the motor car, a favorite spot for speed trials and record runs. In its 25 years, it had become a grand tradition. In 1928, to celebrate the 25th anniversary, Daytona city fathers scheduled a series of races on the beaches, along with the traditional speed trials. These races would also become a tradition.

Stutz was represented by four cars: three sleek new Black Hawk speedsters and Old No. 4, a veteran of the 1927 speed wars. Strangely enough, it was always No. 4 which turned out to be the fastest car, even beating its own teammates.

By this time Moscovics and his engineers had the hot new engine working flawlessly. They had even switched to aluminum pistons and a compression ratio as high as 6:25 to 1. It was the highest in the industry, and something almost unheard of in 1928. Guesses now were that the Stutz engine was churning out as much as 140 or 145 hp.

There was one problem at Daytona for Stutz. Once a car was entered, it could not be altered. So the Stutz drivers and engineers had to figure out which gear ratio would be best for both the beach racing and the speed trials. As it turned out, they chose a ratio which would prove to be almost too low.

The lower ratios made it easy for Stutz to dominate the races. But when the speed trials began, it was apparent they were too low. The Auburns were also much faster than before, and the Auburns had opted for the higher ratios. It meant they suffered in the racing, but did better in the speed trials.

And it was the speed runs that drew the big headlines. The beach, the sand, also played a part. One day the sand would be smoother and harder than other days. Success was partially determined by what kind of sand one had on the day he ran.

When Wade Morton, driving an Auburn, set a new record of 104.347 mph in a two-way run on the mile, it was time for Moscovics and his team to worry. If only they had opted for a higher ratio.

The Stutz drivers tried and tried. The best a Stutz could do was 103.5 mph. Then someone mentioned that the Auburns had a new no-back-pressure bypass muffler. Someone on the Stutz team took a fast look at the rules.

The cars were allowed to run stripped, even if they must be stock. There was nothing that said you couldn't strip off the muffler and exhaust pipe. On the last day of the speed trials, Old No. 4 showed up on the beach with no exhaust pipe, and took one more try.

As the Stutz approached the mile mark, people said the engine was screaming so loudly that it sounded as if it were about to explode. It didn't. It turned in an eye-bugging 112 mph!

That had been with the wind. Now for the return run against the wind. It was fast enough to leave an average at 106.53 mph — and the Auburns could not top that.

Moscovics could now paint a sign on the side of his Stutz: "America's Fastest Stock Car." His pride was showing.

Then came those two incidents — or was it three? — which ripped the Stutz glory flag to shreds.

The first was the great Stutz-Hispano Suiza duel on the track at Indianapolis. It was to become one of the most talked-about and bitterly disputed events in American motor car racing history. It took place on April 18, 1928.

It all began at a dinner for wealthy motor car enthusiasts, when somebody began arguing about the relative merits of American and European cars. Somehow it ended up with a $25,000 bet between Moscovics and his friend Charles T. Weymann, of the Weymann Body Co., the maker of the lightweight Weymann bodies Stutz was using.

Stutz would pit his Black Hawk Challenger against a Hispano Boulogne model, also a stock production semi-sports car much like the Challenger, but

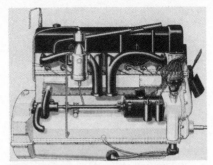

The vertical eight engine with overhead cams and valves.

with a much bigger engine. The Hispano was also longer and heavier. The Hispano had a 480-cubic inch engine, which had its best performance at lower rpm. The Stutz, with 298 cubic inches, was the high-rev engine.

Moscovics was willing to gamble that his high-rev engine (coupled with the low slung worm drive), although outgunned in brute horsepower, would be able to outcorner the Hispano and eventually wear the big Hispano out.

There are many versions of what actually happened. One version has it that the Hispano people, well aware of what they were up against, substituted a faster and more powerful race car for the Boulogne model and kept it tied up in customs so long nobody was able to check it.

The more likely version is that what happened to Stutz was simply one of those freak, "one in a million" accidents which never happened to the Stutz Challenger engine before or afterwards. A lock nut on a valve failed, allowing a valve to drop into a cylinder and destroy the engine. It happened at 140 miles. Up to that time the Stutz had been running according to plan, and probably would have worn the Hispano down, just as Moscovics had planned.

The race had been scheduled as a 24-hour run but, with Moscovics' agreement, the Hispano was flagged down after 19 hours and 20 minutes. It had made the run at an average of 70.14 mph. It probably slowed down after the Stutz was out, but it might be remembered that a Stutz roadster in April, 1927—even before the Challenger engine had been developed —had run 24 hours on the same track at 71.352 mph.

But Stutz was able to salvage a bit of glory from the debacle when Moscovics made one more challenge. He agreed that he had lost his bet, but challenged Weymann to run his Hispano against a substitute Stutz for four and a half hours to finish the 24 hours. Weymann agreed. This time Moscovics showed the Hispano what a Stutz could do. Although the Hispano, with its higher torque at low speed, shot out in front just as it had done in the first run, by the end of 40 laps the Stutz had not only caught the Hispano but was a lap in front. By the end of the run, the Stutz was three full laps ahead.

The only trouble was that nobody paid any attention to the second part of the race. The Stutz had lost the "official" race and Moscovics lost his bet. That was the part that would go down in the record books.

This was shattering enough to the Stutz reputation, but one week later came a terrible tragedy. Frank Lockhart, the blazing star of the racetracks, had not been satisfied with winning at Indy and shattering track records all over the country. He wanted to win the world land speed record.

With the help of Stutz engineers in the Stutz plant, he had been building a twin-engined car to make his attack on that record. True, the engines he had chosen for his run were Miller racing engines, but Stutz had built the chassis and the car bore the name "Stutz Black Hawk Special." For all practical purposes, as far as the public knew, it was a Stutz.

At Daytona, while running at what was believed to be well over 200 mph, the twin-engine car crashed and Lockhart was killed instantly. The blow was so heavy that Stutz officials declared they were halting all racing efforts.

Was it the end of the Stutz climb back to glory? Well, not quite. There still was the highly touted 24-hour Le Mans race in France. In racing circles it had already become one of the most prestigious races in the world by 1928. It was an open secret that Moscovics had planned to be there with his hot new cars. In fact, he had hardly been able to wait.

And now it was an empty dream, because of the tragedy in Florida.

But there would be a Stutz running at

Le Mans after all. The sponsor of that Stutz was none other than Charles Weymann, the man who had won the $25,000 bet from Moscovics—the man who had been so certain the Hispano-Suiza was a better car than a Stutz.

Weymann knew that the Stutz mechanical failure at Indy had been a freak, one-in-a-million accident. He knew that if it hadn't happened, he would have been in trouble. If he needed any more convincing, he got it in that brief second run, where the Stutz ran off from his Hispano.

As for what happened at Le Mans, the record books show that Weymann's Stutz came in second. But what a second!

The favored cars were those of the British Bentley team, three of them. They had won the race the year before. But the Stutz gave them a furious battle. In fact, near the end of the sixth hour, the Stutz had fought its way into the lead, and held it. Weymann's drivers fought off every challenge of the Bentleys.

The Bentleys were faster on the straights but the gallant Stutz, due to its low slung worm drive rear end, was faster in the turns.

The decisive factor in the bitterly fought duel was the gearboxes. The Bentleys were equipped with four-speed gearboxes, a "must" for the wild battle going on around the zig-zag turns of a road race. The Stutz had only a conven- tional three-speed transmission, and the French drivers were forced to rev the Challenger engine unmercifully in second gear. But the Stutz engine took all that punishment without a whimper.

It is almost a miracle that the Stutz gearbox lasted as long as it did—20 hours. Even when top gear on the Stutz gearbox went, Edouard Brisson, the gutsy French driver, never gave up. He continued to run in second gear, with the Stutz engine virtually screaming. Top speed in second gear was 68 mph, with the engine turning nearly 5,000 rpm.

Perhaps everyone, including Brisson, expected the engine to blow at any moment. It didn't. It hung in there tight enough to take second place. Who can say that this was not a moment of glory for Stutz?

The Bentley drivers could only say a prayer of thanks that the Stutz had not been equipped with a decent four-speed, road-racing transmission.

Of course, one doesn't get headlines by taking second place, no matter how glorious the battle may have been.

One thing was certain: even if the official racing days of Stutz had been halted, Moscovics and his engineers had produced what was, for the moment, one of the greatest motor cars of all time.

It was a world class machine.

The twilight years: 1928-1936

The DV-32—the ultimate Stutz! It was the ultimate, at least, in concept and essence, if not the master of such an amazing record of performance as that turned in by the earlier Stutz Black Hawk Challengers.

There the DV-32 stood in the spring of 1931, with a twin overhead cam engine and four valves per cylinder, for a mind-boggling total of 32 valves on a straight eight engine rated at 156 horsepower at 3,900 rpm. Some published ratings gave it 161 hp.

With dimensions of 3⅝ x 4½ producing 322 cubic inches, it would develop a muscular 300 pounds of torque at 2,400 rpm.

Cadillac, a year earlier, had more or less trumped everyone with an unbelievable V-16 with 452 cubic inches, for which 165 hp was claimed. Packard would introduce a magnificent V-12, successor to the earlier Twin Six, with 445 cubic inches and a claimed horsepower of 160. On the horsepower to cubic inch ratio, Stutz was still tops.

Standing on a 134.5-inch wheelbase, the DV-32 was available in a Speedster, a two-passenger coupe, a five-passenger sedan and, on a 145-inch wheelbase, a seven-passenger sedan. A wide variety of custom bodies was also offered.

The new 32-valve engine was topped only by the mighty Duesenberg J with the same engine configuration — 32 valves and twin cams on a straight eight design. The two engines, offered for passenger car use, were unique in American motor car history.

34

Their difference in size prohibited the Stutz engine from challenging the Duesenberg on its own ground, since the Big J had 420 cubic inches and a claimed horsepower rating of 265. Nobody, at that time, had even tried to match it — but probably, inch for inch, the DV-32 Stutz came the closest.

Fred Duesenberg, the great self-made engineer, had helped design the Stutz cylinder head. It should be noted that, in offering the mighty 32-valve engine, Stutz also continued to offer the same engine in a 16-valve version.

Chassis and body styles were identical on the two lines of cars, but prices for the DV-32 ranged from $4,995 for the Speedster to $5,395 for the seven-passenger sedan—and more, of course, for custom bodies. This placed the new Stutz in the Packard and Cadillac price class.

The SV-16's, meanwhile, were priced considerably lower, ranging from $2,895 to $3,895.

It was a magnificent and challenging concept, this new DV-32, but it was never able to meet the requirements of the marketplace. It was introduced in mid-1931, just as America was heading for the bottom of the worst economic depression the country had ever experienced. In that climate, it could never succeed.

The new Stutz "era" — which began with the introduction of a radical new design in 1926, the Vertical Eight Safety Stutz—had started with a bang. First year sales not only met but exceeded expectations. Everything Frederick Moscovics touched seemed to turn to gold.

If only things had continued that way —but they didn't. After that one banner year, when some 5,000 Stutz cars were made, and most of them sold, the whole picture began to come unraveled.

Accurate production and/or sales figures for Stutz are a bit hard to come by. The R.L. Polk Co., the perennial keeper of motor car statistics, reported that only 3,692 new Stutz cars were registered in that record year, 1926. That was a good year for Stutz. Polk records show 2,906 new Stutz cars registered for 1927, and 2,430 for 1928. The Polk register shows no Stutz figures after 1928.

By using serial number sequences provided by the Stutz Motor Car Co. at the time, total production was:
- 4,835 in 1926
- 3,312 in 1927
- 3,516 in 1928
- 1,492 in 1929, not including the Blackhawk line introduced that year.

After 1930, serial number sequences or accurate production figures are hard to find. At least one reputable Stutz historian has suggested that total Stutz production after 1930 did not exceed 700. This appears a bit low.

The serial number sequences that are available suggest that some 1,042 cars were made between 1931 and 1934:
- 537 for 1931
- 105 for 1932
- about 150 for 1933
- 250 for 1934.

Most Stutz historians agree that 1934 was the last year of production for Stutz, and cars numbered and sold in 1935 and 1936 were leftovers from previous production. There is also the possibility that the 1931-1934 serial number sequences contain some duplications, with unsold cars from one year being renumbered for the following year.

Even going back to the 1926-1929 figures, before the depression hit, one does not have to be a genius to see that something was drastically out of kilter at Stutz. These were supposed to be boom years.

The easiest explanation is to blame it on the racing disasters early in 1928: the loss of the match race with Hispano at Indy; the death of racing idol Frank Lockhart during his big try for the world land speed record at Daytona; and the relative failure at Le Mans.

But to lay all, or most, of the blame on these factors is to suggest that the average car buyer did, indeed, base his decision to buy on what a particular make of car was doing on the race circuits. If this were true, how about Packard and Cadillac?

Perhaps a better reason was that Stutz had always built expensive cars and was a relatively low-volume producer. Perhaps, after the Bearcat period, Stutz managers had never been able to revive

1929 Five-passenger Sedan as pictured in the Stutz-Weymann catalog.

that great image, that all-elusive "mystique." And, with production only in the low thousands—or hundreds—it is difficult to maintain the nationwide exposure so necessary for public acceptance.

Moscovics, and Stutz, had tried hard. Moscovics had produced a magnificent motor car in the Stutz Vertical Eight. He had brought a radical but viable concept to the motor car scene. It proved that, from a standpoint of performance and durability, it was qualified to match the best. Its performance record was simply fabulous, but somehow it wasn't enough.

And then there was the Blackhawk episode, which should not be confused with the magnificent Black Hawks (two words), which had performed so well. The Blackhawk chapter is a strange one in Stutz history.

Obviously disappointed in the sales showing by Stutz after 1926, someone in the Stutz command structure was apparently looking for another way to recoup, and did so by coming up with a completely new line of less expensive cars. Introduced in January, 1929, they would not even bear the Stutz name.

Actually, in a sense, there were two lines of cars, although both used the same bodies and chassis and sold for the same prices. The only difference was the engines. One of the engines, a six, was almost identical to the Vertical Eight, with overhead cam and valves, but with two cylinders lopped off. The other was a somewhat mundane flathead eight.

There is some mystery as to why two engines were offered, when they were so nearly the same in performance and power. The six, with 242 cubic inches, was rated at 85 hp; the eight, with 268 inches, was rated at 88. The six obviously had a performance factor nearly as high as the eight because of its overhead cam and valve arrangement. It was even suggested that the six would outperform the eight, but Stutz salesmen and sales literature did not admit it.

The new Blackhawks, riding on a 127.5-inch wheelbase, sold for prices ranging from $1,995 for the four-passenger coupe to $2,735 for a four-passenger Speedster. A five-passenger sedan sold for $2,395.

Obviously, the new line of cars did little to overcome the Stutz sales slump and, after two years, the Blackhawk name was dropped, as well as the 3 x 4¾ flathead eight engine. The six, more in the image of Stutz, was offered for two more years.

We have been unable to find authentic production figures on the lower-priced, Stutz-made Blackhawks, but available serial number sequences indicate that about 1,000 of the sixes were made in 1929, plus 250 of the eights. No serial number sequences are available for 1930 or later, which raises the possibility that those sold in 1930 and later were leftovers from 1929.

In the meantime, another major "happening" had taken place at Stutz. Frederick E. Moscovics had departed. He had lasted three years with the company.

It was Moscovics who had brought that radical new concept in motor car engineering to Stutz in 1925, and nursed it to perfection as probably the best performing motor car on the American scene for at least 1927 and 1928. But when the sales figures failed to match its technical performance, somebody had to be blamed. Apparently the accusing finger was pointed at Moscovics. In any case, for reasons which have not been clearly spelled out, Moscovics resigned from the presidency of Stutz in January, 1929, and left the company.

After 1929 the Stutz story becomes a confusing one, especially when considering the small number of cars being made. One area of confusion was the Blackhawk episode.

It should be remembered that when the new Vertical Eight was first introduced in 1926, it came with a 3 3/16 bore by 4 1/2 inch stroke, for 287 cubic inches. By 1927 the engine had been bored out to 3 1/4, giving 298 inches and increasing the horsepower rating from 92 to 95. By 1929 the engine had been bored out again, to 3 3/8, for 322 inches and 113 hp, in which form it would continue through 1930.

It was in April, 1931, that the "Ultimate Stutz," the DV-32 appeared. The single cam engine remained in production—now called the SV-16 to differentiate between it and the DV-32—but the specifications on the standard engine remained the same. In fact, the only difference between the SV-16 and the DV-32 was in the cylinder head and cam drive.

The whole difference, then, became simply a matter of what Stutz ad men called "volumetric efficiency." Loosely translated, it meant more oomph per cubic inch—about 60 percent more, in fact.

Of course, some estimates on the single cam engine, when tuned for racing in those glory rich years of 1927 and 1928, may have gone as high as 140 hp or even more. It doesn't matter, as the ad men continued to rate the SV-16 at 113 hp and the DV-32 at 156 hp, or 161, your choice.

In any case, adding to the complexity

of the Stutz picture—if not the confusion—was the fact that in the early 1930s the Stutz was offered in as many as 28 body styles. Many of them, of course, were custom bodies. The more standard ones were built by Weymann.

Stutz may not have produced many cars in the 1930s, but styling had kept pace with the industry. The Stutz machines of that period were among the most beautiful classics ever produced.

It has been indicated that, after those freak and tragic incidents in 1928, with Stutz more or less officially withdrawing from speed and racing activities, the assault on the glory trail had ended. But it hadn't, not quite.

Even if the Stutz company was withdrawing, it did not keep a few individuals not connected with Stutz—but well aware of what Stutz cars were capable of doing—from mounting assaults of their own—using cars bearing the Stutz name.

After the magnificent showing by a Stutz at Le Mans in 1928, when it was obvious the Stutz would have won if it had been equipped with a proper four-speed road-racing transmission, it was inevitable that someone would wonder how a Stutz would do if it were outfitted with such a transmission.

At the time, French pride was suffering. France, the home base for the world-famous Le Mans race, and the country which had once so proudly dominated the racing scene, had been forced to submit to the ignominy of seeing a powerful team of British Bentleys kidnap the glory two years in a row.

Without a French car capable of challenging the Bentleys, the French turned to Stutz. If the drivers were French, it would restore at least a measure of glory to the French flag.

Louis Chiron, one of France's top drivers, and Edouard Brisson, a co-driver of the Stutz in 1928, had seen what a Stutz could do during the 1928 race. They were able to sell a wealthy French sportsman on backing a team of three Stutz cars for the 1929 race.

They quickly ran into trouble. By 1929, with interest in racing more or less gone, the Stutz chassis had been stretched to 134.5 inches, and made much heavier to carry the luxury bodies being ordered. Such a chassis could never be competitive at Le Mans, and the rules demanded stock cars.

Moscovics was gone, but the new president, Edgar S. Gorrell, had enough pride in the Stutz image to cooperate. He produced a special run of a 127.5-inch lightened chassis with speedster bodies. He even revived the old Bearcat name for them.

To make it stock, and legal at Le Mans, at least 25 of the cars had to be built — and it was done. Sadly enough, few Americans would ever get to see the exciting new revival of the Bearcat, since it was aimed for export only and never advertised in the U.S. In any case, Chiron and Brisson had their Le Mans cars.

Then someone came up with the idea of superchargers to give the gutsy engine even more pep, keeping in mind that the competition would be coming up with new tricks. The supercharger really was not new. Even Moscovics, before he left, had talked about superchargers, and at least one Stutz engine had been equipped with a blower for an assault on Pikes Peak (it had won). Everyone knew what superchargers had done for the Duesenbergs and Millers at Indy.

But there wasn't enough time to work out a proper installation and test it adequately before the Le Mans race. When the three Stutz machines showed up in France, only one of them had a blower. As events would prove, the bugs had not been worked out.

It was a gallant fight, that 1929 Le Mans race, but destiny had not decreed it to be a Stutz year. For one thing, the Bentley engineers had, indeed, been up to new tricks, and the Bentley team showed up with still faster and more powerful cars than in 1928.

Even then, the Stutz cars, with their French drivers, may have made it if they had not been plagued with mechanical problems, something Stutz machines had usually been able to avoid.

The supercharged Stutz encountered problems early in the race. The supercharger failed to work properly at first, and the car had to be called into the pits repeatedly for adjustments to the supercharger set-up. All chances of winning were lost in those pit stops.

When the machine finally began to whine, the driver apparently over-revved it while in the lower gears in the turns. A rear main bearing was damaged, allowing oil into the clutch. When the clutch began to slip, the car had to be called in for good.

The second Stutz developed ignition trouble, and also had to be called into the pits repeatedly for adjustments. By the time it was running smoothly, it was too far behind to catch up.

The third Stutz split a fuel tank on the rough track and ran out of fuel. It had to be retired.

At the finish, only one of the three Stutz machines was still running — the num-

Trim, racy lines seen in this 1930 Stutz Cabriolet defy its large, masculine dimensions.

ber two car which had been plagued with ignition trouble. But this machine showed what a Stutz could really do, by passing one car after another. If only it had had more time. It managed to fight its way back to fifth place as the race ended. It was a magnificent showing—if you were willing to forget about the four cars that came in ahead of it.

But there was something else happening that year. Believe it or not, when the 33 cars lined up at Indy for the "Big 500," there on the track was a Stutz.

After several years of restricted engine size at the Indianapolis track, with the squeeze forcing it all the way down to 91.5 cubic inches for several years, 1930 was the year in which the lid was blown off. Engines all the way up to 366 inches were allowed. It opened the gates for stock cars.

It was a stock Stutz Torpedo Speedster out there on the track in 1930, driven by L.L. Corum. The machine made top lap speeds of up to 94 mph, and averaged 85.340 mph to take 10th place. This was quite respectable, considering that the Stutz was running with an almost completely stock chassis, weighing some 1,500 pounds more than the racing chassis being used by most of the other cars, including the other "stocks."

All this proved that the Stutz still had a lot of growl left, and that it could run the Indy 500 in the fastest of company. The winners that year were the fabulous Millers.

Now, near the marque's end, there surfaced the "Ultimate Stutz," the DV-32.

Somehow, even though Moscovics was gone, Stutz management never completely forgot the performance image of Stutz. After the introduction of the 32-valve engine, Stutz management bowed once more to the performance image by introducing the Super Bearcat, a stubby speedster on a super short 116-inch chassis. The cars were sold with a guarantee of 100 mph.

Despite this sporty configuration, the DV-32 was seldom raced. This may, at least partly, have been due to the adverse economic times. Stutz officials were busy in a desperate fight to keep the company alive. There was neither time nor money for playing around at the races.

In addition, the opposition in Europe had been busy making their competition cars faster and more powerful, year by year. A Stutz no longer really had a chance at a place like Le Mans. Or did it?

Edouard Brisson, the Frenchman who had so nearly seen a Stutz triumph at Le Mans, was still around. When he heard about the new 32-valve engine, his ears perked up. Maybe the Stutz still had a win coming. So it was Brisson, with a DV-32, who made one more try in 1932.

Nobody will ever know what might have happened if the Stutz had run the entire race. As it was, Brisson had determined to play it safe, not to push the Stutz, and allow the madmen to tear their cars —and, perhaps, themselves—to pieces.

He was running behind the pack when, in the early stages of the race, he rounded a corner to face a melee of smashed cars. One driver, in an effort to avoid a smashup, was spinning in the center of the track. There was no way for Brisson to avoid hitting the spinning car. The Stutz was out of the race. A Stutz had sung its last song of challenge at Le Mans.

Meanwhile, back in the U.S., Stutz was losing another, more important, challenge. E.S. Gorrell had done a creditable job of trying everything:

• He had tried to make some of the most magnificent cars that had ever borne the Stutz name. In that, he had succeeded.

• He had tried to maintain the image of brilliant performance for Stutz motor cars. In that, too, he had largely succeeded.

• He had fought a desperate battle to keep the Stutz Motor Car Co. alive. In that, he had failed.

It was a combination of the bitterly cruel depression, the vanishing market for high class motor cars, and the high cost of constantly making new models available, to keep abreast of the competition, that deprived him of the possibility of succeeding in that last fight.

Near the end, in the 1935-1938 period, in a final effort to salvage something, the company introduced a small commercial vehicle with radical design. Its engine, transmission and rear axle— the entire power package — were mounted at the rear. But even this was not enough to save Stutz. The year 1936

1931 Cabriolet with straight eight engine, 4-speed transmission, and vacuum-assist hydraulic power.

was the last in which the great Stutz motor cars would appear on the market, and the last for the company. In 1937 it would be bankrupt.

Perhaps there will always be some who insist that the total contribution of Stutz to motor car history in America was relatively small — unless one is willing to consider the image.

It is simply a fact, which nobody can wipe away, that a magnificent sports car concept in the early years—a car called the Bearcat — would forever live in the memory of men to whom cars were more than transportation. By the same token, nobody would ever be able to wipe from the record books the glorious story of performance written by the famed Stutz White Squadron in the years around 1915, when the Stutz name reigned supreme on the racetracks of America. All this was the legacy of Harry C. Stutz.

Nor can anyone erase the record of those final glory years, centered around 1927, when Stutz cars of a new breed climbed to the peaks. This was the legacy of that dynamic engineer, Frederick E. Moscovics.

In image, performance, quality and endurance, the Stutz name had been to the top of the mountain: Stutz, the car with guts!

Editor's note: The spelling of the name Moscovics has been Americanized over the years, with the use of the letter "c" rather than "k," as in Moskovics, the more traditional spelling. The popularized version was retained for this chapter on Stutz. Fred Moscovics himself, however, was quoted as preferring the original version with the "k."

40

II
DUESENBERG

Birth of the legend: 1876-1905

It was in the fall of 1928 in a small manufacturing plant in Indianapolis, Indiana, that one of the most dramatic events in the history of the American motor car was taking place.

The mightiest American motor car that man had ever seen was being born — a machine that, in time, would come to be proclaimed king of them all. It was a motor car upon which more superlatives would be showered than any other car in American history, then and now.

It was a motor car which would bear the aura of sable and mink. It would come to be treasured almost like the crown jewels of Czarist Russia.

All this, despite the fact that it was not a car destined to make history in the sense of mass production, which had made the American motor car supreme. In fact, when the totals would be counted, the production figures were pitifully small: less than 500 for a production run of eight years.

There would be, of course, men who argued that this fabled machine was something less than perfect. After all, is there anyone so foolish as to suggest the perfect machine — a motor car without a flaw—has ever been made (or ever will be)?

But it is a fact that the machine taking final shape in that Indiana shop was the most powerful, the fastest, the most spectacular and, in many ways, the best passenger car ever made up to that time — and, many will argue, since. It was unique in its incorporation of mechanical, engineering, metallurgical and quality features, which clearly set it into a class by itself.

Then, and even more in years to come, it would be called sensational, colossal, superb, fantastic, magnificent and legendary—just for a start.

One cannot tell the story of the car without telling the story of the Duesen-

The Duesenberg brothers, Augie & Fred, in 1925.

berg brothers, Fred and August, who were largely responsible for creating that mighty machine. But the story extends far beyond the dimensions, or the greatness, of the "J."

Long before the Model J was born, the Duesenberg brothers, working as a team, had achieved what few others had achieved in the world of designing and building magnificent racing engines. Then there was the Model A Duesenberg passenger car which, some knowledgeable motorists claimed, outshone the "Big J" in many ways.

The Duesenbergs also designed and built the first marine engine in the world to drive a boat faster than 60 mph. They built the first American racing car to win the Le Mans Grand Prix in France. They built cars which three times won the Indianapolis 500. They were the first to successfully use a supercharger in a winning race car at Indy. They built race cars that stormed under the checkered flag at prestigious race tracks all over America.

Prior to that, they designed and built pioneering motor cars for the public under the name "Mason," starting around 1906. Modified Masons ran in and won races around the country. Even before that, Fred modified an early day Marion and won a race in it.

Still earlier, it had been bicycles: Fred set a record for the two-mile run—a record that stood for years.

It all started at Kirchheide, Lippe Detmold, Germany. There, in December of 1876 and 1878, respectively, Frederick and August Duesenberg were born. According to Duesenberg family history, as traced by the late Col. Earl Haefner, it was the dream of Louise Duesenberg's oldest son, Henry, to travel to America to "seek his fortune." His mother, a widow, nixed the idea—at least until Henry was 21 and could take off on his own.

He left behind a weeping mother, certain she would never see her eldest son again. But his glowing accounts of life in the "new world" persuaded Frau Duesenberg to sell her property in Germany, pack up the youngsters still at home, and take off for America.

Fred was eight and Augie was six when they arrived in the U.S. The family settled down on a farm near Rockford, Iowa, where the youngsters did their growing up. Without the boyhood dream of elder brother Henry, the Fred and Augie story, as we know it today, would never have taken place — at least as far as the U.S. and the creation of all those motor cars are concerned.

According to the Haefner account, none of the family noted any exceptional mechanical ability on the part of Fred while he was a boy. It was probably a case of latent, or dormant, genius waiting to be freed. For when Fred was 17 and got his first job with an implement dealer who sold, erected and repaired windmills, his natural talent for things mechanical burst quickly into being. Folks said he was a whiz at repairing balky windmills.

In this period, the bicycle had become the latest mania. Here was the first machine to liberate man from the boundaries set by his feet—to give man, woman and child mobility beyond the measure of footsteps. Even the horse and buggy was far too expensive for the average working man of the day.

It was the next logical step, after serving a three-year apprenticeship with the windmills, to graduate to the bicycle. Fred opened a bicycle repair shop in Rockford around 1897, and Augie was taken in as a helper, or partner. Now it was Augie's turn to show that in his fingers lay a natural "bent" for making things go. The great partnership had begun.

By this time, Fred had started entering bicycle races around his hometown area. When he became dissatisfied with the bicycles available for racing, he designed his own — the beginning of his long, inventive career. Proof that he had been able to "improve the breed" came in 1898, when he set a world record for the two-mile bicycle run at 4:24. It was a record that would stand for 14 years— not a bad omen for things to come.

The next step was to get more speed out of the human-powered "machines." The first crude motorcycles were beginning to appear on the scene. Since Fred didn't have one, he designed a motor of his own and made one. It was another big stride in Fred Duesenberg's career.

There is little in the record to indicate how successful the first Duesenberg-built motorcycle was, but it didn't really matter for, almost at the same time, the "real thing" was chugging into view—the first of the early day motor cars. Most of them were primitive, unreliable, one-cylinder affairs, but they were enough to fire the imagination of a man like Fred Duesenberg. It was time for his love affair with the two-wheelers to fade, as the new-fangled chug buggies came onto the scene.

The record of what happened during the next couple of years has become a bit muddled but, considering the nature of Fred Duesenberg, it is almost certain he had further contacts with internal combustion engines and the early horseless carriages. With motor car repair shops virtually nonexistent, it is probable that he repaired a few at the bicycle shop.

But, most important, one of the early day motor cars that was beginning to make a name for itself was the Rambler, being made by the Thomas B. Jeffery Co., of Kenosha, Wisconsin.

Jeffery, like many early motor car makers, had started out by manufacturing a bicycle. It, too, had been called the Rambler. Fred had known and ridden the Ramblers during his bicycle career. Switching from Rambler, the bicycle, to

Rambler, the motor car, was a logical step.

The new Rambler automobile quickly caught on and almost overnight climbed into one of the leading positions in the infant industry. It was, perhaps, inevitable that the presence of the Rambler in Kenosha—which wasn't too far away—acted like a magnet, attracting Fred Duesenberg. He ripped up his stakes in Des Moines and obtained a job with Jeffery as a mechanic and test driver. This was around the end of 1902.

It is almost certain that, during Fred's two years with Jeffery, he soaked up every detail in the design and manufacture of the nimble little machine. The experience almost inevitably set his brain to whirling with dreams of someday making a car of his own.

By 1904, Fred had reached the point at Jeffery where he felt there was little more to be learned. Pulling up his Des Moines stakes had not been that final after all, and he returned "home."

By this time the new-fangled automobile had begun to establish itself to the point where there was demand for servicing, repairs and parts. Another industry was being born, and Fred was in the middle of it all.

After returning to Des Moines, Fred worked, for a time, with Hoopes Brothers as a machinist. When a man named Cheney Prouty established the Iowa Automobile & Supply Co., Fred went to work for him as superintendent of the machine shop. Things were staring to jell in earnest now, in more ways than one.

For one thing, Duesenberg was getting his first taste of motor car racing. It was during this period that Fred acquired his first motor car, a used Marion. It was a four-cylinder, air-cooled machine with the engine mounted crosswise in the chassis, Franklin style. When Fred heard that a motor car race was being organized for the Mason City (Iowa) Fair—the year is believed to be 1905 — he promptly went to work to prepare his Marion for the race.

There probably wasn't a great deal a man could do in that early era to "soup up" one of the primitive chug buggies, but it was a mark of the racing genius-to-be that Fred devised an early day exhaust header system for his four-cylinder Marion, switching to one pipe per

The famous Duesenberg insignia could be found on various parts of the car.

cylinder instead of one for four exhausting through a manifold.

Beyond that, he stripped the car for action, removing the body and leaving nothing beyond a tiny perch atop the fuel tank amidship to sit on.

The record shows that Fred Duesenberg, driving the car himself, won the race, crossing the finish line 50 feet ahead of a Ford driven by Fred Newkirk.

Fred Duesenberg had won the first motor car race of his career — but not his last. He was, indeed, off to the races!

In the meantime, according to research by Fred D. Roe, a Duesenberg historian with the Auburn-Cord-Duesenberg Club, Fred had become acquainted with a prominent attorney in Des Moines, Edward R. Mason.

The story goes that Mason and his sons had brought their own motor car and other machinery to Fred to be repaired. Fred became a friend of the family — enough so that he was, on occasion, invited to the Mason home for a Sunday dinner.

According to Roe, it was over one of these Sunday dinners that the subject came up about the future of the American motor car industry, such as it was in 1904 or 1905. Fred was bold enough to suggest that he had some ideas of his own about making a motor car. The elder Mason, suggesting that Duesenberg put his ideas on paper, said, "We'll see what can be done." Fate was making great strides now.

The legend takes off, in high gear: 1905-1914

*C*ol. Earl Haefner's Duesenberg *family history and other sources confirm that neither Fred nor his brother August ever finished high school. Nor did either of them ever attend an accredited school of engineering.*

Fred Roe's research indicates that, largely at Edward Mason's suggestion,

Fred did work his way through a drafting course with the International Correspondence School.

In any case, it is a measure of the astounding intellect of this unusual man that, even without a formal education, Fred Duesenberg became Iowa's first member of the American Society of Automotive Engineers. In time, he would become one of the most articulate and respected members of that society, traveling as an equal among the university-trained engineers of his day.

With opportunity knocking at the door, Fred Duesenberg was ready to go. In fact, most indications are that he had already done the design work on his engine. It turned out to be a two-cylinder opposed 5 x 5 for an early day "square" configuration, plus overhead, or valve-in-head, valve action.

Duesenberg was not inventing, or pioneering, the use of the overhead valve action, for David Dunbar Buick had used it at least as early as 1903. The Marion that Duesenberg had converted into a race car had used valve-in-head action, and this may have been one of the factors which influenced him to travel that route. But it was significant that Fred had recognized the advantages of this design so early, because it was a feature that would be important in all his future successes to come—and would, in time, be incorporated into virtually every motor car engine in the world. Most engines being made in 1905-1906, however, did not have this feature.

While Fred designed and built his engine, and put his ideas about a motor car to go with it on paper, Mason tackled the job of lining up capital to finance an automobile making enterprise. This was one time when the designer and maker of a new motor car would forego the honor of having his name borne by the product.

The Mason Motor Car Co. was born.

When the Duesenberg-designed Mason appeared on the market in the early summer of 1906, the announcement descriptions gave it as a 90-inch wheelbase, five-passenger machine weighing 1,750 pounds. The transmission was planetary and the drive by chain, following the accepted practice of the day.

The engine was mounted lengthwise, amidships, under the driver's seat. Top speed was listed at 40, and the price was $1,350.

There was little that was startling or innovative about the new entry into the motor car market, except that it was probably one of the best built cars in its class — plus the fact that Fred, influenced by his racing experience and the desire for a machine that would "go," had built a lot of power into a relatively small machine.

With only two cylinders, but a big bore and stroke, the new engine boasted 196 cid and 24 hp. In size and power, it was more engine than many of the fours then being built. It was bigger and more powerful than the famed Model T Ford, still to come, with four cylinders, 176 cid and 20 hp.

The engine enabled the early Mason ads to boast: "The fastest and strongest two cylinder car in America." A stronger boast followed: "Takes any hill in high gear."

It did storm at least one hill. On July 4, 1906, only a few weeks after the Mason appeared on the market, Fred entered one of them in a hill climbing contest at Des Moines, organized by the Iowa Automobile Club. A published report said: "The Mason won easily against all competitors." The competition, the report stated, included a four-cylinder car rated at 40 hp. Incidentally, the report did not state whether the Mason went up the hill in high gear.

Another early stunt to prove the power and toughness of the new car was to drive it up the steps of the State Capitol in Des Moines, both forward and backwards. But there was more to come.

One of the most widely held assumptions of the day was that winning car races was one way to sell motor cars. People wanted a car that would outdo the competition, the thinking went. Ford, Buick, Peerless and many others had taken a crack at it.

Never one to back away from such challenges, Fred hoisted the body off one of his Masons, stripped it, prepared it for racing, dubbed it "The Goat," and went racing.

If anybody needed proof that Fred Duesenberg was able to build a good motor car, they soon got it. The little Goat, during the next three years, blazed a path of glory to places as far as Chicago, Milwaukee, Kansas City and even San Antonio, Texas. After winning a series of hill climbs in the home area, the car:

- In June, 1907, set a perfect score in a reliability run to Chicago and Milwaukee.
- In September, 1907, won three races against more expensive, four-cylinder cars.
- In August, 1907, set a new speed record on the run from Kansas City to Denver, Colorado.
- In the same month, won all events at the Oldfield Meet in Des Moines.
- In August, 1908, won a 1,000-mile reliability run to Chicago.
- In July, 1909, was the only two-cylinder car to finish the Glidden Tour.
- In April, 1910, set a record in winning a 121-mile match race in Kansas.
- In 1910 (the year before the big annual 500-mile race was inaugurated at Indianapolis), won a 10-mile free-for-all handicap race on the new Indianapolis race track.

A company ad boasted: "The Goat has been the undisputed speed car in its class, the fastest two cylinder car in America and many times victor over high priced and high powered cars."

In perhaps the most grueling race of all, a 24-hour endurance run held at Milwaukee in September, 1907, the Goat failed to finish, but not because of motor or machine failure. After running for seven hours, for reasons not clearly known, the Goat went out of control and crashed through a fence. Fred, as driver, suffered a broken collarbone and was out of the race.

It is possible that the crash was due to the crippling arthritis which had afflicted Fred's hands as early as his teen years. Gripping the wheel of a bucking race car for seven hours may have been beyond the endurance of those crippled hands. It is known that Fred soon left the driving — when it came to racing — to men with better hands than his.

In later years the arthritis became so severe that doctors were forced to break the bones in his hands to enable him to retain some use of his fingers. It was an

A Mason runabout, the first passenger car designed by Fred Duesenberg. It was named for Edward R. Mason, the financial backer who bankrolled Fred Duesenberg's first project in making motor cars for the public.

affliction he was forced to bear—but he still had full use of his brain, plus the nimble and gifted fingers of his brother Augie.

How well did the new Duesenberg-designed Mason sell? How much of a success was it, from a business standpoint?

The record is not complete. It is apparent that the company was never able to organize a nationwide network of dealerships and give the machine a truly hefty push, saleswise, on a national basis. However, the car quickly earned a reputation as one of the most reliable, toughest and most powerful machines in its class. It was marketed in places as far as Milwaukee, Kansas City, and other so-called regional markets.

Research by Fred Roe has turned up the fact that in 1908, after the Mason was considerably improved, approximately 1,500 machines were sold. About 95 workmen were employed in the factory. By comparison to some of the more successful makers even in that early time, it was a relatively small operation.

Perhaps Mason, in accepting the challenge of raising the capital to start the project, had considered that his job was done, and that the responsibility for promoting and selling the motor car would be carried out by others. Perhaps he even expected Fred Duesenberg and his brother August to do it.

But the Duesenberg brothers, despite their brilliance as mechanics, engineers and designers, were not hot-shot salesmen or promoter types. The job of promoting sales and providing the financial wizardry to send a fledgling company to the top required a man like Billy Durant, or John North Willys.

In any case, by 1909 Mason and his associates, as backers of the Mason, were ready to sell out. The man who took over the company was Fred L. Maytag.

Maytag, the man who made a success out of making and selling high quality washing machines, undoubtedly believed he could repeat his success with motor cars, but it was not to be. After taking over the Mason Automobile Co. late in 1909, the company lasted only another five years.

Fred Duesenberg retained his connection with the firm, as chief engineer, at the beginning, but when Maytag decided to move his operations to Waterloo, to be near his other enterprises, Fred and August decided to remain in Des Moines.

The car itself remained a Duesenberg design, and both four and two-cylinder machines had become available.

Fred had designed and built a four-cylinder engine, with the aim of making it the powerplant for the new model Masons. Like the highly successful twin, it was a good one and a powerful one. But the small company had found that the cost of manufacturing it would be too big a financial load, so it contracted for 500 four-cylinder motors from the Excelsior Motor Co., of Chicago. Thus, under pressure of the marketplace, the Duesenberg influence on the Mason-Maytag automobile designs was fading.

But this didn't mean that the brothers had stopped working on engines. They were obsessed with power and speed.

One of the first four-cylinder designs the brothers worked on, as early as 1908, was an overhead cam. Then they came up with another unorthodox valve action design which, for its time at least, brought even more spectacular results. It was something which, for the next few years, would be the Duesenberg trademark: the famed "walking beam" engine.

It was a masterpiece of simplicity for a valve-in-head construction. It was also a gem in performance, power and reliability. Actually, the valves would turn out to be horizontal, in relation to the cylinder, but the valve ports were in the head and thus qualified for valve-in-head classification.

The big difference was that instead of operating the valves with pushrods, the normal practice, the Duesenberg brothers came up with extremely long—nearly a foot long—rocker arms mounted not on the top, but on the sides of the engine block, with the upper ends of the rockers bearing directly on the valve stems and the lower ends directly on the camshaft.

Once again, it was not a Duesenberg invention. It was an adaptation of an old steam engine design. But in adapting the design to an internal combustion gasoline engine, the Duesenbergs probably brought this layout to its peak of perfection. The proof would come in the performance.

Most mechanics and engineers who have examined this design agree that the performance boost came not only from the fact that the engine breathed through the head, but that the design allowed what were probably the cleanest and most symmetrical combustion chambers ever seen to that time. The design eliminated the so-called "dead pockets" so common in early day engines, in which much of the explosive force of the fuel combustion was wasted in a push against immovable cast iron.

In short, it was the closest thing to a "hemi-head" that anyone had seen to that date. And while the compression ratio of the early Duesenberg walking beam engines is not known, it is almost certain that it was higher than on most engines then in existence.

By the end of 1911 the Duesenberg brothers had been able to test the new engine to the point where they were satisfied. They were ready to go to the races.

There is some confusion as to the size of the new Duesenberg engines. The available record indicates they started out with 3¾ x 5, which would have been a 221-cubic-inch engine. Another record shows 3¹³⁄₁₆, for 228 cubic inches.

A 1911 Maytag. This was still a Fred Duesenberg design carried over when Fred L. Maytag bought out the Mason company and changed the name of the car to Maytag.

Still another shows 3.875 x 5, for 236 cid. The engines were relatively small, but powerful. Part of the confusion on size may have been due to a constant reboring of the engine to squeeze out more power.

Estimates on the horsepower of these engines have varied, with at least one source indicating 58 bhp. Other sources have gone higher. But even 58 was a healthy chunk of power for such a small engine in 1912.

Proof of what the new engine could do was not long in coming. A Mason racer with the Duesenberg engine won the Wisconsin Trophy race at Milwaukee in 1912. The car then took the Pabst Trophy. Venturing further afield, the Duesenberg engine won in such prestigious races as Elgin and Brighton Beach.

One of the best examples of what the Duesenberg-Mason could do came when the brothers took their car to Galveston for the Cotton Carnival races in August. At this meet, with Harry Endicott at the wheel, the little car started by winning 15-mile and 25-mile races. It was only the beginning. The big race on the program was a 200-miler, a so-called free-for-all open to cars up to 600 cubic inches. The Duesenbergs decided to challenge the big boys, and entered the race.

It was a grueling run, lasting more than three hours. While the Duesenberg-Mason did not win it, when the checkered flag went down on the winning car (a Simplex Zip), the Duesenberg was right behind, in second place. Seven minutes behind, in third place, was a Mercedes.

What is so exciting about second place? Simply this: the Simplex had a 452-cubic-inch engine, virtually twice the size of the Duesenberg engine. The Mercedes was even bigger, at nearly 600 inches.

Most old time race fans remember that the famed Indy 500 began as an annual event in 1911. What they may not remember is that almost every car in the race that year was a monster. The winning Marmon six, with 447 cubic inches, was actually one of the smaller cars entered.

In 1912, the year the Duesenberg brothers began their racing career in earnest, it was almost the same. Some historians have suggested that it was the size of this formidable competition that frightened the Duesenbergs away from Indy that year. What could a little 230-inch engine do against such monsters? The fact is that they did take one of their new Duesenberg-Masons to Indianapolis, with Lee (not Barney) Oldfield as driver. But the Duesenberg engine blew up in practice, before the race, and the car never got a chance to run.

Fred Roe has suggested that the engine failure may have been due to boring out the engine cylinders too much, making the cylinder walls too thin. It would have been an effort to squeeze a bit more power out of the engine to make it competitive with the "big boys." The Duesenberg engines did quite well in other races that year, even the long ones.

But one of the significant factors in that 1912 race at Indy was the fact that a 300-cubic-inch Mercer took third place and ran only about two miles per hour slower than the 490-cubic-inch National that won it.

The Duesenberg brothers could not have missed this significant fact, and it encouraged them to take another crack at it in 1913, especially since a new rule at Indy limited engine size to 450 cid.

Up to this time the theory had been: the bigger the engine, the faster you go. In the early days this had, to a large extent at least, been true. But now, for the first time, builders of race cars were forced to recognize the old (it was new, then) formula about the ratio of weight to power to speed. To over-simplify the formula: if a 500-cubic-inch engine, rated at 200 hp and in a car weighing two tons, could go 100 mph, why couldn't a 250-cubic-inch engine, rated at 100 hp and in a chassis weighing only one ton, go equally as fast?

Since a 300-inch Mercer had done so well in 1912, why couldn't a 350-inch

As a publicity stunt, a Mason was driven up the steps of the Iowa State Capitol Building.

Duesenberg-Mason win it in 1913?

There is nothing to indicate that this is what Fred Duesenberg was thinking, but the record shows that they did come up with a 4.316 x 6 Duesenberg walking beam engine for 1913 with 350 cid, and with their sights on the checkered flag at Indy.

Such reasoning may have been sound, but there are many other intangible factors in a 500-mile race that can cost you the win. There are so many that the Indy track has come to be known as "heart-break alley."

But there it was. For 1913 the Duesenberg brothers managed to qualify not one, but four cars in the big 500. And, for a while at least, there was a Duesenberg-Mason in first place.

But that fast car, driven by Willie Haupt, began to blow tires and the clutch began to slip. When it was over, the Haupt car had managed only 9th place. The other Duesenberg-powered cars were not in the running.

Adding to the disappointment was the fact that one of the 300-inch Mercers had moved up to second place. The winning car, a Peugeot, had a 448-inch engine, just a hair under the limit.

Certainly, the Duesenberg brothers could take consolation in managing to finish and place in such a grueling race —a feat which has always been a triumph, then and now. It also helped that coming up behind Haupt was a whole string of prestige machines: Peugeot, Isotta Fraschini, Stutz, Case and Mercedes. All were bigger than the Duesenberg-Mason.

But the biggest consolation of all came from the fact that, in other prestigious tracks around the country, the Duesenberg engines were still winning. With that respectable showing at Indy and the other wins to garnish it, the time had come when big time race promoters and race car makers could no longer afford to ignore the "country boys" from Iowa.

People who wanted powerful and fast engines began beating the proverbial path to the door of the Duesenberg brothers' shop.

One of them was Commodore J.A. Pugh, who wanted a marine powerplant big enough, fast enough and powerful enough to win the international Harmsworth Trophy boat race in England.

When the brothers quoted a price of $50,000, Pugh never hesitated. The result was a monstrous 12-cylinder, in-line engine with a bore of 6½ inches by 7½ stroke and a crankshaft more than 10 feet long. The horsepower rating was a mind-boggling 600.

The brothers made three of the engines. Two were mounted in the Commodore's boat, Disturber IV, and the third was a spare. The Disturber was shipped to England to challenge the greatest of the world, but World War I erupted, involving England. The race was cancelled, and the Disturber was shipped back to the U.S.

But the boat still managed to make history. In a trial run, the craft was clocked at an astonishing 62 nautical miles (69.12 land miles) per hour. It was the first time a boat had ever been propelled faster than 60 mph, and a new world record was set.

How could the Duesenberg brothers, men with no formal engineering training, pull off such feats? The answer is that, on rare occasions, men are born who are endowed by nature with a genius that allows them to tower over the mob.

The early day history of the motor car has several such stories. One of the best examples is Jesse Vincent, another unschooled, self-taught engineer, who designed the famed Packard Twin Six.

By the end of 1913, the Duesenbergs had moved to St. Paul, Minnesota, where they set up a shop to build engines. Powerplants were custom made for anyone who wished to buy them for race cars, boats, airplanes and even a tractor. Almost all the engines they built for the next few years followed the famed "walking beam" design.

Before this phase of their career ended, they built a giant V-16 aircraft engine so powerful that it took three of the biggest dynamometers to measure its power, which was pegged at 800 hp. The big engine was intended for the Army and Navy. Four were built, but the war ended before they could be put to use.

In spite of these and other commitments, the Duesenberg brothers continued to build race car motors. These motors always occupied a "first love" position.

Up to this time, all of Fred and Augie's achievements in the field of motor cars and racing had been under the name "Mason." But 1914 changed all that. From then on, the name painted on the sides of the fleet and spirited motor cars on the race tracks was "Duesenberg."

The struggle to win Indy: 1912-1920

It was July 4, 1914, when a mud-spattered race car with a battered, improvised mud shield and an unconscious passenger, bucked and roared across the finish line of the nationally touted Sioux City 300-mile race just 40 seconds ahead of its nearest challenger. The car was a four-cylinder Duesenberg equipped with the famed walking beam engine. The driver, who would one day be one of the most famous men in the world, as America's top flying ace in World War I, was Eddie Rickenbacker.

The passenger, a riding mechanic as required in those days, was Eddie O'Donnell, who would one day be a famed race driver on his own. He had been struck on the head just a few laps before the finish by one of the big hunks of rock-hard mud being hurled by the tires of the racers in a constant barrage that battered machine and man.

"I didn't know whether he was alive or dead. The last thing I could do was stop," said Rickenbacker.

He didn't. To keep the car going, he grabbed the handle of the oil pump with one hand, taking over the mechanic's job of pumping up the dangerously low oil pressure to keep the engine running. With the other hand, he clung to the steering wheel of the bucking car as it leaped crazily down the rutted track.

It had been a grueling race, and Rickenbacker had not been slated to win it. There were several more powerful and faster cars in the race, including a Mercer running hard on his heels. But perhaps the driver of the Mercer, Spencer Wishart, had not been willing to throw the last ounce of caution to the wind on that dangerous track, as Rickenbacker was doing — even refusing to stop to take care of his injured companion.

For Rickenbacker, the race was a

"must" to win. The Duesenberg racing team was broke. If they didn't win, they wouldn't eat.

The team was in one of its periodic slumps. It had raced at several meets without a win. There hadn't been enough money at Sioux City to rent rooms to sleep in or a garage to house the racers. They had parked the cars under the stands, and the men had slept on the ground. Meals were down to a milkshake with a couple of raw eggs whipped in. Luckily, they had enough tires and spare parts to put the three Duesenbergs in good condition for the race.

When the race started, the pounding of the speeding cars soon made the gumbo track a rutted and gouged hell road, with the ruts grabbing the wheels of the flying cars and sending them bucking like crazy, miniature toys.

It was one of those flying chunks of gumbo that had been hurled against O'Donnell's head. Aware of the hazard from practice laps before the race, Rickenbacker and his mechanic had fashioned a wire screen mudguard, but it had been battered to a shapeless mass.

When O'Donnell came to in the pits, he discovered that he and Rickenbacker had won $10,000. Another of the Duesenbergs had come in third, putting an additional $2,500 in the team kitty. "We were suddenly rich," said Rickenbacker.

"I took the team to the best hotel in Sioux City. We soaked the gumbo off in brimming tubs of hot water and went to buy the best food in town," he recalled.

It was a typical story of the up-and-down fortunes of the early day Duesenberg racing team, which operated mostly on a shoestring and hoped for better days like that one on July 4, 1914.

The Duesenberg racing saga had begun back in 1912, when Fred and Augie Duesenberg sent their first four-cylinder walking beam car into the racing wars. It ran under the name of Mason — the name of the backer of the car they had originally designed for road-passenger use.

But what they wanted more than anything else was to win the Indianapolis 500, the annual race which had only begun in 1911, but had rapidly gained prestige as the biggest and richest automobile race in the country.

In 1914 the Duesenbergs were operating under their own name for the first time. They signed up a gutsy and savvy young driver named Eddie Rickenbacker, who had just started making a name for himself on the mostly dirt tracks around the country.

Young Rick had actually driven, as a relief driver, in the first Indy 500, in a car that placed 11th. In the 1912 race he had driven the same car, a Firestone Columbus Red Wing, and was running in fourth place in the 44th lap when an engine bearing burned out.

The Duesenbergs had squeezed a bit more "oomph" out of their engine by boring it out to 4.40. With the long six-inch stroke, it gave them 360 cid. But the 1914 Indy race was dominated by powerful European cars that were imported for top American drivers or, in some cases, driven by foreigners. Delage and Peugeot took the first four places. The best an American car could do was fifth place, for the great Barney Oldfield in a Stutz. Rickenbacker managed to bring the Duesenberg in 10th, just barely in the money.

That was one of the reasons why the big win at Sioux City on July 4 had been so important, for morale and the pocketbook.

In the Indy 500 for 1915, a Duesenberg moved up on the leaders and finished in fifth place, the best showing to date for a Duesie. At the wheel was Eddie O'Donnell, the mechanic who had been knocked cold at Sioux City. Rickenbacker had deserted the Duesenberg team at the end of the 1914 season, to switch to Maxwell, and Fred Duesenberg quickly promoted O'Donnell to driver.

It was, perhaps, poetic justice that Rickenbacker's Maxwell failed to finish the 1915 race, going out with mechanical problems on the 103rd lap, while his former riding mechanic was wheeling a Duesenberg to fifth place. It was even more ironic because Rickenbacker had

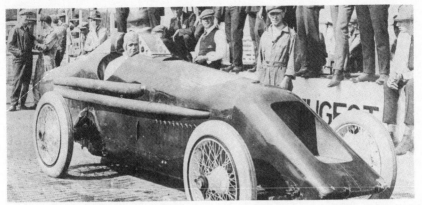

Tommy Milton in the Duesenberg 16-cylinder racing car which established an American 1-mile straight away record of 156 mph at Daytona Beach, Fla., in April, 1920. (Photo courtesy Indianapolis Motor Speedway)

confessed, on many occasions, that it had always been his big dream to win at Indy.

He never did. But some old time race fans have suggested, with a good deal of logic, that if he had stuck with Duesenberg he might have made it.

Other things had also been happening at Indy in 1915. Officials had cut the engine size limit down to 300 cid. They had started and run the first two years with the monster limit of 600 inches. For the next two years it was 450. Now it was 300.

In an effort to match the big boys, the Duesenbergs had been squeezing a bit more size and power out of their engine by bigger bores. They had inched it up to 360. Now they would have to reverse the process, all the way back to 3.980.

It must be said, to the eternal credit of the Duesenberg brothers, that they were able to get even more power and speed out of the smaller engine.

Rickenbacker, no slouch of a driver, had managed an average of 70.83 mph in taking 10th place in 1914, running with the 360 cid engine. In 1915, with the engine cut back to 299 inches, O'Donnell averaged 81.47 mph.

There was a constant, never-ending battle to keep up with the opposition. Constant tinkering with carburetion, breathing, valves and chassis improvements was necessary. It was the only way to keep from being left behind, in the dust, as progress and speed moved up, year by year.

Incidentally, in the 1915 race another Duesenberg, driven by Tom Alley, who had placed third in the Sioux City race in 1914, came in 8th with a 79.97 mph average. Even this was better than Rickenbacker had been able to do in 1914.

A bit of luster was added to the 1915 showing at Indy by the fact that a Duesenberg driven by O'Donnell had won the 103-mile Glendale road race in California on February 3. A Duesenberg driven by Ralph Mulford, one of the top drivers of the day, won a 300-miler at Des Moines on August 7. Duesenbergs were also running strong in other races around the country.

Then came 1916, the year in which the Duesenbergs finally got a whiff at the big win at Indy. They couldn't grab first place, but they took second in a race that was cut to 300 miles due to the war.

The average speed of that No. 2 Duesie, with Wilbur D'Alene at the wheel, was 83.24 mph. It was just a fraction of a mile less than the 84 mph average set by the winning car, a Peugeot driven by Dario Resta.

Some old time race fans believe this was the year in which the Duesenbergs finally had the power and speed to win it, if they had had a more experienced and gutsy driver at the wheel — say, for example, Rickenbacker, or even O'Donnell, who had left the Duesenberg team to join Rickenbacker at Maxwell.

To its credit, it must be said that D'Alene drove a good race. As the race wore on and he gained confidence, D'Alene picked his way through the pack, moving to the front. He passed them all, except Resta. What if he had driven a Rickenbacker-type race from the beginning?

For 1916 the Duesenberg name got a boost when O'Donnell, before he joined Rickenbacker, won the 300-mile Corona road race in California on April 8, driving one of the hot Duesenbergs. On April 15 he took a win in the 150-mile Ascot race at Los Angeles. In fact, the record shows that Rickenbacker took over the wheel of a Duesenberg late in the season, on November 30, to win a 150-mile race at Ascot.

Duesenbergs scored second-place finishes in two 300-mile races at Tacoma and Cincinnati that year. Altogether, the year 1916 proved that as long as the Duesenberg brothers kept trying, their cars would be top contenders.

As for 1917, who knows what might have happened had there been an Indy 500 that year? There wasn't. World War I had started in Europe in 1914, and by 1917 the U.S. was involved. The 1917 and 1918 Indy races were cancelled.

But other things had been happening with the Duesenberg brothers. When they moved their shop to St. Paul in 1913, they went into the business of designing and building engines for anyone who would buy one. They had contracted with Commander Pugh to build giant marine engines which propelled his Disturber to a world water speed record.

A short time later, the hot Duesenberg engines attracted the attention of engineers at the Loew-Victor Engine Co. Soon the Duesenbergs were associated with the Chicago company in the design and building of marine engines. Eventually the brothers closed shop in St. Paul and moved to Chicago to work with Loew-Victor.

Later, but still during the war, the Duesenbergs, together with several New York businessmen, formed the Duesenberg Motor Co., moving the site of operations to Elizabeth, N.J. The brothers and their staff designed and built aircraft, marine and automobile engines for use by the military forces of the U.S., England, Italy and Russia.

As the war ended, the Duesenbergs sold their interest in the Elizabeth plant and spent a short time in Newark at more engine development. Then came the final move to Indianapolis. There is little question that Fred, driven by his obsession with the Indianapolis Motor Speedway, was happy with this move. But

Here is a shot of the famed Eddie Rickenbacker, taken in 1914 when he was captain of the Duesenberg racing team. This was the car he drove in that 300-mile win at Sioux City, IA. With him is his riding mechanic, Eddie O'Donnell. (Photo courtesy of the Indianapolis Motor Speedway, Speedway, IN)

beyond that, at this period in motor car history, Indianapolis was second only to Detroit as a home for U.S. car makers. The Duesenberg brothers still hoped one day to design and build their second passenger motor car — this time, under their own name.

Somewhere along the way, as the Duesenberg motor building project grew and prospered, the brothers acquired an engineering staff. One man on that staff was a brilliant young engineer named C.W. van Ranst.

Caught up in making the four-cylinder walking beam engine into a winner, it was as early as 1915 that van Ranst laid out a 16-valve version of the four banger. That meant, in simple language, four valves per cylinder. To do it, the young engineer simply added another camshaft to the other side of the engine, together with a second set of the giant, walking beam rockers. Now it was a double walking beam.

The first prototype of this engine was installed in a chassis and fired up, but it was wrecked on the first trial run. The brothers were so busy with war work that the project was shelved, but when Indianapolis Speedway officials announced a series of fall races — to be called the Harvest Classic — the Duesenbergs dusted off the 16-valve design and hurried several of the engines to completion.

Four cars with the new engine were entered in the 100-mile event, and took second, third, fourth and sixth places. The second-place car, driven by Hughie Hughes, was only seconds behind the winner. It wasn't a win, but it was close, and it proved that the extra valves added some four to five miles per hour to the top speed. A few extra squirts of speed were the "something extra" always needed to keep up with the pack, for others were also improving their engines — and there was always the possibility of refining a bit more speed into the new engines.

Who knows what the Duesenbergs, with the new engine, would have done at the 1917 Indy 500—if there had been one?

During the war, as the Duesenberg plant began making engines for war use, van Ranst took the 16-valve design, beefed it up to 4¾ x 7, put a reduction

gear on it, and offered it to the government as a trainer plane engine. Rated at 125 bhp, it was approved, but never reached large scale production.

Shortly after the war, Tommy Milton, one of the rising stars among race drivers, took one of the 16-valve racing engines, put it into a race car chassis and went to Sheepshead Bay. Milton set new absolute speed records for distances up to 300 miles, and for one 25-mile stretch averaged 116.2 mph.

Who said a Duesenberg engine wouldn't go? The average speed of the last Indy 500 had been 84 mph.

It was not long after this that a stock Roamer roadster, equipped with a Rochester-Duesenberg engine based on the 8-valve design, took off on a blast down Daytona Beach and set a new stock car speed record of 105.1 mph — the fastest stock car in America.

A Duesenberg engine in a stock Roamer? That calls for an explanation. The Duesenberg brothers were in business to make money, too. Since there were, at this time, dozens of makes of cars still in production with four-cylinder engines, Fred offered his four-cylinder walking beam engine design for sale.

The Rochester Motors Corp. bought the design and offered the engine to car makers. According to Jerry Gebby, one of the country's top Duesenberg historians, the Rochester-Duesenberg four-cylinder engine was used by the Biddle, Disbrow, Kenworthy, Meteor, Revere, Richelieu, Romer, Shaw and Wolverine at one time or another. Some of these makes offered the Rochester-Duesenberg as an option, since it was more expensive than standard engines.

Perhaps one reason Fred Duesenberg decided to sell the old four-cylinder design was because, at long last, something much bigger was in the works: nothing less than a straight eight engine, and plans to put a long-dreamed-of Duesenberg passenger car on the market. Duesenberg was far from finished with racing, or building race engines. In fact, in all his plans was the hope, if not the intention, that the new eight would also be suitable for racing — modified, perhaps, but a race engine nonetheless.

There has been a lot of debate among historians about how and why the Duesenbergs became interested in straight eight engines. Such an engine for passenger car purposes was virtually unknown in the U.S., but that didn't mean the Duesenbergs didn't know anything about one. The monster engines they had built for Commander Pugh as early as 1914 had been straight twelves!

During the war, together with Loew-Victor, they had designed and produced an in-line, eight-cylinder marine patrol engine. They had built, under license, a Bugatti-designed engine which, for all practical purposes, was two in-line eights paired together. After that, they designed a successful V-16 of their own. During the war, they probably got to see virtually every type of engine the government was interested in, foreign and domestic. In short, the Duesenbergs and their staff knew all about in-line eight engines—perhaps as much or more than anyone else in the country.

Nonetheless, when Fred and Augie started work on the first in-line eight for motor car purposes, racing or otherwise, they were still hung up on the old walking beam valve design that had served them so long and so faithfully. When the first prototypes of the Duesenberg motor car eight were built, they still incorporated this design.

But in the end even Fred Duesenberg had to recognize that there was something better. It was time for a Duesenberg in-line eight, with overhead valves and overhead cam, to be born.

Certainly it was no accident that, when the in-line eight took shape, it would—in racing form—wind up with dimensions of 3 x 5¼, for 296 cubic inches of displacement. After all, wasn't the engine limit at Indy 300 inches? For passenger car use, it was a bit smaller, at 2⅞ x 5.

In 1919, when the first post-war Indy 500 was being programmed, the Duesenbergs started work on three of the new eights for their racing team. They managed to complete the cars just in time for the race.

The squeeze of time undoubtedly contributed to the disaster that followed. In hurry-up trial runs, two of the cars burned out connecting rods. The third, which Tommy Milton managed to qualify — again, just barely — went out

Here's a 1919 version of the Duesenberg racing cars. The Duesenberg brothers were never very proud of their record for that year since not a single Duesenberg entered in the Indy 500 even finished, and two were wrecked with tragic results. In the picture is race driver Ira Vail showing the car to actress Anita Stewart. (Photo courtesy Indianapolis Motor Speedway)

after 50 laps. Milton had been trying to nurse the car along, well aware of the fact that he had a new, unproven engine under his hood. But there was no use being in a race if you didn't try to win it. So he tried, and blooey.

The first eight-cylinder Duesenberg racing cars utilized the splash oiling system that had been used successfully for many years on the walking beam fours. The Duesenbergs, remembering all those miles at high speed in the races, had thought the old system would do for the eight. It wouldn't. The new engine, at racing speeds, was turning around the 4,000 rpm mark, far higher than the old four banger. A few laps at that speed caused the "bottom ends" to come apart.

The Duesenbergs and their staff quickly made tests to find out what happened, then devised a new pressure oiling system. After that, the new Duesenberg eights would go. The Duesenberg men had known all along that the new cars were fast — until the con rods let go. Now the drivers could stomp on the gas.

But the whole story of the 1919 race hasn't been told. Although the new eights were finished just before race time, five other cars in the race used the old style Duesenberg walking beam fours. If the new eights couldn't capture any honors, perhaps the old fours could salvage something.

They didn't. In fact, disaster was hardly the word for what happened. Arthur Thurman, driving a Duesenberg-powered Thurman Special, flipped soon after the race started, killing him and seriously injuring his mechanic.

Near the half-way mark, a Duesenberg-powered Roamer Special driven by Louis LeCocq burst into a furious blaze when the fuel tank exploded. Both LeCocq and his mechanic burned to death. According to Al Bloemker, a Speedway official, these were the first fatalities in competition at the Speedway since 1911.

To compound the tragedy for the Duesenbergs, both fatalities had taken place in Duesenberg-powered cars. The other three fours went out with mechanical failures. Wilbur D'Alene managed to keep his car in the race well past the half-way mark, when an axle broke.

With all this disaster piling up, it would seem that public esteem for the Duesenberg name would be at its lowest ebb. Some small comfort could be taken from that fact that, in the case of the two worst tragedies, the cars had not been running under the Duesenberg name.

Tommy Milton, the brightest star on the Duesenberg team despite the failure of his new eight in the Indy race, managed to reclaim a large measure of glory for the Duesenberg name later that year. With a few more months to work the bugs out of the new engine, he took it to the famed Elgin road race in August, and ran away from the field to win it handily.

If the old fours were, in fact, finished, they went out in a blaze of glory. In November of that year, Milton took one of the 16-valve fours to the Sheepshead Bay track and set 19 new speed records in the under-300 cid class, topping 117 mph for a mile, and averaging 113 mph for an hour.

It was a heroic performance for Milton. In September, less than two months previous to the Sheepshead record runs, his race car caught fire while running in first place in the Uniontown 225-mile race.

Milton managed to put his car into a spin, throwing the flames away from himself and his mechanic. That move, witnesses said, certainly saved both their lives. In fact, both were severely injured, Milton so badly the doctors wanted to amputate one of his legs. Tommy said no—and in November was setting new speed records, even if he had to hobble to his car on crutches.

While lying in the hospital recovering from his burns and wounds, Milton schemed up another project. How about going for the absolute world land speed record with Duesenberg engines?

Milton suggested the idea to Fred Duesenberg. The speed ace had enough knowledge of the game to know it would not be possible with a single engine, not even one of the new in-line eights. But how about coupling two of the engines together, side by side?

Fred bought the idea and started putting the car together. It was at least partly financed by Milton's savings from race wins. It was an odd-ball machine, with both engines connected to the rear axle by separate ring gears and pinions. But it would go!

Tommy Milton finally got his world record in 1920, but not before someone almost beat him to it.

The someone was Jimmy Murphy, another young and ambitious driver. A Milton protege, he had been promoted to driver at Milton's urging, but was kicked off the team by Fred Duesenberg because he cracked up too many cars.

Milton interceded and got Murphy reinstated. That should have made Murphy and Milton loyal friends for life, but it didn't. The world record car was shipped to Daytona. Meanwhile, Milton went to one more race meet to try to replenish his wallet, emptied by the building of the car.

Before Milton could arrive, and with the engines of the "new double-barrel" machine running beautifully, Fred Duesenberg suggested that Murphy take it out for a trial run. Murphy, sailing down the beach, couldn't resist opening the machine up. When he stopped, he found he had been going more than 151 mph, breaking Ralph DePalma's 1919 record of 149.875 mph. It was unofficial, of course, for the official timers had not been present, but that was a technicality the newspapers ignored as they blared, "Murphy Breaks DePalma's Record."

When Milton arrived in Florida and saw the headlines, he exploded. So this was how he was to be repaid for helping Murphy. Milton had invested his hard-earned savings in the project, and this young upstart wanted to steal his glory.

It is not hard to understand Milton's

anger. He was quoted as saying, "I could have killed him (Murphy)."

Murphy's only defense was that Fred Duesenberg had told him to make the run, and Fred was boss.

Milton finally calmed down enough to dismantle and rebuild the engines, fine-tune them, and take off for a run of his own — this time with the official timers on station.

As Bloemker told it in his book, "Under Tommy's superb guidance, the big Duesie thundered through the timing traps at 156.046 miles an hour." Tommy Milton had his record, and this time it was official. A Duesenberg was the fastest motor car in the world.

Now the Duesenberg brothers could once more turn their attention to the big one that had constantly eluded them: the Indy 500.

A flash of glory at Indy and LeMans: 1921-1927

*A*t last! *After 12 years of sweat, frustration, bitter disappointments, a series of heartbreaking "almosts" and, perhaps, a few tears, Duesenberg finally had a victory at Indy. The year was 1924.*

Not only did the winner's flag come down on a Duesenberg, but it was a heart-thumping race, the kind from which legends spring.

It was not a race where the winner and runner-up were half a lap or more apart. Nor were the laps so confusing that nobody really knew who was ahead. It was, rather, a clawing, fighting, bucking race in which No. 1 and No. 2 seemed to be only feet apart in the turns, desperately vying for that all-important lead.

And somehow, it seemed, Joe Boyer, who drove such a masterful race and flashed that Duesie to victory, had some kind of mysterious reserve of power and speed to fight off every challenge. The Duesenberg straight eight engine was making a strange, high-pitched sound.

He and his car seemed to be capable of going even faster than the blistering pace he was setting. It became such a spectacular fight because he was trying to save his tires for that last assault on

the winner's flag. He was using blinding speed on the straights — a speed which absolutely nobody could match — then easing off on the turns, taking them wide. That precious rubber just had to last.

Fred Duesenberg also had to be given credit for a masterful decision of strategy: switching drivers in the middle of the race.

The Duesenberg team started four cars in the 1924 race, three of their latest creations and an older, back-up car. One of the four went out early with a broken steering arm. Another, starting from the second row and driven by Joe Boyer, quickly showed that it was the fastest car on the track by blasting past all the front runners. Then a tiny key sheared on a vital engine accessory, and the car was out.

That left L.L. Corum in the last of the new cars, and Pete DePaolo, now a rookie but destined for his own share of racing glory, in the slower back-up car. To Fred Duesenberg's race-wise eyes, it was clear that DePaolo didn't have the speed to match the pace, and Corum wasn't using his.

Corum was a good race driver, but at Indy a "good" driver is not enough. Victory has virtually always gone to the gutsy, the brilliant, and the daring — the singular breed of men who are more than just good.

Fred Duesenberg knew he had the fastest car in the race. But it was running in the pack, apparently with no chance of victory. The year 1924 would go down as another bitter disappointment, unless something drastic happened.

Fred quickly made his decision. He would make that "something drastic" happen.

Joe Boyer, the man who had driven such a dazzling race until his engine conked, was sitting on the sidelines, glumly watching the speeding cars go past. He was clearly in the dumps because his chance at victory was gone.

At this point, according to Al Bloemker, an Indy staff official, Fred Duesenberg tapped Boyer on the shoulder and said, "Maybe we can still win. Get your goggles and be ready when Corum comes in for fuel and tires. *I want you to finish this race in his car."*

Boyer did exactly that. Well aware of the mysterious source of power and speed under the hood, and with nothing to lose, Boyer began one of the most brilliant and masterful runs for the glory that Indy has ever seen.

On the straights came that blinding, matchless speed. He passed one car after another. On the turns he eased off just a bit, to hoard the rubber.

Not only was he passing his rivals, he was forcing them, in desperation, to take chances in the turns that they probably did not want to take. They were ruining their tires. Within 20 minutes after getting behind the wheel, Boyer had moved all the way up to third place.

He was pushing Jimmy Murphy, in a beautifully performing Miller, until Murphy ruined a right rear tire and was forced into the pits. That left only Earl Cooper, in another of the fast riding Millers, out in front.

Cooper was another crafty and brilliant driver. As the Boyer-driven Duesenberg moved up on him, he fought desperately to stay in front. The boiling pace cost Cooper a tire, and he was forced to pit.

When Cooper roared back out on the track, he was determined to gain back the precious No. 1 position. In the last 50 miles of the race Cooper, the pursuer now, drew up to within 11 seconds of Boyer, and the sensational battle began.

Only 30 miles to go, and Cooper had closed the gap. In the turns he seemed to be running only feet — or was it inches? — behind Boyer. In a last ditch try at taking Boyer in a turn, Cooper was making his maneuver to pass the speeding Duesenberg when another tire went. His last chance at victory was gone.

The murderous pace had even been more than Boyer had wanted. He could now ease the throttle and save his tires for the last precious laps to the winner's flag. No. 1 at last!

Actually, Boyer had something under the Duesenberg's hood that made him the unquestioned master in the power and speed category. His desperate fight had been to stay ahead of the madly careening Millers, yet save his tires. He had done it.

The big win at last! Joe Boyer is shown in the cockpit of the car that finally won an Indianapolis victory for the Duesenberg brothers. At least part of the secret of success was the fact that this machine was supercharged — the first successful supercharged racer to run in the famed 500 mile race. (Indianapolis Motor Speedway photo)

What was the "secret weapon" that enabled him to set such a blistering pace?

The answer: nothing less than the first successful supercharger ever to run on a winning car at Indy. Fred Duesenberg would have to get most of the credit for that coup, too.

The principle of superchargers, or blowers, had been around for a long time. Men named Roots, Philander and Francis had invented a rotary blower to superheat furnaces in iron foundries as early as the 1850s. Village blacksmiths had been using simple, hand-turned but geared-up blowers to super-heat their forges for years.

As early as 1906, Lee Chadwick, builder of the Chadwick motor car, put a blower on a Chadwick Six and made the car do some pretty sensational things. But Chadwick went broke, and his cars disappeared from the scene before anybody paid much attention to the idea.

Then came World War I, the first war in which airplanes played a decisive role. Pilots quickly learned that the "on top" position was one of the most important factors in air victories. But when they tried to climb "on top," their early day airplane engines ran out of breath. So aircraft engineers, both in Europe and the U.S., pulled out the old blower idea.

The idea worked, when the blowers worked. But there were a lot of bugs in the blowers.

The Duesenberg brothers had been involved in the building of airplane engines during the war, and had come in contact with virtually every new development, including those involving blowers. It was, perhaps, inevitable that Fred Duesenberg would sooner or later grab onto the blower idea to put him in the "on top" position with a race car.

Even before 1924, the Duesenbergs had been experimenting with the supercharger for several years. They tried and tried until they had a blower that wouldn't explode at high speed. Then they had to try and try again to devise a drive system that could stand the shock of rapid speed changes so essential on a racing engine.

When they finally had the blower problems licked, they found the engine burning up. They had to start experimenting all over again to find out what

combination of blower volume, blower speed, compression ratios, pistons and valves would take the punishment and still bring in more power and speed.

They had to do all this in utter secrecy, to keep the opposition from finding out what they were up to. Not even the workshop mechanics knew what was going on.

Even after the 1924 Indy triumph, Fred would have liked to keep the secret locked up, but it was impossible. The rules said the cars had to be submitted to the Speedway technical committee for a displacement check. The committee checked, and the blower was no longer a secret.

Not only had the winning car been equipped with a blower—all three of the "newer" cars had them. That was why Boyer had been blasting the opposition from the start, until the vital key sheared in the drive system of his supercharger.

In the 1924 race DePaolo, the rookie on the Duesenberg team, begged for a supercharger on his car. But the Duesenbergs had decided that the blowers were still a bit of a risk, and they wanted at least one back-up car in the race without the supercharger.

Pete had driven a conservative race, saving his tires, and managed to bring his Duesie in sixth. As a reward, in 1925, he was given the Duesenbergs' number one car—another supercharged straight eight with, perhaps, a few more improvements.

DePaolo rewarded Fred Duesenberg by giving him another victory, the second in a row for the big "D." In addition, he set a new speed record for the race, posting an average of 101.13 mph, and became the first driver in Indy history to average more than 100 mph!

By zeroing in on 1924, because it represented the zenith of everything the Duesenberg brothers had been fighting to achieve for so long, we have skipped another major triumph which, in many ways, glowed just as brightly as the big Indy win.

For this story, we have to go back to 1921. The glorious Grand Prix victory for Duesenberg at Le Mans, in France, came in July, 1921. It was the first time in history that an American car had won that Grand Prix in Europe.

Perhaps the only reason American cars

After 1927 no Duesenberg-powered car managed to win at Indianapolis, but in 1931 a Duesenberg did manage second place with Fred Frame as driver. By this time the cubic inch displacement limits had been lifted and the days of the finely tuned but tiny engines were gone. (Indianapolis Motor Speedway photo)

were invited to run at Le Mans was because this was the first racing after the great war. France had come very close to losing the war, and the American "Doughboys" had arrived on the battlefields in time to help save France from defeat. French-American friendship was probably at an all-time high.

Besides, France had a great team of Ballot racers. France and other European countries had always dominated the Grand Prix. The Germans were out of the picture. What did the French have to fear by inviting the Americans?

They had the Duesenberg brothers and Jimmy Murphy to fear, that's what.

Murphy, one of the gutsiest of a new breed of brilliant drivers, was involved in a crash during practice runs—through no fault of his own—and ended up in the hospital with a broken rib. But on race day he was all taped up from hips to shoulders, determined to drive, pain or no pain.

There was plenty of pain, and more. The race became one of the toughest, and roughest, in racing history. The course, laid out over 10.7 miles of French roadway, quickly went to pieces.

Stones flew like shrapnel and a number of cars were wrecked. Cars went out with broken chassis parts, fuel tanks

punctured, and radiators were blasted by stones. So many tires blew, nobody could keep count.

But when it was over, there was Jimmy Murphy in the battered Duesenberg out front. His car was a shambles. A tire was flat. The radiator, ruptured by a flying stone, was empty. The overheated engine was smoking, and on the verge of exploding—but it was still running.

Murphy managed to nurse the engine, and the car, through the required "safety lap" at about 40 mph. But he had averaged 78.1 mph for the entire 321.78 miles, despite the horrible roadway and the punishing ordeal. His Duesenberg was 15 minutes — not seconds — ahead of the second-place Ballot, and the Ballots had been favored to sweep the race.

It was a day of glory that would be savored for a long time by the Americans, especially a pair of German-Americans named Duesenberg. But the French wouldn't even play the American anthem. Ernest Ballot, of the Ballot team, mounted a public soap box to shout that French cars were still best, and challenged the Duesenbergs to a rematch. But the race was over.

Then came 1922. Some Duesenberg fans insist that, from a technical standpoint, this was the peak year for Duesen-

59

berg supremacy in building race cars, even if they didn't win at Indy.

Or did they? When the Indy results were posted, Duesenbergs had swept seven of the first 10 places—eight, if you counted the winner. Some folks said it was a Duesenberg. Some said it was a Miller. Some called it a Miller-Duesenberg.

The driver was none other than Jimmy Murphy, who had performed so heroically for Duesenberg at Le Mans.

It is a strange story. Both Tommy Milton and Jimmy Murphy, separately, came to a parting of the ways with Fred Duesenberg. Milton, at least, had become upset over money matters. Perhaps that was part of Murphy's reason as well.

In any case, the stage was set for the great Duesenberg-Miller rivalry — one might call it a war—for American racing supremacy during the 1920s.

The Duesenbergs had started in the racing game around 1912, not counting Fred's 1905 run in the 1903 Marion. Miller was also an old time engine and carburetor man, who became seriously involved with racing engines around the 1915-1920 period. The Miller story is also a saga of glory and wins at Indy.

When Tommy Milton left the Duesenbergs, he went to Miller and contracted for Miller to build him a special engine. The order included all the best features he had picked up from top racing engines, including the Duesenberg.

As the Milton-Miller engine began tearing up the tracks, Jimmy Murphy decided he wanted one too. He had purchased his Duesenberg shortly after the Le Mans win, so Fred Duesenberg couldn't object when Murphy slipped his new Miller engine into the Duesenberg chassis. This was the car in which Murphy roared to glory in 1922.

It was in another Miller-powered car that Milton himself blasted to victory at Indy in 1923. Even if a few of his ideas had been snitched from Duesenberg, Miller and his staff had to be credited with bringing the in-line eight to a certain plateau of perfection — a plateau high enough to give the Miller-powered cars almost a clean sweep at Indy: first, second, third and fourth place, not to mention seventh. It was utter disaster for the Duesenbergs, after their great triumphs

in 1921 and 1922. A lone Duesenberg managed to come in 10th.

One of the reasons, perhaps, was that after the 1922 race, the year Duesenberg had made such a sweep, Speedway officials once more lowered the engine size. The limit of 183 cid was cut all the way to 122. Miller had gotten the jump on making the switch.

The Duesenberg shops barely managed to finish three cars with the new engine configuration for the 1923 Indy race. It was so close that one car left the Duesenberg shop shortly after midnight on the morning of the race, and just managed to qualify at dawn. The other two left the shops a few minutes later and became entangled in early morning traffic, mostly people trying to get to the track. They never arrived in time for the race.

The only possible excuse for the poor showing of that single entry, driven by Wade Morton, was that the car was so new and tight they never had a chance to break the engine in properly before the race, or even race-tune it. Maybe they were lucky to take 10th.

As if the Indy debacle were not enough, the Miller-powered cars won nearly every important race in America that year.

Is it any wonder that Fred Duesenberg, still short of his dream of an Indy victory, would decide to put top priority on the only secret weapon he had left —the supercharger?

In 1924 and 1925 it was the Duesenbergs' turn to bask in glory. After that, it was Miller's turn again.

Barely had the word "supercharger" echoed through the pits at Indy in 1924 when Harry Miller raced back to California to begin work on a supercharger of his own. Miller had his superchargers in time for the 1925 race, and they were good ones—but not quite good enough to beat DePaolo in the Duesenberg. At other tracks around the country that year, Miller and Duesenberg split the honors.

Then the Speedway managers came up with a ruling that would affect every race car builder in the country. The cubic inch displacement of Indy racers was slashed once more, this time all the way down to a 91-inch limit!

An engine that size was little more than

Jimmy Murphy posed for this picture in France after winning the prestigious French Grand Prix at Le Mans in 1921. (Photo courtesy Fred Roe)

a toy. Could men like the Duesenbergs, Miller and others take an in-line eight and squeeze it down to such a size? It sounded almost impossible.

But they did it. Not only did they do it, they ended up with just about the most perfect little jewels the world had ever seen. The Duesenberg had a 2.286 bore by 2.750 stroke, and the Miller a 2.1875 bore by 3 inch stroke. Both were supercharged, of course.

The arguments in favor of the tiny engines had been largely safety, to reduce the furious pace being set by hot drivers in hot cars. When the results were in for 1926, the first year of the new "midget formula," the top speed had been reduced by all of about five miles per hour.

The Duesenbergs and Millers may have been pretty evenly matched in the 1926 Indy race, but now Miller had a secret weapon of another kind. This time it was in human form, a rookie driver named Frank Lockhart. One of the hottest drivers of his decade, he blasted his Miller out front and stayed there, except for pit time, until a downpour of rain forced officials to end the race at 400 miles.

Nobody knows, of course, what might have happened in that last 100 miles, but it was a good Lockhart win. Pete De-Paolo, the top Duesie driver that year, was running fifth when the race stopped.

At the 1927 Indy race Lockhart was in the pole position, with a posted time trial speed of 120.100 mph.

When the race started, he was out in front. The pace he set was so furious that

it was not long until almost every one of the top cars was knocked out by mechanical trouble. Then, at the 300-mile mark, Lockhart's engine blew.

Now it was time for Lady Luck to smile on another rookie and a Duesenberg.

It was said that the Duesenbergs trained and lost more race drivers than anyone could count.

• Some of them drove to glory in Duesenbergs.

• Some of them, like Milton, fell out with Fred over money. It was said that, despite his considerable successes, Fred Duesenberg was almost always broke, or nearly so.

• Some of them, in certain years, simply lost faith in the Duesenberg cars.

• Some succumbed to more glamorous offers from other team captains. When Miller's fortunes rode high, it seemed that drivers deserted Duesenberg in droves.

In any case, as the top cars and drivers went out of that 1927 race, one by one, here came George Souders, a rookie running his first race at Indy, to take over the number one spot in a Duesie.

Duesenberg had the number two spot nailed down, too, with another Duesie driven by another rookie, Bennie Shoaf, cruising along behind Souders. With only three miles to go, an axle on the Shoaf car failed and the Duesenbergs had to be content with Souders' win.

It was the Duesenbergs' third win at Indy in four years—but it would be their last. They continued to run, and provide

61

top competition, for years to come. A Duesenberg won third place in 1929, fifth in 1930, and made a "comeback" to place second in 1931.

But things would never be the same at Indy again. In 1930, succumbing to pressure from the motor car manufacturers, Speedway officials finally relented from their 91-inch rule — a rule intended to slow the cars down. From now on, engines up to 366 cubic inches would be allowed.

The days of the little jewel-like 91's were ended. Gone was the edge from that sharply fought Duesenberg-Miller battle for supremacy on the speedways in the roaring twenties.

But while the race track activity had been going on, the Duesenberg brothers had become involved in another project which would, in many ways, overshadow even those bitterly contested races on the Indy track. For the second time in their lives, and for the first time under their own name, the Duesenbergs were up to their ears designing, building and marketing a passenger car.

The times and record of the Model A: 1919-1926

*I*t was a strange sight.

Not only was a big car roaring around the famed Indy 500 track in the darkness of night, but something weird was going on: a man was perched on the left running board and front fender of the moving car, chopping a hole in the side of the hood while another man drove.

When the hole was big enough to admit an arm, the man on the fender reached to the engine and unscrewed a spark plug. Then, with compressed gases spewing violently from the open spark plug hole, the fender-riding mechanic managed to ram in and screw home a new spark plug.

After that the motor, which had been missing due to a cracked spark plug, roared back into action on all eight cylinders, picked up speed and roared on, at times reaching speeds up to 105 mph.

By the time it was over, the car had been on the track and running 50 hours and 21 minutes, covering an amazing 3,155 miles at an average speed of 62.63 mph. It was a speed-endurance record that would stand for 10 years.

The spark plug change stunt had been born of necessity, because the announced intention of the sponsors of the run had been to run more than 3,000 miles non-stop. The plug change had taken place with the car slowed down to about 55 mph.

In order to fuel, lubricate and service the speeding car while moving, it had been equipped with a reinforced running board rail on the right side. Another car, designated as the service car, had matching reinforcement on the left side.

In action, the drivers of the two cars eased alongside each other, matching speed, while fuel, oil, water and, perhaps, a sandwich for the drivers were passed from one car to another. Even drivers were switched. If the cars bumped a bit during the transfer, the reinforced running board rails gave protection from damage.

Everything worked except the tires, which began to show carcass fabric long before the race was finished. Despite all the preparations for a non-stop run, the endurance car was forced to a halt twice for tire changes. The best they could do was keep the engine running at a simulated 40 mph while the changes were made. But the stops did, of course, detract from the total average speed.

This machine, roaring through the night, was nothing less than a Duesenberg Straight Eight passenger car. The time was April 27-29, 1923. The purpose was to prove that the first Duesenberg passenger car model to appear on the market was the fastest, toughest and best that money could buy, and that it could live up to the slogan proclaimed by the advertising brochures: that it was "built to outclass, outrun and outlast any car on the road."

Most of the people who bought them and drove them agreed it was true. Some connoisseurs of old cars were still saying it more than 50 years later.

In any case, at last there was a fine passenger car carrying the Duesenberg name. It was the car of which the Duesenbergs had been dreaming for so long—promising to build it and planning for it during all the years when they had been fighting the battles of the racetracks.

The brothers first started design work on a straight eight engine as early as 1916, during the time when their primary efforts were directed to building engines for aircraft, boats, and other machines during World War I.

One of the best and most reliable of those engines of war had, indeed, been just what they now proposed to put in a passenger motor car: a straight eight known as the Navy Patrol Engine, developed for patrol boat use. A straight eight for passenger car use was unheard of, up to that time.

The Duesenberg brothers had a dual purpose in designing an in-line eight for motor car use. They could use it for racing or for passenger cars.

Their famed walking beam engine, which had performed so brilliantly for many years on the racetracks, was reaching—or had reached—its peak of potential, even in its final, 16-valve version. Fred Duesenberg was willing to drop the walking beamers if he could come up with something better. And maybe, just maybe, Fred had already seen that "something better" in an overhead cam design.

Duesenberg did not invent the overhead cam design. A few engine designers had been playing around with it, including Peugeot and Mercedes in Europe and, among others, Louis Chevrolet in the U.S. It had already shown promise in racing engines, but was virtually unheard of in passenger cars.

The Duesenbergs had their first in-line eights ready, but barely, for the first postwar running of the Indy 500 in 1919. There were racing successes from 1920 on, culminating in the glory years at Indy in 1924 and 1925.

Obviously, the overhead cam design would be good enough for a passenger car.

In the midst of all the racing activity, Fred and Augie, acting as engineers for

Model A engine showing overhead camshaft and bevel drive, rocker arms and valve springs.

the newly formed Indianapolis-based company using their name, managed to put into production the first Duesenberg passenger car for the market.

The original prototypes of the new in-line eights weighed in at 296 cubic inches, obviously with the 300-inch limit at Indy in mind. But when it came time to design the first passenger car model, it would be 2⅞ x 5 inches, for 260 cubic inches, and thus smaller than the racing engine.

That was quickly switched, however, when Indy officials, for the 1920 race, reduced the engine size limit to 183 inches. It forced a quick downsizing. In 1923 the racing formula was squeezed down again, this time to 122 inches. By 1926, the limit was dropped all the way down to 91 inches.

Through all this, the passenger car engine remained at 260 cid.

While the racing engines would come in with three valves per cylinder, two exhausts and an intake, the passenger straight eight would have a more conservative two-valve design.

In keeping with the exacting standards Fred Duesenberg had set for the new passenger car, the combustion chambers were completely machined, completely round, becoming the closest thing to a "hemi-head" that anyone could find in that day. The valves were set at an angle. The cam and valve train were driven by a vertical shaft and spur gears. Pistons were lightweight aluminum alloy, as in the racers.

The massive crankshaft was, in effect, two four-cylinder crankshafts joined at the center with the throws of the two sections at right angles with each other. Latter day engineers would scorn such a design, but it worked—and worked well — especially later, when the Duesenbergs added special mercury tube balancers.

Another interesting feature was that the carburetor was mounted on the right side while the intake manifolds, ramshorn shaped, were on the left side, drawing air through a passage in the cylinder head for heating purposes. This was a valuable feature in a day when gasoline quality was notoriously poor, with raw "ends" remaining unburned until the engine was very hot.

All this was only the beginning. Fred Duesenberg had not earned his spurs in the racing arenas without learning a great deal about metals and special alloys, and things like the importance of light, unsprung weight.

Through the use of special molybdenum steel, he was able to hold the weight of the rear axle down to 230 pounds, compared to 430 for a Cadillac axle of that day. "But it's stronger," Fred insisted, and was able to recall later that only one of those axles had ever failed. The front axle, following the same principle, was lightweight tubular, special alloy — and it was strong.

For the transmission, Fred selected something he had learned about while designing massive aircraft engines during the war: fully ground Maag gears, a three-speeder.

Even on the frame, Fred drove relentlessly in his battle for light weight, using special heat-treated chrome nickel steel for the side rails. Despite the size of it all, with a wheelbase of 134 inches for the standard model and 141 for the seven-passenger limousine, Fred wanted a car that would perform — no heavy freight wagon.

Fred obtained that performance in what, normally, would have been a very large car, through what we know as the "horsepower to weight" ratio. The 260-cubic-inch Duesenberg engine was rated at 90 hp (some ratings had it at 100).

How did the Duesenberg compare with other cars selling in its price class? The monstrous Locomobile being sold in 1924 had a horsepower rating of 93 for its giant six, but a huge cubic inch displacement of 525, more than double the Duesenberg's. The Pierce-Arrow for the same period showed 100 hp for a giant T-head six with 414 cubic inches.

In the all-important weight picture, the Duesenberg weighed in from 3,900 pounds for a roadster to 4,350 pounds for a seven-passenger limousine. Locomobile weight ranged from 4,957 to 5,722 pounds and Pierce-Arrow from 4,500 to 5,060 pounds—and Pierce-Arrow used aluminum bodies.

When it came to bodies, the Duesenberg brothers wisely decided to stay out of the field. As a new independent maker with a projected low production rate, the body building would be left up to the custom shops. The result was that Duesenbergs had bodies by Bender, Biddle & Smart, Fleetwood (then still independent), LeBaron, McNeer, Rubay, Schutte, and Millspaugh and Irish.

As was appropriate for a low production luxury car being made in Indianapolis, the Duesenbergs arranged to have every chassis given a road test on the famed Indianapolis 500 Speedway before being delivered to the body maker.

Since the testing was done without the body weight, the rear ends were loaded with iron or cement blocks to simulate that weight. Any engine or chassis, or any component thereof, which failed to give a perfect performance in the track test was immediately replaced. It was probably no accident, considering its heritage, that the finished Duesenberg incorporated several "firsts" for the American passenger motor car industry:

• The first production straight eight.
• The first production passenger car with overhead cam engine.
• The first with completely ground transmission gears.
• The first with lightweight, tubular front axle.
• Of major importance, the first hydraulic brakes.

Fred and Augie had been experimenting with hydraulic brakes for several years—on race cars, of course—so they

Fred Duesenberg and his wife are shown in a 1920 prototype. The engine depicted here is a prototype eight-cylinder walking beam engine that never entered production. (Fred Roe photo)

didn't have to be told about the advantages. It's been suggested that if Fred Duesenberg had been foresighted enough to patent the brakes, he would eventually have made enough money to keep him out of financial troubles the rest of his life.

The first Duesenberg hydraulic brakes were equipped with cut-offs to each wheel, allowing the driver to cut off the fluid to any wheel when a leak or breakdown took place. He could continue driving with brakes on three, two or even one wheel.

Perhaps the one overriding characteristic of the Duesenberg motor car was quality—the insistence on only the best. Fred and Augie had known from the beginning that they were laying their reputation on the line with a passenger car. Every part and component had to be the best that could be made or ordered.

Which, of course, raises the question of who actually built the Duesenberg Straight Eight. The answer is much the same as it had always been, during all the years of designing and building motors and race cars. Fred and Augie decided what was needed, and then the parts were made.

If the parts could not be made by hand with chisel, file and welding outfit, or by the machine tools available in the Duesenberg shops, castings or billets were ordered for machining. The unfinished castings, or forgings, were either finished by hand or by machine work in the Duesenberg shops. When it came time to put the Straight Eight into production, there was a bit less hand work, a bit more ordering of castings and forgings, and a bit more of the semi-production type machine work in the Duesenberg plant. In no way could the new Duesenberg be considered an "assembled car."

On every part Fred Duesenberg ordered, he specified exactly what he wanted by way of special steels and alloys. Only the finest and strongest materials available would be used; they would be finished to as near perfection as the best craftsmen could manage.

On the other hand, the engineering methods would have driven a university-trained engineer to tears. Former Duesenberg employes told stories of how Fred would say: "Make this a bit shorter"; "Make that shaft a bit longer"; "Put a 30 degree bend in that bracket."

In any case, the motor industry fraternity had come to recognize the abilities and accomplishments of Fred Duesenberg. Thus, when the Duesenbergs made the announcement of their long awaited car, the leading motor magazine, *Motor Age*, said: "You couldn't kiss it off by simply saying, 'Here is another car.' " For, the magazine suggested, "The fame of Fred Duesenberg as a race car designer and builder has hardly a parallel, and now this master designer enters the passenger car field with a design incorporated in which are many of the design and structural features evolved as answers to problems presented by the race track."

Nobody could say exactly what the Duesenberg brothers expected from their new enterprise. Certainly they hoped, and believed, it would succeed. But equally certain — with the expensive materials and quality being built into the new car and with price tags ranging from $6,500 for a two-passenger roadster to $7,800 for a seven-passenger limousine—no mass production could have been expected. Cadillacs at that time were selling for prices ranging from $3,100 to $4,600. A Model T Ford was as little as $364. Only the huge Locomobiles, the prestigious Pierce-Arrows, and the limited-production McFarlans sold for as much or more as the new Duesenberg.

The Duesenberg Straight Eight got its first public showing at the Sixteenth Automobile Salon at the Commodore Hotel in New York in November, 1920, but the showing may have been a bit premature.

The plant to build it didn't even exist,

and the prototype engine in the show car was of the old side rocker (walking beam) design. By the time the brothers agreed on a production design, it was the new overhead cam engine. As for the factory, construction did not even begin until February, 1920, in Indianapolis.

According to Fred Roe, author and historian for the Auburn-Cord-Duesenberg Club, not more than half a dozen of the new cars were assembled in 1921, and probably none of them was registered in that year. For all practical purposes, 1922 was the first production year.

Figures on actual production, compiled by various sources, do not always match, but most Duesenberg historians agree that total production on the new Straight Eight, for the five years of its production life, was between 600 and 650. Roe's figures show a total of 644:

- 148 for 1922
- 240 for 1923
- 26 for 1924 (a year of financial troubles for the company)
- 128 for 1925
- 56 for 1926.

Perhaps as many as half of the 1926 machines were classified as 1927 models and sold after 1926.

Since, according to Roe's research, the plant had originally been designed for a production capacity of up to 2,500 cars per year, the project must have been a bitter disappointment to the brothers and their backers.

During the five to six years of production on the Duesenberg Straight Eight, the company went through at least one bankruptcy and at least one threatened bankruptcy. The operation was in an almost perpetual state of financial emergency, especially after 1924 when the Duesenberg brothers, after a "reorganization," were forced to take over most of the active management.

Layoffs and re-hirings became almost routine, especially in the latter years. When a few orders came in, the workers worked and got paid. When orders stopped, workers were "furloughed." The process cost the company some of its best workers. They found other work, and were not available when recalled.

Almost certainly, one of the reasons for the slow sales—aside from the high price of the car—came from the fact that such

The beautiful and large seven-passenger Model A Touring of 1922-23. (Fred Roe photo)

a small organization never had the money or the manpower to set up a proper sales organization with a chain of dealerships throughout the country. There were many parts of the country where folks had never heard of a Duesenberg, much less seen one in a dealer's showroom.

In the final sense, none of these problems would affect the quality or performance of the machines themselves. Fred saw to that.

Perhaps what really set the new Duesenberg Straight Eight apart from other luxury cars in the same price class was its heritage on the racetracks. The Duesenberg brothers would not build a car that was not fast, nimble and powerful. All those years of racetrack experience were deeply ingrained in their instincts.

The 3,155-mile speed and endurance test on the Indy 500 oval was proof enough. The fact that the car in stock form, in its lighter-bodied models, could crowd 100 mph—and hit 90 mph even with heavier bodies — assured that it could outrun virtually any production car being made in the U.S.

The model designation "A" was seldom used when the car was introduced, or in the early years of its career. Company ads preferred to refer to it as "The Original Straight Eight," or the "Duesenberg Straight Eight." After Jimmy Murphy scored his sensational triumph in the 1921 French Grand Prix at Le Mans, Duesenberg ads began referring to the car as "The Grand Prix Car." The car was, however, referred to in company records as the Model A in the latter years of its production. As time passed, Duesenberg fans have come, more and more, to the usage of "Model A," if for no other reason than to differentiate between it and the Model J.

There is also the matter of superchargers on the Duesenberg A. At least some

Featuring a body by McNear of Boston, MA, the second body mounted on this chassis, this 1926 Model A Duesenberg was meticulously restored by Vic Benischek of Albuquerque, NM, over a five-year period. (Fred Roe photo)

of the customers who bought Model A's were well aware of the role superchargers had played in the Duesenberg racing picture, beginning with the surprise triumph at the Indianapolis Speedway in 1924. So, they asked, why can't we have superchargers on our cars?

They could, and a few of the passenger car models were fitted out with the blowers. There is conflicting evidence about whether any of them were actually sold to customers, and most Duesenberg historians say only about three cars got the blowers. There really wasn't very much to the supercharged Model A story.

How many of the Duesenberg Model A's have survived? Some published reports have said 100, but most historians have said the number is nearer 50. Duesenberg historian Fred Roe believed about 35 complete or semi-complete A's existed in 1982, with 15 or 20 incomplete.

A final question leaves many disturbing thoughts: with so much going for it, why did the Duesenberg Model A fail to sell?

There are several answers. First, the Duesenberg brothers were superb mechanics, self-made mechanical engineers. Fred would have to be ranked high among the greatest. But they were not salesmen.

Nor did the company ever have the money or personnel to properly organize a sales department and dealer network. The Duesenberg team lacked a brilliant organizer, such as John North Willys in the Willys-Overland enterprise.

It might be safe to say that if potential buyers had known then what we now know about the Duesenberg Straight Eight—the superb Grand Prix car—the enterprise may well have ended differently. The nimble, fast and well-performing thoroughbred might have achieved the success it deserved, and the great legend named Duesenberg might have been born some six or seven years earlier.

The mighty "J" is born: 1926-1930

The time had come: the time to create a "motor car incomparably superior to any other car which may be bought," its maker unashamedly declared.

It would be a car that would fulfill that promise in such measure that, more than half a century later, motor car lovers still call it the greatest motor car ever made—then or now.

In its time, it was the fastest, most powerful, roadworthy, elegant and durable car made, and just about the biggest.

From a historical standpoint, the car would give birth to a legend more durable than that surrounding any other single model of car—unless, of course, one wished to consider the Model T Ford, a machine so vastly different it almost belonged in another world. Such legends do not endure without at least some measure of substance.

Under the sponsorship of Erret Lobban Cord, Fred Duesenberg was about to bring forth the Duesenberg Model J, and create an automotive legend. The gestation period was 1926-1928. The machine was first shown to the public at the Motor Car Salon in the Hotel Commodore, New York City, in December of 1928.

Perhaps nobody knows for certain the exact moment or place in which the idea for the Model J was conceived. We do know that the first Duesenberg production model, the "A," was nearing the end of its production period in 1926. Fred had been considering a new model and had done some preliminary planning but, because the Duesenberg Motor Co. was in financial trouble, he lacked the capital to build it.

Cord had come to Indiana to take over the troubled Auburn Automobile Co. He had boosted that ailing company with a dramatic recovery, and was seeking new worlds to conquer when his eyes cast upon what was left of the Duesenberg enterprise.

He was well aware of Fred Duesenberg's engineering genius, the fabulous record of his racing machines and the sound, trail-breaking engineering behind the Model A.

The team was a natural: Cord, the jet-propelled promoter, and Duesenberg, the man who could engineer the best in motor cars, racing or otherwise.

Most historians agree that by the time Cord took over the nearly defunct Duesenberg company in 1926, he had glorious visions of a motor car that would be the greatest ever built. Fred had his own ideas of a new Duesenberg, but the dimensions of Fred's dream were, perhaps, of a smaller scale than those of Cord.

Reporters of the motoring world have recorded that Cord told Fred to build the biggest, the best, the most powerful and the fastest passenger car that could be built. Fred Duesenberg was not a man to object to a bit of upgrading on his own dream.

The historical fact is that they did it: a car that weighed in with a super long 153.5-inch wheelbase (also 142.5), and a giant straight eight engine that churned out a whopping 265 hp. (Some old car fans have disputed this horsepower rating.)

This was 1928, when the biggest Pierce-Arrow, one of the most prestigious makes of its time, had a giant 414-cid six rated at 100 bhp and a 138-inch wheelbase. The Packard Custom Eight had a bit more impressive statistics, with a 384-cid engine rated at 106 hp and a 143-inch wheelbase. The Cadillac of that year offered 341 cid, 90 bhp, and a 138-inch wheelbase on its biggest model.

Then there was Walter P. Chrysler, whose young company had just announced the Chrysler Imperial 80 with the bold boast that it was "America's most powerful motor car." It had an impressive 112 hp and a wheelbase of 136 inches.

Now, suddenly entering the picture was a mighty motor car with 265 hp, on a 153.5-inch wheelbase!

The average motor minded newspaper reader who picked up his Sunday paper in December, 1928, and saw the story of the new Duesenberg, would have to do some fast and drastic gear shifting in his mind to grasp the immensity of what he was reading. Perhaps he might be forgiven if he suspected the newspaper's typesetter had made an error with the horsepower figure.

But there it was. As if the horsepower figure wasn't enough, how about the headlines shouting that this fabulous new car would do 89 to 90 miles per hour *in second gear,* and that it would go 116 to 120 mph in high gear, depending on the body style and gear ratio of the rear axle?

The owner of a 1928 Cadillac or Packard was lucky if he could see an honest 80 mph on his speedometer in high.

Not that any motorist needed, or could use, all that speed on the comparatively primitive roads available in 1928. But just the fact that it was there was impressive enough, even if Fred Duesenberg had been required to borrow the brick-paved Indianapolis Motor Speedway to prove it.

How had Duesenberg done it? How was it possible for him to extract 265 hp from 420 cubic inches when Pierce-Arrow engineers, with their long vaunted T-head design, had been able to obtain only 100 hp from an engine of virtually the same size?

Perhaps the biggest single factor in the enormous power of Duesenberg's new engine was a feature which would not come into common use until two new generations of motorists would be born: nothing less than the overhead cam—not one, but two, with four valves per cylinder. In addition, the completely machined combustion chamber was of a design that very nearly qualified as the "hemi-head of the 1920s," decades before Chrysler produced such spectacular results in the 1950s.

In the 1920s it was a design reserved almost exclusively for the best racing cars, which probably explained why Fred Duesenberg used it. He hadn't been building some of the best racing engines in the world for nothing. Duesenberg knew only one system for making motors or motor cars: the best, the most powerful and the fastest.

Those wise in the ways of high-powered motors might suggest that a motor as powerful, fast, spectacular and intricate as the new Duesenberg would also be temperamental, hard to tune, hard to keep tuned, and relatively short-lived.

It is true that, if one wished to count every one of the 265 horses under the hood, the unique powerplant would require the best of tuning. On the other hand, the engine would prove to be remarkably durable. Several hundred of the mighty Duesenberg J's are still with us today, and some of them are driven quite regularly. It is not uncommon to find owners who can document complete turnovers of the 100,000-mile odometer—on a few of them, twice or several times.

In any case, it was inevitable that a machine with such spectacular statistics would produce an equally spectacular storm of publicity, first in the motoring publications and then—after being shown at the Salon in New York and in other major cities — by newspapers reaching into the far corners of the country.

America in 1928 or 1929 was, perhaps, just reaching the first plateau in its fabled "love affair with the motor car." It had long been every man's dream to own a car, but it was only in the "roaring twenties" that this dream began to come true for the masses.

Even if millions had to be satisfied with a $400 Model T Ford, a four-cylinder Chevrolet National or a Star Model M, those millions could still dream of the fast and the powerful.

Just one example of the attention given to the new dream machine was the seven pages of description, with 22 illustrations, in the magazine *MoTor* for December, 1928.

There was plenty for the magazine's technical editor, Harold T. Blanchard, to describe and illustrate. He called attention to the massive breathing capacity of the big engine, provided by the overhead cams and four valves per cylinder. One might have suspected, with four valves per cylinder, that the valves would have to be chopped down to diminutive size, but Fred had been able to arrange for 1½-inch intake valves and 1⅞-inch valves for the exhausts—no puny valves, to be sure.

The specially designed ignition system operated with two breakers and two coils, with the spark plug located in the exact center of the combustion cham-

1929 Duesenberg Lebaron dual Cowl Phaeton Model J. The Wallace automobile from the Barbour collection.

ber—more of the "hemi" design.

Backing all this up was a massive crankshaft with five main bearings, with extra large dimensions of 2¾-inch mains and 2½-inch connecting rod bearings. The huge crankshaft was not only statically and dynamically balanced, but equipped with a unique mercury tube balancing system. The connecting rods and pistons were aluminum, but the rods had steel caps.

The drive was by a twin disc clutch and a specially designed three-speed transmission incorporating a unique "internal-external" second gear design so silent that many drivers would forget to shift into high. After all, if the car went faster in second than most competitive cars would go in high, how was one to know?

Shifting was by long sliding actuators, which allowed the shift lever to be mounted on the toe board rather than in the center of the floor, where it might interfere with somebody's feet.

The final drive was through a massive torque tube with two special yoke-mounted rubber stabilizers at the front to eliminate shock or vibration at the rear axle from being transmitted to the engine or body. The torque tube also provided the front mounting of the flexible hoses for both the hydraulic brakes and the automatic chassis lubrication system, thus eliminating the need for these lines at each rear wheel.

The single universal joint at the front of the driveshaft was another unique design, based on eight rubber balls imbedded in sockets which allowed flexibility but complete freedom from shock or vibration.

The rear axle gear was of the hypoid design, one of the earliest for passenger car application, allowing an extra two inches lowering of the body height. To reduce unsprung weight, special alloy tubular steel was used for the axle housings, with special steel casting for the central housing.

In the rear axle design, as on virtually every component of the big car, Duesenberg reduced weight by using special alloys, or aluminum, while still providing what was termed at least a 50 percent greater margin of strength than was necessary. Despite the car's enormous size, Fred was able to put the big

machine on the road at around 5,000 pounds for the four-passenger phaeton, very little more than competitive cars of much less power and size.

The brakes were also unique. Fred Duesenberg had been a pioneer, actually an innovator, when it came to the use of hydraulic brakes for passenger car use. He had been using them for years on his racing cars.

On the new Model J, the hydraulic cylinder for the front brakes was mounted vertically, atop the king pin, thus allowing a single piston and a single adjustment. The king pin, incidentally, was mounted on ball bearings, both upper and lower, the lower bearing carrying the weight and the upper the side thrust. It was a design that could be used only on the most expensive cars. The bearings were so well sealed they needed lubrication only once a year.

Chassis lubrication was taken care of by a system which was not only central —operated by a pump which forced lubricant through tubes to all spring shackles and chassis bearings—but also automatically operated by the rotation of the fuel pump cam. The system was timed so that it automatically gave every bearing a shot of lubricant every 80 miles. Signal lights on the dash told the driver when the system had completed a lubrication cycle, and also told him when the system was empty and needed refilling.

More warning lights on the dash, operated by clock type reduction gears from the same drive that drove the lubricator, told the driver when it was time to check the battery and change engine oil. Who invented the so-called idiot lights?

Another indication of how thoroughly every detail had been covered was the fuel pump. It was of special design, with double bellows and a double cam. An ordinary fuel pump, company literature pointed out, would provide plenty of fuel for all normal requirements, but the Duesenberg engineers wanted to make absolutely certain the big engine would never be starved for gasoline, under the most extreme conditions of high speed or acceleration.

Drivers who viewed the colossal machine felt a bit of apprehension, at first, about the "muscle" required to steer,

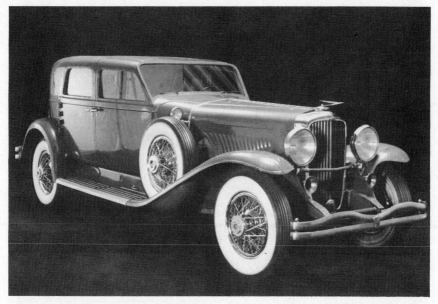

1930 Duesenberg Model J Sedan by Murphy. The Model J was built between 1929 and 1936. The Murphy company alone was responsible for building more than half the bodies for all the Model J Duesenberg chassis that were produced, a figure estimated at 470.

clutch and brake such a motor car. They were in for a pleasant surprise when they tried it and found that one didn't have to be a "horse" to drive the new Duesenberg.

Blanchard, the *MoTor* writer who gave the Duesenberg the seven-page report, was one of the first to note this. "Steering is easy, clutch and brake pedals have a light action, while the brakes are unusually effective. The car takes turns beautifully and with a full sense of security," he wrote.

For anyone suggesting that a car of such size would be slow on the acceleration side, Blanchard reported he could go from 10 to 80, in high gear, in 22 seconds. After all, the engine put out 374 pounds of torque at 2,000 rpm.

No wonder word quickly spread that "nobody passes a Duesenberg unless the driver of the Duesenberg is willing to be passed."

Gordon M. Buehrig, who would become famous as the designer of the celebrated Model 810 Cord, suggested that the Model J was a miracle in another sense: in that such a highly complex and well engineered car—the epitome of the best the American motor car industry

could produce—was brought into being by a company whose payroll was less than 50 persons (including all employees, from the president to the floor sweeper).

Someone may suggest that much of the Duesenberg was farmed out: parts, components and, of course, the bodies. But there is no disputing the fact that every part of the machine was designed, engineered and, to a large part, machined in the Duesenberg plant. All fitting and assembly took place in the plant. Beyond all this, there was scarcely a part used that would fit any car except the Duesenberg.

Take the engine, for example. Cord had also bought the Lycoming engine building plant, which became a part of the Auburn-Cord-Duesenberg complex. It was only logical that the building of the Duesenberg-designed straight eight engine would be assigned to the Lycoming branch.

The engines were completed, assembled and block tested at Lycoming. They then went to Duesenberg, where they were completely torn down, re-assembled and retested much more severely than at Lycoming. Every engine, even after being bedded into its chassis, was required to run 500 miles on the Indianapolis Speedway before being declared fit to be sold as a Duesenberg.

Any engine, or part, that failed these final tests was simply scrapped.

Any story of the Duesenberg Model J must include a discussion of the bodies. As with the earlier Model A, the big "J" was designed in chassis form only, although the chassis included radiator shell, hood, dash, fenders, running boards and lamps, including the rear fender-mounted tail lamps.

Such a layout guaranteed that all Duesenbergs would remain Duesenbergs, and recognizable as such, no matter who made the body. Having said this much, one can also suggest that, of the entire production run of the Model J, from 1928 to 1936, no two cars were exactly alike.

It is true that some were very similar. Some body makers produced a run of, say, half a dozen of a certain body style. They might even complete the bodies "in the white," a term used for bodies that were unpainted and untrimmed. Then the buyer could decide on the color and the trim he wanted. But those "differences" extended to the hardware as well as the trim. Many of the bodies were, indeed, of the "one of a kind" variety: ordered, styled and finished to meet the specifications of the individual buyer.

In June, 1928, as the Model J was nearing its final form, the company sent out to the leading body makers specifications with scale sketches of the chassis, along with invitations for the body makers to submit design proposals for the giant chassis.

Duesenberg wanted proposals, and at least some bodies, on hand for the December introduction. It was no accident that some of the pre-announcement designs accepted by Duesenberg came from some of the top names in the custom industry: a phaeton and several sedan designs from Derham; a convertible roadster and a convertible sedan from Murphy; a phaeton by LeBaron; a town car by Rollston; and a town cabriolet by Holbrook.

Later, more names were added to the list, including Judkins, Weymann, Brunn, Walker, Willoughby, La Grande, Dietrich, Locke, Bohman & Schwartz, and Hibbard & Darrin—virtually the entire galaxy of great body makers.

Singer Wayne Newton has his 1930 Duesenberg Model J Convertible Roadster on loan to Harrah's Automobile Collection. The gigantic 420-cid eight-cylinder engine was rated at 265 hp. This little gem sold new for around $14,500.

The bodies came in phaetons, sport roadsters, convertible coupes, convertible sedans, convertible victorias, speedsters, sport sedans, fixed top coupes (both two and four-passenger), cabriolets, town cars, town limousines and formal sedans, or any other specific body style or type a customer might want.

In the early months, Duesenberg salesmen showed the various design proposals to their customers. After the order was booked, Duesenberg shipped a chassis to the designated body maker.

Later, Duesenberg set up its own body design department. Gordon Buehrig, who had been working as a stylist at General Motors, drove to New York to see the new designs at the Motor Car Salon. He immediately fell in love with the new Duesenberg, declared it to be the hit of the show—which it was—and decided he wanted to design bodies for the new machine. He went to work as chief body designer in 1929 at the "munificent" salary of $300 per month.

P.A. Derham, from the body building firm of that name, came to Duesenberg to act as a liaison man between Duesenberg, the customers, and the custom body shops. He helped work out engineering and structural details. With this system in place, Duesenberg publications claimed that "Duesenberg maintains a custom designing and body engineering organization second to none in the world."

The system now was for Duesenberg to create body designs of its own, subject to customer approval, then hand

*1929 Duesenberg J long-wheelbase Willoughby
Berline.*

them to the custom builder. There was
never any intention of actually building
the bodies at Duesenberg. In any case, as
Buehrig recalled later, he ended up designing roughly half of the bodies that
eventually found their way onto Duesenberg chassis. The practice became,
more or less, for the body maker to ship
the bodies to Indianapolis for mounting
and fitting at the Duesenberg plant.

Most people who look at a Duesenberg J come away with the impression of
how low and sleek it appears. This is, at
least partly, an illusion. The overhead
cams on the big straight eight engine actually dictated a hood that had to be a bit
higher than the designers may have liked.
It was proof of their artistry that they
succeeded in producing the "low and
sleek" effect despite the hood height.
They were helped, of course, by the fact
that the hypoid rear axle gave them an
extra two inches with which to play.

Who bought the Duesenberg J's? First,
a buyer had to have money—a good deal
of it. The chassis alone was priced at
$8,500. Bodies started at $2,500 and ran
as high as $10,000, depending on the
whims of the customer. A few of the
Duesenbergs sold for as much as $20,000.

You could, at that time, buy a new
Model T Ford for as little as $385. The
most expensive Cadillac models, complete with bodies, sold for around $5,500
to $5,700. One of the cheaper Cadillacs
was as little as $3,350.

With everything about the Duesenberg engineered, built and calculated to
appeal to the socially and financially elite,
it is obvious that this is where they went.
First, to the social elite, and then the ce-
lebrity crowd. A few ended up in the
hands of rich mobsters.

On the other hand, not every family of

the so-called "four hundred" would rush
to buy a Duesenberg. The name, after all,
was somewhat of a newcomer to the
"elite" market. Pierce-Arrow, Packard
and, to a large degree, Cadillac were already well entrenched into this market,
and buying habits in this group did not
change quickly. It is probable that at least
some members of the social crowd considered a car with so much speed and
power as being a bit on the vulgar side.
Who needed that much "oomph"?

While it was not yet true in 1929, the
first year of sales for the great car, the
cruel economic depression would crash
home with full fury by 1930. It would,
inevitably, have some effect on the sale
of cars in the luxury class—if, for no other
reason, than that some of the elite would
decline to buy the most luxurious of cars
because it smacked of flaunting their
wealth in the face of so much poverty.

Relatively few of the new Duesenbergs found their way overseas. Pride
undoubtedly dictated that Europeans
with money would stick to their Rolls-
Royces, Isotta-Fraschinis, and Mercedes.
The Duesenberg was so big, powerful and
imposing, however, it was inevitable that
some would go to Europe, even in chassis form so that the best European body
makers would have an opportunity to
body the audacious machine. Sadly, most
of the European-bodied Duesenbergs
were destroyed by war.

King Alfonso of Spain bought a Duesenberg, as did Prince Nicolas of Ro-
mania, a racing and sports car enthusiast.
It is significant that when King Alfonso,
who owned some 30 motor cars, was
forced to flee into exile, the one car he
selected to go with him was his
Duesenberg.

A staff member to Prince Nicolas was
quoted as saying, "His Royal Highness
considers that the Duesenberg is the
world's finest automobile today, from
every point of view."

A measure of the overpowering presence of the great motor car came from
France, of all places, when the Duesenberg was declared the finest car on display in luxury car exhibitions at Cannes
and Pau in 1930—not, perhaps, because
the French wanted to hand this acco-
lade to an American car, but because they
could hardly avoid it. Perhaps someone

remembered that a Duesenberg had won the French Grand Prix in 1921.

It was becoming apparent that Fred Duesenberg—the child immigrant from a small village in Germany, the small town boy from Iowa, the one time "shoestring" manager of a motor car racing team, the builder of fast racing cars—had come a long, long way to the very pinnacle of the motoring world.

"There is a very simple and completely accurate explanation for the excellence of the Duesenberg engine and chassis," Gordon Buehrig said many years later. "Fred Duesenberg was a genius."

A mightier Duesenberg, and the final years: 1932-1936

If Fred Duesenberg had sent shock waves through the auto industry in 1928, by announcing a 265-horsepower passenger car at a time when the best of the industry was struggling to reach 100, imagine the excitement he created when he raised the ante to 320. It took a supercharger to do it, but he did it.

A supercharger, coming from Fred Duesenberg, should not have been a surprise, considering that he had been one of the world's pioneers in their use. He was the first man to put a successful supercharger on a race car—and with spectacular success, including three wins at Indy.

In June of 1932 the announcement came from Duesenberg that henceforth the mighty Model J would be available with a supercharger, with a horsepower and performance rating that would, once more, soar into the realm of the "unbelievable."

Back in 1928, when the Model J first appeared, people were amazed that the fabulous new car would do 90 miles per hour in second gear, with something like 116 to 120 mph in high. The 1932 announcement had to be mind boggling. The new Model J, called the SJ when the supercharger had been added, actually topped 100 miles per hour in second, and played around the 130 mph area in high — perhaps even more when equipped with one of the lighter bodies.

The top makers of other luxury cars had also made some strides in horsepower and performance since 1928. Packard, Pierce-Arrow and Lincoln had all weighed in with highly sophisticated and powerful V-12 engines. The Packard boasted 160 bhp; the other two, 150 hp. Cadillac had trumped everyone, it seemed, with an unheard of 16-cylinder, Vee-type engine with a displacement of 462 cubic inches but a somewhat modest horsepower rating of 165.

The Duesenberg, while relatively big, was smaller than the Cadillac or the Packard, and had only eight cylinders. It did, though, have a 420 cid.

Duesenberg had done it without upping the size of the engine at all, merely beefing up some of the internal bearings and moving parts so they could take the extra pounding a supercharger would bring.

The supercharger itself, only 12 inches in diameter, was mounted upright on the right side of the engine and was propelled by a worm drive and a specially "cushioned" driveshaft. The cushioning may sound like a minor detail, but it was actually one of the most important factors in making a supercharger work without tearing itself up during rapid acceleration or deceleration — mostly deceleration. It was one of the first things Fred had learned when he started playing with superchargers, and it was the secret of his success.

The rotor turned at six times motor speed, which meant that at 4,000 engine rpm, the supercharger was turning 24,000 rpm — not sensational in terms of what later superchargers would do, but enough to boost the manifold pressure by five to eight pounds at speed, ram that already phenomenal horsepower rating from 265 to 320, and keep the Duesenberg far ahead of the pack in both performance and power.

Spectacular and sensational as the new engine may have been, it also contained elements of personal tragedy for Fred Duesenberg himself. Tragedy was about to strike the man who had, for the most part, been the inspiration and creator of the Duesenberg saga.

One version of the story has been told by William H. Beckman, an engineer and draftsman who had left Duesenberg shortly after the development of the "J" and taken a job as engineer for Johnson Motors, in Waukegan, Illinois. Early in July, 1932, just after the sensational new "SJ" had been announced, Beckman received a telegram from Fred, asking Beckman to meet him at the LaSalle Hotel in Chicago to discuss some "very important" business.

Duesenberg never kept the appointment, and Beckman never learned what the very important business was. On July 2, while driving one of the new "SJ" models through the Ligonier Mountains in Pennsylvania, the veteran engineer and driver lost control of the big car and crashed. Taken to a hospital at Johnstown, it had seemed that his injuries were not critical. But he developed pneumonia and died on July 25.

It has never been determined what caused the crash. It was well known that Fred had suffered from severely crippled hands nearly all of his adult life. At the time of his death, his hands had been described as "clawlike," with no power to move the fingers at all. Chester S. Ricker, a close friend, described how Fred had been forced to wrap "knots" of friction tape onto the steering wheels of the cars he drove, in order to be able to drive at all.

In spite of this, he was known to enjoy driving cars fast. It is quite possible that a combination of fatigue, the crippled hands and, perhaps, a bit too much speed from the eager new supercharged car may have combined to cause him to lose control on the winding mountain road at night.

In any case, the death of Fred Duesenberg sent a kind of shock wave rippling through the motor car engineering profession, the great circle of friends, the men of racing, the Indy 500 fraternity, all of whom had known him so well and loved him so much.

Chester Ricker, in a tribute published in *MoTor,* called Fred "the Grand Old Man of motor racing." He added: "Few men were better known or better liked in the automotive industry. He never saw obstacles. He always seemed to find a way out."

When they carried Fred Duesenberg to his grave in Indianapolis, there were few dry eyes among the crowd of people who came to bid him farewell. Perhaps most fitting of all the tributes was the great floral arrangement they laid upon his grave, as a flight of airplanes dipped in salute over the gravesite: an arrange-

Greta Garbo's Duesenberg J Victoria, still basking in all its glitter and glory.

ment in the form of a checkered flag, that coveted symbol of victory at Indy.

Fred Duesenberg would have liked it. Now, with Fred gone, it was up to Augie to carry on. Augie had not been directly associated with the Duesenberg enterprise during the development of the "J" and "SJ."

Instead, in a small building across the street from the Duesenberg factory grounds, he had continued to work with the racing fraternity in the development of racing cars. It was all centered around modifications of the Model A engine, now that the cubic inch displacement limits at Indy had been raised.

One of these creations had scored fifth place at Indy in 1930, and in 1931 came very close to bringing another victory to Duesenberg, placing second with Fred Frame at the wheel. He was only seconds behind the winner.

Why was the mighty Model J engine, or the sensational SJ, never called upon to show what it could do on the racetracks — at Indy, for example? The answer is simple: it was too big.

When Indianapolis race officials lifted the limits in 1930, they didn't lift them all the way. Their purpose had been to allow stock car engines, in modified form, of course, back into the racing picture. The new limit on cubic-inch displacement, while extremely liberal compared to the limit of 91 inches during the late 1920s, had a ceiling of 366 inches.

The big Duesie was 420 inches. No matter how badly folks might have yearned to see the mighty J in action on the tracks, it was not to be.

But the big "SJ" engine was destined to reap at least one measure of glory on the speed-endurance circuit—on the Salt Flats of Utah. It would prove, decisively, that the big Duesenberg engine was very fast indeed, and very tough.

It all began under another name and another banner — Pierce-Arrow — and with a man named Ab ("Iron Man") Jenkins.

For three successive years, beginning in 1932, Jenkins had set new world records for the 24-hour endurance run in cars powered by modified Pierce-Arrow V-12 engines. He had earned the title "Iron Man" because he insisted on running the entire 24 hours alone, without a relief driver.

On his first run, he had been unable to obtain "official" timers, and his sensational new record of an average of 112 mph for the 24 hours was not officially recognized. It didn't really matter. In 1933, after tinkering his Pierce-Arrow machine up a bit, and with official timing, he boosted the record to 117.77 mph.

In 1934 he was back again, having squeezed still a few more horsepower out of the magnificent Pierce-Arrow V-12, and shoved the record all the way to 127.229 mph. This included stops for fueling and tires, which meant that while he was moving, he was moving very fast indeed. The engine was turning out 235 bhp.

Before Jenkins had started the speed runs on the Salt Flats, none of the world speed record people had ever heard of the place — or were not interested in traveling to a very hot hell-hole out in the western desert of the U.S.

But in blasting all those records, Jenkins had, inevitably, attracted attention to the Salt Flats. Motor car speed record attackers began paying attention. It was almost inevitable that an Englishman named John Cobb would come to Utah to try to smash Jenkins' records.

Cobb had to use a huge modified airplane engine to do it—a Napier rated at 450 hp—but he managed to up the record to 134.85 mph.

Jenkins was in a trap. A canny, self-made mechanic and engineer himself, he realized that he had squeezed the Pierce-Arrow engine until not another ounce of power or speed could be forced out of it. If he wanted to break Cobb's record, he had to look elsewhere for an engine —and there was the mighty Duesenberg SJ, king of them all.

At 320 hp, it was not quite a match for the monster 450 hp Napier but, since it also wasn't quite as heavy, it might do in a lighter chassis. Besides, maybe with his own knowledge of engines — together with what Augie Duesenberg knew about them — they could squeeze a bit more oomph out of the Duesie.

Anybody who knew Augie Duesenberg should have been able to predict that one. How could Augie have resisted? After tinkering with the magnificent SJ

1932 Duesenberg Model J.

engine, they came up against a fact which almost anybody who knew Fred Duesenberg should have been able to guess. Fred had done such a thorough job of engineering that there wasn't a lot that could be done to make it better. Then someone came up with the idea of equipping the big SJ with dual carburetion and ramshorn-shaped intake manifolds — one for each four cylinders, but still with the supercharger ramming in the air.

Suddenly, Ab and Augie found that they had an extra 60 horses on their hands. The dynamometer needle started reaching toward the 400 mark.

After making and installing a special streamlined body and a flat 3 to 1 rear end, they cranked the new machine up and found they could top 160 mph.

When they actually began cracking at the record, though, a few bugs began to show up. On the first try, a crankshaft bearing blew. In squeezing out all those horses, they had put a bit too much stress on the bearings.

That wasn't going to stop them. After they designed a new set of special bearings, they were back again. This time everything went fine until one of those truly unpredictable things happened: the aluminum crankcase split.

After a new crankcase came try No. 3.

With the mighty Duesenberg running flawlessly, and topping 160 mph at times, Jenkins managed to bring the 24-hour endurance record back to America at 135.47 mph. He crossed the finish line at more than 160 mph.

The run was made in 120 degree heat, a tortuous run for any engine, covering 3,253 miles in 24 hours. There were stops for tires and fuel every 400 miles.

This time Jenkins allowed himself the luxury of a relief driver, Tony Gulotta, giving Tony a share of the glory. For one entire hour during the run, the mighty car had averaged, officially, a record 152.145 mph.

Those records for cars in the Duesenberg's class would stand for years. If anybody needed to know which was the fastest motor car in the world, all one had to do was point west — to Utah — and Duesenberg.

In 1935, the year in which Jenkins, Augie Duesenberg and Tony Gulotta put on the record-breaking production out on the Utah Salt Flats, the speed of the winning car in the Indy 500 was 106.240 mph. That was for 500 miles, not 3,253 — and it wasn't quite that hot (over 100 degrees) at Indy, either.

When a few Duesenberg owners heard about the ramshorn manifold trick, and what it did to the fabulous SJ, they demanded to become the owners of such "options" too. That is why, among the big Duesenbergs still surviving around the country, one can lift the hood on a few of them and find ramshorn manifolds. Those who own the cars own some very fast hardware, even for the 1980s.

While shouting about the glory in Utah, what was happening to the Duesenberg enterprise back in Indianapolis—in terms of production, sales and the state of the business—has been more or less ignored.

With Fred's death, the spark plug was gone. Augie had been brought back into active management of the Duesenberg production shops. He was doing his best, and it probably would have been good enough under ordinary circumstances.

But, since 1929, the Duesenberg project—in fact, the entire American motor car industry—had been operating against the background of a cruel economic depression that was squeezing the motor car industry in a vicious grip. One proud make of motor car after another was sinking into the morass—bankrupt, broke and gone, never to return.

It would be easy to say that the great depression also killed Duesenberg. That, however, is an oversimplification. Duesenberg now was part of the Auburn-Cord-Duesenberg empire built by E.L. Cord, which included Lycoming engines and aircraft projects. It was on the Auburn-Cord end of the motor car business where the volume in production and sales lay, even though the company had always been comparatively small. It could be said that if the Auburn-Cord end failed in the depression, it would drag Duesenberg down with it, even if Duesenberg was still profitable.

That raises an interesting question, on which there has been some difference of opinion. At least one Duesenberg historian, one-time chief designer Gordon Buehrig, insisted that the Duesenberg operation remained a profitable one — barely, but paying its way.

The Duesenberg J was never intended as a volume production car. When the plant was built, it was designed for a possible volume of 2,400 cars per year. It is probably safe to say that Cord and Fred Duesenberg obviously hoped for a higher rate of production than they achieved.

When Cord gave orders to make the Duesenberg J, he had intended it as the flagship luxury car of the line. He would make his money from the Auburns and Cords. If the Duesenberg operation made a profit, or broke even, fine. Even if it showed a loss—as long as the losses were bearable — it would be tolerated in return for the prestige it brought, at least as long as the remainder of the empire was profitable.

General Motors had done this with Cadillac; Ford with Lincoln. Most historians agree that both lost money during the depression and would have gone bankrupt if they had not been part of a larger empire. Packard, an independent, and the prestige car of the 1920s, would have gone broke if it had not brought out a lower-priced car and cashed in on the prestige of the senior cars. Pierce-Arrow, the prestige car of an earlier period, also tried a low-priced model, but went broke nonetheless.

In the case of Cord, his "empire" was too small. His razzle-dazzle methods had made it go while the country was prosperous. But when one considers that his Auburns and Cords were also, in a sense, prestige cars—certainly not in the Model T Ford class — he did not have a viable base when the depression hit.

By 1933 he was losing $2,300,000 per year. For a small manufacturer with a small base, he was rapidly heading for disaster. He scraped up another $1,000,000 to make a last ditch try with another razzle-dazzle model.

Actually, there had been plans to make a smaller, less expensive Duesenberg. Gordon Buehrig had been put to work on a design. Deep into the project, he was called to Cord to turn the "small Duesenberg" into what would become the 810 and 812 Cord — a classic in motor car design, but with no chance to save the company. When that project added to the disaster, in 1935 and 1936, Cord sold the remnants of his empire and got out. The new owners had little interest in producing motor cars—Auburn, Cord or Duesenberg. It was the end.

The last of the mighty Duesenbergs were assembled late in 1936. Several of the cars were shown at the auto shows for 1937: a convertible sedan by Rollston in the New York auto show, and a

Jack B. Nethercutt's "Twenty Grand" Duesenberg was a Rollston-bodied company showpiece built for the 1933 World's Fair.

Rollston JN sports sedan (with fender skirts, narrower running boards, smaller headlamps and 17-inch wheels) in Chicago. No more cars would be produced in 1937.

How many Duesenberg J's and SJ's were made? Only 470 cars were produced from 1928 to 1936, including 36 SJ's built between 1932 and 1936.

With the number so small, it is easy to suggest that it wan't even a production car, especially since the entire production crew was often less than 50 men. It was virtually a hand-built machine.

But the Duesenberg J occupied a unique and very exclusive niche in the production and sales picture. With such a small work crew, and with the price remaining so high to assure that each car would more or less pay its way even at a meager production rate, it was just possible to keep the operation going even during the cruel depression.

There might not be enough buyers with enough money to keep Cadillac, Packard or Pierce-Arrow operations profitable — with production numbering into the hundreds, or thousands — but there would always be enough people with money to buy 470 Duesenbergs in eight years. That was only 60 cars per year.

It is probably a reflection of the unique position occupied by the "Big D" that a car so expensive, so exclusive, has one of the highest survival rates of any car ever built. Duesenberg historians claim that some 360 Duesenberg J's still exist, including at least 227 of them in more or less complete condition. Perhaps as many as 160 of them are still driven more or less regularly.

Is it possible to make an honest assessment of the fabulous Model J, which has virtually become a legend? It has frequently been called the greatest motor car of all time. Can this be true?

Stock cars with more horsepower, performance and speed have been produced since 1936. Some might insist that cars of more advanced styling, more elegance, have been made. But styling and design, like art, are a matter of taste — and, thus, timeless.

It is, perhaps, safe to say that never has a motor car so vastly superior in power and performance, in comparison to its contemporaries, been placed on the market. There might be a few exceptions, but if so they were far less in numbers, and in production for a far shorter period of time than the mighty J.

It is only when one considers the audacity of the concept, the incredible performance of the engine, the size, the finish, the sheer quality of every part, the enormous symphonic impact of the finished product in its entirety, that one must be willing to consider that it may be true — that the Duesenberg is, indeed, the greatest motor car of all time.

In all, Fred and Augie Duesenberg

1934 Duesenberg Supercharged J 107 Dual Cowl Touring Car.

made a unique pair in the history of the American motorcar.

- They designed and built one of the most powerful of the early, pioneering motor cars, the Mason.
- They developed a unique concept in engine design, the walking beam valve engine, which powered some of the fastest race cars in America in the period 1912-1920.
- They developed the first straight eight racing engine and the first production straight eight passenger car.
- They built the first American race car to win at Le Mans, in France.
- They built a machine which set a world speed record on the sands of Daytona Beach in 1920.
- They built a marine engine that set a world speed record in 1914.
- They designed and built the first successful supercharger for racing cars.
- They did pioneering work on hydraulic brakes.
- They built racing cars that three times won the Indy 500, plus others that came in second so many times.
- They—mostly Fred—designed and built the mighty Duesenberg Model J, widely acclaimed as the greatest passenger car ever made.

In speaking of great motor cars of the past, it has been the vogue to remind ourselves of the so-called "mystique" which may have been generated by, or which surrounded, a certain make or model of car. Mystique is the embodiment of respect, admiration, recognized greatness, envy, the acknowledgement of quality, and the devoted craftsman-ship which made it all possible.

Pierce-Arrow, in a time long before the Duesenberg Model J, was one of the first of the great cars to be blessed by an aura of mystique. During the 1920s, it was Packard which probably shared most of the honors; then Cadillac, in still later years. In other lands, cars like Rolls-Royce, Mercedes and perhaps a few others basked in the magic.

And then there is the Duesenberg Model J. It would be impudent to try to assign this car its share of mystique on a scale measured by a mathematical formula. Mystique, by its very essence, defies such ratings. Suffice it to say that whenever and wherever lovers of great cars gather to talk about value, performance, horsepower, torque, pistons, valves, gears, all the assemblage from which great motor cars are created, the name Duesenberg is always one of the first names to be heard.

Could Fred Duesenberg have left a finer legacy?

Author's note: The author must acknowledge the valuable assistance of the Auburn-Cord-Duesenberg Club in the preparation of this chapter. Special thanks go to Fred Roe, of Holliston, Massachusetts, Duesenberg historian for the ACD Club, who most generously provided historical material and pictures, and checked this material for accuracy. Roe completed a Duesenberg book of his own, *Duesenberg, The Pursuit of Perfection,* published in 1982 by Dalton Watson and distributed by Classic Motorbooks.

III
FRANKLIN

The beginning of the story: 1897-1903

There was something in the wind which made it all possible.

The soothing breath of air which cooled the sweat-flushed brow of the summer plowman could also miraculously cool the tortured, blistering iron made hot by countless explosions of gasoline and fire.

It made possible the story of the Franklin, the most successful air-cooled automobile in American history.

The word "successful" is used in the business sense, for there was never any question, from beginning to end, that the use of air as the only agent to cool the Franklin automobile engines was a total success.

The pity was that the Franklin makers, salesmen, advocates and users had to spend so much time proving it — being forced to demonstrate, over and over again, that primary air cooling was really successful. The makers of water-cooled motor cars and their salesmen, who outnumbered the air-cooled forces by far, waged constant war, psychological and otherwise, to sell the American public on the idea that air cooling could not possibly work.

Some wag said that from the time the first Franklin was built, until the last one, some Franklin driver was kept busy somewhere — in a desert sink-hole, trekking across a vast wasteland, climbing the steepest hills and the highest mountains—just to prove that Franklins stayed cool and would run forever.

The question should be a moot one now, after a little German beetle named the Volkswagen became one of the greatest automotive success stories of all time — and did it with an air-cooled engine.

Of course, all automotive engines are air cooled. Fords, Buicks, Chryslers and Cadillacs do it by using water (or cool-

An early survivor of H.H. Franklin's efforts is this 1904 Type A.

ant) first, to absorb the heat from the blistering cylinder walls and then, via radiator, use air to cool the water.

"The only difference is that they do it the hard way, and we do it the easy way," a Franklin advocate will say.

And, of course, he is right. There are no radiators, no water pumps, no hoses or clamps, no anti-freeze, no cracked cylinder blocks from freezing — all of which add to the weight of a motor car and provide sources of trouble to the car owner.

Other things, too, helped make the Franklin a unique automobile, especially in the earlier years. One was the obsession, based on scientific principles, of keeping a car light — especially the unsprung weight, in a time when most people didn't know what unsprung weight was.

The Franklin used a wooden frame because it was lighter and more flexible than a steel one. Full elliptic springs were used on all four wheels.

The full elliptic springing system defied all accepted engineering principles by scorning the use of radius rods, trusses, stabilizers or torque arms. The only logical thing about the suspension system was that it worked.

In fact, the suspension system — coupled with the extreme light weight of the cars — worked so well it allowed Franklin drivers to do things with their machines that owners of the heavy, monster cars could not dare to attempt.

Because of the extreme light weight and super-flexible springing, Franklin drivers could maintain speeds over the atrociously rough roads of early day America that were unthinkable for their heavier, more ponderous cousins. Owners of the nimble-footed Franklins entered long distance, cross-country races against much heavier and more powerful cars — and won. The Franklins danced, light-footed, over boulders, ruts, mud and ditches which left their heavier rivals either stuck in the sand or mud, or lying on the roadside with broken springs or frames.

It was enough to make the drivers of some of the heavier, more powerful machines lose their faith in logic, and curse at the fates which decreed such madness. To Franklin owners, it was supreme logic that was on their side, not madness.

Then there was the matter of tires. In a day when people considered themselves lucky to travel 50 or 100 miles without a puncture or blowout, the little Franklins rolled on, using the same tires, without flats—simply because their light weight, coupled with the super-nimble springs, placed so much less strain on the tires. It was said that Franklin drivers spent less than half as much time patching tires as the drivers of conventional cars. It was another reason why Franklin drivers, in those long, grueling road races, so often showed their heels to competitors, the big-power machines, at the finish line.

The Franklin was a lusty, healthy and viable piece of machinery, and there is, indeed, a story behind it: why and how it all came about, and who did it.

The most fateful day in the beginning of the Franklin story came in June, 1901, when an engineer and inventor named John Wilkinson, who had designed and built a four-cylinder, air-cooled automobile, made a visit to the H.H. Franklin Corporation in Syracuse, New York, driving his experimental machine. When the machine attracted the attention of Herbert H. Franklin, manufacturer and developer of "die casting" light metals, Wilkinson suggested, "Why not take a ride with me?"

Without hesitation Franklin accepted, and the Franklin story began.

To do justice to the story, we must go back to 1897, a time when Wilkinson, an engineering graduate of Cornell University and now in the bicycle business, began experimenting with the construction of an automobile engine. It was a four-cylinder, air cooled, at a time when virtually all other American experiments in this line were one or two-cylinder engines, most of them water cooled. It should be noted that 1897 was only one year after Henry Ford completed his first "quadricycle."

During the next four years, Wilkinson perfected his engine to the point where he could install it in a four-wheel vehicle. He became more or less a common sight, chattering about town on test drives.

He had also made connections with a

group known as the New York Automobile Company, which had been formed for the purpose of bringing onto the market a self-propelled motor vehicle. The company had not been a dynamic, driving force, and little or nothing had been done up to the time of the fateful meeting between Wilkinson and Franklin. The company had, in fact, paid Wilkinson no salary for a year.

Some students of the Franklin story have said that at least part of the fault lay with Wilkinson, an excellent engineer, inventor and designer, but not a man who could push a product and make it go from a business standpoint. What was needed was a man with push and imagination, to organize the project and sell the product. Such a man Wilkinson was destined to meet on that fateful day in June.

Meanwhile, friends and associates of Wilkinson said his was a mind teeming with mechanical ideas and inventions, but also with a mania for simplicity: doing things the easiest and most simple way, the right way.

When he was asked, some years later, why he had chosen to make his engine an air-cooled one, his reply was simple. "I don't recall," he said, "just any special reason except that I could see no reason why air cooling shouldn't work and lots of reasons why it would be an advantage."

Of course, Wilkinson did not invent air cooling. Other early day engine makers had also tried and made it work, but perhaps no one made it work better than Wilkinson did.

For maximum cooling effect, he placed his four-cylinder engine crosswise in the chassis, up front with an air scoop opening at the front of the hood, where normally a radiator would be installed, to scoop in the air. The engine was a valve-in-head, with the intake valves operated by vacuum, or automatically, while the exhaust valves were operated by push rods, in the conventional fashion.

Bore and stroke were 3¼ x 3¼, an early example of the "square" engine. Many of the early day engine developers used this square configuration, but — because there is very little engineering literature on the subject for that period —we may never know why. We do know that around 1910 the trend was toward long stroke engines. It was a trend that

The chassis of the first production model Franklin, shown after it was restored by the Smithsonian Institution.

would last a long time before the square engines made their comeback in the 1950s and 1960s, in a day predominated by the high-speed V-8 engines.

One thing is certain: the early day engines turned at such relatively slow speeds — 750 rpm, in the case of Wilkinson's engine—that it would be useless to compare them to the latter day "square" engines which came into their glory at the rate of 4,000 rpm and higher.

Getting back to Wilkinson's "new" air-cooled engine, when he was asked 17 years later to describe the first engine, he wrote that he had used a "surface" carburetor, a term usually applied to an evaporator, tank type carburetor, one of the earliest forms of carburetion.

Ignition was of the high-tension, vibrator coil type, powered by batteries, with DeDion spark plugs being used. In a letter written to D. Beecroft, of *The Automobile,* Wilkinson said that he himself built the rear axle and frame, as well as the engine. The first model had no clutch, since he was using a compressed air starting system of his own invention, for which he had obtained a patent. As he opened the air throttle, the vehicle started to move and the engine started to run. The drive was by chain, from engine to rear axle.

Such was the state of the art, as used in Wilkinson's engine, at the time of his meeting with Franklin and that historical test ride.

Which brings us to the other half of the two-man combination: Herbert H. Franklin. Not only was Franklin to give his name to the new machine, but he would give something of his own character, as well. There would always be a certain distinction about the car and the people who owned them. For a large part, they would be people of stubborn independence, often men of accomplishment, who had fought for their success and independence.

Franklin was born in 1866, on a farm near Lisle, New York, some 50 miles from Syracuse. His father was a school teacher turned farmer, who hoped his son would show an interest in the family farm. The younger Franklin did his share of the farm work, but never with relish, as if he instinctively knew he was not destined to be a farmer.

Young Herbert acquired what education was available locally. He attended the Lisle Academy, often walking the five miles to school and back. He was born with a cleft palate and a speech impediment, but with an extremely sharp mind. Since he could not speak fluently, he was forced to develop, at an early age, the ability to express himself extremely well on paper—to write forcefully and clearly.

Failing to like farm work did not mean that Franklin was averse to work. By the time he was 19, after graduation from the Academy, he obtained a job in a nearby town, in a shop making sleighs. His job was sanding the wood, but he quickly proved that he was destined to be more than an ordinary smoother of wood.

Young Franklin quickly noted that the workers, paid by the day, did a good deal of loafing. He asked his boss if he could be paid by the sleigh, rather than by the day. The result: Franklin worked harder and earned more pay than the other workers. The further result was that soon the other workers asked for the same conditions, and the shop began turning out more sleighs, faster. The boss liked Franklin's idea so well he offered to make the young man his foreman but Franklin, seeking new worlds to conquer, moved on.

His next job was with a newspaper at nearby Coxsackie. Here, once more, it quickly became apparent that Franklin was not destined to be a common typesetter, printer, advertising man or reporter. Within six years he had learned every job on the paper, then took over as proprietor.

But the newspaper business failed to hold his attention. When he met a man who had invented the process of pressure casting small aluminum and zinc metal parts, called "hydrostatic molding," Franklin sold his newspaper, bought out the rights to the new process, and went into business. He renamed the process "die casting," and it should not take any old car fan more than two seconds to recognize the significance of the name or the process. For years there has hardly been an automobile made anywhere that has not used die cast parts: door handles, hinges, brackets — you name it. In the new process, Franklin had unerringly picked a winner.

At first, after the H.H. Franklin Company was incorporated in 1895, it was a struggle. One of the first items to be marketed was a corrugated match striker. Later, the company made small machine and appliance parts. By 1901, Franklin could report, "The company is already a solid institution" and was paying dividends to its stockholders.

Perhaps it was not only by "chance" that Franklin accepted the invitation to ride in Wilkinson's new vehicle on that June day in 1901.

"I have been watching developments (in the automotive field) since 1893," Franklin wrote to a friend that year. If this were true, his interest in self-propelled vehicles dated back to the year when the Duryea brothers made their first successful run with a gasoline machine. Little had been known about this machine, however, until the second Duryea machine won the famed Chicago race in 1895, usually called the first automobile race of America. It is possible that Franklin had been watching published accounts of motor cars in Europe, notably France and Germany, where developments were ahead of the U.S.

How do we know?

Franklin was a prolific and articulate correspondent, and his letters prove his enchantment with the motor car. So prophetic were some of these letters, it is difficult to believe they were written as early as 1901.

In a letter to a friend, written on August 8, 1901, a few weeks after seeing the Wilkinson machine, he said: "Before long I expect to be doing things in the automobile business. It is the coming business."

He added, "I am convinced that as a business proposition now is the time. It is neither too late nor too early. It is IT! "Maybe you think the automobile is a fad. But don't. As a factor in the industrial and financial operations, it has come as a permanent fixture. Its development and progress is as certain as the sun. It will be a recognized article of commerce the world over and as staple as whiskey. For utility, for pleasure, in war and in peace, its position is assured."

Heady stuff, that — a vision of the future spread out as clearly as if it had already been written in the history books, only this was 1901 and those history books were yet to be written.

A few days later Franklin wrote to a business man with the Hallwood Cash Register Company in Columbus, Ohio, and revealed more of his plans.

He wrote, "In this business (motor cars), as in all others, there are going to be leaders. At the start it may not be so much a question of the 'best' construction as it will be the best way. The best way will get the construction right. It is the fellows who go in intelligently that are going to win.

"Good construction does not necessarily mean business success. It depends on the pushers. And in the long run these wise-headed pushers will get the best things."

The above paragraphs reveal a good deal about the man, Franklin, who was about to jump into the automotive industry. First, they reveal supreme confidence in himself as a business man. Second, they reveal his philosophy that simply producing the best automobile, from a construction standpoint, would not alone ensure success. On the other hand, he was saying, if you did things right all the way, part of being right would be having a good machine.

He added to that philosophy later by saying, "Great perfection, rather than cheapness, is the essential feature now. As I wrote you, we are especially fortunate in having engineers who thoroughly understand the business and whose experience has been practical."

This, of course, was after his ride in the Wilkinson machine. Certainly, the ride had been an unqualified success,

otherwise Franklin would have washed his hands of the four-cylinder, air-cooled machine.

For one thing, virtually all American cars being placed on the market at that time were one and two-cylinder machines, mostly with water cooling. Here was a machine, air-cooled and with four cylinders, proving to Franklin's demanding standards that it could be perfected and sold.

Wilkinson and Franklin apparently agreed that before it could be successfully marketed, it needed additional improvements. The engine needed better carburetion and a clutch. The air starter, while it worked, had not been perfected to the point where it could be placed in the hands of the average operator.

In any case, a letter written by Franklin in October, 1901, made two things obvious:

• First, Franklin had persuaded Wilkinson to drop his connection with the New York Automobile Company, and place his machine at the disposal of the H.H. Franklin Company for production.
• Second, it was agreed that Wilkinson would produce a new prototype of the machine to go into production, incorporating modifications which would make it ready for the public.

In another letter, on October 11, Franklin wrote: "The assembling of the machine was completed about 1:30 p.m. on October 1. I was anxious for the engineer (Wilkinson) to give it a thorough test inside so the public would not see the thing balk. But I was at lunch and he ran the machine out doors and made for the country without testing. He went down into the valley and then off to the hills. He came back and I went out with him. We made 12 miles through the country over all kinds of roads. We have been running the machine ever since and not a single hitch or balk. Day before yesterday the engineer took his wife and made a roundabout trip through the country, taking in the worst hills in this vicinity. He was gone four hours and made about 60 miles."

Here were incredible results, and Franklin knew it. "The automobile people here say we have them all stopped. The machine is not noisy. It controls perfectly and is fully as elastic as a steam

A 1905 Franklin runabout shown during the 1961 meet of the H. H. Franklin Club.

machine."

This was heady talk. The bugs and balks Franklin had expected in the shake-down cruises had not developed. Now all that remained was to get the machine into production and onto the market.

Although the H.H. Franklin Company was a profitable concern, it was obvious that a jump into such a major venture as automobile production would require new capital. Franklin wrote more letters that fall, offering stock in the company for sale to selected friends and business associates at $100 per share.

He used the "soft sell" approach in his letters, assuring his correspondents that they had the "opportunity" to buy stock if they wished, but that the project would go ahead regardless of whether they bought stock or not.

From the record, it is clear that stock was sold. Capitalization of the company was raised from $100,000 to $250,000, and the project began to jell. One of the men who not only gave financial backing at this time, but engineering assistance as well, was Alexander T. Brown, a local Syracuse man, the "Brown" in the Brown and Lipe team producing various types of gears for industry and motor cars. The new Franklin automobile boasted a Brown and Lipe steering gear.

To get production under way, Franklin rented additional space on November 14, 1901, just six weeks after completion of the new prototype model. One historical brochure, published by the company several years later, recalled that the original production crew consisted of Wilkinson and two men, and that the cost of the first machine was $1,100.

The first "production" model came off the assembly line — if it could be called an assembly line at that point — on June 19, 1902. This was just a year after Franklin had taken his ride in Wilkinson's experimental machine.

The first Franklin machines had the "square" dimensions of 3¼ x 3¼. Wheelbase was 68 inches and weight was 1,000 pounds. The engine was rated at 10 horsepower, although it obviously produced more brake horsepower than that. The machine was fitted with an Apple electric generator to supply current for the electric ignition. This was one of the first such uses of a generator in a time when most machines relied on dry cell batteries or magnetoes. Speed of the machine was rated at 15 miles per hour.

The first production machine was sold to S.G. Averill, of New York City, for $1,200. Averill had been a classmate of

Wilkinson at Cornell, and had been following with interest the development of the new car by his college friend.

Averill drove the car under its own power from Syracuse to Albany, a distance of 150 miles — no mean feat for a fledgling machine. By the time he arrived in Albany, a rainstorm was pouring down, so he loaded the car onto a river boat for shipment to New York City, down the Hudson River. He later entered the car in several reliability runs, where he made good showings against imported machines.

In a letter written several years later, Averill claimed that he had been able to drive the little Franklin 30 miles per hour, which meant that the rating of 15 mph was extremely conservative. Perhaps Franklin and Wilkinson were so cautious because of the strict speed laws governing the early cars, with people of the horse factions raising loud outcries against the "mad speeders" in their new-fangled automobiles.

Production was slow getting under way, however, and only 13 of the new machines were produced in the last months of 1902. By 1903 production took a jump to 184 — still pitifully small compared to present day mass production—but in 1903 a healthy output for a new company.

In a letter written several years later, answering questions about the early days of his company, Franklin wrote: "We never made a car we didn't sell and the company made a profit every year from the first, including 1902."

By 1904 production had climbed to 718 cars. Things were moving.

During the first year the only model available was a little two-seater runabout, but during 1903 a "light tonneau" body was added, to make the car a four-passenger "touring." As was typical of the day, the second seat was merely an "add on" feature, fitted to the rear of the seat of the runabout.

From the very first, the little Franklins turned out to be much more lively machines than their makers claimed. When their owners allowed it, they took the bit in their teeth to show what spunk they had.

The Franklin business office, under the influence of Franklin himself, quickly took advantage of this performance by printing a brochure labeling the Franklin car "The Surprise of 1903."

"People were surprised when the Franklin had the temerity to enter the Yonkers Races and were again surprised when the little 10 horsepower Franklin ran away from a 16 horsepower French car and established a world record for motor cars of its class," said the brochure.

It added that people were further surprised "when one Franklin entered six races on the Pacific Coast, winning four of them and taking second in another and a third in the other. This magnificent performance proved that the Franklin principle of cooling its cylinders by air, and the Franklin way of building its cars throughout, is right — triumphantly right."

The brochure ended with a glowing blurb, describing the Franklin car as "sensitive as a woman and as strong as a giant."

What a car it would have to be to live up to that slogan!

In any case, one of the most unique motor car enterprises of the twentieth century had been launched. Men had created a make of car which was to acquire a mystique all its own and an army of Franklin partisans who would stoutly defend their beloved machines forever.

The crowning years: 1904-1906

*I*t was at 1:40 p.m. on September 3, 1904, when a little two-passenger runabout, carrying two weary but happy men, chugged into New York City after one of the most amazing performances ever delivered by a motor car up to that time.

The little car had just completed a run from San Francisco to New York in 32 days, 23 hours and 20 minutes, smashing the previous record by a whopping 28 days—almost cutting it in half.

Just the fact that the trip had been completed at all, at a time when roads in the great wilderness between the two coasts of America were mostly dreams, was a sizable accomplishment. Precious few automobiles had even made the trip at all.

It meant climbing rocky mountain trails where huge boulders had to be rolled out of the way, splashing through bridgeless streams and rivers where a false move might plunge you into water over your head, clawing through gullies with walls steep as cliff sides, grinding through endless stretches of burning sand, running out of gasoline in spots where a messenger had to be dispatched — by horse or by foot — to get a new supply. Gasoline service stations hadn't yet been invented.

The men who did it were L.L. Whitman and C.S. Carris. The car was a Franklin, a make that had been on the market less than two years, and which incorporated an air-cooled engine. This was a feature that would make the car one of the most controversial machines in America for years to come.

Such a performance should have ended for all time the question as to whether air-cooled cars could take it. Franklin officials apparently felt the same way. They announced in ads, boasting of the cross-country record, "We believe FRANKLIN has settled the air cooling question forever."

But such was the nature of the American automotive industry that the Franklin would be forced to stand almost alone against its competitors, year after year, forced to prove over and over that the spunky little air-cooled machines had "stuff."

It was a test of loyalty that set Franklin owners and drivers apart as a stubborn, independent breed of men — and a few women — who extracted a certain satisfaction in doing their own thing, in their own unique automobile.

After a slow start, things were happening more quickly at the H.H. Franklin Manufacturing Company by the time the spunky little runabout made its spectacular trip across the continent.

By 1904, production was running at the rate of 718 cars per year. Part of the slow start was due to the fact that the company's boss, Herbert H. Franklin had vowed that when he placed an automobile on the market, "It must be right." "Right" meant reliable, durable, salesworthy.

In John Wilkinson, the inventor, designer and chief engineer for the new car, Franklin had a business partner who matched him well. Wilkinson had a dual mania for simplicity and quality, with a genius for making things work.

But any new machine, especially one with features so different, was bound to have a few bugs, no matter how carefully made. Improvements, at the beginning, were constantly added. Miles S. Amick, who traced the early technical history of Franklin, noted in examining surviving examples from the very first years that something "different" was found on almost every one of them. But they ran.

The engine of the new Franklin was unique in more ways than merely being air cooled. It was one of the first four-cylinder engines to be placed on the U.S.

market, and the fact that it was a valve-in-head made it the first overhead-valve four in America—certainly, the first air-cooled, overhead-valve four.

Most automobiles being placed on the market in the U.S. at that time were one and two-cylinder machines. At low speed, they had a tendency to "leap" or "jump." It was only at higher engine speeds that they would smooth out a bit.

Wilkinson had reasoned, and rightly so, that with a four-cylinder engine of relatively small size, he would not only have more power but smoother power. Drivers were able to operate the engine at lower rpm's, without the disagreeable "leaping."

Since Wilkinson had chosen to go the air-cooled route, the lower engine speeds were important, for it would mean less heat developing in the cylinders and combustion heads. Later, as the motor car industry developed, Franklin engineers were forced to find ways of running their engines much faster, but for now low rpm's were an important factor in keeping the air-cooled engine cool.

Incidentally, the Franklin company claimed only a modest seven horsepower for the first Franklins, but it soon became obvious that the engine was doing better than that and the claim was jumped upward to 10. In a few years the Franklin people would have a good deal to say about exaggerated horsepower claims for other makes.

Although Wilkinson had designed — and the Franklin plant built—their own engines, the Wilkinson-Franklin team was fortunate in those early years in being closely associated with the Brown-Lipe engineering team, which actually occupied quarters in the same building where Franklin had been operating his die casting business.

In a day when the steering mechanisms of most cars were among the most crude parts of the linkage, the Franklin was able to boast a solid, gear-driven steering set-up. The Brown-Lipe team also produced the planetary transmissions and rear-end differential gears which found their way into the early Franklins.

Wire wheels, with 28 x 3 tires, were mounted on the first Franklins, but by 1904 wheels had been switched to wood, artillery type. The early Franklins were among the first cars to use a belt-driven dynamo, or generator, to generate current for a storage battery.

All of the early Franklins, with the four-cylinder engine mounted crosswise in the chassis for maximum cooling, used chain drives. For the first models, Franklin bought bodies from the John Leggett Carriage Shop in Syracuse, but by late 1904 and 1905 the company was making its own bodies, with aluminum, carrying out the Wilkinson mania for light weight.

During the first two years the Franklin ignition system, designed by Wilkinson, consisted of an exposed cam-type shaft with make-and-break brushes for each cylinder. It was crude but it worked. In late 1904 a Herz timer was adopted.

Did the early cars have frames of wood, or of steel? Most Franklin purists have assumed that all Franklin frames were all wood, from the very beginning until near the end, in the 1930s.

Actually, the evidence is contradictory up to the 1904-1905 period.
• The 1904 *Handbook of Gasoline Automobiles* listed all Franklin models for that year as having "angle iron" frames.
• In 1905 the Handbook listed the Models A and F as having angle iron frames, but on the Models E and B it stated "angle iron and wood." For the models D and

This picture shows a beautifully restored 1906 Model G Franklin. The man in the picture is the late Carl Doman, a long-time engineer with the H. H. Franklin Company and who attempted to keep the company alive after its bankruptcy.

C, it stated simply "wood."
• By 1906 it listed "wood" for all models.

One picture of the first Franklin sold, with body stripped off, shows it with the angle iron frame. With bodies on, the early Franklins appear with the body sills. In the frame-only picture, the springs bolt to the steel frame.

The January 20, 1904, issue of *The Horseless Age,* in describing the Franklin, stated, "The frame consists of 2 inch light steel angles reinforced by a wood sill." The October 4, 1905, issue of the same magazine gave a more detailed description for the upcoming 1906 models: "The (frame) sills are laminated and made of specially selected second growth ash, which is seasoned very slowly. The laminations are laid up in white lead and over the top is placed a strip as wide as the sill, also laid in lead, which effectually prevents the possibility of moisture entering between the laminations. To these wood sills are fastened four full elliptic springs which render the running gear unusually flexible and the car smooth riding."

Miles Amick, in a series of articles on the early Franklins, published in *The Antique Automobile* in 1955 and 1956, said, "The frame was of wood with a sub-frame of angle iron, to which the motor was bolted by two steel cross arms." The evidence indicates Franklin was using a combination "wood-steel" frame structure at the beginning, but by 1906 had gone to all wood.

When the Franklin first appeared, it was available only in a runabout model but by 1903 came the Model B, essentially the same car as the runabout, or roadster, but with an added rear seat, or "tonneau," to make it a four-passenger vehicle later known as a touring. The runabout, with no previous model designation, was now called the Model A, to distinguish it from the B.

By 1904 the engine, although basically the same, had a new ignition system, adjustments for the overhead valves and a new oiling system. The wheelbase had been stretched to 78, six inches longer, with heavier, longer springs. Entrance to the rear "tonneau" was through a door at the back. Horsepower was listed as 10.

Early in 1904, Franklin made its first major model change, with a larger car— known as the Model C—and a much larger engine mounted up front, lengthwise, with a flywheel designed as a fan to cool the engine. *The Horseless Age,* in its January 20, 1904, issue, described the new Franklin as having "the most powerful air cooled engine ever made." The *Handbook of Gasoline Automobiles* listed the horsepower as 24, and gave the almost unbelievable dimensions of a five inch bore by a four inch stroke.

If these dimensions are correct, Wilkinson and his men had brought forth not only a "square" engine but one considerably "oversquare." This was an almost unheard-of design at the time. The cubic inch displacement would be a whopping 314 inches. The wheelbase on this larger car was 96 inches, and the weight of the car was listed at 2,000 pounds.

Little is known about this unusual machine — neither how many were made, nor how they performed. We know of none that has survived, nor does the H.H. Franklin Club register list one.

A photograph of the car, shown in an outdoor setting, was published in the January, 1904, issue of *The Horseless Age.*

One suggestion is that very few Franklins of this model were produced, although it remained in the catalogs through 1905. No reports on its performance are available. Perhaps Wilkinson encountered some cooling problems with the large bore, for it was a com-

monly accepted engineering principle of those early years that when a bore grew too large, it became difficult to induce cooling out in the middle of all that volume. That would be especially true in an air-cooled model. In any case, the Model C was a major change of direction for a company less than two years into production, and it was a considerable achievement that such a machine was produced at all.

By 1905, another major change in engine design appeared for Franklin, with a feature so unique that many Franklin fans are not even aware of it. This time it was a mind-boggling design of three valves per cylinder, with two valves located in the normal position in the cylinder head, and a second exhaust valve located opposite an exhaust port in the cylinder wall near the bottom of the piston stroke.

The intake valve, of course, was located at the top, and now the intake valves were push-rod operated. This in itself was a great improvement.

Why the third valve? The answer is, simply, to improve the cooling.

Why was this necessary, when the original air-cooled designs were such spectacular successes? Certainly, no engine that was prone to overheat, or to fail from overheating — especially while crossing the summertime desert—could have survived the grueling cross-country run in 1904.

All this is true, and the air-cooling design had been successful, but Wilkinson and his men were constantly improving the cooling, especially as they sought to produce larger, more powerful engines which developed more heat. The third valve was designed to open just as the piston passed the cylinder wall port, just prior to reaching the bottom of the piston stroke.

Wilkinson claimed that this design allowed 70 percent of the exhaust gases to escape at the bottom of the power stroke, leaving only 30 percent to be pushed out on the normal exhaust stroke. The purpose was to remove the exhaust gases at the point where they had reached their highest temperature, thus leaving less heat inside the cylinders and allowing the engines to run cooler.

The third valve, the Franklin people

claimed, was so successful it allowed them to announce a horsepower boost and an even cooler running engine. It would remain on Franklin engines for seven years, during which time the engineers were to learn a great deal more about cooling an air-cooled engine.

Horsepower on the old standby 3¼ x 3¼ engine for the smaller cars was now rated at 12. Franklin had also introduced an intermediate 4 x 4 engine on which the rating was 20. Meanwhile, horsepower on the big bore Model C, still listed in 1905, was boosted to 30.

Another unusual feature which came as a result of the triple valve design was the necessity for an extra exhaust manifold and two exhaust pipes, a sort of "double header" arrangement, although both exhaust pipes fed into a single muffler.

During this period, Wilkinson and the Franklin engineering staff were phasing out the old planetary transmission and going over to the sliding shift gear boxes which fit in better with the new parallel engines with drive shaft.

Meantime, Wilkinson, with his mania for keeping things light, was making use of a great deal of aluminum, as well as wood for the frames. The central housing for the rear axle differential was aluminum, a design some engineers considered impossible. The engine crankcase was aluminum, and it was about this time that Franklin began to make its own bodies, using a great deal of aluminum in their construction.

But Franklin engineers during 1905 were also at work on another major engineering step — a six-cylinder engine. The significance of this move can be seen from the fact that many makes were still struggling along with one and two-cylinder machines, and had not yet progressed to the four. Now Franklin was preparing to put a six on the market.

There is a bit of mystery about the exact date on which the new six went into production. The October 4, 1905, issue of *The Horseless Age* mentioned the car in announcing the new Franklin models for 1906, but added: "A description of the Model H, the new six cylinder car, is reserved for a later issue."

The November 16, 1905, issue of *The Automobile* also mentioned the new six-cylinder car and gave a brief description, but showed only the fours. The new six was described as the Model H, a 30 horsepower machine with a 4 x 4 bore and stroke; in other words, another "square" engine. But the description was sketchy, and there were no pictures.

Some years later, when the editors of *The Automobile* wrote to the H.H. Franklin Company and asked for the date on which the first Franklin Six appeared, Franklin officials were unable to come up with an exact date. The purpose of the inquiry was to determine the validity of Franklin's claim to have built the first six-cylinder automobile in America. The answer has not been found, and it is possible the six did not actually appear until early in 1906.

The model and engine picture was a bit confused now. The lineup for 1905 included four cross-engine models, each with a slightly different body style:

- The Model A, the old standby roadster or runabout, with an 82 wheelbase.
- The Model E, known as "The Gentleman's Roadster," was essentially the same as the A except that it had a bit of a hump at the rear, somewhat of an early built-on "turtle back," or luggage space. Wheelbase was listed at 74.
- The Model B had an 82-inch wheelbase and rear "tonneau" seats entered through a rear door.
- The Model F was essentially the same as the Model B, with the same wheelbase and rear seat, but there were no doors. Entrance to the "tonneau" was gained by tilting the front seat forward.

Next in line was the intermediate car, the Model D, with the 4 x 4 engine mounted parallel up front with shaft drive, riding on a 100-inch wheelbase. The hood was of a barrel design, to become known as the "stovepipe."

At the top of the line was the Model C, carried over from 1904. It had a 110-inch wheelbase and the engine boasting 30 horses.

At the bottom of one full page boosting the 1905 lineup, the Franklin ad writers declared, "It is exhilarating to be three or four years ahead of the rest of the motor world. Hadn't you better get in line with the Franklin and see how it feels?"

Announcement of the 1906 line included the small "Gentleman's Roadster," with the old standby 12 horsepower, 3¼ x 3¼ engine. It was the last of the cross engine machines. Miles Amick, in his 1956 article, stated that he had been unable to find any evidence that this machine ever went into production in 1906. It is possible that some of the 1905 models were left over and sold as 1906 models. In 1975, however, the register of the H.H. Franklin Club listed two 1906 Model E cars.

The new light car for 1906 was the Model G, in both runabout and light touring cars, still using the small 3¼ x 3¼ engine which had proved so trustworthy, but in an "in-line" design. The Model D was carried over from 1905, with the 20 hp, 4 x 4 engine. At the top of the line was the Model H, the new six-cylinder car.

The Franklin register for 1975 showed no surviving Model H for 1906, and only one for 1907, indicating that production on this model was very low. All engines for 1906 were practically identical in design, according to articles in both *The Horseless Age* and *The Automobile,* except for size and number of cylinders. For durability, all Franklin fours had five main bearings; the six had seven.

In announcing the new 1906 models, the Franklin people joined the "battle of horsepower" with a new twist. Instead of boosting horsepower ratings higher to keep abreast of the compitition, the Franklin ad writers now invented a new term: "Franklin Horsepower."

Most old car fans are familiar with the confusion surrounding horsepower claims for the early years of the automotive industry. Nobody really knew, when the manufacturers spoke about horsepower, whether they were talking about actual power, performance ability, or the ALAM formula based purely on an engine's bore (which had little relationship to actual "power").

The brake horsepower rating system, far more accurate, was still in the future. In fact, an effective, accurate system of measuring true power and performance had not yet been invented.

Franklin engineers had no reliable means of measuring the power of their engines, but the engineers, test drivers,

This is an early ad picture of the 1906 Model H, Franklin's first six-cylinder machine. Note the long "stovepipe" hood.

customers, people who had been winning hill climbing contests and races against much larger cars, had a "seat of the pants feel" that their car was delivering just a bit more than most of their competitors. Part of this extra performance was undoubtedly due to the light weight and the extra flexible springs. Regardless of where it came from, it now had a name: "Franklin Horsepower."

Said the Franklin ads: "Many motorists have been greatly disappointed and they will continue to be disappointed in the performance so long as horsepower is graded by figures, rather than ability."

Thus, boasted the ads, "Twenty Franklin Horsepower equals 30 of any other kind. Thirty Franklin Horsepower equals 45 or more of the average American sort."

This was a bold challenge to Franklin's competitors but, the ad writers reminded their readers, it was a 10 horsepower Franklin that had shattered the cross-country record in 1904.

And now, in 1906, a Franklin was about to do it again.

The Franklin people claimed they had built the first six-cylinder engine in America, certainly the first six-cylinder, air-cooled engine. In choosing that machine for the grueling attempt to set a new cross-country record, they were hurling one more challenge at their competitors. They would prove that air cooling was a success even with the longer engine, with six cylinders in a line to keep cool.

Chosen to make the 4,100-mile run were the same men who had done it in the plucky little Franklin runabout in 1904: L.L. Whitman and C.S. Carris. There also would be two relief drivers, so the car could keep going constantly.

Only two years had passed since the

earlier run, and little progress had been made in the construction of roads. Most of the distance was still a trackless plain and wasteland.

To prepare their car for the cruel grind, the men removed the rear "tonneau" from the car, replacing it with a large hamper and a steamer trunk to hold supplies, clothing and gear. An extra gas tank was installed, and the men ended up by carrying two extra spare tires, five inner tubes, an extra set of batteries, extra brake linings, extra spark plugs, a bag of tools, a bag of nuts and bolts plus small parts, an axe, a shovel, pulley blocks, two stout hickory poles (for prying the car out of ditches or mud holes) and 150 feet of strong rope.

Some of the trip was smooth sailing, with the new Franklin Six cruising along at speeds near 50 miles per hour. But most of the time, the miles came only by torture.

Even the start was a bad one. They encountered a flood after leaving San Francisco, forcing them to make a long detour with a loss of 10 hours right at the beginning. Then came the rocky climb over the Sierra Mountains.

In Nevada, the test was crossing Humboldt Lake, with the car breaking through the crusted lake bed into quicksand below. At one point, wrote Whitman later, "It took us seven hours to go 17 miles. Yet the motor did not overheat." He suggested that a heavier car would never have made it. The Franklin, despite its larger size and greater power, weighed in at only 2,200 pounds, thanks to all the light weight engineering. Even the air cooling contributed to the weight saving: no water jackets, no radiator, no gallons of water.

For hundreds of miles, the car traveled across the trackless sands of the Nevada desert where, Whitman wrote, "You can cook an egg in the sun and the sand is so hot it burns your feet through the leather shoes."

A water-cooled car would never have made it here, suggested Whitman. Even if you had been able to keep such an engine cooled by constantly replacing water that boiled away, or evaporated, "Where would you get the water?"

Then came endless stretches of wilderness where the men had to hire guides to show the way across the trackless plains. There were no roads. In other places they found wagon trails with ruts so deep they were impossible to use. Sometimes they traveled for miles, bouncing over railroad ties — the only roads available, and the only bridges. There were miles and miles of mud; often they were able to proceed only by use of the block and tackle, hitched to fence posts.

In Wyoming, after bouncing through one washout after another, the rear axle finally broke. They had to send for a new one from Cheyenne—another 28 hours lost. They forded one stream after another—no bridges. It was on one of the fords that the air-cooled Franklin engine became water cooled. They plunged into water so deep it reached the cylinders and stalled the engine.

The men got out their hickory poles and pried the car forward through the water, inch by inch. Once on dry land again, and dried out, the engine fired and took off.

In one clay-bottomed creek bed the car got stuck again, in a place where plenty of manpower was available. A crowd of men volunteered to literally lift and carry the car to the far bank.

After passing Cedar Rapids, Iowa, the weary travelers met a new kind of danger: deputy sheriffs, armed with pistols, who ordered them to halt. Some miles earlier, the deputies informed them, they had forced a horse and buggy off the road, breaking the buggy pole. The farmer had telephoned ahead with his complaint, and wanted money for a new buggy pole. Highway robbery? It didn't matter—they had no time to fight the case. They paid and rolled on.

In Pennsylvania, just as the crew was congratulating themselves for reaching comparatively "civilized" country, disaster struck. This time it was not for lack of a bridge, but for missing a bridge that was there. The relief driver took a curve too fast, missed the bridge, and plowed into a stone abutment on the far side of a gully.

The car was severely damaged, with the front axle and springs bent. But the wooden frame had survived the impact and, above all, the precious engine had escaped damage. This time it took 36

Here is a "worm's eye" view, from the bottom, of a 1905 Franklin chassis, showing the double exhaust pipe which resulted from the three-valve-per-cylinder design.

hours to repair the damage—another big loss of time.

After that final smash-up, and with home base almost in sight, wrote Whitman, they almost "flew" the rest of the way. The big six-cylinder engine, roaring a lusty, air-cooled song of power and speed, headed for New York.

During the trip, said Whitman, the four men had done "pretty near all that a motorist could do, except get killed."

When they reached New York, one of the men was so exhausted he fell asleep in a bathtub — taking his first hot bath since the trip started — and almost drowned.

The new six-cylinder Franklin had not only beaten the old record, the car had shattered it. The time was 15 days, 2 hours and 12 minutes, compared to 32 days for the old record.

Up to this time, reported Whitman, only eight cars had crossed the continent under their own power. Until 1906 the fastest time had been the record set by the little Franklin runabout in 1904. Now the record had been chopped in

half, by another Franklin.

The air-cooled engine had stayed cool under the worst torture the primitive roads and desert could hurl at it, at 120 degrees or more.

As for breakdowns and repairs, except for the bridge smash, the only major breakdown had been the broken axle, which had given way only after the most unmerciful pounding. There had been a leaking gas tank, three spark plugs had been changed, one spring was replaced. As for the engine itself, it had never faltered except when drowned in water.

Now, with the applause of the country ringing in their ears — and to prove beyond all doubt what the battered car could do—the crew turned around and headed back to Chicago, a distance of 1,000 road miles, to smash their own record for that stretch. They even ran half the distance, 500 miles, without the fan.

Looking at the fantastic cross-country run, the newspapers of America sounded their praise.

• The *Boston Herald* said: "Speaks volumes for the construction and reliability of the air cooled motor."

• The *Scientific American:* "It is doubtful whether any but a powerful lightweight car could equal the record which has just been made."

• Said *The Automobile,* perhaps America's most influential motoring magazine: "It has added a strong argument in favor of the air cooled car of high power."

Whitman himself added the ultimate postscript: "What about Franklin air cooling now?"

From barrel hood to droop-snoot: 1907-1910

*I*n January, 1908, the H.H. Franklin Manufacturing Company staged a lavish show at the Alhambra Hotel, in Syracuse, New York, as a debut for the company's 1908 motor cars—but two toy automobiles almost stole the show.

One of the little toys, weighing only one pound, represented a Franklin. The other, weighing one and a half pounds, represented Franklin competitors.

The two little cars were mounted on steep, uphill inclined tracks, side by side, with a string and a counterweight

mounted over a pulley to pull the little machines up the steep "hills."

When you used counterweights of equal size, the Franklin went shooting nimbly up its hill, while the "competitor," using the same weight, crept laboriously and slowly up its own hill. To make the competitor go up the hill as fast as the Franklin, you had to add 50 percent to the counterweight.

On the face of it, the demonstration would seem to be unfair, except that it dramatically illustrated a point

Franklin engineers, salesmen and ad people had been trying to tell prospective customers ever since 1902. The Franklin weighed about 50 percent less than competitors in the same engine power class. This paid off in fuel economy, less tire wear and, above all, the ability to negotiate roads the heavier cars could not travel.

Another exhibit at the 1908 show demonstrated how well balanced the Franklin machine was. A Franklin car, weighing 2,050 pounds, was perched on four weight scales, with one wheel resting on each of the scales. The readings on the four scales varied less than 17 pounds.

To show the extreme flexibility of the full elliptic springs on all four wheels, another demonstration had a Franklin with its right front and left rear wheels resting on large blocks of wood, some 10 inches high. The other two wheels rested firmly on the ground. Few makers of competitive cars could accept the challenge from Franklin to match this feat.

It took stunts like these to "sell" people on the idea of buying Franklins because the competition had never ceased the drumfire of criticism aimed at the air cooling which set the Franklin apart.

In 1908 Franklin was in the middle of its "stovepipe," or "barrel" styling period, so-called because of its unusual hood design which resembled a stovepipe or barrel more than a conventional motor car hood.

It was not a feature that would attract many buyers because of its beauty. Franklin designers were not indifferent to styling, but in a choice between beauty and functional efficiency, the efficiency demands always came first.

The engineers had determined, when they made their switch from the cross-mounted engine to the longitudinal engine mounting, that a tunnel — stovepipe, if you prefer — was the best hood design for cooling four or six cylinders in a row. It was a wind tunnel, with a fan up front to send the wind past the cooling fins on the individually cast cylinders.

Use of the stovepipe hood design came as early as 1904, when Franklin introduced its first "big cylinder" engine in the Model C. This car was the first to have the engine mounted lengthwise in the frame.

As the "stovepipe" era continued into 1906, the engine incorporated a three valve per cylinder design, with one of the two exhaust valves located down below to remove hot exhaust gases at the bottom of the power stroke and, thus, improve cooling of the engine.

For 1907, the car and the engine remained largely unchanged, with only minor improvements. One more body style was added: a roadster, as a companion to the touring in the middle-sized

The H. H. Franklin Manufacturing Company plant as it appeared in 1910, after growing steadily from 1902.

Model D, with a 4 x 4 engine. Carried over from 1906 were the small cars, the Model G, with a 3¼ x 3¼ engine, in both the touring and runabout body styles.

At the top of the line was the bigger six-cylinder car, 4 x 4, weighing only 2,400 pounds for its comparatively large engine, and selling for $4,000. The price of the Model G was $1,650 for the roadster and $1,800 for the touring. The Model D, with both cars weighing 1,900 pounds, sold for $2,800.

For the 1908 model year, Franklin announced its next big engineering changes in August of 1907. There were two major improvements in the engine — one of them another "mind-boggler" — and a new valve design that was unprecedented.

The more orthodox improvement, aimed at improving still further the efficient cooling system, was a change of design in the cooling fins on the cylinders. Previously, the fins had been part of the cylinder casting. Now the outside of the cylinders had been cast smooth, without fins, and the outside surface of the cylinder was machined. Then a thin sleeve, containing machined fins and made of phosphor bronze, was shrunk over the cylinder. The new feature accomplished two things:

- First, because the fins were thinner and machined, it allowed more fins and more cooling area.
- Second, because phosphor bronze was a better conductor of heat than cast iron, it carried the heat away faster.

The new valve system, however, was something else.

In a very early period, Franklin engineers had recognized the advantages of the "square" engines, such as the 4 x 4 configuration. From the beginning, they had used machined combustion chambers of almost perfect spherical design, a feature that was to be "invented all over again" in the 1950s.

For the 1908 models, the engineers wanted to increase the size of the overhead valves to improve engine breathing and cooling. The problem was how to do it without losing the spherical combustion; there wasn't room.

The surprising answer was to use a single valve port in the center of the combustion chambers, and put two valves in the same hole!

The intake valve was a hollow, thin-walled cone with a tapered, flaring lip matching the contours of an ordinary poppet valve. The upper portion of the valve narrowed to a sleeve, somewhat like an oversized valve guide, which it was. The exhaust valve was a conventional valve which fit inside the cone, or sleeve valve, with the beveled edges of the valve head exactly fitting the flared tip of the cone.

To close the valve-within-a-valve, two springs were used, one larger outside the other, each with its own "stop" or keeper. The inside — exhaust — valve was operated by a conventional overhead rocker arm, working against the end of the valve stem. The inner — intake — valve was operated by a second rocker arm with a fork, straddling the inside valve stem.

When the intake valve was pushed open, it compressed both springs and carried the exhaust valve with it. When the exhaust valve was opened, the intake—or coned valve—remained closed. The intake and exhaust ports were arranged so that when the exhaust valve opened, the exhaust gases escaped through the hollow cone of the intake valve, but when the intake valve opened, the two valves acted as one conventional valve, both moving together. (Many people believe that Chrysler introduced the spherical combustion chamber in 1951. In fact, the Chrysler design used two conventional valves, side by side.)

The least that can be said about the Franklin design of 1908, aside from the fact that it worked, is that it demonstrated once more that Franklin, in Wilkinson and his crew, had a stable of the most imaginative engineers in the world.

Meantime, Franklin was also making widespread use of die castings, in which the company had pioneered, for such things as main bearing and connecting rod caps. It was another contribution to weight saving and heat dissipation.

It should also be pointed out that despite the "unbelievable" new valve design up overhead, the engine still retained the third valve down below — which meant that the engine had just about the most unorthodox valve system in existence. But it all worked.

To improve the carburetion on this strange engine, the engineers came up with a double wall on the lower exhaust manifold, from the auxiliary valves, then leading the hot air to the carburetor. This design helped vaporize the poor quality gasoline available at the time.

The engine was also increased in size, with the bore of the smaller engine going from 3¼ to 3⅜ x 4, and the engine now rated at 18 horsepower. The larger four was now 4¼ x 4, again introducing a slightly "oversquare" engine, but not as drastic as the earlier attempt in 1904. The six-cylinder engine had the same bore and stroke as the larger four, thus also being slightly oversquare. The larger four now had a rating of 28 horsepower, while the six jumped all the way to 42.

For 1909, the Franklin engine and model lineup remained largely the same, with only minor refinements and improvements.

The radical change in engine design and air cooling system for 1910. For the first time the cooling fins were vertical, surrounded by jackets, and the flywheel converted to a "Sirocco" type fan to suck air through the jackets and the air ducts.

One forward looking feature came in the new design of a complete worm and gear steering gear for one of the most stable steering devices on the market at the time. This was the work of the Brown and Lipe gear team, which had contributed so much to the early Franklins.

Perhaps this is the time to take an objective look at the Franklin air cooling system. Although direct air cooling in the Franklin engines was a success, and instance after instance of tough tests can be cited to prove it, not every Franklin was a "miracle machine," or never broke down, or *never* overheated.

The truth is that there was never a make of motor car or engine that *never* broke down or failed. Even in our day, after decades of improving and refining their products, the makers of Rolls-Royce or Mercedes motor cars, or Cadillac, if you will, know that their customers sometimes experience breakdowns and failures.

It really does not compromise the claim of success for Franklin to say that Franklins sometimes broke down, or even overheated. Usually, it was when the engine was out of tune, out of time, being abused by inexperienced drivers or, possibly, after prolonged use under dirty road conditions when the cooling fins got choked up with dirt because the driver failed to clean them out.

But the water-cooled engines of those days had just as many, usually more, failures or cases of overheating—often, for the same reasons, but also because water cooling systems were not always adequate to do the job.

From such a perspective, one can say that Franklin direct air cooling was a success. The cooling system worked at least as well as the cooling system of competitive water-cooled cars — and usually better. But with Franklin owners so greatly outnumbered by the "water coolers," and with the constant sniping by the competition's salesmen and advocates, each verified case of a Franklin "failure" was amplified and spread throughout the land.

As a result, one of the greatest engineering dramas of all time was being played at the Franklin engineering laboratories. There, under constant pressure from the competition, Wilkinson and his men were forced into a never-ending battle to improve their product — mostly in the area of cooling. The engineering group probably spent more time on this problem, and knew more about thermal engineering, than any similar group anywhere in the world. With them, it was a way of life, in order to survive.

It was inevitable, with so much work and effort being put into the constant research on air cooling, that from time to time there would be another true breakthrough or major improvement.

It was such a breakthrough that came for the 1910 models.

From the outside, the cars looked much like the 1909 models. The stovepipe hoods were still there. It was when you opened the hood to look at the engine that an experienced Franklin man, accustomed to the older designs, would gasp with surprise.

From the very first Franklin air-cooled engines in 1902, the cooling fins on the cylinders had always been of horizontal, circular design. Now, however, the cooling fins were vertical — running up and down the cylinders, from top to bottom. Each cylinder was covered with a jacket, enclosing it.

At first glance, it would seem to be impossible to cool such an engine — that the jackets would keep the air out. A shroud that covered the engine, to a point two-thirds of the way up the sides of the cylinders and closely surrounding the cylinder jackets, seemed to make the cooling job even more impossible.

The secret of success in the seemingly impossible design was that the top of the air jackets was open. In addition, the flywheel of the engine, at the rear, had been transformed into a big "Sirocco" type turbine air blower—or, in the case of Franklin, a turbine air "puller."

Since the only air intake was at the front of the engine and there was no place else for the air to go—being blocked by the jackets and shroud — it had to enter through the top of the jackets and travel downward through the vertical air fins. The Sirocco type air turbine created the suction to make the travel thus, as the Franklin engineers decreed it should.

It is the Sirocco type air blower, or suction fan, that is today recognized by engineers as the most efficient mover of air—and is incorporated in most modern air conditioning systems.

Anyone with the slightest knowledge of air cooling in gasoline engines recognized that this system had to be better. In the first cross-engine models, there had been nothing except the finned cylinder exposed to the air. How had the little machines stood up to the grueling tasks thay had performed, such as the record-breaking cross-country run in 1904?

The explanation, of course, was that the early Franklin engines had turned at relatively low speeds, and the little cars had been "overpowered" to the extent that the engines seldom had to work hard, or labor. Thus, a great excess of heat was never generated to be dispersed. Wilkinson, with his insight into the cooling problems of the day, had designed them that way.

But, living in a competitive world, Franklin engineers were also faced—as the years went by — with demands for more speed and power if they were to remain abreast, or ahead, of the competition. With engines working faster, and harder, with more and bigger explosions inside the cylinders, there was more and more heat to be carried away.

The new system, introduced in 1910, did this very well. With minor changes and improvements, it remained as the Franklin cooling system for 12 long years. Wilkinson and his men would eventually make further breakthroughs in the battle to improve air cooling, but for now —and for years to come—they had won

David Doman of Ann Arbor, MI, and his daughter, Sara, in a 1910 Franklin Model G Roadster (David is the son of the late Carl Doman).

a great victory.

Many motorists who had driven Franklins from the beginning were to swear that the Franklins built in the next half dozen years or more "were the best damned Franklins ever built."

Internally, Franklin engines remained virtually unchanged. For the third year, the single port "valve-within-a-valve" was used in the spherical combustion chamber. The fact that Franklin engineers were able to retain this system for three years running was another indication that they had somehow solved almost "unsolvable" problems in making the hybrid system work under high temperature conditions. The third valve, down below, was also retained for 1910.

What about the fuel economy factor of the Franklin design? The "scientific light weight" of the design had paid off in the ability to negotiate roads impassable to heavier cars. It had paid off in the Franklin's nimble ability to scramble up hills. It had paid off in less tire wear — and it had also paid off in fuel economy.

From the very beginning, Franklins were able to outperform their competitors in the economy runs.

As early as 1905 a Franklin had won an economy run on Long Island. On February 25, 1908, a Franklin scored another triumph in the Long Island Auto Club economy run, by running 242 miles with an average of 26.5 miles per gallon. This was extremely good mileage, considering the carburetion available in that day.

But the best was still to come. On May 7, 1909, in an economy run sponsored by the Automobile Club of America, a four-cylinder Franklin touring, carrying

The top-hat Franklin brougham for 1908 was discontinued after one year, but one survives in the Harrah Collection in Reno. (Courtesy Harrah's Automobile Collection)

five passengers, scored an astounding 36.6 miles per gallon. On July 11 of the same year, in an economy run at Buffalo, N.Y., a Franklin ran 46.1 miles on one gallon of gasoline.

On June 30, 1913, a Franklin set the most amazing economy record of its era by running 83.5 miles on one gallon of gasoline—but that story will be told later.

Meanwhile, Franklin dealers and owners continued to enter contests of the most "impossible" nature to prove, over and over, that Franklin air-cooled engines could do things their water-cooled competitors could never do.

For the March 2, 1909, Kansas City auto show, for example, a Franklin dealer issued a challenge to his competitors to see whose car could run the farthest, wide open in low gear. Several drivers of water-cooled cars accepted the challenge but in the run they dropped out, one by one, until only the Franklin was still running.

After 60 miles, the Franklin driver stopped, but not because his car failed. He locked the Franklin, with its engine idling, in a closed garage for 60 hours to prove the foolishness of critics who said a Franklin had to be moving — and catching moving air—to stay cool.

To prove the fallacy of claims that a Franklin would overheat in a tail wind, the Kansas City dealer put his Franklin in reverse and drove it for 12 miles, with no overheating.

In 1908 a team of five Franklins were entered in the famed Glidden reliability run. All five cars turned in a perfect score.

There are pages and pages in the record books of similar Franklin performances. Such tests should have sent customers flocking to the showrooms to buy. The tests did sell many Franklins. But somehow, perhaps because the Franklin was almost alone in the air-cooled field, with almost every other car on the market water cooled, masses of buyers remained skeptical.

During the early years, Franklin had produced some very unusual body designs. In 1907 the catalog offered a strange appearing "landaulet," with pictures illustrating it, but present day Franklin Club experts can find no evidence that they were actually produced or sold.

In 1908 Franklin added an extremely top-heavy brougham, which has been nicknamed the "telephone booth." There is proof that this model went into production, for one still exists at the Harrah Collection in Reno.

Strangely enough, Franklin put this ornate body on the small Model G chassis, with the 3¼ x 4 engine. Normally, auto makers put unusual and ornate bodies on their most expensive chassis, which would have meant the big Model H six-cylinder car. The brougham was dropped after one year. Part of the reason may have been its high, top-heavy design, which may have been unstable on the extremely flexible Franklin chassis. In negotiating turns, or traveling in a high wind, it might have been a bit of a hairy experience.

For 1909, in place of the brougham, a town car was added to the line. According to Franklin serial numbers, only 20 of the town cars were built in 1909, although the number increased to 81 in the next year.

Again, however, instead of placing the town car body on the big chassis, Franklin engineers used the small, 3⅜ four-cylinder machine. The price on the town car for 1909 was $2,850. It was the most expensive Franklin, except for the Model H six-cylinder touring, priced at $3,750. In 1910 the town car price jumped to $3,200.

Prices for the smallest touring, the 1909 Model G, were $1,800. It was the cheapest of the Franklin line. In 1910, the same model had a price drop to $1,650.

Other models ranged higher. The town car, incidentally, had a model designation all its own — the Model K — while the truck was called the Model L.

Otherwise, the lineup for 1909 and 1910 was the Model G, for the small touring and runabout; the Model D, for a larger roadster, using the medium 4¼ x 4 engine; and the big Model H, the six-cylinder touring and roadster.

By this time the H.H. Franklin Manufacturing Company had grown from a tiny workshop employing a handful of men in 1902, to an aggregate factory site of 15 connecting buildings, with 236,085 square feet of floor space, employing 1,500 factory workers in 26 different trades, plus 157 office workers.

Production of Franklin cars, while never reaching the mass production status of the top makes, continued to grow until 1908 and 1909, when they dipped sharply. They recovered again in 1910. According to serial numbers provided by the Franklin company later, the total reached 1,112 in 1905, climbed to 1,304 in 1906, and went up to 1,522 in 1907. At this time, a depression struck the country, and Franklin sales dropped. Production was listed at 1,143 in 1908 and plunged to 611 cars in 1909. But in 1910 production recovered and went all the way to 2,045 cars, the highest record to date for the top air-cooled car of its day. The new, improved cooling system may have helped the recovery.

By late 1910, for the 1911 model year, the company was prepared to make its next major change, this time mostly in styling. Perhaps by this time Franklin officials realized that the "stovepipe" design was not the most attractive. In any case, the company reached across the sea to France, to borrow a hood design from the famed Renault, and entered what was to be known as the "Renault period," a styling motif that would last through 1916.

The breezy teenage Franklins: 1911-1916

*I*n the fall of 1908, a young man named Ralph Hamlin, struggling to make a living selling Franklin cars in Los Angeles, heard that a group of promoters was organizing an automobile race from Los Angeles to Phoenix, Arizona.

When Hamlin said he would like to enter the race, one of the promoters impatiently suggested that he forget about it.

"A Franklin couldn't cross the desert," he told Hamlin.

It was like a red flag in front of the proverbial bull.

The race promoter's rash statement started Hamlin on a five-year crusade to prove that Franklins could cross the desert—and do it better and faster than most other cars.

The idea behind the race was to dramatize the need for better roads. At that time there were practically no roads at all, no bridges, not even markers to show the way across miles and miles of sand. Hardly anyone attempted to make that trip by motor car, let alone making a race out of it.

Hamlin entered the first Los Angeles to Phoenix race. He lost, but not because his Franklin couldn't cross a desert. He failed to make a trial run, to learn the way, and spent one night wandering in the desert, going around in circles.

The next year Hamlin was better prepared. He had learned the way, and he arranged for an experienced desert man, Clayton Carris, who had helped set the cross-country record in a Franklin in 1904, to go with him as co-pilot.

Hamlin failed again, but not because he got lost. He ran over a railroad crossing so fast his rear axle housing crashed into the rails, smashing the housing beyond repair.

Competition was getting tougher. Only four cars had entered the first race, in 1908. In 1909 it was 10 cars at the start, and only four finishing.

By 1910 there were 14 entries. The progress of the motor car had reached the point where you had to win races and competitions to prove your car was worth selling. Interest in the race had grown to the point where a special railroad train was laid on to carry spectators. There was even a band to play at every stop.

In the 1910 race, Hamlin finally

proved his Franklin could cross a desert. He placed second — only 32 minutes behind a big, powerful Kissel Kar. It was a good showing, but not good enough.

The tenacious Hamlin was back on the starting line in 1911. His car, a Franklin Model D, had the six-cylinder, 4 x 4 engine rated at 38 horsepower.

Once again, he had to be satisfied with second place. The race was won by a big National with a 5 x 5 $^{11}/_{16}$ engine, known as the "Monarch of the Road." Nationals had placed third and fourth in the famed Vanderbilt Cup race, and ad writers were boasting that in major races around the country, Nationals had won 22 first places, 27 seconds and 23 thirds.

Then came 1912. As Hamlin wrote, years later, "I now had two good seconds to my credit and it was high time to bear down, win the race and quit fooling around."

That is exactly what he did.

The odds were the toughest of all. More new cars were in the race: Buick, Cadillac, Mercedes and Simplex, to name a few. All were more powerful and faster than Hamlin's Franklin—and, instead of using the latest model Franklin, Hamlin decided to stick with the same car he had run the year before.

Hamlin ran the route ahead of time, finding out just how fast his Franklin could go over each stage. He knew he could not outrun his competitors, but he also knew that the 500-mile route had been changed, with some very tough stretches included. It would be on the roughest roads, in the deepest sands, where his light car with the super-flexible springing would have the advantage. Hamlin planned his race to outrun the big, powerful cars in the rough going, not the smooth sailing—and that was exactly the way it worked.

Since much of the race was to be run at night, he equipped his car with a huge searchlight powered by a special generator. It was capable of lighting up the road for 200 yards.

Twelve drivers lined up near midnight on October 26. Before the start, bad news arrived. Heavy rains had filled some of the usually dry gullies with water. It was a new hazard. But the cars

took off anyway, one by one, started at intervals.

One of the first cars to start was a Buick. It was a period when Buicks were burning up the tracks with amazing racing triumphs, but the Buick had gone only a few miles when it crashed because the driver was not able to see the road well enough.

The searchlight on the Franklin saved Hamlin from crashing into the smashed Buick lying in the roadway. A few minutes behind Hamlin was a Mercedes. Its driver failed to see the wreck and crashed into it, putting the Mercedes out of the race.

One by one, the cars ahead of the Franklin were picked off by Hamlin: first, a Hupmobile, then a Cadillac. Hamlin's strategy of driving all-out on the rough stretches was paying off. The super-flexible Franklin could take it. The heavier cars could not.

Shortly after daybreak, Hamlin sighted a cloud of dust ahead. It was a big Simplex, running in first place. Hamlin knew he would never have a chance to catch the car on a smooth road, but these roads were far from smooth. Slowly, the Franklin crept up on the more powerful car. At Brawler, 200 miles from the start, the two cars were almost neck-and-neck. A waiting crowd cheered them on.

They had said a Franklin could not cross a desert, but Hamlin was counting on that very desert to give him the edge he needed. He counted on the heavier car to bog down. When they hit the bottomless sands, it happened.

In the sand, wrote Hamlin later, "It was plow, plow, plow and dig, dig, dig." For the lighter Franklin, it meant less plowing and less digging.

When the big Simplex finally bogged down for good, and had to be pulled out by horses, the Franklin forged ahead.

In Hamlin's words: "I began to feel that the motor out in front of me was almost human and seemed to know the effort it would have to make before it reached its goal and was putting out every ounce of strength to do it.

"My Franklin was doing all that it knew how to do; never was there a car that would stand such abuse and do such constant work. Deep sand, rough trails, they became no more difficult than smooth roads as we sped on."

Running through a sandstorm left Hamlin's face cruelly cut, but his spirits were high. At Yuma the cars remaining in the race were impounded for the night. The race would resume in the morning. But Hamlin was out in front, and determined to stay there.

Next day the problem became water, with the usually dry gullies and rivers running full of water. On the Agua Friar River Hamlin saw a railroad bridge and was tempted to use it. But the rules forbade use of railroad bridges, so he wrapped his magneto in rubber and suffered the ignominy of being pulled through the water by horses. The rules did allow this. Back on dry land, the Franklin cranked back to life and sped on.

By the time Phoenix could be sighted, the Franklin was 43 minutes ahead of its closest competitor, the Cadillac. The big Simplex was still in the race, but a long 50 minutes behind the Cadillac.

Hamlin had finally achieved his dream, a victory five long years in coming.

The Franklin had performed flawlessly. The only mechanical problem had been one flat tire. Of the car itself, and the "freak" air-cooled engine,

Hamlin wrote: "The car in which I had made the trip finished in perfect condition and not a single mechanical adjustment had been made. The motor never faltered, even though at times we were running on low or intermediate gear for as much as a half an hour in a stretch."

With victory in his hands, Hamlin called it quits. He had promised his wife that after he had won the Los Angeles to Phoenix race he would stop racing. He kept that promise.

Publicity from his victory, to top off his two second place wins in the two previous years, finally paid off. Prospective car buyers — some of them, at least — were willing to gamble their money on a car which could beat the big boys across the desert.

Franklin business improved. The air-cooled cars were shipped to the west coast by the railroad car load. As the most successful Franklin dealer on the west coast, Hamlin was invited to visit the factory in Syracuse.

He got to know Herbert Franklin, John Wilkinson, and other top Franklin men. In the future, Hamlin would play an important role in the history of Franklin—but, for now, Franklin history and development would continue.

In the year 1911 the appearance of Franklin cars changed, suddenly and dramatically. The stovepipe was gone, replaced by a sloping, coffin type nose that strongly resembled the French Renault.

Franklin designers made no effort to deny that they had been influenced by the famed French car. But, except for the hood styling, there was little to compare between the two cars—especially in the mechanical area. The Renault was a conventional water-cooled car, with a more or less conventional suspension.

Under the "Renault" hood on the Franklin was the famed air-cooled engine, coupled with full elliptic springing and the flexible wooden frame. The engine remained much the same as in previous years, except for one major change: the "valve-within-a-valve" was gone.

Some might call it a step backward,

since it had been considered a big technical step forward when it first appeared. Now, in describing the move back to the conventional side-by-side, two-valve system with normal rocker arms and push rods, The Horseless Age for August 3, 1910, said simply, "The reason given (apparently by Franklin spokesmen) for reverting to the original construction is that it enables more silent operation to be obtained."

Since air-cooled engines are normally just a bit noisier than their water-cooled cousins — where the water jackets and the water itself tend to muffle engine noises—the reason may sound just a bit thin.

The valve-within-a-valve system had worked, and worked well. Otherwise, Wilkinson and his staff would never have certified it for production. Nor, if it had been a troublemaker of any propor-

During the early teens, the Renault-type nose was incorporated into the Franklin lines. A 1911 Franklin Touring Model M is shown.

tions, would they have kept it for three years.

Perhaps it was a source of some problems other than a bit of noise. In any case, the device was gone, and one year later —for the 1912 models—Franklin engineers dropped the other unconventional feature: the third valve down below.

Thus, by 1912 the Franklin engine, aside from its air cooling, was a more or less conventional powerplant with overhead valves.

Now for the surprise.

For years, Franklin engineers had worked to improve the cooling of their air-cooled engines. For the 1910 models, they had claimed a great breakthrough in engine cooling, by changing the cooling fins from lateral—or horizontal—to vertical, with shrouds and envelopes to prevent the air from going anywhere else than through the fins. They created an efficient Sirocco type fan in the flywheel at the rear, to suck the air through the vertical ducts.

Now, as the surprising switch, Franklin engineers said their engine was running too cool.

The whole thing proved once more that thermal research in the Franklin engineering laboratories never ceased. While the Franklin men, led by Wilkinson, may have been stubborn about their air cooling principle, they were willing to learn.

The air cooling, they needed. It was the one major difference between Franklin and almost all other cars—the feature that set Franklin cars apart as something different, unique, a point of pride to owners who often spent their money on a Franklin purely as an act of defiance against the conventional.

In any case, in a 62-page booklet, *An Analysis of Franklin Motor Car Construction,* issued by the company in 1912 —the year they dropped the third valve —Franklin engineers revealed just how much they had been learning about the cooling of engines.

They had learned, for example, that an engine running about 100 to 150 degrees hotter than the conventional water-cooled engines was a more efficient engine. Taking a pot shot at the water coolers, they suggested that when the water in a water-cooled engine reached 212 degrees it boiled, turned to steam— and had no value at all as a coolant.

If the water in a water-cooled engine turned to steam, the cooling system had lost all of its efficiency. If you didn't shut off your engine immediately, cool it down and get new water, the temperature would simply run away—up to 400, 500, 600 degrees, burning up parts and melting bearings. You were immediately a candidate for a new engine.

In air cooling, the Franklin engineers pointed out, air did not lose its cooling properties when the temperature ran above 212 degrees. To sum it all up, their research showed that a slightly hotter engine was more efficient. If you could control that temperature, and consider normal temperature at around 300 to 350 degrees, you had a more efficient engine —especially in the area of fuel economy — with the added advantage of doing a better job of burning the poor grade of fuel available in those days.

It was a neat trick, if you could pull it off. The engineers at the water-cooled car companies didn't have a chance at it. The Franklin people, using air, did—and, they were now saying, they had learned how to do it.

The proof lay in the fact that Franklin drivers at this period were turning in some of the most astounding fuel economy records in history. On May 1, 1914, for example, the company organized a mass, nationwide economy run by Franklin dealers throughout the country.

On that day 94 Franklin dealers, driving as many Franklin cars, set out on an economy run. When the results were announced, it was found that the cars had averaged 32.8 miles per gallon. Some got as many as 50 to 55 miles per gallon.

A few months prior to this, S.G. Averill, who bought the first production Franklin in 1902, made headlines by driving a specially prepared Franklin roadster over the roads of Long Island in a test monitored by the Automobile Club of America. He had managed to drive his Franklin 83.5 miles on a single gallon of gasoline. It was an unbelievable record — and it had been made possible by the new "hot engine" principle.

Of course, in making a higher temperature "normal operating temperature" for a Franklin, Wilkinson and his men were forced to seek ever better materials for their engines — especially valves. One trick to keep valves from burning up was to use oxy-acetylene welding to fuse a

The car which set the amazing gasoline mileage record of 83.6 miles per gallon. At that time in 1913, it belonged to S. G. Averill, the man who had bought Franklin's first production car in 1902.

thin strip of cast iron around the lip of the valve.

Incidentally, in changing from the round, barrel type hood to the Renault style hood, Franklin engineers retained the function of the hood as a wind tunnel to channel the air through the cooling ducts. They simply found that a hood did not have to be round to serve as a wind tunnel.

But with this system — and all air blocked off from the cylinder unless the tunnel system was working — Franklin owners had to be warned not to run their engines more than a minute or two with the hood open.

For 1911, the first year of the Renault hood design, Franklin continued making four basic model lines:
- The big Model H, the six with the 4½ x 4½ engine.
- The Model D, the smaller six, with the 4 x 4 engine.
- The Model M, a four-cylinder with the 4 x 4 engine.
- The baby of the family, the Model G, with the 3⅜ x 4 engine.

Body styles included torpedo phaetons and tourings for the H; tourings, limousines, torpedo phaetons and landaulets for the D; tourings, torpedoes, limousines and landaulets for the M; and a touring and a roadster for the smaller G.

For 1912 the model lineup remained much the same, except that the big six engine was dropped and the 4 x 4, six-cylinder engine was used for both the Model H and the Model D. A new, smaller six was introduced, with a 3⅝ bore and a 4 inch stroke. The 4 x 4 was retained for the Model G, and the smallest engine, the 3⅜ x 4, was used only in a runabout.

That year was the first in which Franklin officials began designating their cars by series. The Series One appeared in 1912.

For 1913, however, three separate series were announced: Two, Three and Four. Since there were so few changes in the cars themselves, this mostly served to confuse future historians of Franklin models. The major improvement in 1913 was introduction of an automatic starting-lighting system.

The old car fans who believe the "Startix" system used on several makes of cars in the 1930s was the first automatic starting system might do well to look at the Franklin Dyneto system for 1913. As long as the ignition system remained switched on, the starter would automatically restart the engine if it stalled, simply by pushing on the accelerator.

It was for the Series Four cars of 1913-1914 that Franklin engineers looked at their complicated engine lineup, and decided they had been producing a lot of engine "clutter."

Suddenly, Franklin had only one engine: a powerplant called the Six-Thirty — six cylinders and 30 horsepower. Franklin engineers, who had already moved slightly away from the "square" or "over-square" design of earlier years, had opted completely for an under-square engine, following the trend of other makers. Its size was 3⅝ x 4.

Although there were no big mechanical or cooling breakthroughs to talk about, there was a considerable change in the design of the engine. The intake manifolds and carburetors were moved from the right side of the engine (viewed from the rear) to the left side.

Along with the switch came a change from the right hand steering wheel to the left, following the unstoppable trend set by Henry Ford in 1909, when he swung his weight to the left. When the Model T became the car of the people, there was no stopping the trend.

Series Five Franklins, introduced late in 1914, differed little from the Series Four cars. For the Series Six machines,

One of the strong points of the Franklin air cooled car was its super flexible suspension system, shown being put to the test by Purdue University engineering students.

introduced early in 1915, however, considerable changes were made. The hood, while retaining the Renault styling, got smoother, more rounded lines. The "honeycomb" grille in the air opening up front was replaced by more handsome bars.

Rear axle drive gears were changed from bevel to spiral. The heavy, old style Dyneto starter-generator was replaced by a new model, 40 pounds lighter. The body was somewhat larger and a bit more "streamlined," if such a term could be applied to any body made at this period.

For the Series Seven, appearing in mid-1915, few changes were made except that the overhead valves on the engines for the first time had covers to protect them from dirt and dust. Due to the unique, separate cylinder construction of the engine for cooling, this had to be done with individual covers designed to interfere as little as possible with cooling. It was in the cylinder head area where cooling was most critical.

Series Eight Franklins, introduced late in 1915 and continued to late in 1917, were the last of the Renault period cars. They were little changed from the Series Seven cars. There were some refinements, such as a new, enclosed type universal joint. The hand crank was gone from its fixed position out front. It was a move in the direction of reliable electric starting, which eventually would see no crank at all.

Some of the closed cars of the Series Eight also pointed toward the future with a semi-wraparound windshield.

By the end of the Renault period, late

in 1916, the Franklin could be bought in five body styles: the touring, coupe, sedan, berline and roadster. All had a single motor, known as the Model M, instead of the confused motor lineup when the series started. Prices ranged from $1,900 for the roadster to $3,100 for the elaborate berline, which could almost classify as a sort of town car, or enclosed limousine, for its day.

It would be difficult to say, at this point, whether the Franklin enterprise, from a business standpoint, was a great success. There was no question but that the Franklin, as the almost exclusive exponent of the air-cooled type motor car, had come a long way.

But production, measured against the leaders—or even the secondary leading group of cars — remained small. Although it is difficult to give accurate yearly figures, because of the different dates on which the various series were introduced, production fluctuated from a low of less than 1,000 cars per year to something near 3,000.

In view of the remarkable performances being turned in by Franklin cars — in reliability, driveability and economy, especially during this Renault period — it is difficult to understand why production figures remained so low.

During this period, on September 14, 1914, the Franklin organization set up still another "torture test" to prove again that Franklins could take it.

The plan was for Franklin dealers throughout the country, driving a total of 119 cars in low gear, to go 100 miles over some of the toughest roads in their individual parts of the country.

The routes took the cars over hills, rutted roads and up mountains. One car climbed to 7,500 feet on the Continental Divide. When it was over, only three cars had failed to finish the 100 miles in low gear. One had ignition trouble. Another suffered a broken oil line. The third ran out of oil, which the driver failed to notice, and had bearing damange.

The remaining cars finished their runs without the slightest sign of overheating. It was a test few water-cooled cars could have passed, for it was considered more or less normal for a water cooler to overheat if run in low gear for a long period of time.

None of the 116 cars required any oil to be added and, of course, no water. The average running time, in low gear, was from eight to nine hours—a cruel grind, indeed.

Over and over, Franklin cars came through with colors flying high at the end of the tests. Still, people seemed to be afraid to buy Franklins.

Time for a change: 1917-1927

Perhaps the most important single event in the history of the Franklin Automobile Company, from its beginning in 1902 to its end in 1934, was the big "rumble" of 1924-1925.

It threatened to rip apart the very foundations of the Franklin management structure. It caused the departure of the man who had given birth to the first Franklin, who had built it with his own hands.

He was the man who had nursed the Franklin automobile through all the pioneering years, established the engineering principles which set the Franklin so far apart from the so-called conventional machines, and made the Franklin name synonymous with something different, unique, distinctive.

The man was none other than John Wilkinson.

For years afterward, he would not even speak to H.H. Franklin. Yet they continued to live only a few blocks apart in Syracuse, New York.

Strangely enough, hardly a word of the internal dispute leaked out to the public at the time. Readers of the motor journals of that period didn't know that anything unusual was going on. The story was finally revealed by Franklin officials, years later.

What terrible event took place, which brought about the rupture of friendship between two men who had worked so closely together for nearly a quarter of a century?

The truth is, it started with a sort of dealer's revolt—and, really, that is not too strong a word to use for what happened.

A 1914 Berline seven-passenger. Note the early "wrap-around" windshield. This was also one of the most expensive in the so-called "Renault Period," — $3,100.

Franklin had its loyal dealers, men who had been with the company for years. Many of them had probably become involved in a sort of "love affair" with the car which dared to be different.

But automobile dealers of that day, as in any day, were in business to make money—or at least make a living—and they were having trouble selling Franklins.

Part of the difficulty, of course, was the most unique feature of the Franklin: its air cooling. The makers and sellers of the conventional water-cooled machines had never ended their warfare against the Franklin.

Perhaps the dealers were willing to accept the air cooling factor. It was, after all, their major selling point in talking to prospective buyers. They probably realized that without air cooling, you wouldn't have Franklins at all.

The feature which really triggered the "revolt" was styling: the fact that Franklin not only was different, but looked different. Most car buyers of that day, like car buyers today, were suspicious of anything as different as the Franklin. They preferred to go with the crowd.

The styling feature which had made the Franklin so "different" had been mostly the hood. Franklins started out with a front that became known as the "shovel nose." Then came the round hoods, known as barrel hoods or stovepipes, and in 1911 the Renault-type hood, borrowed from the French Renault.

Perhaps it would have been acceptable for a year or two, but Franklin designers used it for six long years and, in a modified form, until 1922. This "droop nose" styling was different from anything else on the American market and, as years went by, its critics felt it left a good deal to be desired.

During the first years, the Renault hood had a patched-on look to it. The bodies had a vertical firewall, but the rear contours of the hood did not match the outlines of the firewall, and left several inches of the firewall exposed.

In 1917, the designers took care of that faulty design by making the hood meet the shape of the body, and rounded off the squared corners. It now had a rounded, sleek effect that would almost qualify for streamlining honors—but it still had the droop nose effect. It was still different, very different.

With the car to be introduced for the 1922 model year, Franklin designers, under the influence of Wilkinson, finally decided to do something about the hood. They did it by going what some critics called "half way" to meet the clamor for conventional styling. But, the same critics loudly scoffed, the new half-way measures made matters worse, instead of better.

The scoffers dubbed the new model "the horsecollar," and said it was so ugly only a mother could love it. The new styling had the appearance of having a radiator, and was conventional at least in that respect. But it resembled a horsecollar, sloping backward from bottom to top as if it had been bashed, or knocked backwards. The body, even in an age of ugly motor cars, was almost as unlovely as the hood. It was during this so-called "horsecollar" period — 1922-1924 — when the dealers' revolt came to a boil.

Perhaps the leader of the revolt — it really had no organization—was one of the oldest, most loyal and successful Franklin dealers on the list: Ralph Hamlin, of Los Angeles. Hamlin was the persistent driver who fought a five-year battle until he finally won the annual Los Angeles to Phoenix race.

Many years later, long after Franklin was no longer on the market and the only Franklins still being driven were those belonging to members of the H.H. Franklin Club, Hamlin discussed the revolt.

His comments were recorded by Thomas H. Hubbard, one of the club's historians. "What motivated those people in Syracuse? Why did Franklin always have to do things the difficult way? Why was I, Ralph Hamlin, forced to spend so many years trying to prove the merits of air cooling, wooden frames, and so on, when it would have been so much easier just to move with the crowd?"

After all, as Hamlin pointed out, the name of the game was to make money. You couldn't make it by bucking the crowd, single-handed.

Hamlin had said the same thing back in the days when it counted—in the early 1920s, while on a trip "back east" to the Franklin factory.

This 1924 s 10-C "horsecollar" Brougham was one of the last models made before the big styling change of 1925.

He managed to catch Herbert H. Franklin alone on the terrace of a country club where they had gone to lunch, and unloaded his woes in no uncertain terms: either Franklin had to "fix things" or he, Hamlin, would switch to another make of motor car. This, coming from one of the oldest and most loyal Franklin dealers, was strong language. Franklin had been hearing much the same thing from other dealers. This time he not only listened, he made a decision to act.

First, he asked Hamlin if he knew of a body designer who might come up with a design Hamlin could live with. Hamlin did — the Walter H. Murphy Company, of Pasadena, California—a body builder which had already done some custom work on Franklins to make them look more "conventional."

Franklin authorized Hamlin to contract with Murphy for a prototype model. In the meantime, Franklin also ordered a prototype in the east.

This one was from J. Frank deCausse, operator of a custom body shop and a gifted motor car designer. The order was to create a design that would follow conventional styling concepts of the day and also be up to date.

In a few months both prototypes stood there, to be judged by their merits. It was the deCausse design which got the nod, perhaps justifiably so, because the eastern designer had come up with cleaner, more handsome body lines. The Murphy design seemed a bit out of proportion.

One thing was certain about the deCausse design: it didn't look like a Franklin. In fact, the transformation was so complete that almost anyone seeing the car on a street would scarcely have given it a second glance. The hood and "radiator" lines looked like those of an Oldsmobile or Lincoln. Of course, the "radiator" was a fake — nothing but an air grille — but you couldn't tell it by looking.

The radiator design included a simulated radiator cap and a lion ornament. To purists, the real-looking radiator was exactly what was wrong with the new Franklin. You couldn't tell it was a Franklin. The distinctive Franklin look was gone.

To men like Hamlin, the change was welcome. Perhaps now the car would sell.

But one of the purists—the most important purist of all—was John Wilkinson, the man who had created the Franklin. Wilkinson turned thumbs down on the new design. Normally, that would have been enough to relegate it to the junk heap. The engineering and design departments, under Wilkinson, had always been autonomous. They told the salesman what he had to sell.

H.H. Franklin, president and majority stockholder, had control only over sales and finance, until now. Exercising his prerogatives as "the boss" for the first time, he overruled Wilkinson and said the new design would go into production.

Historian Thomas Hubbard could find no record of what was said and what took place in the confrontation between the two men. The fact is that Franklin had the authority and, for once, was stubborn enough to assert it. It was probably the first time he had overruled his friend Wilkinson.

As a result, Wilkinson walked out of the Franklin plant forever. People who knew the two men said they never spoke for 20 years, although as age mellowed them they eventually patched up their quarrel before they died. By that time Franklin, the motor car, was gone.

Perhaps there could have been another way, a middle ground. If only, as Hubbard put it, "they could have come up with a stylist who could have produced a design that would be both beautiful and yet different, it might have done the trick."

In any case, the Franklin had its new car design, but was minus its chief engineer — the man who had completely dominated the engineering and design of the car up to this point. For better or worse, Franklin would have to travel on the deCausse design.

In discussing the bitter argument, we have jumped a bit ahead of the story. As the so-called "Renault" period ended, the new Franklins introduced in July, 1916, for the 1917 model year, had a comparatively major styling change. The hood had been rounded off and made to "fit" the body, but it still had the "droop nose." This was the Series Nine.

The first of them, the 9-A, was produced through 1917 and 1918, when it became the 9-B, on which production continued until June, 1922. For reasons known only to the Franklin engineering department, the size of the engine was reduced a bit, to 3¼ x 4, with a horsepower drop from 35 to 30.

At this time Franklin was still boasting of its "Scientific Light Weight" which, the ad men said, enabled Franklin to obtain more performance with less engine. One reason, obviously, was to keep alive the old Franklin tradition of economy. There was little doubt that the Franklins of this period were, for their size, just about the most gas miserly of any machines on the road.

The Franklins consistently delivered better than 30 miles per gallon. In 1919 a Franklin won the Los Angeles to Yosemite Valley economy run, with a rating of 49.9 ton miles per gallon. No other car was even close. Here was at least one feature that helped sell Franklins.

A factor on the minus side of the slate for Franklins of this period was the difficulty in starting them in cold weather. The major cause was the fact that an air-cooled engine had to use a heavier weight of oil and, when the temperature dropped around the zero mark, it became extremely difficult for the starter to turn the motor over.

Franklin engineers solved the problem on the Series Nine cars by a unique combination:

• An electric heater coil in the carburetor throat, which gave absolute vaporization of gasoline before it entered the combustion chambers of a cold engine
• A bypass system which automatically shut off and bypassed the heater chamber after the engine started and warmed up.

Most Franklin fans believe that if Franklin had switched to a 12 volt electrical system, such as that used by the Dodge of this period, it would also have helped with the problem.

Prices on the Series Nine cars ranged from $1,800 to $3,200 for the 1917 model year, with Franklins available in 11 body styles ranging from a two-passenger roadster to a seven-passenger limousine. One unique styling feature for Franklins of this period was a sharply pointed Vee-type windshield on the sedans and broughams.

During the six-year period of the Series Nine cars, prices rose slowly. In 1922, the last year of the Nines, prices ranged from $2,300 for a two-passenger runabout to $3,800 for a touring limousine.

By the time the Series Nine Franklins bowed out, a total of 59,500 of them had been made and sold, making this the biggest of the Franklin series, numberwise. It was in production the longest — six full years.

In 1922, after months of experimental work in the engineering shops, the Wilkinson-directed engineering team came up with another major engineering achievement. It meant an entirely new Franklin engine, incorporating another major advance in the cooling efficiency of the direct air cooling system. In principle, if not in design, it was very nearly the type of air cooling that would be used in future years by a car called

Volkswagen.

The new Franklin was known as the Series 10. The major change consisted of moving the Sirocco type cooling fan from the rear of the engine, where it had served the double purpose of flywheel and fan, to the front of the engine. In cooling principle, it meant pushing—or blowing — the air through the cooling fins rather than pulling — or sucking — the air through.

It was a revolutionary change as far as capacity to move air was concerned. Any mechanic or engineer in the field of thermal dynamics knows that it is easier, by far, to push air than to pull it. Cold air, coming in through the front of the engine, is far more efficiently moved than hot air coming out the rear after passing over the hot cylinders.

The dramatic difference was revealed in a service bulletin issued to Franklin mechanics soon after the change was made. Although the new fan at the front was smaller than the old one, by three inches in diameter, at 20 miles per hour it would move 1,250 cubic feet of air per minute — compared to 486 cubic feet with the old fan. At 50 miles per hour, the speed of maximum efficiency, 5,500 cubic feet of air per minute went whooshing through the blower system, compared to 2,200 cubic feet in the old system.

Due to the smaller size of the blower, and an improvement in blower design, Franklin engineers also gave the engine a substantial power boost, simply because the new air blower consumed much less of the engine power available. It meant more power to be applied to the wheels. It was another cooling breakthrough of major proportions.

A brilliant young engineer who had just joined the Franklin staff, after graduating from Cornell, had been largely responsible for the big coup.

Progress had been made in engineering schools over the years, and when young Paul Williams joined the engineering staff, he immediately recognized that the "pull" system of moving air was far less efficient than the "push" system. He told Wilkinson and his staff as much—and, as a young upstart, he was more or less told to mind his own business.

Custom bodied Sedan Landaulet, Series 11-A for 1925, based on the DeCausse design after the big styling change. (Photo courtesy Long Island Automotive Museum)

Williams did exactly that — the business of improving Franklin cars — by taking a Model 9 Franklin, then being produced, blocking off the fan, and driving it that way for an entire year without damaging the engine. He said it only overheated when driving slowly through heavy traffic.

He then demonstrated, in the engineering laboratory, how much more air could be moved by pushing rather than pulling. The old heads were finally convinced, and the new Series 10 Franklins came into being. The hiring of Williams, if nothing else, proved that any engineering staff needs new blood occasionally — especially if they were brilliant young chaps like Williams.

The cooling system "reversal" was only part of the story. The entire engine was redesigned, from front to back. A heavier crankshaft with seven main bearings was now used, with case hardened bearing journals. Larger camshaft bearings were introduced for longer wear.

The oiling system became a high pressure system, forcing oil through the crankshaft and engine at 30 to 35 pounds pressure. This in itself was a cooling factor, as any race driver could attest. Some race engines were designed with oil coolers, or radiators, to help cool the engines.

The compression ratio of the new Franklin engine was raised to 4.44 to 1, by using a piston one-sixteenth of an inch higher. All the changes, added together, were so great that even a child who looked under the hood of the Franklin saw that an engineering "revolution" had taken place.

In 1921, when the first prototypes of the new Series 10 Franklin were completed, the company sent several of them on a cross-country tour, headed west, to work the bugs out of the new machine. Even at this comparatively late date, as the men traveled west they reached empty territory where often the only road markers were dabs of paint on a rock. There were long stretches of desert sand where, young engineer Williams reported, you almost had to steer by the stars. Williams was on the test team to make sure the new "baby" he had helped create was a good one.

The trip proved that the new Franklin, as almost any model did, had its weak points. To keep the weight of the cars down, Wilkinson had used aluminum for the steering gear housing. It was one time aluminum didn't work. The housing cracked on both test cars when the going got rough, and they had to switch back to cast iron.

With heavier sedan bodies and higher speeds, the test engineers found that leaf spring breakages were coming much too often. They solved that by using snubbers, shock absorbers, for the first time. The trip paid off well by getting most of the "bugs" worked out of the car before it was placed in the hands of the buyers.

After the new machine was placed in production, a major bug showed up: a serious vibration in the transmission. It was so bad that customers were returning their cars and refusing to keep them. It threatened a shut-down of the assembly lines just when the company desperately needed to sell as many cars as possible to recoup the costs of development of the new model.

This time the company was rescued by a man who had never been to engineering school, but had been around the Franklin company from the very beginning. He was John Burns, a "born mechanic" who had helped John Wilkinson assemble the very first experimental Franklin back before the company was organized. Burns had been used as an engineer and trouble shooter over the years.

Louis Stellman, boss of the engineering crew under Wilkinson, was storming at the transmission shop for producing what he called "inferior" transmissions. The transmission shop tightened up on production clearances and quality. Still, the vibration persisted.

It was Burns who looked for the trouble elsewhere. He knew, as everybody in the shop knew, that in making the big change in the engine — moving the cooling blower to the front — they had adopted the solid coupling for the transmission, with the clutch and transmission unit bolted directly onto the engine block. Previously, there had been a flexible coupling between flywheel and transmission. Burns suspected that the trouble lay here.

He tried to tell his colleagues, but they impatiently told him to go away and leave them alone. They had headaches enough.

Instead of "bugging off," Burns bugged in by working after hours and nights to design a clutch plate incorporating a vibration damper with springs. He then took one of the cars on which the vibration was worst, secretly installed his new clutch plate, and took the car out for a spin. The vibration had vanished, as if by magic.

Now it was Burns' turn to invite the bosses, those highly educated engineers, for a ride in his "cured" vehicle. After that, when a troublesome bug developed, the cry went up in the Franklin shops: "Call John Burns." On more than one occasion, veteran Franklin men remembered, John Burns pulled scorched Franklin chestnuts out of the fire.

In fact years later, long after the Franklin company no longer existed and Franklin lovers were trying to restore their antique Franklins and keep them running, the old cry for John Burns went up again. This time he was called upon to edit a trouble shooter's column in *The Air Cooled News,* the publication of the H.H. Franklin Club.

It was called, simply, the "John Burns Column," and many a neophyte Franklin owner was guided over the rough spots on how to keep his Franklin going by the old veteran who had done it so many times while the machine was in production. When he died in 1957, there was many a Franklin owner who shed a silent tear. Other Franklin technical experts kept the column going, but they

John Burns (left) and John Wilkinson (right) had been engineers with the company from the beginning and together assembled the first Franklin. Carl T. Doman (standing) joined the firm later and played a major role in the final years.

continued to call it the "John Burns Column" to honor the veteran who knew how to make Franklins go.

In the end, when the bugs had been worked out, the Series 10 — although derided as the ugliest Franklin of them all—turned out to be, mechanically and performance-wise, the best machine produced to date, to bear the Franklin name. Williams, the engineer who helped bring it into being, said many years later that, in his opinion, it was the best of all Franklins — if you didn't mind a horsecollar.

Then came that big "revolt," the big styling change, and the departure of John Wilkinson. One cannot help but wonder if the coming of brilliant young men like Williams, the star performance of men like Burns, didn't help Herbert Franklin make his decision in the showdown with Wilkinson. Perhaps he decided that Wilkinson, while a brilliant engineer, had become a bit too rigid—and that it was now up to younger men to lead the way.

Meanwhile, the production picture at Franklin had been going through its ups and downs, with the trend slowly but steadily improving over the years. It was 1915 before production topped the 3,000 mark—at 3,217. The next year was even higher: 3,817.

In 1917, the year when Franklin stylists finally smoothed out the lines of the Renault hood, a big jump came—all the way to 8,985. The next year, 1918, was a war year, when all manufacturers were required to cut back on production. Franklin production dropped to 6,689. But in 1919, with the war over, the fig-

ure began climbing once more—to 9,334. In 1920 Franklin production for the first time topped the 10,000 mark, going to 10,552.

Then came an economic depression in 1921, sending the figure downward again, to 8,536, and to 8,052 in 1922. In 1923, as the country recovered from the depression and Franklin had the bugs worked out of the Series 10 cars, production topped 10,000 again, at 10,130. In 1924, however, another slump appeared for Franklin, dropping the figure all the way down to 6,075. This was the year of the "revolt." Perhaps part of that slump was tooling up for the the biggest change in the company's history.Now that Hamlin and his compatriots had won their battle and got what they wanted, a more "conventional" car, did it also win the battle of the salesroom?

The answer, sadly, was "no."

This 1927 Franklin 11-B Walker coupe is pictured while in temporary outdoor storage at the time of a recent auction. (Photo courtesy of Harrah's Automobile Collection)

The big change in styling did not produce the sales "miracle" the dealers had hoped for. It is true that in 1925, the first year of the new Series 11-A, production did recover to 8,595, but in 1926 came another drop, to 7,606. In 1927, the last year of the Series 11-B, production barely topped the 8,000 mark, at 8,103.

The Franklin, despite its impressive engineering achievements — and now with its conventional look — was still a car hard to sell. Such was the pressure from the water-cooled motor cars, which now overwhelmed Franklins by thousands to one. Such was the fate of a small company which dared to be different, to produce a car unique among the masses.

Some Franklin friends have suggested that the big styling change simply came too late. Franklin purists have insisted, as Wilkinson so stubbornly did in 1924, that it was a mistake to make the Franklin look like other cars. Perhaps, as historian Tom Hubbard suggested, the ideal solution would have been if Franklin could somehow have been different and beautiful, too.

In any case, the years of the most beautiful and most powerful Franklins were yet to come.

The decline and fall of Franklin: 1928-1934

For years, people had been saying that the Franklin was an "old man's" car, slow and stodgy. It was dependable as the day is long, but a lousy performer.

Then, in November, 1929, along came Cannonball Baker to prove it wasn't so. Driving a Franklin with an engine of a revolutionary design, he zipped across the continent — from New York to Los Angeles, some 3,259 miles — in 69 hours and 31 minutes, establishing a new record.

There had been a lot of years and a lot of Franklin history since Franklin had owned any sort of record like this.

Economy runs, yes. Durability runs, to prove the efficiency of air cooling, yes. But a speed run of this kind, no.

It had taken a revolution in air-cooled engine design to do it. Actually, in a sense, the engineers had been forced to go back where they had started.

The very earliest Franklins had horizontal cooling fins, and little else, to do the cooling.

Then had come one step after another:
• First, a fan.
• Then a shroud, to direct the air, and a suction fan at the rear.

• Then, hailed as the greatest breakthrough of them all, up to that time, the Sirocco type fan up front, blowing the air down through vertical fins.

All these things had worked — and worked well — especially the last system. But during the 1920s, Franklin de-

This 1928 roadster, a sweet little boattail number, swept the Best of Show honors at several prestigious car shows during the 1970's.

signs had gradually slipped away from the principle of "scientific light weight," while the size and power of the engines remained on the low side.

Horsepower, in the 1922-1927 period, remained around the 32-35 mark. When one considered that the cooling system ate up a good portion of that, perhaps even the most loyal Franklin owners had some cause to complain of poor performance.

Franklin management finally decided to do something about it, and hired an aircraft engineer named Glen Shoemaker, with experience at McCook Field, to do something about the Franklin reputation as an old man's car.

Shoemaker did it by going back to the beginning, with horizontal cooling fins.

Then, instead of blowing the air up, back and down, he simply blew the air down an air passage alongside the engine, with deflectors to force the air into one simple turn, sideways into the cooling fins.

Then he made one final redesign of the cooling fan that had been reworked so many times. Despite its smaller size after the old flywheel days, it had remained quite large and, with "forward" scoops, or blades, it had been eating up as much as 20 horsepower just to drive it.

Shoemaker reversed the air scoops, or blades, on the fan from forward to reverse, and proved that it would move more air with less power. He reduced the fan from 15 to 12 inches in diameter, and showed that the new fan design moved more air than the old one—and used only from four to six horsepower. This in itself was a major power boost for the anemic engine.

Then, with the bore increased from 3¼ to 3½, increasing the size of the valves and raising the compression ratio, Shoemaker presented Franklin with a very hot engine indeed. Franklin engineers claimed thay had raised horsepower by as much as 76 percent in one jump, all the way to 90 and 95—and, with an extra little "supercharger" gadget, tapping air off the cooling system, up to 100 bhp.

The Franklin engine had grown up. This was the engine that made it possible for the record-breaking "flight of the Cannonball."

With the compression ratio raised to

1930 Franklin convertible sedan owned by Charles A. Lindbergh, the world-famous trans-Atlantic flyer. Lindbergh favored air cooled motor cars because his famed Spirit of St. Louis was also air cooled.

unheard-of 8.5 to 1 on one special Franklin engine, and using standard premium grade gasoline bought at service station pumps, Baker went to Pikes Peak and smashed a series of records.

The performance of the sensational new engine led the blunt spoken Baker, who was used to driving very fast cars, to comment: "That old waffle iron was the greatest car I ever drove. That snub nosed baby would run forever."

Franklin engineers, of course, were not ready to sell an engine with 8.5 to 1 compression ratio to the public, but it was quickly apparent that with the new engine, Franklin had suddenly become highly competitive again.

The new engine was "hot" in more ways than one. In a paper presented to the Society of Automotive Engineers, Franklin engineers Carl Doman and Ed Marks described how they had tested the cooling system on the new engine by running the engine at full throttle for four hours in a "hell box" where air was preheated to 165 degrees. The engine had to use this oven hot air for "cooling," and the cooling system still worked. In fact, it got so hot inside the hell box, it set off the automatic sprinkler system, dousing the engine and test equipment.

When they dismantled the engine after that grueling hot run, they found it was still in perfect condition.

Not satisfied with the red hot six-cylinder engine, Shoemaker got the green light to go ahead with the development of a V-12, the "ultimate" Franklin engine. Here again the new super cooling system, with the new type fan and side draft cooling, were used. It took some doing to design such a cooling system for a complicated V-12 engine, but it was done and worked just as it worked on the six.

It is almost impossible to give a detailed description of every series and body style made by Franklin, especially in the later years when series, models and body styles proliferated. But with the Series 12 cars for 1928, Franklin engineers took the first steps to improving the performance of the lethargic engine by stretching the stroke from 4 to 4¾ inches, while leaving the bore at 3¼. This increased the cubic inch displacement from 199 to 234, and raised the horsepower to 46. It was a sorely needed boost.

Another change, very significant from a historical standpoint for Franklin, was the use of a steel frame in 1928. The Series 12 Franklins were brought out in two wheelbases, 119 and 128 inches, with the longer car using the steel frame. It was the first time, since the very beginning, that Franklin had used steel instead of wood for the frames. The change was made necessary by the need to lower the car and use drop frames.

For 1929, Series 13, Franklin offered three models:
• The 130, on a 120-inch wheelbase.
• The 135, on a 125-inch wheelbase.
• The 137, on a 132 inch wheelbase.

For the two larger models, the engine was beefed up once more, this time by increasing the bore to 3½, thus bringing the cid to 274 and the horsepower to 60.

It was in 1929, for the 1930 model year, that Franklin engineers perfected the hot new side draft engine, with the big leap to 95 and 100 bhp. In basic size, however, the engine remained at 274 cid right to the end of Franklin motor cars.

The 1930 Franklin was the Series 14, again on several wheelbases and models. Although some cosmetic work was done on the bodies, especially the hoods, grilles and windshields, Franklin body styling had remained more or less static since the introduction of the Model 11's.

In 1931, for the Series 15 cars, bodies for the lower priced lines remained much the same, but the top-of-the-line six, the Model 153, had a flashy new body, with low, sleek lines. It was, perhaps, the most handsome Franklin to date.

In the meantime, a dark cloud was hovering over the Franklin operation—the same cloud that was over the entire motor car industry. It was nothing less than the beginning of the country's worst economic depression in history.

Franklin managers and engineers were meeting that threat in almost the same manner that most other motor car makers were doing: by making the best automobiles they had ever made, and hoping the cloud would go away.

With Franklin, the results were doubly tragic because it had always been a comparatively small, high overhead operation. It was expensive because, despite the low production volume, Franklin engineers had always insisted on making almost every engine and chassis part in their own shops.

The results were that quite early in the depression Franklin found itself in deep financial trouble. Part of it came from development costs of the new side draft six engine and the V-12 engine, the latter not yet on the market. In addition, Franklin had borrowed heavily from the banks in 1929 to finance an expansion program, going in debt some $5,000,000.

Franklin officials felt justified in doing this because 1929 had been the high point of the boom years of the 1920s, with production and sales reaching their all time record high of 14,432. Things looked bright for the future.

But when the depression hit, the shock waves battered Franklin very quickly. In 1930, production dropped all the way to 6,043, which was even less than the 1928 figure of 7,770. This was a comedown— and it was only a beginning.

One problem was that Franklin had no low priced car, as Ford, General Motors and Chrysler did, to fall back on in hard times. All emphasis with Franklin had always been with quality. In 1929, that peak year, the cheapest Franklin had sold for $2,210. In that year you could buy a new Ford for as little as $435. Chevrolet's new model sold for $525, or you could buy a Plymouth for $675.

Franklin had tried to make a move into the low priced field in the early 1920s, setting up an experimental shop to produce a four-cylinder car to sell for less than $1,000. A prototype of the "Model Z" was actually built and tested, with excellent results. Some of the men who worked on the project said it outper-

A 1933 Franklin Olympic, one of those hybrid cars fashioned by mating a Reo Flying Cloud body to a Franklin engine, grille and hood.

formed its big sister six. But the car had never gone into production because the company lacked the funds to build the entirely new factory that would have been required.

In 1931 Franklin production dropped to 2,851 units. There was no money coming in to pay the bankers on the huge expansion loan of 1929 — which had permitted the company to gear up for production above the range of 15,000 cars per year.

Costs were slashed. Workmen by the hundreds were laid off. It was not enough. Late in 1931 the banks forced Franklin to accept a new manager, Edwin McEwen, who became known to Franklin employees — those who were left — as "The Undertaker."

The arrival of McEwen forced the retirement of Herbert H. Franklin, the man who had created the company and had led its management from the start. Then McEwen cut the engineering staff, which had probably accumulated more experience and knowledge of air cooling than any other group in the world, from 125 to 11 men. Production crews were slashed just as savagely; the few who re-

mained had their pay cut to the bone. One workman who lived out of town complained it cost him more for carfare to get to work than he earned.

One problem McEwen had to face was what to do with the new V-12 engine, developed but not in production. It had been scheduled for a 137-inch wheelbase and was expected to drive a car weighing 4,000 pounds.

McEwen, obviously believing the depression would end shortly, followed the same path being taken by Cadillac, Packard, Pierce-Arrow and Marmon. He gave a go-ahead to production of the new car, but ordered the wheelbase stretched to a whopping 144 inches and, of course, a larger body.

Another major move ordered by McEwen was to sever connections with the Walker Body Company of Amesbury, Massachusetts, which had been making Franklin bodies during the 1920s. Bringing body making operations back to the Franklin plant did not make for good results. Franklin workmen were no longer trained in sheet metal work and body quality, especially for the big V-12, suffered severely. Constructing the body largely by hand, with makeshift production facilities, resulted in a great deal of lead being used, adding to the weight of the already heavy car and bringing a further reduction in performance.

For the new big chassis, McEwen ordered steel frames and dropped the full elliptic springs which had been a Franklin trademark from the beginning.

Then McEwen made another drastic move by virtually scrapping what was left of Franklin engineering features. He ordered into production a special car to be known as the Franklin Olympic, the Series 18, on which the only Franklin feature remaining was the air-cooled engine.

He contracted with Reo and the Hayes Body Corporation to buy complete Reo Flying Cloud chassis and bodies. Although the Franklin tradition had been destroyed, the results were good, from a performance standpoint. Since the Reo combination weighed about 1,000 pounds less than the Franklin six had weighed, and with the hot new Franklin 100 hp side draft engine, the new Franklin Olympic became a bit of a "hot rod" for performance. With the handsome body lines and styling of the Reo Flying Cloud Six, it was not a bad car. It wasn't a Franklin but, for those seeking performance, it would out-perform the Reo.

The first of the Franklin Olympics were placed on the market on October 22, 1932, as 1933 models, with the same car as the Series 18-B, begun in July, 1933. For the 1934 model year came the final Olympic model, the 18-C, beginning in January, 1934.

For Franklin purists, if there were any left with enough money to buy one, production had continued on the conventional Franklins—the Airman Series, with the full elliptic springs and the conventional body.

Then there was the highly touted V-12, on which Franklin engineers had begun development as the "dream car." Now, though it had become something else, it was at least on the market, having been introduced on April 1, 1932.

When Franklin engineers had begun that engine development, they had known it was to be a car designed to compete with the "big boys," so they were in a performance, or horsepower, race. They designed the basic engine

crankcase and blocks so that they could be adapted to three engine sizes: one for 340 cubic inch displacement; a second for 398; and, if necessary, a third at 452 cid.

The latter engine would have been a formidable machine indeed. Since it was never built, however, one can only guess what its horsepower rating would have been. McEwen, making the decision, took the middle ground and the engine went into production with a 3¼ bore and a 4 inch stroke, for the 398 cid size. When its horsepower was measured, it weighed in at 150 bhp—not sensational, but quite an engine for its day.

Coupled with the huge 144-inch chassis and the big, virtually handmade body, the new engine did not quite produce the performance one might have expected. It was said that the hybrid Franklin-Reo-Olympic could outperform its big sister in all categories except top speed, and it took a two-speed Columbia rear axle to give the big car a slight edge there.

Another area where the big car suffered was in gasoline mileage, where Franklins had always been famous for economy. The big V-12 got as little as five miles per gallon, and seldom more than 10.

On the other hand, people who have driven the big twelves, especially the later ones, after bugs and body defects had been corrected, have reported that it is a fine motor car. Tom Hubbard, of Tucson, Arizona, one of the country's top Franklin historians and restorers, wrote a description of his own V-12.

Hubbard said: "The lack of the full elliptic springs and tubular axle, the use of

The first Franklin engine to challenge the performance superiority of their competitors was the new six-cylinder side-draft machine which produced as much as 100 horsepower.

a conventional rigid chassis frame instead of the unique and very clever flexible frame system, the extra size and weight in violation of the Franklin tradition of 'Scientific Light Weight' — all are shortcomings which make the V-12 something of a step-child in the Franklin fraternity.

Another "gimmick" Franklin engineers came up with in the final years was a "supercharger." A real supercharger— a blower to blow the intake mixture into the motor under pressure, rather than to force the engine to suck it in, as conventional engines do — does wonders to increase performance of an engine. In the case of Franklin, the supercharger was a bit of a fraud.

Some historians have suggested that Franklin used the term mostly for advertising purposes. Actually, the gadget was nothing more than a small attachment for drawing off a bit of the forced air draft from the efficiently operating air cooling system, and feeding it into the carburetor. The high speed and expensive blower needed for a true supercharger just wasn't there. Some drivers who have test driven Franklins equipped with the so-called supercharger have said they could tell little difference when the "supercharger" was switched on or off.

In any case, the cars made in those last desperate years — produced in the shadow of impending tragedy — were simply the best, the most beautiful and the most powerful machines produced in all of Franklin history.

But there was little that the quality, beauty and performance of these magnificent machines could do to stop the falling axe. Production and sales continued to plummet. The figure in 1931 was 2,851 Franklins. By 1932 it dropped all the way to 1,905. In 1933 there was another nosedive, to 1,011.

There could be only one end to the story.

Company officials — those who were left — went through the motions of giving a last ditch styling facelift to the 1934 models. It was the first major styling revamp in several years, and gave the 1934 models a sharply vee'd and sloping grille, similar to that of the big V-12. The 1934 models were "different," but it was largely a futile gesture, and they might

Impressive 1932 Franklin convertible, a Series 16 model.

as well have saved the money it cost. Only 360 of them were made before it all came to an end.

The banks holding the notes on the Franklin loans, dating back to 1929 and before, called a halt to any further drain on resources.

Herbert Franklin said then, and repeated it later, that the Franklin Motor Company was still solvent in 1934, and could have been saved. He may have been right. The figures seem to dispute that but, in any case, he no longer had the power to make the decisions. The banks, acting under bankruptcy laws, closed the factory doors in the spring of 1934.

There are a few "postscript" notes to the Franklin story, however. For one thing, all Franklins made during the so-called "classic period," beginning in 1925 and lasting until the end of Franklin production, have been granted classic status by the Classic Car Club of America— all, that is, except the hybrid Olympic.

A goodly number of Franklins produced during this period were delivered, in chassis form, to the custom body makers, and thus became something more than production classics. These custom machines proudly bore names such as Dietrich, LeBaron, Willoughby, Derham, and others. They are the most desirable of all Franklins.

In bringing the Franklin story to an end, one faces the painful task of putting a reasonable "why" into the failure of such a long, enduring and unique story.

The easiest and most reasonable answer is, simply, the economic depression. Franklin was not the only motor car enterprise killed by that disaster.

But a post-mortem on a car, and an enterprise, as interesting and as "different" as the Franklin story calls for further comment. Some Franklin fans, including Tom Hubbard, have suggested that when you measure the Franklin story by all the yardsticks which governed the motor car story of America, "It should never have happened at all, but it did."

Part of the explanation must, inevitably, come from the fact that in any society there are always a few men and women who feel the subconscious urge to be different, to attach themselves to the unique.

Such people bought Franklins, and made the whole impossible story possible.

Which raises the question as to exactly what kind of people they were.

There is no easy answer. There are only clues as to the curious "mystique" which attracted people to Franklin. The famed American novelist, John O'Hara, was not a motor car specialist but he was aware of the Franklin "mystique," and spoke of it in a lecture at Rider College in 1959.

In speaking about the way a novelist creates characters for a novel, O'Hara said, "In the Twenties if you said a man owned a Franklin you could not be talking about the kind of a man who owned a Buick, although some Buicks cost the same amount of money as some Franklins. The Franklin owner would not be wearing an Elks' tooth, nor a Rotary Club button. He might wear a Masonic pin, but not a Shriner's. The Franklin owner was more likely to be a tennis player than a golfer, a doctor rather than a real estate agent, a college man than a non-college man, and a much more independent thinker than a Buick owner.

"He would be more likely to own securities than a Buick owner, whose money would be tied up in personal enterprises. It would be out of character for a Buick type man to own a Franklin; it would not be quite so much out of character for a Franklin man to own a Buick. In any case the novelist has told the reader that Jones owns a Franklin, therefore, Jones will behave as a Franklin-owning Jones will behave. And if he behaves in a way that is out of character, either the novelist has been wrong in providing him with a Franklin, or he, the novelist, must explain and make credible the acts that are out of character for the Franklin-owning Jones."

Perhaps this provides a clue as to why that tiny handful of Americans supported and made possible the Franklin story for so many years, returning over and over to buy Franklins—perhaps even in times, or years, when they had reason to be less than completely enchanted by their machines.

Some auto historians have suggested that the late, post-1929 Franklin engines had become so good, and their performance so impressive, that if the economic climate had been a bit more favorable, those air-cooled engines might have forced the so-called trend makers of the motor car industry to take another look at air cooling.

Other historians, in looking at the Franklin story, have suggested that one reason for the failure in the 1930s was that Americans had lost their enthusiasm for air-cooled cars.

This is sheer nonsense. It would make just as much sense to say that during the depression Americans had lost their taste for all automobiles, because they ceased to buy them. It was simply a lack of money which kept Americans from buying Franklins, just as it kept them from buying Fords, or Cadillacs.

It wasn't air cooling; in the end, it took the Volkswagen to prove that.

In its own way, Franklins proved it too. During the depression, the U.S. Army was looking for engines that "could take it" in their tanks. They bought a few Franklin engines for testing purposes, and found they were the only engine that could do the job in those hell-hole engine compartments of the tanks.

But during the depression, even the

A 1934 Airman Club sedan, series 19-A. The smaller Franklins got a major styling revamp for the front end but it was a "last gasp." Only a handful were made. It was the end.

U.S. Army did not have enough nickels to keep Franklin going.

Historian Tom Hubbard wrote a fitting epitaph for Franklin when he said, "The Franklin Company earned its own keep in a highly competitive business for 32 years. It was never dependent for its support upon the fruits of other enterprises or the whims of rich men. Its contribution was an important one and the heritage it left places it among the honored names of the industry. Perhaps it is well that it did not survive beyond its time."

What Hubbard was saying was that if Franklin had somehow found a financial godfather and managed to survive the depression, the product would almost certainly have undergone such changes, such "cheapening," that things would never have been the same again. The end may only have been postponed, as it was for Packard.

The Franklin "mystique" would have been gone, and those unique men described by John O'Hara could never have endured that.

Editor's note: In the preparation of the Franklin story, the assistance of the following is gratefully acknowledged: the Detroit Public Library, the H.H. Franklin Club, and especially Thomas H. Hubbard, Dr. George S. Boyer, William Drake, and the others without whom this chapter would have been impossible.

IV
KISSEL KAR

Grounded in the German tradition of workmanship and quality

They called it the Kissel Kar, and the machine was as solidly German as its name.

The men who conceived her, brought her into being, were George and William Kissel, sons of a pioneer German farmer who had gone far beyond the soil to create a sizable industrial and mercantile empire. These men were well grounded in the German tradition of honest workmanship and solid quality.

The Kissel industries had already begun the manufacture of gasoline engines for farm and shop use. It was only a short step to the motor car.

Then, to add another German influence to the Kissel Kar, there was the chief engineer, Herman Palmer, a man bred and born in Germany, trained as an engineer at the University of Cologne. Inventor, creator, craftsman, Palmer was a man who left his mark on the Kissel during its entire existence — except at the very beginning.

And then there was the coach builder, J. Frederich Werner, the man mostly responsible for the styling, the craftsman-

ship and solid durability of the Kissel bodies. Werner was a man trained in the artisan craftsmanship tradition which created coaches fit for a king — which had, indeed, created coaches for kings.

What was this Kissel Kar, which had its beginnings in 1906—not at the birth, but still in the pioneer era of the motor car? How did this motor car, which was destined to create a considerable chapter in the history of the motor car, come to be?

One of the most revealing answers is provided in a feature story printed in the *Milwaukee Sentinel* in May, 1906. Datelined Hartford, Wisconsin, the story was published under the headline, "Hartford Opens City's Gates."

It said: "This city is experiencing one of the most phenomenal runs of prosperity in its history. On every hand evidence of activity and thrift is apparent. Merchants and manufacturers, men of law and clergy, retired farmers and business men, all are joining hands in an endeavor to promote the welfare of Hartford. Chief among these who are

1907 Model "C" KisselKar. At a time when most motor cars were one- or two-cylinder machines, the Kissel started out as a four. And, while others were chain-driven, the Kissel had a shaft drive.

doing so much for this city is the firm L. Kissel & Sons."

The story told how Louis Kissel and his sons owned and controlled the Hartford Plow Co., the Kissel Manufacturing Co., the Hartford Electric Co., and were stockholders or directors in many other local firms.

The Kissels, the story pointed out, had their own lumber processing plant, stone quarry and sand pits. They were building houses at the rate of 40 or 50 per year, and had already built 500 houses.

A significant item in the news story was that "they (the Kissel enterprises) are manufacturing a large amount of farm machinery. The last three years they have had their gasoline engines made by the Western Malleable and Grey Iron Co., of Milwaukee, but *are now making the engines themselves."*

The biggest news of all, however, was the announcement that one of the latest additions to the Kissel empire was a project to begin the manufacture of automobiles.

"The Kissel Automobile Co. will make about 25 runabouts and about 15 touring cars this year. They will be equipped

with a new plant and machinery for making 1,000 cars next year."

This last announcement, by itself, probably did not create much of a stir in 1906. New automobile making enterprises, with equally glowing promises of the future, were springing up all over the country—and dying just as fast. The difference here was that the Kissels had a reputation for getting things done when they promised to do so. There was a smell of gasoline, motor oil and engines in the air in Hartford. One of the better motor cars was about to appear.

The 1906 dispatch from Hartford added: "At the present time this concern (L. Kissel and Sons) is advertising extensively for men with families to locate here, and to all such they will sell them a cozy home on easy terms, give them employment at good wages, and to those who are not masters of some trade, competent instructors will be furnished them free."

This is the background. Perhaps one of the next links in the chain came about because of the family car.

As a wealthy leader of his community, it was probably inevitable that Louis

The 1912 KisselKar "50" semi-touring is an impressive motor car. Complete with top, gas lamps, adjustable shock, tire pump and tool kit, plus numerous other items, it sold for $2,350.

Kissel was one of the first to own a motor car. The family machine was a White steamer, which fascinated two of the Kissel sons, George and Will. For a time, as sub-dealers, they even sold a few of the Whites in their area, a part-time project while working in the farm implement and engine business.

The Kissel plant was equipped to make gasoline powered engines, mostly one-cylinder, for farm or shop use. But one day the two Kissel brothers got together with a pattern maker in their plow factory, and contrived a four-cylinder automobile type engine, with a 3¼ bore with four-inch stroke.

When they cranked it up, the engine not only ran but ran so well it produced 18 horsepower. Now they had an automobile type engine, but no automobile. This, inevitably, led to the next link: "Let's build one." They bought the necessary parts and ended up with a vehicle of 82-inch wheelbase.

With the new engine in place, recalled Will in 1971, the brothers found that the car operated better than most of the early motor cars puttering around the Hartford area — so well, in fact, that it put ideas into their heads: "If we can do this well, why not go into the business?"

Why not, indeed? Together with their father and the other two Kissel brothers, Otto and Adolph, they were already engaged in just about everything else. The fledgling motor car business seemed a natural. They incorporated, with $15,000 cash capital, on June 5, 1906, as the Kissel Motor Car Co. George A. Kissel was president and William L. Kissel, secretary and treasurer. At first it was only a piece of paper and that one home-made motor car, but in time it would overshadow the entire Kissel enterprises.

Their first machine had shown the Kissel flair for the innovative. At a time when many — if not most — motor cars were one or two-cylinder machines, the Kissel started out as a four. At a time when most motor cars were chain driven, the Kissel machine had shaft drive.

The next move was to produce a more refined prototype, one more adaptable to production. It was true they had built their first four-cylinder engine for that first machine, but the Kissel plant, at the beginning, was not equipped to put such

an engine into production. The second Kissel, the prototype of the one they now planned to produce for sale, used a Beaver engine, rated at 35 horsepower. The car had Timken axles, a Warner transmission and a radiator which resembled the Pope-Toledo, a car the Kissel brothers admired.

The newly created Kissel Motor Car Co. had scarcely announced the birth of their new car when it attracted the attention of the McDuffee Automobile Co., of Chicago, distributors for the Stoddard-Dayton, already one of the leading motor cars of the day. A bit on the expensive side, the Stoddard-Dayton machine was rather difficult to sell.

The McDuffee people offered the Kissel brothers a contract to purchase 100 of the Kissel-built machines if they could produce them to sell for $1,850 stripped, or $2,150 fully equipped — a price about $200 below that of the Stoddard-Dayton. The stipulation was that the machine must be just as good as the S-D, though priced lower.

The Kissel brothers promptly accepted the challenge, stipulation and all. It meant they had to give up their preferred Pope-Toledo type radiator styling, but the brand new Kissel firm produced the car, met the price and the quality, yet made a $25,000 profit. This was no mean pot of gold in 1907.

Then there was the matter of the car's name. The most authentic account attributes it to a dream of Mrs. William Harvey, wife of the president of the McDuffee Automobile Company.

When the first negotiations between the Kissel brothers and the McDuffee firm took place in 1906, the story goes, a conference of the directors was held in Chicago. A discussion arose about a name for the car. The name "Wisconsin," the car's home state, was proposed, but it was decided to stick to the family name of the company producing the car—Kissel. The formal christening was postponed, but a week or so after the conference Mr. Harvey wrote to the makers, reporting that in a dream his wife had hit upon the idea of spelling "car" with a capital "K" and adding that to the name. It thus became Kissel Kar, or KisselKar, both being used at various times — a catchy Teutonic name that was to attract the fancy of many a car buyer until World War I.

Another quirk of fate in the Kissel history had come in 1906, as the Kissel motor car was being born. A traveler through Hartford happened to look out of the window of his train to see the Kissel factories looming against the small city's background. The young man was billed at the moment as a musician, but after leaving the train he applied for a job at the Kissel plant and was hired.

The powerful four-cylinder engine of the 1912 "50" was rated at 50 horsepower.

At first he was only another worker around the plant, until the foreman began to notice that this unassuming stranger seemed to know a great deal more about machinery—how to figure stress, for example—than any ordinary laborer had a right to know. When they inquired into his background, they discovered that he had been trained as an engineer at the University of Cologne, in Germany.

After this was disclosed, Herman Palmer was put to work in the engineering department. It was only a matter of time until he became head of the Kissel Kar engineering department, a post he would hold to the end, adding inventions and engineering features of his own to the Kissel engine and chassis. His achievements grow in stature when it is considered that he had had no previous experience in the building of motor cars.

So many circumstances created the Kissel organization. A look at the background of the body builder, J. Frederich Werner, is a vignette of the German tradition that could produce a machine like the Kissel. Born in an age of craftsmen and kings, Werner could recall a time when his father, a master coach maker, had made coaches fit for a king; and he

did make coaches for a king—Ludwig II of Bavaria, in the era 1864-1886.

These were the days when a coach could be a thing of beauty and strength, almost a work of art. The men who made them were taught their trades as a craft, with the painstaking exactitude of creating a master artist.

Young Werner followed his father's footsteps and learned the coachmaking trade, starting as a lad of 14, but fate — and the marching of time — was bringing changes to the world of coach making. Progress-minded mechanics had begun playing with machines called internal combustion engines, installing them to drive the coaches, sending the horse off to pasture. There was still work for the master coach builder, but it was a different kind of coach they were building now — coaches drawn by engines.

After seven years of painstaking training as a coach builder, three as an apprentice, and four in a technical school, young Werner found himself working at the Opel works in Russelsheim, Germany, one of the pioneer plants of the auto industry. Once again he was working on coaches for kings, personages like Kaiser Wilhelm II, of Germany, Czar Nicholas II, of Russia, and the King of Siam.

But this was not enough to hold a young man with a bit of adventure in his heart. When young Werner received an opportunity to take an assignment with that old time wagon and carriage company in America — Studebaker — he jumped at the chance. For whatever reason, he remained there only a short time, moving next to a fledgling manufacturer in Iowa. In 1908 he saw an ad in the Chicago papers, placed by the Kissel brothers, telling about the need for a body engineer in Hartford.

When he approached the Kissels, he was hired and placed in charge of the new body building shops for the latest Kissel Kar. His future was tied to that of the Kissel Kar for the next 22 years.

Thus in 1908, with an able engineer and a master coach builder on the staff, plus enterprising managers in the persons of George and William Kissel, the Kissel Motor Car Co. had the ingredients to write its pages in motoring history.

But we have moved slightly ahead of our story. It was in 1907 when production of the Kissel Kars began in earnest. By the fall of that year, production had increased to the point where 92 completed cars rolled out the doors of the plant during the last quarter, with a dollar evaluation of $185,000 — again, no mean achievement for an infant company.

In this early period, before the Kissel body shop had become a reality, the company bought its bodies from Zimmerman Brothers, in Waupon, Wisconsin, a company that made sleighs for use in this north country. As a result, the early Kissel Kars bore out the sleigh "motif," with the graceful sleigh type bodies.

The basic design of the 1906 prototype continued through the 1907 production, except that the wheelbase was lengthened to 98 inches. For 1908, the body styling was changed, moving away from the McDuffee-Stoddard-Dayton imposed styling. The new radiators took on more of a standard "hip roof" form that was typical of the period. Bodies were bought from Charles Abresch & Co. of Milwaukee, an arrangement that continued until sometime in 1909, when the Kissel firm got its own body shops into operation.

Another change in 1908 was to move the radiator back over the front axle, together with the engine and machine weight, to provide a more balanced center of gravity and make for easier steering. The rear springs were now half elliptical, replacing the previous scroll type rear frame horns.

By 1909 the company was ready to make its next big move, running with the leaders in the industry: production of the first Kissel Kar six.

This was a bigger car, on a 128-inch wheelbase, with the "big six" engine, 4¾ x 4¾, rated at 60 horsepower. This was near the top for the industry although, in truth, it must be said that horsepower measurements in those days were not always accurate or scientific.

The addition of a six had been comparatively easy, for cylinder blocks were still cast singly, or in pairs, so the same cylinder blocks used on the four could also be used on the six. You simply used three blocks instead of two, bolted to the top of a longer crankcase, which was always separate in this period.

The Kissel Kar line still included two fours, one light and the other "regular." The light four, designated the LD-9, had a 4¼ x 4¼ engine and rolled on a 107-inch wheelbase and on 32-inch tires. ("D" meant touring car body.)

The "regular" four touring car, designated the D-9, had a 4¾ x 4¾ engine and rolled on 36-inch tires, as did the Big Six. The regular four and the Big Six shared the same bore and stroke, with engine blocks, pistons, and connecting rods interchangeable.

With this line of cars the Kissel Motor Car Co. was ready to move into the ranks of the top auto makers of America.

The middle years: 1910-1919

I t was in 1910 when Harvey Herrick won the Los Angeles to Phoenix race, setting a new record of 15 hours, 44 minutes for the 483-mile run. He clipped three hours off the 1909 record, and finished 46 minutes ahead of his closest competitor. Herrick's car, a machine with low seats and gasoline tank set behind them at a rakish, forward angle, was a Kissel Kar Semi-Racer.

In 1911, when President Theodore Roosevelt made a trip out west, he was photographed in a big, sturdy touring car: a Kissel Kar.

These two events, seemingly unrelated, gave evidence that the Kissel Kar, a machine which had been in production only since 1906, had arrived with a bang.

- *The race proved that a Kissel Kar could stand up to the best of them. The cars left far behind included one of the famed Mercers.*
- *And nobody, in those early days of the motor car, would dare to offer the President of the United States a tour in a car which lacked prestige.*

The men running the Kissel plant had determined that theirs would not be just another "assembled car." In just a few short years, Kissel had set a track record which put it in the class of auto manufacturers to be reckoned with.

By 1911 the young company was able to announce: "Since the publication of

In 1904 Kissel introduced a detachable sedan top, which in combination with KisselKar touring models, was offered under the name of "The All-Year Car."

our 1910 catalogue, we have added a drop forge plant and an aluminum and brass foundry, which enables us to manufacture practically the entire car within our own factory. We have also added a large body building plant." A ferrous metal foundry was on the way, which would enable Kissel to cast its own engine blocks.

One major body change in 1911 was to offer a double drop frame, which enabled Kissel to lower its machines. It gave the Kissel Kar lower, more rakish lines than most of its competitors, in a day when most automobiles rode high. It would be years before many of the other cars would adopt this feature.

To accommodate customers in the rugged hinterlands, Kissel continued production of a "Western Special," still using the straight frame to give extra clearance on the worst of the roads in the rugged west.

In 1912 the big innovation in the automobile marketplace was "electricity." This was the age when most people still lighted their homes with kerosene lamps, and most of the automobiles equipped with headlamps used acetylene lighting systems. They were reliable, if a bit troublesome.

But the trend had started to the little glass bulbs which glowed when you turned a switch, drawing power from bulky "wet batteries" which, in turn, were charged by the new "dynamos," later called generators.

Kissel made its first move into the field

of electricity by offering, on the Big Six for 1912, electric side and tail lamps powered by a storage battery. The big upfront headlamps still relied on the old standby, acetylene. For 1913 Kissel offered electric headlamps on the entire line of cars, with combination electric and kerosene side and tail lamps. The kerosene lamps were still there, as a safety feature, if the electrics conked out.

But something even bigger than this was electric starting. Auto engineers had been trying to come up with an efficient system that would eliminate the hated crank which had, until then, not only left a trail of broken and bruised arms but effectively barred most women — except the hardiest Amazons — from the seat behind the wheel. It was one of the reasons why, in that day, if you saw a woman driving an automobile, the odds were heavy that it was an electric car.

Cadillac was credited with making the big breakthrough in 1912, with the first efficient and practical electric starting system. Late in 1913, in time for their 1913 line of cars, Kissel engineers were ready to offer a similar system. This was a fast-breaking trend which could not be ignored, and Kissel had moved so fast it was able to offer the electric starting a full year ahead of most of its competitors. It is a credit to Palmer and his small Kissel engineering staff that he was able to move so fast.

Another new feature during this period was four-speed transmissions. Top gear, in effect, was an overdrive, which gave the Kissel Kar a quiet, smooth operation almost unknown in motoring at this time. It created a feeling of luxury car performance.

But all was not smooth sailing at Kissel. Perhaps it was visions of mass production, with Kissel Kars near the top of the industry, which led the Kissel brothers to set up a branch factory in Milwaukee where a new model, the 6-48, was assembled.

This time the Kissels produced an assembly car. Bodies were bought from Charles Abresch & Co. of Milwaukee. They also went outside the Kissel plant for an engine, purchasing a Wisconsin six-cylinder engine with the block cast in one piece. The engine had dimensions of 4 x 5½ — an extremely long stroke. But it was that "en bloc" casting of the engine which proved costly. It was a process which taxed the ability of the industry's best engineers at this time. When the Wisconsin engine heated up, it had a tendency to create tensions which, in turn, resulted in broken crankshafts or camshafts. Such performance was rough on the Kissel reputation for quality. It was the steady performance of the old reliables still being made in Hartford — the 4-40 and the 6-60 — which saved the Kissel fortunes.

The big seven-passenger 6-60 touring car, on a 142-inch wheelbase, was one of the biggest and most impressive motor cars being made at this time. That long wheelbase gave the machine a stability and a ride which made it possible to drive the car at high speed and long distances —when the roads permitted.

By mid-1915 Kissel was ready with a still newer line of engines. There was a 4-32, at 3⅞ x 5½; a 4-36, at 4½ x 5½; and a 6-42, at 3⅝ x 5½. Perhaps the most notable feature of these new engines was that they all were cast "en bloc": one-piece blocks. They were proof that Kissel engineers had whipped the problems which had plagued these larger castings for so long—a major engineering triumph.

The other major feature of these new engines was the commitment to the long stroke principle, in contrast to the old "square" dimensional engines of the earlier Kissel Kars. Some modern engineers have argued that the engine makers of that time erred in relying so heavily on the long stroke engines but, when one considers the fuels then available, and the fact that road conditions often demanded slower engine speeds, perhaps those early day engineers were wiser than we think. One also must consider that the delicate balancing required for high speed, short stroke engines was still a developing art in 1915.

Meanwhile, one of the most important developments in Kissel history was being worked out in the Kissel body shop, under the direction of Fritz Werner and Will Kissel. It was a new "convertible" body style, to become known as the "All Year" body.

This new body style was to become one of the most talked-of motor car features in the industry for the next half dozen years. It was enough of an innovation that Will Kissel and Werner applied for a patent, which stated: "The object of this invention is to provide an automobile body which shall be readily convertible from an open to closed condition, and vice versa, without sacrifice of elegance, rigidity or strength."

The Patent Office thought well enough of the idea to grant the patent.

The design was simply an open, touring type body upon which a rigid upper, glassed-in body could be fitted in winter. You could buy the two-door touring car without the All Year body at regular price and then, for $300 to $350 extra, purchase the sedan half-body. (Although Kissel continued making an ordinary, four-door touring car of lighter construction, which cost $515 less than the combination type, Kissel advertising was heavily pushing the All Year models.)

Other body, or top, makers had thought of this idea before, and had produced winter glass-windowed enclosures which could be partially ventilated by sliding glass panes. Such cheaper versions, selling for prices of $75 to $100 or more, had gained some popularity. When one considers that the Kissel version cost $300 or more, there had to be a reason for the hefty difference in price —and there was. It lay mostly in quality, built into the combination by Werner's body shop, starting with the extra thick, heavily reinforced lower structure designed specifically to receive the heavy duty, rigidly built upper enclosure.

In contrast, the cheap accessory type enclosures being sold were drafty, cold, leaked rain, and rattled. The Kissel Kar All Year body was something else. The lower half of the combination, aside from the thick walls, carried well-designed fittings for the upper half *which did fit*. Plate glass windows slid down into slots in the lower bodies, and there were dome lights which worked. When riding in one of the Kissel winter bodies, you were scarcely aware that this was a "convertible job."

So sturdy, in fact, were these upper-lower bodies when fitted together that Kissel ads were able to call them "Gibraltar" sedans—and no one was able to dispute the claim.

In addition to the regular touring-sedan body, the convertible combination type body was also available on the roadster, making a coupe, and for the victoria top touring car, making it a town car with the All Year enclosure only over the rear tonneau. This last model provided a touch of elegance and luxury to the Kissel line.

The Kissel Kar convertible body types sold well enough that several other makers entered the field. At that point, Kissel advertising men felt called upon to boast of "Kissel's original idea that changed the motoring habits of the nation."

One of the drawbacks of the All Year body system was the problem of where to store the top in the summer. Some Kissel dealers complained that they were being expected to provide storage space during the summer.

By 1921 the regular sedans had become so entrenched in the public's buying habits that Kissel, along with the other makers, dropped the dual convertible system. But it had been a notable contribution to motoring history.

By the year 1916, competition had grown stiffer in the automobile industry, and the sixes were becoming standard in the medium price range. To meet this competition, Kissel brought out a 117-inch Kissel Kar six, 11 inches shorter than the big 6-42 and at least 300 pounds lighter.

For this car the Kissel shops produced a new, refined six, somewhat smaller at 3¼ x 5, but well enough built that Kissel ad men touted the new car and the new engine as the "Hundred Point Six." The new 6-38 was listed at prices from $1,095 to $1,850, which made the car a real "buy" in its class, designed to meet the growing competition.

Said the ad men: "In no other car in its class is there such an engine — a Kissel-built wonder that will develop 52 horsepower and pull a load 50 to 60 miles an hour — such rapid acceleration — perfect fitting together of co-related parts — liberal employment of bushings — compactness—doing away with all grease cups, but two, oil bolts being substituted—chrome vanadium steel springs —shock absorbers are unnecessary—22

coat finish."

The car did, indeed, have quality features.

Kissel was able to place the car in production just in time to assemble 250 units for the 1916 model year but, by the next year, it was a huge success. Over 4,000 units of the 1917 models were delivered, starting July 1, 1916. With this solid, compact six on the boards, the fours were gone for good, as well as the 6-42.

No Kissel story would be complete without mention of the Kissel Kar Double Six. In 1915 famed Packard engineer Jesse Vincent developed the highly successful V-12 engine that become known as the Twin Six. When the Twin Six began to sell by the thousands, other makers of prestige cars felt called upon to answer in kind.

Kissel's entry in the 12-cylinder field was made possible by the development in Indianapolis, by the Weidely Motor Co., of a 12-cylinder engine which went the Packard Twin Six one better by incorporating overhead valves. This was engineering with a vengeance—if it had worked. It was said that this engine developed up to 103 bhp, making it more powerful than the Packard.

Unfortunately, the big Weidely did not have the thorough engineering behind it that the Packard engine had. There were lubrication and carburation problems which were never completely whipped.

Several other makes of cars had joined Kissel in offering the big Weidely engine in the years 1917-1919, but by 1920 the troublesome Weidely had faded from the picture. As far as is known, only one of the Kissel Kar Double Sixes has survived, out of some 800 made during 1917 and 1918.

Fortunately, the troubles of the big twelve did not rub off on the Hundred Point Six program. These tried and reliable sixes, developed in the Kissel shops by Palmer and his assistants, continued to sell well at volume prices. After the shift to "en bloc" construction in 1915, Kissel had a proven engine design which lasted — with minor bore, stroke and compression changes—until 1928.

By 1918 this engine had been refined to the point where Kissel owners throughout the country were able to

Well-heeled conservative buyers of 1920 could opt for custom-built bodies.

boast of their smooth operation. It was largely achieved by close matching of parts, with pistons and connecting rods being weighed until variations of no more than an eighth of an ounce were tolerated. The vibration-free engine was capable of driving the Kissel Kar at speeds up to 60 miles per hour for hours on end. It was probably the high point of engine development from the Kissel factory.

Another unique feature of the Kissel six engine was the fact that its intake manifold was cast as an integral part of the block, instead of the usual "bolt on" type. This was done to give better and quicker vaporizing of the fuel.

Engine development in the industry had just about reached the point at which one of the greatest limiting factors in further efficiency was the low grade gasoline then available. All engine manufacturers were battling this problem of poor vaporization, especially during the period before an engine reached proper operating temperatures. The Kissel "in-block" manifold worked at least as well — and probably better — than the usual designs.

Still another factor in the success of the basic six design was the method used at the Kissel factory to "limber up" or "burn in" the engines before they were installed in a chassis.

Each Kissel engine began its break-in period being driven by — not driving — reversible dynamometers, which allowed the engines to turn without being subjected to the heat and stress of internal combustion. After a run-in period, when the engine was finally cranked, it was allowed to idle for several hours. Finally, the last test came: the engine was forced to pull the dynamometer, producing electricity, as a test for performance and horsepower.

Thus, Kissel was able to deliver a motor car to the customer without the requirements — almost universal in those days — of requesting the owner to treat the car gently for 1,000 miles or more as a break-in period. It was much later, in the 1930s, before the Ford Motor Co. claimed a coup by telling customers they need not worry about a break-in period for the Ford V-8. Somebody forgot that Kissel had done it more than a decade earlier.

Another contribution from the Kissel factory at this time was the introduction of the Stewart vacuum gasoline feed system. Pressure feeds (or gravity systems), to provide gasoline from tank to carburetor, had been one of the universal headaches of the early motor car industry.

The motorist with pressure feed had

to rely on either a temperamental air pump attached to the motor to pump air into the tank at the rear, forcing it up front, or do some hand pumping every time the pressure got a bit low in the tank. The slightest air leak in the pressure system meant more frequent pumping, and many a motorist cursed as his car stalled for lack of gas, just when he needed power most.

The Stewart vacuum tank system, providing an amazingly simple and reliable answer to the gasoline feed problem, was developed in the Kissel shops by Webb Jay, a race driver, inventor and engineer. The Kissel Kar, naturally, was the first automobile to adopt it, but the feature became almost instantly popular until practically every motor car made was using the system.

Kissel history would never be complete without mention of Kissel trucks. Kissel had built its first trucks as early as 1908. By 1912 four different truck chassis were offered, with a giant 180-inch wheelbase, five-ton "Dreadnaught" at the top of the list. Kissel made almost every type of truck, some with custom, made to order bodies. There were fire trucks, beer trucks, ambulances, police wagons —you name it. Some of the trucks used the well-tested six-cylinder Kissel engines; for others, Kissel went outside its own shops and used Wisconsin or Waukesha engines.

As World War I began in Europe, Kissel obtained a contract to build trucks for the Greek government, so it was natural that, when the U.S. became involved in the conflict in 1917, a contract for 2,000 trucks would be awarded to an established firm like Kissel. The Army truck, however, was not a Kissel design. It was the famous four-wheel-drive design from the Four Wheel Drive Auto Co., of Clintonville, Wisconsin, which had started out making four-wheel-drive passenger cars.

The first contract was completed, swelling the Kissel work force to its largest point in history, with 1,400 men on the payroll. The Army followed with an additional contract for 1,500 trucks, but by this time the Armistice had been signed, and the second contract was cancelled. Kissel, like other war contractors, was forced to return to the

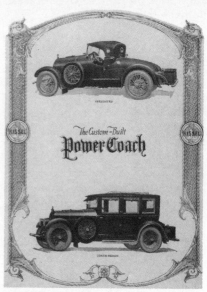

Quoting from this 1921 sales brochure, "Only by riding in a Kissel Power Coach can you appreciate its finality of engineering developments and coach body exclusiveness."

peacetime competition of the marketplace.

By this time Kissel had the reputation for building solid motor car bodies which, when it came to quality of construction, need take a back seat to nothing in the industry. They were not called Gibraltar bodies for nothing. A reporter at the Chicago show had noted it in 1916, when Kissel first introduced the All Year bodies. In writing for *Automobile Topics,* the reporter said: "The All Year Kissel was conspicuous not so much by reason of its immediate development from a pioneer design, as because of its workmanlike construction."

If the Kissel bodies were lacking something, perhaps it was in the styling flair. Then a new figure appeared on the Kissel stage: Conover T. Silver, the New York distributor for Kissel. Silver, whose flair for styling was largely influenced by some of the latest designs from Europe, had already persuaded several other manufacturers to produce models bearing his styling recommendations. After he took on the Kissel line in 1917, he immediately began persuading Kissel management to produce a line of "Kissel-Silver Specials."

Kissel agreed to give it a try. The first three Kissel bodies showing the Silver-

European influence were a seven-passenger touring, a Tourster with just two wide doors, and a Silver Special Speedster. When these models were introduced at the 1918 New York show, they all attracted favorable attention, but it was the speedster which drew all eyes and quickly became the most popular car at the show.

It was easily the most eye-catching, sportiest automobile Kissel had ever produced, and it was destined to carry a nickname that would be remembered for generations to come — the Gold Bug. Kissel, with a solid reputation for quality tucked safely under its belt, had now scored a clean styling triumph.

The Gold Bug name came about through some razzle-dazzle promotion by W.W. ("Brownie") Rowland, automotive editor for the *Milwaukee Journal*, to whom the Kissel company loaned one of the speedsters for his annual tour of Wisconsin highways.

Rowland took off on his tour in a yellow Kissel speedster and, through his column, offered a prize to the reader who would come up with the most appropriate name for the sporty machine. After some 500 entries had been received, "Gold Bug" was announced as the winner.

Rowland also staged a race between the Gold Bug and an airplane, between Marshfield and Milwaukee. The race was a bit of a phony because a handicapping system was used — considering speeds available, road conditions, etc. — and the results were a three-hour head start for the Gold Bug. With this handicap, the Gold Bug won. The Kissel people never boasted much of this victory, but the loud publicity cranked up by Rowland certainly did the Kissel cause no harm—especially when, at the end of his summer tour of 4,978 miles behind the wheel of the Gold Bug, he announced in his column that the doughty machine was "one of the best all around cars in its class."

One unique feature of the speedster was a drawer which pulled out of each side of the body, just to the fore of the rear fender, to reveal extra little jump seats extending beyond the edge of the fender. Such a seat would be impossible from a safety standpoint today, but an eye-catcher it was — and remains even today, when one of these Gold Bugs is displayed at a show.

Meanwhile Silver, who had inspired this sporty styling coup for Kissel, faded out of the picture. Perhaps because the war had curtailed passenger car production, making it impossible to make a good profit, he dropped his Kissel franchise and the Kissel factory took over the New York territory. The styling trend Silver had started, however, was to remain with Kissel for years to come — the years of the most beautiful Kissels. It was during the war, in 1918, when the Kissel brothers decided to drop the name "Kissel Kar." The name, someone suggested, was too German and — during a war against Germany — carried possible connotations reflecting on the patriotism of its makers. The car became, simply, Kissel.

With a new name and a new styling trend, Kissel was ready to move into the post-war era, with the "Roaring Twenties" to come.

The final era: 1920-1930

The hill, they said, was the graveyard of many an ambitious motorist's fondest hopes.

It was Baxter Hill, on the outskirts of Los Angeles. It had one block with a grade of 17 percent rise, followed by another with the devilish rise of 29 percent.

Some drivers just looked at the hill and gave up.

Most drivers were happy if their cars would groan and grunt to the top in low gear.

And here was this crazy character in a Model 55 Kissel, who said he was going to the top in high gear. He promised to carry two passengers, and that the transmission would be locked in high gear.

"We know how you'll do it," a skeptical bystander said. "You'll slip the clutch."

In answer to that one, the man simply took the clutch pedal off!

Then he took off. The well-tuned Kissel engine, bellowing its song of defiance, not only carried the car to the top in high gear, but did so at a speed of 21 miles per hour at the top.

The year was 1923. The Kissel motor car was in the period of its greatest

Kissel coach designs were fashioned a year in advance of production. 1921 Tourster.

achievement.

Another Kissel took a crack at Powell Street Hill in San Francisco, a hill so steep the streetcars had to use cables to climb it. The Kissel made it.

Still another Kissel climbed to the 6,250-foot peak of Yosemite Valley Road, locked in high gear—the first car officially recorded as having done this.

On November 12, 1923, a Kissel 55 phaeton, with standard equipment and driven by H.L. Nicholson, claimed a new record on the Phoenix to Los Angeles run: 694 miles in 20 hours and three minutes, cutting an hour and 15 minutes off the previous record.

Still another record for high speed and long distance travel was claimed for a Kissel: from Los Angeles to San Francisco and return—878 miles in 26 hours and 18 minutes. This time, there was a new gimmick: the Kissel did all this with the transmission locked in second gear.

The purpose of the hill climbs, the races and the record runs was to prove that the Kissel engine would not overheat and could take all that high speed wind-up for hours on end, at top rpm's.

The engine, called the "Custom Built 6-55," had a 5⅛ stroke and 3⁵⁄₁₆ bore, and was rated at 61 bhp. It was the same basic engine design chief engineer Herman Palmer and his crew at Kissel had introduced in 1916.

During the intervening years, there had been changes in bore, stroke, compression, carburetion, manifolds and lubrication, but always with the same basic and reliable six-cylinder, L-head design. The engine had been tested, proved and improved over the years so that from now, in 1922, until the engine was phased

out in 1928, the design had been refined to its highest peak of performance and reliability.

Perhaps the ultimate achievement of this engine came at the Ascot road race where a Kissel, with the chassis shortened by two feet and the engine slightly modified, challenged the best of them. In the elimination trials the Kissel roared across the finish line only six seconds behind the two leaders—a Duesenberg and a Frontenac. This was competition with a vengeance.

In the race proper, a 250-mile run, the gutty Kissel stuck with the leaders again, and was dogging the heels of the Duesenberg and Frontenac until it was involved in two collisions. The car had to go to the pits for repairs, losing vital time and depriving it of any chance of victory.

But they got the Kissel back on the track, and it became one of 19 cars—out of the original 49—to finish the race. It took 11th place, despite the time lost in the pits. At the finish, according to a report made to the factory later, "there was not a car at the track which came through the race which sounded as good or better than the Kissel."

Actually, Kissel management had never made any serious attempts at racing or record runs. The Kissel goal, the managers said in a 1923 salesman's guide, was to build the kind of car a buyer would build for himself if he had his own auto factory.

But the Kissel performances in these hill climbs, endurance runs and races gave a glimpse of what might have been achieved if the Kissel factory had really gone after the glory.

These brilliant performances by the

Kissel 6-55 engine seem to give the lie to a statement published in 1955 by the *Milwaukee Journal,* that "engines were never the Kissel Kar's strong point."

To back up this statement, the *Journal* printed a reported conversation between George Kissel, president of the Kissel Co., and a Kissel dealer who had suggested more emphasis on what was under the hood of the car.

Kissel reportedly replied: "The less said about that, the better."

It was this "legend," never completely confirmed but oft repeated, which has led people to say that Kissel engines were somewhat less than the greatest.

In 1961 Ralph Dunwoodie, of the famed Harrah Collection of old cars, interviewed Herman Palmer, the man who designed and perfected the Kissel engines. Dunwoodie asked Palmer about George Kissel's statement.

Palmer replied that Kissel probably did make the statement, but never meant it to imply that the engines were inferior.

In Palmer's opinion, "...he meant it primarily to mean that in selling, the salesman should capitalize on body design because of their European flair and styling lead in the industry. After all, it is the appearance and lines that attract would-be buyers initially." The Kissel statement, said Palmer, had been twisted to imply that the engines were inferior.

Palmer knew he had designed and produced a good engine and, although he may never have said it himself, outsiders who have studied the Kissel history and know what limited facilities Palmer had to work with, know that the 6-55 engine was an achievement which ranked with the best.

No better proof of this could be found anywhere than in a statement to come many years later from an Australian owner, Henry Berthold, who reported that he had driven his 1928 Kissel 6-55 Speedster 300,000 miles before an engine head cracked.

It was in the field of styling where Kissel held an indisputable lead in the motor car field until near the end of the Kissel motor car venture. It had started with the Kissel speedster, dubbed the Gold Bug, which had "stolen the show" at the New York auto show in 1918.

When Kissel switched back to civilian production after World War I, the company announced it would concentrate on a single chassis, with a 124-inch wheelbase, and phase out the Hundred Point Six. The new "motif" was dubbed the "Custom Built Six," a continuation and expansion of the "Silver Special" line, with a few changes.

Kissel had placed so much emphasis on the All Year transformable bodies that, when the industry began its switch to closed bodies, the company had to struggle to keep up with the trend. In the first months of post-war production, Kissel was still bridging the gap with leftover convertible All Year bodies but, by July, 1920, Kissel was ready with its first real post-war sedan bodies. Again, the new bodies bore the distinctive Kissel touch, with a Staggered Door Sedan which had one door up front on the driver's side and a door in the middle on the other side for the passengers. It was a unique idea.

By the following January, Kissel had begun to catch up, with new sharp-edged bodies which were high style and abreast of the vogue. To add practicality to the short-bodied five-passenger open car, there was a new Tourster with four doors instead of two, and a body which lent even more of the "sports" flavor to the family type car. The car featured individual fenders, aluminum step plates in place of running boards, a low-slung trunk, and two side-mounted spares. This was an eye-catching machine indeed. There was similar treatment for the Gold Bug speedster, with six-wheel design and slicked-up fittings that made the Kissel speedster even more eye appealing.

By July, 1921, Kissel was able to show a sedan with the same sporty lines, including a stagecoach type bustle over the gas tank at the rear. It bore the name "Coach Sedan."

The results of this styling razzle-dazzle paid off when, after a dismal start during the short-lived economic depression following World War I, sales began to climb and reached 2,133 units during 1923. The Kissel cash register was now tinkling on the profit side again, in a healthy spurt which lasted two years.

But the star of the Kissel line during this period was the Gold Bug speedster, which received wide publicity as celebrities, movie stars, and others joined the list of purchasers. They included Al Jolson, Mary Pickford, Douglas Fairbanks, William S. Hart (the cowboy hero), Fatty Arbuckle, Eddie Duchin, Greta Garbo, Rudy Vallee—all very big names in their day, when movies were king. There were purchasers like Amelia Earhart, the famed aviatrix. But the real tribute came when Ralph DePalma, one of the race champions, selected a Kissel as his private car.

The winds of change were blowing in other directions, too, in the auto industry. The years 1923 and 1924 saw a big controversy over four-wheel brakes. When Rickenbacker announced them for 1923, some competitors slapped back with direct advertising, slamming the four-wheel brakes as unsafe.

But it was a trend so strong it could not be held back. Chrysler, late in 1923, announced not only four-wheel brakes but four-wheel hydraulics. The Kissels had always been quick at spotting a trend, and they saw the Chrysler move as the face of the future. Even when Vincent Bendix, creator of the widely used Bendix brakes, appeared personally to present his case for four-wheel mechanical brakes at Kissel, the Kissels said no and opted for hydraulics—first as optional equipment, then as standard.

The hydraulics functioned better than the mechanical four-wheel brakes offered by Packard, Buick, Oakland and Cadillac—in that order—and it was only a few years until almost the entire industry had switched to hydraulics. Once again Kissel had correctly sensed the trend.

The next big change at Kissel — for 1925 — called for a heart-rending decision. It was an era when most of the smaller, independent auto producers largely made what were called "assembled cars," with the producer buying his engines and major parts in the marketplace.

It was not that these parts were not good. There were engine makers such as Lycoming, Continental, Waukesha, Herschel-Spillman and others who had reputations for making sturdy, reliable engines. Often the engines were made to the specifications of the buyers. There were equally good makers of clutches,

transmissions, rear axles, and other parts.

Perhaps some of the faults in assembled cars lay in the fact that such parts, or components, were not always properly mated, or matched, giving less than the best performance and service. In some cases it was the weakness of the bodies or auxiliary parts—made by the makers of the assembled cars — which were less than first rate and caused the assembled cars to earn that "less than the best" reputation.

The tag had been tacked onto Kissel at various times, but Kissel fought back with a vengeance — and with a clear conscience. Kissel catalogs and ads boasted that "ninety-five per cent of our parts are made in the Kissel shops." A brochure published by Kissel showed the step-by-step process by which Kissel engines were manufactured.

In their eagerness to slap down the "assembled" label, around 1920 Kissel ad men began to boast of their "Custom Built" engines and cars. Meanwhile, in truth, Kissel—like General Motors, Nash and other top makers—found it to their advantage to buy some parts from specialized makers.

But using that "custom built" tag made it easier for competitors to use Kissel as a target, and more difficult for Kissel to defend. Kissel did defend the claim by pointing to the solid, careful construction of Kissel bodies, the painstaking assembly, run-ins and breaking-in of the engines to show that what was meant by "custom built" was the method and quality of custom cars.

"It can be said that Kissel builds his motors to Custom-Built standards as every operation in the building and assembling is done with the greatest care for accuracy," one Kissel brochure declared. In this statement, the Kissel claim was nearer to the truth.

The factor which brought about that heartbreaking decision by Kissel was the fact that, in the mid-1920s, the industry —especially above the middle price range — was moving to eight-cylinder engines. Lincoln and Cadillac could boast of exceptionally good V-8 engines, while Packard had a magnificent straight eight. Kissel had refined and improved the 6-55 until it was undoubtedly one of the best sixes in the industry. But time had

The New **KISSEL** $**1485**
Custom Built Phaeton

The 1923 Custom-built Phaeton could go from 5 to 60 miles per hour in 30 seconds " . . . with no vibration point between these speeds . . . ," and sold for $1485.

begun to run out for sixes in the market-place, in the price range above, say, the spot dominated by Buick at lesser cost.

On the other hand, Kissel production at this time was below the 2,000 per year mark, making the Kissel enterprise a small one when compared to Ford or General Motors. Even independents like Dodge, Studebaker, Hudson or Nash were giants by comparison. The costs and facilities for developing a new eight-sylinder engine in the Kissel shops—one that would uphold the tradition of the 6-55—were simply beyond the reach of such a small operation.

There was no other choice. Kissel managers swallowed their pride and selected Lycoming as the basis for a new eight-cylinder engine.

In truth, Kissel did not purchase a complete engine. This would have been too much of a surrender of principles. Instead, it bought an engine block with crankshaft from Lycoming, to which was fitted Kissel's own aluminum cylinder heads, lightweight Lynite pistons and connecting rods, with a special over-sized oil pump and 12-quart aluminum crankcase.

The engine was then assembled in the Kissel shops, but such care was taken in balancing the crankshaft, the pistons and connecting rods that the new Kissel eight engine—to be known as the 8-75—turned out to be a superior engine to the original Lycoming. In fact, it was so perfectly balanced that it became one of the silkiest engines in the industry for smoothness.

Kissel continued to label its car a "custom built" automobile. The fact was, that with all the special parts and special care given to the balancing and assembly of the engine, Kissel could very well claim it as a Kissel engine.

The new Kissel 8-75, the first eight in the Kissel stable, was a good one. Even with wheelbases lengthened to 126, 130, and 136 inches to make room for the longer engine, the new models, especially the 126-inch speedster, were snappy performers. Owners reported they had an easy 85 miles per hour at their command, and not even the highly touted Lincoln V-8, known as one of the fastest cars on the road, could pass the Kissel 8-75 speedsters.

Kissel, in truth, now had two lines in production, for the shops continued to turn out the tested and reliable 6-55—and, according to owner reports, the Kissel sixes made in these last years were the best ever.

But now it was in the Kissel body shops, pride of the Kissel enterprise, where the battle to uphold the Kissel reputation for styling was being fought. To stay abreast of the new trend to all-weather closed bodies, there was a distinctive two-door brougham for 1925. In 1926 there was an "All Year Coupe Roadster," which today would simply be called a convertible. This model, while boasting low, sporty lines, was shorn of frills and sold for prices ranging from $1,695 for the six to $2,095 for the eight. This made the closed model competitive with the open tourings, normally the cheaper models.

It was one of the few times in Kissel

history that Kissel reacted to slower sales by attempting to meet the competition with less car and lower prices. But sales in 1924 had dropped to 803 units, and the company lost money. The new eight, together with the new body styles, boosted sales back up to 2,122 in 1925.

By January, 1927, Kissel took still another step toward meeting the competition by introducing a smaller eight, also with Lycoming block — the 8-65, with dimensions of 2⅞ x 4¾, compared with 3³⁄₁₆ x 4½ for the earlier big eight. Kissel ads, without hesitation, referred to the new car as an "Economy Eight." The new, smaller eight was fitted to the six-cylinder chassis at 125 inches for most models, with 132 inches for the longer sedans. For the 1927 models, wheelbases for the 8-75 stretched to 131 and 139 inches.

When the time came for the 1928 models, the Kissel body shops, still maintaining the Kissel standard of quality and workmanship under Fritz Werner, moved to meet the new trend to higher hoods and lower roof lines. The radiator was raised and narrowed. The low belt line on the closed cars, a distinctive Kissel feature for seven years, was gone. The radiator temperature gauge was moved from the radiator cap to the dashboard. The effect was to give the Kissel bodies a wider, lower look.

Meanwhile Kissel pride, no longer so sensitive, allowed Kissel management to buy a six-cylinder engine from Lycoming too. The famed 6-55, the engine which had made those historic hill climbs and endurance records, had reached the end of its days.

One of the final moves in the engine department was to increase compression and make other refinements in carburetion and manifolds of the big eight until they were able to classify the engines as the 8-90 — for a claimed 90 bhp. Moreover, a limited deluxe edition was bored to 3¼ inches. These were called the "White Eagle Deluxe." For the Speedster Special, the ads claimed "115 horsepower — 100 miles an hour." This was an all-time peak in Kissel performance.

Only 100 Kissel chassis were set aside for the 1928 White Eagle, with that extra muscle in the engine compartment, special luxury fittings and, on the rear of the sedan and tourster models, two rakishly hung spare tires. On the radiator cap was hung a heavy — three-pound — metal eagle, the only time a factory-specified mascot was ever used on a Kissel motor car.

For these special models, prices ranging from $3,185 to $3,885 were asked, compared with a price range of $2,295 to $3,585 for the regular 8-90 series. It was, some said, a hefty price increase for the special fittings and somewhat more powerful engine.

Strangely, despite the apparent exclusiveness of these special models, which should have made them collectors' items from the beginning, only one of the early White Eagles, a brougham sedan, is known to survive today.

For 1929 the Kissels were given a completely new look, and all three lines — both sixes and eights — were called the "White Eagle Series by Kissel." The radiator and hood lines were flatter, wider and higher. An eagle, on a black panel, was embossed across the front of the water tank above the radiator core. The closed bodies had a finely striped, wide beltline. Fenders appeared with long sweeping lines. It was, by judgment of many connoisseurs of fine cars, the most beautiful that Kissel had ever made.

Meantime, behind this facade of new models, engines and styling, was the slow, steady march of financial disaster. It was now stalking Kissel as it had stalked so many of the well-known makes in the industry — especially the smaller independents, which had not been able to keep up in the burgeoning age of mass production.

In earlier years Kissel management had boasted of small production, saying it had never been their intention to produce numbers but to build a car as an owner himself would want to build it, then sell it for a price to cover the costs of such manufacture. But the time had come when the engineers in the shops of the mass producers were able to guarantee a considerable level of quality built into even the cars that were turned out by the hundreds of thousands.

Thus, when the mass producers were able to build cars of comparative, or nearly comparative, quality — such cars

as Buick, Chrysler, Nash, Studebaker —
and sell them in the marketplace for
prices far below Kissel prices, was it any
wonder that Kissel sales and fortunes
began to falter?

One of the major factors in this squeeze
on the small, independent producers was
the growing use of gigantic presses to
stamp out body parts by the thousands.
Only the giant producers could afford
these monster machines. Kissel never
owned one, but beat out the body parts
by hand or by trip hammer—a slow, expensive and time-consuming process.
Before the 1929 models, the Kissel
fenders were rolled on the company's
own novel fender rollers—a once good
method, but no longer competitive.

In the early years Kissel fortunes had
risen rapidly, and the Kissel Kar had once
ranked among the top seven. Then came
the middle years, when quality, innovations and reliability kept the company
going. There was the brief, heady success of the Hundred Point Six in 1916-
1918, which set a Kissel record of 4,000
units for the 1917 model year. World War
I—with big orders for trucks—also had
given the company a financial boost.

The first hint of disaster came on the
heels of that war when, just as Kissel and
other manufacturers were struggling to
convert to peacetime production, a short
but crippling economic depression
struck. When this financial crisis hit in
1921, inventory values dropped so
sharply that Kissel managers were forced
to go to the mortgage markets for help
—for the first time in Kissel history. The
company at this time was sound enough,
and had assets enough, that it had little
trouble getting the $750,000 in bonds
needed to get momentum started again.

As the short depression ended, so did
Kissel troubles — for a time. The production total rose to 2,024 in 1923. Then
sales dropped again, to revive slightly in
1925. But by 1926, a slow but certain
decline had set in:
• 1,972 units in 1926
• 1,147 in 1927
• 1,068 in 1928, the year that the 1929
  White Eagles were brought out
• 889 in 1929.

Then came disaster. Sales were down
to 221 in 1930. A new, far greater, economic depression had begun, destined
to kill many a bigger producer than Kis-

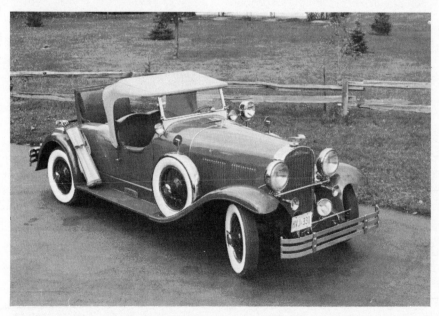

One of the best-known KisselKars is the 1929 Kissel White Eagle Speedster 8-126. This was one of two
Eagles in the Harrah's auto collection, which was purchased by Ron Fawcell in 1978, and totally
restored.

sel. In Kissel's final calendar year, production of passenger cars was down to 93 cars, 16 of them so-called 1931 models.

There was, in addition, some production of taxicabs, funeral coaches and commercial vehicles. In the last years, Kissel had relied more on this type of vehicle to keep employees at work and the production lines going. It had not been enough. By 1929 and 1930, the banks would lend no more money.

In March, 1930, when the handwriting was on the wall for all to see, George Kissel entered into a contract with Archie Andrews, promoter of New Era Motors, and the ill-fated front-wheel-drive Ruxton, to produce 1,500 Ruxtons annually, plus a handful of Kissels. In return, the Kissel Motor Car Co. was to receive $250,000 in new financing. The contract was never carried out, on either side. The details are another story but, in short, to keep Kissel from falling completely into the hands of Andrews, the Kissel brothers asked that the company be placed in receivership. It was.

By this time, the economic depression had taken a hand. It was a depression destined to be far more severe, and to last much longer, than that short depression in 1921. In the atmosphere of financial tragedy which struck the country in 1929, it was impossible to salvage even a fraction of the value of the remaining Kissel assets.

Reorganized as Kissel Industries, the company did make a small comeback, making industrial engines, parts for auto accessory houses, furniture, oil burners and, eventually, outboard motors. A war contract, on the eve of World War II, gave the company a new lease on life until 1942, when George Kissel, the most active force behind the Kissel Motor Co., died suddenly. His brother Will was unwilling to keep it going, and the company was sold.

Thus came the end of a distinctive venture into the motor car field—a vigorous one with a German aura of quality, solidity, tradition and a complete unwillingness to compromise with shortcuts or cheapness.

Today the Kissel name evokes, perhaps, little nostalgia on the part of the general public — especially to those of later generations. Only to those who know the Kissel story comes the lift of spirit, a slight quickening of the heartbeat, when they attend an old car show and hear the throbbing chug of that sturdy 6-55 engine, or catch a glimpse of one of those creatures of Kissel's greatest glory: a Gold Bug speedster or a White Eagle.

At such a moment the whole panorama is there, alive, and it is difficult to tell this afficianado that there will not be Kissels forever.

V
PACKARD

The birth of a thoroughbred: 1899-1914

There it stood, the newborn creature. It was somewhat spindly in the legs, perhaps, and a bit trembly at the knees, like a newborn colt in its first tentative steps.

There are men, born and schooled to the breeding of fine horses, who insist they can see in the lines of a newborn colt the promise of future greatness—the lines of a thoroughbred.

But this was no colt. This was a primitive automobile, born of a new age: the age of the motor car, in its first tentative years. The spindly machine, standing there on November 6, 1899, at No. 2 High Street in Warren, Ohio, was the first Packard.

It is doubtful that anyone present at that moment had the vision or the boldness to predict the great history which lay ahead for the Packard name. Who, in 1899, could see the long line of proud, smooth, powerful motor cars of the future to bear that name?

It would be the motor car of presidents and kings; the prized possession of men of wealth and distinction; the car of pomp and parades; the most prestigious motor car in America during the first half century of the motor age—and, in many respects, the best.

Even without this vision of the greatness to come, it is safe to say there was a certain cocksure confidence present when the first Packard was born. James Ward Packard knew very well what he was doing when he directed the creation of this machine.

He was an engineer, a graduate of Lehigh University with a degree in mechanical engineering. He had already become a highly succesful manufacturer in the field of electrical cables and equipment. Early in the 1890s he had toyed with the idea of creating a motor car and in 1893, together with a friend, had drawn sketches of such a machine.

"Packard 'Thirty' Runabout — 1908"

He and his brother, William Doud Packard, had a three-wheeled French De-Dion-Bouton, brought back from Europe after a trip.

With his engineer's mind, Packard had already examined this machine and made mental note of things that needed improving. The Packard brothers also purchased one of the early products of Alexander Winton, a bright star in the field of automobile manufacturing at that time.

It was the Winton automobile which provided the impetus for the Packard project.

According to one version of the story, in attempting to drive it the 50 miles from the factory in Cleveland to Warren, the machine immediately began to bear evidence of faulty construction. The engine overheated and the drive chain broke. Packard suffered the ultimate ignominy of motorists in that age when he arrived home behind a team of horses on the tow bar. It was after this initial, ill-fated trip that Packard resolved to make a few suggestions to Alexander Winton.

Another version has it that the Packard brothers drove the Winton a year before they felt qualified to give their engineering opinion of the machine. James Packard may have been full of good

The Packard Motor Car, Model K, 25 Brake Horse Power.

intentions when he decided to have his say; Winton might value the judgement of a fellow engineer.

The bristly Winton's response, however, was of another kind.

"If you are so smart, Mr. Packard," he said, "why don't you make a car yourself?"

"I will," replied Packard, and he did.

Some historians say the Winton episode played no part in the creation of the first Packard. Others insist that it did. But the incident undoubtedly took place, and gave birth to a magnificent legend, if not to the Packard itself — or, rather, the "Ohio," for the first automobiles built for sale by the Packard brothers were the products of the Ohio Automobile Co. It was not until 1903 that the firm was reorganized as the Packard Motor Car Company.

Whether or not the Winton snub fired the Packard project, when the Packard brothers set about to produce their first automobile, their methods may have been calculated to do Winton the most harm. They started by hiring two of Winton's best men—George L. Weiss and W.A. Hatcher — out from under Winton's nose. Weiss had helped organize the Winton Company. Hatcher had been Winton's shop superintendent. If this was vengeance, it was vengeance with a sting.

A workshop shed was set aside at the Packard firm, and the men went to work.

The first machine, the Model A, was more or less typical of the spidery, buggy-like machines being built at that time, with a single cylinder, 5½ x 6 engine rated at 12 hp (some sources say 9 hp). Like most cars of the day, it was tiller

steered and chain driven.

Packard's resolve to make a better car than the Winton was evident in subsequent models. In 1900 Packard introduced the steering wheel and an automatic spark advance which other cars would not have for years to come. Not far behind was the H-slot gear shift, also to be copied by other makers.

Above all, the mark of Packard's "better car" was the sturdy construction and reliability built into even the earliest machines. In 1901 Packard entered five of his cars in a New York to Buffalo endurance run and, although the majority of the other cars broke down before the finish, all five Packards crossed the finish line.

Perhaps mindful of the snubbing he got from Winton, Packard took aim at records set by Winton cars and smashed them. When a Winton set a new record for a transcontinental crossing in 1903, a one-cylinder Model F Packard, piloted by Tom Fetch, set out to beat it. Despite almost insurmountable obstacles and impossible weather, the Packard did exactly that — knocking three days off the Winton record.

A year later, when the Winton Bullet set a new speed record on the sands of Daytona, a Packard immediately knocked 8.8 miles off that record.

But this is getting a bit ahead of the story. It was back in 1901 when another legendary "happening" took place that brought into the company a man who would play a bigger role in the destiny of Packard than the Packard brothers themselves.

He was Henry Bourne Joy, the son of a railway magnate, who not only had money and position but was keenly interested in seeing America produce quality automobiles that could compete on an even footing with the European imports which had dominated the scene to this point.

Joy had visited the New York automobile show in 1901 with the intention of buying a steam automobile. He was inspecting one of the steam cars, the story goes, when a pressure gauge on the car burst, showering him and a friend with hot water. The unscheduled shower cooled Joy's ardor for steam.

Joy then turned his attention to one of the well-built Packard gasoline autos at the show, and was inspecting this machine when a fire engine roared past. The driver in charge of the Packard gave one jerk at his crank and popped away in pursuit of the fire engine, leaving Joy behind.

That quick start so impressed Joy that he decided he would like to own one of these machines. He journeyed to Warren, Ohio, where he not only met the Packard makers but joined them. Joy said he could see a bright future for the well-built machines, and was willing to put his money where his mouth was.

Joy induced friends and relatives to join him in investing a quarter of a million dollars in the Packard enterprise, to build a factory that could produce the machines. Joy joined the newly organized company, which soon became the Packard Motor Car Co., as vice president and general manager.

Although James Ward Packard remained on the scene as president, it was Joy who dominated the company and had the heavier hand in the making of policy. It was a strange picture: that of a man, Packard, who brought into being a bright star on the automobile horizon, gave the car his name, then retired to the wings to allow other people to play center stage.

One of the first decisions made by Joy and the new investors from Detroit was to move the Packard Motor Car Company to Detroit. The Packard brothers, with their ties in Warren, withdrew more and more from active participation in the activities of the firm—first William, and later James.

Other changes were taking place too. While James Packard had been more or less satisfied with the old one-cylinder design, which had proved so reliable, improving it from year to year, Joy was dreaming of twins or quadruplets. An engineer was needed to design the new multiple cylinder machines, so in 1903 Joy brought into the firm a French engineer, Charles Schmidt, who had helped design prize-winning race cars in France.

Joy immediately put Schmidt's talents to use in that field. In 1904, winning automobile races was the accepted way of gaining publicity, prestige and buyers for any make of car. Henry Ford had challenged Winton, the leader, with his monstrous "Old 999." He had won fame for the Ford name that way. Now Joy planned to assault the ramparts of the giants too, with a Packard entry. He put Schmidt to work at the drawing boards for the first four-cylinder Packard engine.

The result was the Packard "Gray Wolf."

When Schmidt first appeared with his Gray Wolf at the race tracks, many spectators were tempted to laugh. Most race cars in those days were monstrous affairs, with pistons big as buckets, weighing 2,400 pounds and up, with horsepower ratings from 80 to 90.

The sleek little Packard was streamlined at a time when people didn't think of streamlining, but what really set the new entry apart was its size. It weighed only 1,310 pounds and had a motor rated at only 24 hp. But Schmidt had already learned what race and sports car design engineers were to learn many years later: it was not always brute horses on the crankshaft that won. A small, light car, properly balanced and designed, could get by with a lot less horses.

The little car immediately began giving a good account of itself, often winning against cars with more than twice its power. It was entered in the 1904 Vanderbilt Cup race in New York, which lured some of the famed race cars from Europe. The tiny Gray Wolf was the surprise of the show. It took fourth place, finishing ahead of many of the big European cars, in a triumph of major proportions for the little American upstart.

It was the Gray Wolf that smashed the

Winton speed record at Daytona.

Still later that year, 1904, Schmidt took the wheel of a stock Packard Model L, with an engine based on the same design as that in the Gray Wolf, and set a new record for an endurance run. He turned 1,000 consecutive laps of a one-mile race track at Grosse Point, Michigan, at an average speed of 33.5 mph.

At this point, Alexander Winton—after suffering defeats at the hands of Ford and Packard — withdrew from the racing circuits. Perhaps he was regretting that hasty remark five years earlier, when he challenged the Packard brothers to "show me."

The Packard flag flew high on the race track, but things were not quite that rosy at the factory. Schmidt's first new model for the company, said to be the first four-cylinder production car in America, was the ungainly appearing Model K. This hastily designed car was patterned after the heavy European machines, but it was expensive to make and sold for $7,500. The infant company lost $200,000 in getting the car into production, and sales were slow.

A blooper of this size would have meant bankruptcy for most struggling auto factories of that day. Dozens were falling by the trailside, unable to produce machines of quality or to get them sold. James Packard would probably have been willing to call it quits. After all, he had proved the point that he could make a reliable automobile.

But Joy was an incurable optimist — and he, together with his friends, had the money to back their optimism. Instead of closing, Joy slapped a mortgage on the Packard plant, borrowed $250,000, and brought out the Model L.

This car used basically the same engine as the K, but somewhat smaller. Most important, the Model L was the first car which looked like a Packard — resembling, to a recognizable degree, the automobiles as we know them today. For the first time, the famed Packard creased hood appeared. Production costs had been pared so that the car could be put on the market at $4,850, several thousand dollars less than the K.

Sales and production began to soar. Although only 33 of the Model K cars had been made, production on the L climbed

Packard Model C — 1903

to 250. The following year, with a new and improved model, the N, Packard was able to reduce the price still further — to $3,500—and production almost doubled, to 481 units. Now the profits were rolling in.

In 1907 appeared the most famous Packard of this period: the Model 30, so-called for its 30 hp engine, a hefty 5 x 5½ machine. Production soared well past the thousand mark, and the company showed a profit of $1,000,000. This was a profit four times as great as the gamble taken in 1904. By 1909 the Packard Motor Car Company showed gross receipts of $15,000,000. It was now one of the major producers of automobiles in America, and its reputation was of the best — based on the solid, reliable performance of well-built Packard automobiles. These machines allowed the company to boast, "Ask the man who owns one." It was a unique sales slogan. Men asked, and they bought.

The year 1909 was historic also as the year in which Henry Ford introduced his Model T, "The People's Car." The Model T, introduced at $850, was deliberately aimed at the mass market. Ford's target was also a unique one. He set about to create a mass market, to create the motor age—and he did.

Packards at this time were selling for prices ranging from $3,200 to $4,200. The men behind the company — the Packard brothers, Joy and his compatriots who invested money in the company — were not the type of men who had a burning desire to produce a "people's car."

Their goal was to bring American industry into its own; to produce cars of an equal quality with the European

The 1912 Packard "30" Limousine

models, for men of position and wealth. It is unlikely that they even considered the proposition of a car in every working man's garage. America was a young and prospering country. There were enough people in the "carriage trade" class to assure a highly profitable market for a car like the Packard.

But changes were taking place at the management level, too. The man who had created the first Packard and gave a fine motor car its name, James Ward Packard, had dropped more and more to the rear. By 1909 he was ready to turn the presidency over to Joy and return to his quiet life in Warren.

Joy himself was ready to bring other figures into the burgeoning company. The biggest name to join Packard in this period was Alvan J. Macauley, destined to play a key role in the next great chapters of Packard's history.

Macauley, a graduate of Lehigh and George Washington universities, had been a patent attorney and general manager of the Burroughs Adding Machine Company before Joy lured him to Packard to take over as general manager. Macauley brought with him Jesse G. Vincent, an engineer—perhaps one of the greatest engineers the American motor industry was to see in its first half century.

Packard evolution up to this point had followed—or, more probably, led—the course of the motor car industry. Most authorities agree that production of the early, one-cylinder models had been extremely limited.

• There was a single Model A, the first spidery creature.

• Three Model B's were produced.

• Five Model C's pioneered the steering wheel and the automatic spark control.

• The Model F, Old Pacific, was the car that blazed a trail of glory for the Packard name by setting the historic cross-continent record.

Then came the ill-fated Model K, in the 1903-1904 period. It had been claimed that this was the first four-cylinder production car in America, but with only 33 examples, it could hardly be called "production."

After that, there was the Model L, the success story, then the Models N and S before the famed Model 30.

The Model 30—with a smaller sister, the Model 18, introduced during a short-lived depression to cut prices — remained the backbone of production.

Until the advent of the Model 30, Packard had more or less followed the industry practice of producing one or two basic models. The touring car was the standard bearer. But by 1911, the Model 30 was available in seven body styles.

There were touring and runabout styles, at $4,200, a phaeton, brougham, coupe, limousine and a regal limousine imperial priced at $5,600. The Packard crest had begun to take on the regal bearing of a queen. The coachwork, perhaps a bit more ornate than functional, was among the finest to be seen at the New York automobile show. Even the cheaper Model 18 retained as standard equipment on the closed models a speaking tube and dome light. It could hardly be called a "people's car."

By 1911 Packard had grown to 6,000 employees, with factories covering 33 acres of floor space. The time had come for still another step forward.

This was the period when a "great controversy" raged in the press and the technical publications: the battle of the "fours versus the sixes." Everyone from the mechanic up to the engineers and company presidents argued whether six-cylinder engines were really better than the fours.

At Packard, the switch to the six came without great fanfare in 1912. There were two of them at first: a smaller $4\frac{1}{8}$ x $5\frac{1}{2}$, and a larger $4\frac{1}{2}$ x $5\frac{1}{2}$ rated at 48 hp, with wheelbases up to 138 inches. By 1914 wheelbases stretched to 140 inches and 18 body styles were available.

Packard engineering advances remained abreast with the times. By 1913 Packard engines had forced feed lubrication and electric starters, and followed the trend to the left-hand drive. Electric lights with dimmers, and shock absorbers, were standard equipment. Packard introduced the combination foot-hand throttle controls which other cars later copied.

There were other, less spectacular improvements from year to year, in steering gear, spring suspension, and the growing quality of the coachwork. Packard had some of the finest crafts-

men in the country on its payroll.

Perhaps the single feature which kept buyers coming back to Packard showrooms was an intangible one: quality. The Packard was not only a "gentleman's car," but was of such rugged construction it was well nigh indestructible. It was a combination — fine appointments and ruggedness—which could not fail in an era when breakdowns on the road were still, more often than not, the rule rather than the exception. The cry of "Get a horse" could still be heard by motorists unfortunate enough to land beside the road with a breakdown.

The Twin Six era: 1915-1925

*P*ackard labored, and brought forth twins.

Perhaps it would be more accurate to say that Jesse G. Vincent labored, and produced the twins.

In any case, most auto historians agree that it was one of the most significant events of automobile history, either before or after 1915. The first 12-cylinder engine — an unbelievably compact piece of machinery which, until they saw it, many considered impossible — was officially born in June of 1915.

Henry B. Joy, president of the Packard Motor Car Co., was unabashed in his jubilant announcement of the new creation. "The greatest piece of machinery that ever went onto the highways and the most luxurious carriage," he exclaimed.

Ad flacks working for the company praised "The heavenly twins who have smoothed the earth and made it smaller."

Hidden behind all the pomp and circumstance which announced the delivery of the "Twin Six" to a somewhat speechless automobile world was the

engineer who was responsible for it all, Jesse Vincent. Even his most envious rivals were forced to agree that Packard had managed to capture one of the greatest geniuses the automobile world had ever seen.

Even today it would be difficult to find a mechanical engineer who could match the achievements of this man who never attended high school.

The 12-cylinder bombshell Jesse Vincent created in 1915 was only a beginning.

- *To prove it was no fluke, Vincent played a key role in the creation of the great Liberty aircraft engine of the World War I era.*
- *He created the Twin Six that won world records on land, at sea and in the air. At one time Vincent-designed Packard engines held more records than any other engine ever built.*
- *He created the Packard Twelve during the 1930s.*
- *His genius was also felt in World War II, when great Packard V-12 engines —which still bore the imprint of Vincent's hands—powered the famed PT boats of that conflict.*

The history of the automobile is really two stories: that of the automobiles, and that of the men who created them. Some of these men left their mark by their ability to organize great industrial empires to sell their products. Then there are those — the real heroes, perhaps — whose mechanical genius was such that

they were able to create the machines which made it all possible. The ones who truly stand tall in the crowd are few indeed: a few like Henry Leland, Henry Ford, or Jesse Vincent.

Vincent started his career at the turn of the century as a clerk in a hay and grain commission firm in Pana, Illinois. These

According to company advertising, this 1912 seven-passenger Packard Eight " . . . will out-perform any stock car in the world. This is the conservative statement of a conservative company."

were the days when hay and oats, rather than gasoline and oil, were the motive power which turned the wheels on American roads.

But the age of the machine was being born and somewhere, stirring in the brain of the youthful oats clerk, was the turning of gears and wheels rather than hoofbeats. He abandoned the oats and hay to take a job with a firm of St. Louis engineers, working on developing an adding machine.

Although Vincent had only an eighth grade education, as far as formal schooling was concerned, it became apparent to the adding machine engineers that they had a mechanical genius on their hands.

One of Vincent's first inventions was a method, and the machines, to bore a whole series of tiny holes at once in the adding machine mechanism — all in a single, precision operation. In almost no time, the young man was promoted over the heads of college-trained engineers to become superintendent of the plant.

The adding machine was fast becoming a necessary adjunct to the industrial age, and it was only a short time until Vincent and his team of engineers moved to Detroit to join the Burroughs Adding Machine Company.

Making adding machines was not really the kind of preparation a man needed to design motor car engines, but Vincent had the kind of brain that soaked up mechanical information like a blotter.

The top Burroughs executives had bought examples of the first primitive automobiles—the balky, unreliable machines being built at the turn of the century. The youthful engineer quickly fell in love with the snorting, new-fangled monsters, and appointed himself as superintendent of the company garage, working at night and in his spare time to teach himself the mysteries of pistons, gears and valves.

He bought a machine of his own, and it was not long before Vincent knew as much, or more, about the machines than the men who had built them.

The chain of circumstances which brought Vincent to Packard started with decisions made by Henry Joy. Like James Packard before him, Joy decided—after he had built Packard into a great corporation making great cars — that he was ready to turn active management over to other hands.

Joy spotted Alvan Macauley, who was general manager at the Burroughs Company, and lured him into taking the same job at Packard. Macauley came up with the idea of taking Vincent with him. He knew of Vincent's interest in motor cars, and he decided that, together, they might make some startling history in the automotive field. This was prophetic vision indeed.

In 1910, when Macauley turned up in the post of general manager of the burgeoning Packard plant, it was not long until Vincent was installed as vice president of engineering. Packard now had the manager and the engineer destined to fabricate some notable chapters in the history of the automobile.

Somewhere along the line, Vincent provided himself with an addition to his formal education by zipping through the engineering course of the International Correspondence School. Just before joining Packard, he spent some time in the engineering department at the Hudson Motor Car Company, under the tutelage of another great automotive engineer of that day, Howard E. Coffin.

In his first years at Packard, Vincent spent his time smoothing out the bugs and making improvements in the famed Packard Model 38 and 48 engines, which helped boost them into a spot among the most powerful, most reliable and smoothest six-cylinder engines then being produced.

Early in 1915, at a board meeting, the chief engineer announced, "Gentlemen, I have something to read."

There was nothing boring about sitting through the reading of Vincent's 35-page engineering report because these were no ordinary men, and this was no ordinary report. The men were dedicated to the job of producing the finest motor cars in the country, and the report included the plans for an engine which made them sit up with astonishment—a 12-cylinder, V-type engine: the Twin Six.

Most of the auto proponents of that age were still arguing about the relative merits of the fours versus the sixes. Few of them had advanced to the point of considering a straight eight. But here, exploding from the 35-page report, was the proposal for a twelve! Was it possible? Was it practical?

Sitting around the conference table were executives with enough confidence in their chief engineer to give the word, "Go ahead."

The Twin Six started with another invention of Vincent's—that of having expert pattern makers create the first model out of wood to save time. Within 24 hours, a crew of wood craftsmen were turning Vincent's blueprints into a real model.

From there, the job progressed to the casting and milling of gears, crankshafts, connecting rods, cylinder blocks and pistons of a shape and pattern never seen before.

If any word of what was going on in the Packard shops leaked out, the chances were that few people believed it. A tale bearer with word of a 12-cylinder engine would probably have been hooted off the streets.

Besides, it all happened so fast. Only 10 weeks after the day Vincent read his report, the first Packard experimental automobile powered with the fabulous new engine was already on the test track, undergoing road tests.

Thus, when the word became official that Packard was about to place a 12-cylinder engine on the market, the news caught most automobile experts with their jaws hanging open in surprise.

To remain historically correct, it is necessary to point out that Vincent's Twin Six was not actually the first 12-cylinder engine ever made. Jonathan D. Maxwell, of Maxwell-Briscoe fame, had built a 12-cylinder engine as early as 1903, and managed to make it run. But he was never able to solve carburetor and balance problems, and the engine was not successful.

In 1909 George Schebler, of carburetor fame, designed a V-12 which he drove for several years. It was an unusual design, with the second set of connecting rods grafted onto the sides of the primary rods, instead of having all connecting rods riding bearings on the crankshaft itself. It was also designed to run on either set of six cylinders. You could switch half the motor off to save gas when the going was easy. But this engine also had bugs in it, and was never put into production.

If any inventor wishes to claim a "first" in any field, he really should produce a practical machine adaptable to production and reliable use. By such standards Vincent, with his Twin Six, brought to the automobile world its first 12-cylinder automobile engine.

National and Weidely quickly imitated Packard, with 12-cylinder engines of their own introduced within a year after the Packard bombshell, but neither of these engines came near to matching the performance, reliability and success of the Packard engine. Cadillac decided to stick to its new V-8 design until many years later.

By 1915 the Packard name had become synonymous with great cars. When word of the new engine reached the marketplace, men with cash in their wallets just naturally assumed that if the

"Twin Six" bore the Packard name, it must be good. They lined up to buy. By the end of the first year, more than 10,000 of the multi-cylinder machines had been produced.

By the time production of the multi-cylinder Twin Six ended in 1923, more than 35,000 of the great Packards had been sold.

One of the features of the new engine which took many of the automobile experts by surprise was its compact size. Most of the auto writers who went to the shows to look at the new machine expected to find a gigantic engine, an automobile with an enormous, outsized hood.

Instead, they found the new Packard engine installed under the same hood that had previously covered the six—only six inches shorter! This was made possible by Vincent's use of a 60 degree angle between the engine blocks, compared to the 90 degrees used in the V-8's of the day.

One reporter for the *Automobile Trade Journal* refused to believe a 12-cylinder engine was under the hood until he lifted the bonnet and took a look. "The twelve cylinders are there all right," he admitted in his story. The *Journal* devoted three full pages to the announcement of the Twin Six.

But the new engine had other unique features, too. There were aluminum pistons, an innovation which reduced the weight of all moving parts and reduced

vibration to the point where test drivers, after a trial run in the new car, wrote: "It is as smooth as an electric automobile."

Test reporters amazed their readers with the story of throttling the Twin Six down to three miles per hour in high gear and then accelerating, smoothly and without a shudder or shifting gears, from three to 30 miles per hour in 12 seconds.

The new engine had only a three inch bore compared with the 4½ of the six it had replaced. In fact, with 12 cylinders, the new machine had only 414 cubic inches, or only 10 inches more than the six it replaced.

The engine horsepower rating, at 85 bhp, may sound somewhat timid when one considers the 300 and 400 hp V-8's of later days. But this was 1915, when 40 or 45 hp automobiles were considered high-powered cars.

Still another change in the new machine was the transmission. For a number of years, it had been a Packard trademark for the gear box to be attached to the rear axle but in the Twin Six, the gear box was attached to the rear of the clutch housing.

The machine was introduced in two models: the 1-35 and the 1-25. The first was on a longer, 135-inch wheelbase; the second on a shorter, 125-inch base. It was offered in 13 basic body styles for the bigger car and nine for the smaller model,

1927 advertising art showing the Eight's power plant — one engine that was built to be seen as well as driven.

with prices ranging from $2,600 for the 1-25 runabout to $4,600 for the 1-35 limousine imperial. This was a far cry from the Model T Ford being offered in 1915 for $440.

By the time the Twin Six had reached its final series in the early 1920s, prices had climbed as high as $7,750 for a coupe duplex, $7,900 for a limousine, and a healthy $8,000 for a sedan duplex. These may not have been the most expensive automobiles being produced in the U.S. at this time, but they were close to it. One thing was certain: they were the most sought after, the most sold, and the most succesful of all cars in the so-called "gentleman's car" class.

Twin Six cars found their way to Russia, where Czar Nicholas rode in a model equipped with skis on the front and a special chain traction gear for the rear, to navigate the snows of the bitter Russian winter. Packards were bought and used by royal families in Spain, Yugoslavia and Japan, where mechanics lost control of a Twin Six which landed in the moat at the royal palace. The Belgian king had a whole stable of Packards. An armored model costing $35,000 was made for Chang Tso-Lin, a Chinese warlord in Manchuria.

The full impact of the success of the Vincent-designed Twin Six can best be appreciated when one considers what this engine accomplished. During World War I, when America desperately needed a high-powered aircraft engine to gain supremacy in the air, it was the famed Liberty engine, largely designed by Vincent and derived from the Twin Six pattern, which provided the answer. Even though it appeared too late in the war to have a major impact, aircraft for years afterward still used the big Liberty.

A special Packard with an engine derived from the same design, with Ralph DePalma at the wheel, set a new world record for the flying mile in 1919, at 148.875 mph.

In the same year, a Packard with the same engine was entered in the 500-mile race at Indianapolis. It was leading the pack when a broken front wheel bearing forced DePalma into the pits for a long stop, which cost him his chance at victory. He still managed to finish in sixth place, and the big engine never faltered.

This was a more than creditable showing for a new machine, running against proven racing machines.

On water, it was Gar Wood and his series of Miss America boats, powered by Packard engines, which shattered world records. These Packard-powered boats won 10 of 13 Gold Cup races in which they were entered.

In the air Packard engines, based on the basic Vincent design, set equally impressive records. A Navy PN19, equipped with such Packard engines, established seven world records.

But this was not the complete Packard story. Macauley replaced Joy as president of the company in 1916. The new president, in charge during most of the Twin Six era, was destined to guide the company through its days of greatest glory — through the age of the classics, still to come.

By 1920, despite the success and reputation of the Twin Six, Packard executives decided it was time to start thinking of other machines. Perhaps it was time to produce a smaller machine again. Certainly, a straight six-cylinder engine was much easier and less expensive to build than the impressive twelves.

Thus, the "Single Six" appeared, with a 54 hp engine with dimensions of $3\frac{3}{8}$ x $4\frac{1}{2}$. The cheapest touring model bore a price tag of $2,350, which placed it in an entirely different class than the big Twin Sixes. It was called the Model 116, based on a wheelbase of that many inches.

Twin Six production, meanwhile, continued until 1924, when it was phased out in favor of still another new engine which Vincent and his staff had produced. This was the first Packard straight eight, which appeared in 1923.

Packard lovers with a memory of the stark simplicity of the big straight eight engines used by the company for so many years may consider the use of a straight eight to replace a glamorous twelve as a retreat from greatness.

But Vincent and his men had learned some new engineering facts during the eight production years of the Twin Six. It was now possible to produce the same smoothness, the same performance, the same power from a straight eight design that they had been producing with the complex twelve.

Packard's presentation of the 1927 Six 5-26 Phaeton.

An eight with a design of such simplicity and ruggedness was not only much easier and cheaper to build, but also was capable of surpassing the record of dependability set by the Twin Six. The new straight eight was a design which was to remain in production, without major changes, for 33 years.

In a sense, the new Packard engine was a first, too. As in the case of the twelve, it was not the first straight eight engine ever built. Engineers had been trying to make a successful straight eight since 1903. But these early machines suffered from "crankshaft whip," and there had been balancing problems. Nobody had been able to produce one that would stand the pressure of the marketplace until the early 1920s, when several successful straight eight racing machines appeared, including a Duesenberg.

It was at this time that Vincent and his staff were working the bugs out of their straight eight design. When the new Packard engine was introduced to the public in June, 1923, it was the first successful machine of this design to be placed in series production by a major manufacturer.

The first model, with dimensions of 3⅜ x 5, developed 84 bhp — which meant that, despite its smaller size (358 cubic inches, compared to 414 for the Twin Six it replaced), it was producing virtually the same horsepower. Nobody could argue with that kind of statistic.

Another factor which may have helped development of the new eight was the severe economic depression which struck the country in the early 1920s, which made price a factor even for a Packard. With introduction of the new engine, Packard was able to drop prices at least $500 for most models.

When the new Packard eight appeared, it also offered the innovation of four-wheel brakes, again a first for any major production company. Other makes quickly followed suit, so that by 1925 most American cars had brakes on all four wheels—except Ford, who held out until 1927.

By 1925, with the country once more on the road to economic boom, Packard was the indisputable leader in the field of prestige cars. No other manufacturer could match its reputation or its success. While other makers of luxury cars faded away, one by one, Packard grew richer and stronger.

Now Packard was moving into the era of the classics.

The Classic Period: 1925-1939

I*n the summer of 1932 a long, sleek limousine stood parked at the curb in front of a Manhattan hotel, attracting a small crowd of admirers who stopped to look at its impressive beauty.*

A chauffeur stepped out of the hotel and slipped behind the wheel of the big car. Suddenly, without the sound of a starter or the clashing of gears, the big car glided away from the curb in a movement so silent it left the onlookers open mouthed in surprise.

Was this a new steam automobile, or an electric?

No, it was the new Packard Twin Six —reincarnated. In its rebirth, it was more powerful, smoother and vastly more silent, with automatic valve lash adjusters.

The chauffeur had been indulging in a play of vanity. He had left the motor running, so silently that no one standing there had been aware it was still turning. It was a trick one could pull off only with a Packard.

For the second time in its 33-year history, Packard had made automotive news with a Twin Six. The first time was in 1915, when the sheer impact of a 12-cylinder engine was enough to set the automotive industry on its ear. The second time was in the depths of the country's most brutal economic depression.

The early years of the 1930s were a time when the creation of multi-cylindered cars was part of a gut-ripping battle by the luxury car makers—Packard, Marmon, Cadillac, Pierce-Arrow, Duesenberg, Lincoln, Franklin—to keep their grip on a share of the prestige car market which was slipping away from all of them.

Packard entered the depression in front of the parade. For more than two decades it had been the odds-on leader in the field of "gentlemen's cars," outselling its nearest competitors by a margin of two or three to one.

Before the depression began, the prestige car market had been at least 10 percent of total automobile sales — enough to keep alive a lusty family of great names in motor cars. That market had suddenly slipped to two percent, or even less. It was a situation where everyone in the game, inevitably, was a loser—including Packard.

The only winners were people of the future, of the 1950s and beyond, who became collectors of fine old cars that would be called classics. These people were lucky, indeed, to find one of the luxury cars built in the late 1920s and the 1930s still intact after a depression and a war which sent thousands of the graceful machines to the scrap heap.

The irony of it was that the engineers, the designers, the craftsmen of metal and wood, the skilled upholsterers who created these machines were ill-equipped to fight the new kind of battle they were engaged in: a battle where dollars, not quality or beauty, held trump cards.

In the years of prosperity, no buyer for this class of car ever asked for the price. He merely asked for a motor car. If that car bore the Packard name, that was all he needed, because he knew what the name meant. Nine out of 10 buyers who came to the Packard showrooms to select a car had been there before. When

Packard ads said, "Ask the man who owns one," it was no idle boast.

Now, as the depression gripped the country, the craftsmen fought back with the only weapons they had—their skill and their art—with a determination to build ever finer cars. It was the only way they knew to fight for their share of a market which simply didn't exist any more. The irony of it all: the finest cars in the country's history were being produced at a time when the least money existed to buy them.

Cadillac had introduced a V-16 in 1930. People said it was the ultimate engine. Marmon quickly followed with a gigantic, powerful V-16 of its own. Engineers at Lincoln, Franklin and Pierce-Arrow had twelves on their drawing boards.

After abandoning the first Twin Six in 1923, Packard had scarcely changed models or made any drastic changes during the fabulous years of 1923 to 1930. The magnificent straight eight engine, which bore the Packard banner through those years of prosperity, had been a solid nine main bearing machine, so well built it came as near as possible, for its time, to being indestructible.

It started out at 3⅜ x 5, rated at 84 hp, but by 1926 it had been beefed up to 3½ x 5, with hp upped to 106, where it was to remain until 1930. By 1932 and 1933, when the first of the new Twin Sixes were being sold, the basic straight eight engine had been improved until it was rated as high as 135 hp, or even 145 for a special speedster model.

For the record, it must be stated that Packard also produced a six and a smaller eight.

The six, from 1925 on, was a 3½ x 5 engine rated at 61 hp (in its last form, at 82 hp). The smaller eight, known as the Standard Eight, appeared in 1928 with dimensions of 3³⁄₁₆ x 5, rated at 90 hp. It was also improved until, by the time the

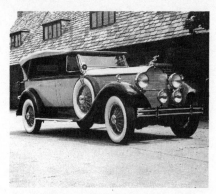

Packard's standard eight "bottom line" models, such as this 1930 733 Phaeton, were priced starting at $2,000 at a time when "top line" Fords were priced around $600.

new Twin Six appeared, it had reached a rating of 120 hp.

The late 1920s were a time when the hoods of fine cars were meant to be raised; the days when gentlemen owners lifted those hoods and spoke knowingly about what was inside.

Packard bodies produced during the last half of the 1920s were—and still are —probably the most solidly built examples of the body building craft the industry has ever seen. The Fourth Series 443 Custom Packards, made in 1927 and 1928, were offered in as many as 20 semi-custom models, by such makers as Dietrich, LeBaron, Rollston, Holbrook and Judkins. In addition, true custom bodies were available from additional classic builders: Derham, Waterhouse, Biddle and Smart, Phillips, Brunn or Brewster. Even the regular production models offered by Packard came closer to being custom than anything seen up to that time, with an almost unlimited choice of colors, upholstery and accessories.

During this period, Packard management held production more or less stabilized by decree, especially for the more expensive models, even when there were long lines of customers clamoring for cars and willing to pay the asking prices. The Packard Motor Car Co., during these years, was profitable far beyond the wildest dreams of its founders.

In the nine years from 1916 through 1924 — largely the years of the highly successful series of Twin Sixes — the company showed earnings of $39,449,824. People had said this was prosperity. Then came the vastly more fabulous years of the Twenties, when Packard equalled that earning record in three years! Men who had invested a few thousand dollars in the company at the beginning were now millionaires. Packards were outselling Cadillacs three to one—despite the fact that Packard officials made no effort to set new production records and, instead, preferred to let their customers wait.

Certainly, Packard could have cut prices and quality, and increased production. But then, argued the men who made them, the cars would no longer be "Packards."

But the era of the golden Twenties had ended, and the company had to face two facts:
- First, the introduction by the competition of such formidable multi-cylinder machines—the 12 and 16-cylinder cars—they could no longer be ignored.
- Second, the impact of a depression such as America or the world had never seen before.

It is quite likely that Packard management, at least at the beginning, did not consider the depression a serious problem. In 1930, nobody expected it to hit so hard or last so long.

This left the problem of the multi-cylindered competition. Even this was no serious problem for Packard managers and engineers because, aside from the fact that they had all those years of experience in the making of the first Twin Sixes, they had never really stopped working with this kind of engine.

Over the years, Jesse Vincent and his team of engineers had been involved in the development of the famed Liberty engine of World War I, based on the original Twin Six design. They had built marine and aircraft racing engines, largely based on that proven design, which had shattered records and won gold cups at a rate no other engine had matched.

Vincent was still active in the Packard shops, despite his title of vice president for engineering. In a sense, to meet the challenge of the multi-cylindered Cadillacs and Marmons, all Packard had to do was reach into the bag and pull out an engine, then start the production lines.

This is why, after Cadillac tossed out the so-called V-16 bombshell in 1930, Packard was able to place its own highly improved Twin Six back in the showrooms within a few months.

Why didn't Vincent come up with a V-16 — or something even more impressive to trump the Cadillac ace?

The truth is that Vincent and his engineers had been tinkering with just about every design under the sun, including a long, straight twelve. They tinkered with it long enough to prove it was not a practical design. The one car built was destroyed, depriving future collectors of one of the rarest of all items: a one-of-a-kind in the world.

Vincent and his staff had long ago convinced themselves that the V-12, due to its geometry, balance and spacing of power strokes, was the most practical of all the multi-cylinder engines for use in a motor car. "Ours is a better engine," they said. It is a boast few engineers will challenge, even today—except, of course, the fact that the V-8, with half the cylinders, has been refined far beyond what was possible in 1930.

The new Packard Twin Six appeared in the auto shows with dimensions of 3⁷⁄₁₆ x 4, with a bhp rating of 160 at 3,200 rpm. Later, in 1934, the stroke was increased to 4¼, with a corresponding jump in bhp to 175. In typical Packard style, the rating was an understatement. The actual horsepower of this magnificent engine, most experts agreed, was much nearer 200.

By comparison, the old Packard Twin Sixes of the earlier period had dimensions of 3 x 5, with bhp rating of 90. The new Twin Six, after an absence of V-12's for eight years, represented a hefty improvement — aside from the refinements which made it much smoother and more quiet.

Although introduced as the new Twin Six, the machine was renamed the Packard Twelve in 1933, and remained in production eight years. The regal machines were available on wheelbases ranging from 132 to 147½ inches, and once more the custom body builders — those that had not succumbed to economic disaster—used the Packard Twelve chassis for some of the finest classic coachwork the industry has ever seen.

There were bodies by Dietrich, Murray, LeBaron, Briggs, Darrin, Murphy, Rollston, Bohman and Schwartz, Brunn and Derham, not to mention the foreign coach makers. These were stately cars which, even today, command an aura of respect wherever they are seen. It was artistry of a type and style never matched before, or since.

These were the cars of presidents and kings. Packard Twelves were bought by customers such as King Gustaf V of Sweden, President Franklin D. Roosevelt, Indian maharajas, and the tinsel queens of Hollywood. They were the odds-on choice of the old line moneyed families, the ones who still had cash for this kind of an automobile, although Packard quality and changeless style made it possible for some owners of the great machines to make do with them for years before new ones were necessary.

Packard leadership in the field of prestige cars never faltered. If admiration and acclaim could have been transformed into gold, Packard stockholders would still have had their dividends. But, as a major market, the demand for the grand machines was gone — gone, because money was gone.

Total production of the magnificent Packard Twelve for the eight years of its existence was only 5,744 — a pitiful figure when compared to the triumph of the first Twin Six, when 10,000 were sold the first year. Production of the big Twelves averaged only slightly more than 700 per year. During the heyday of the fabulous Twenties, Packard had produced almost that many of its luxury line each month, not to mention the smaller models. In only one year, 1937, did Packard Twelve production exceed the thousand mark.

The disastrous impact of the depression can be seen in looking at total Packard sales, which had reached a peak of more than 50,000 units per year in 1928 — and, by 1934, at the bottom of the depression, had dropped below the 7,000 mark. This figure included 960 of the big Twelves. The Packard Motor Car Co., which had been making millionaires of its stockholders, was now in the red for the first time in three decades.

This was the period when other great names in automobiles — Duesenberg, Pierce-Arrow, Franklin, Marmon — were

The car that saved Packard. This was the famed Packard 120 as it appeared for the first time at the auto shows in 1935 to bring new triumph to Packard and save the company from bankruptcy.

wiped completely off the slate by the economic disaster. Even Ford, the richest of them all, was in the red for the first time.

The prestige cars of the big companies — Lincoln, Cadillac and Chrysler — were saved by their association with the cheaper cars. Even so, General Motors almost halted Cadillac production. Without the backing of the giant corporation behind it (especially Chevrolet), Cadillac would certainly have been gone.

Packard President Macauley and his fellow executives were faced with the choice of joining the mass production market or seeing the great Packard name be wiped off the boards. It was then that the famed Packard 120 was born.

Some historians have said it was the most important single event in the history of the Packard Motor Car Co. Others have said the decision to enter the field of mass production, with a competitive motor car, was an invitation to disaster which eventually overtook Packard. Still other students of Packard history, notably Robert Turnquist, have pointed out that it could not have been a mistake for the simple reason that Macauley had no other choice. The decision saved Packard for another 20 years.

It meant that an entirely new concept of engineering and production had to be introduced at the Packard plant — and quickly. This brought into the picture the name of George Christopher, a future Packard president.

Christopher had been a production manager at Pontiac and Buick, and was brought in to introduce the new concepts. The plan was to use the Packard name — built up through all those years of leadership in the luxury car field and through the many records set by Packard-built engines — to sell a competitive machine built to a price.

Packard engineers faced an unpleasant truth at this time: during all the years while Packard clung to tradition — the slow, laborious methods of making fine automobiles — engineers in other companies had been teaching themselves how to build more quality into mass production cars. Buick, Oldsmobile, the new Chrysler Corp., and independents like Studebaker, Hudson and Nash were building cars which, for their cost, offered their buyers a geat deal of comfort, durability and beauty. In short, on a dollar for dollar basis, some of these cars might offer their owners as much as the smaller Packards produced by the old fashioned methods—and at a fraction of the price.

Packard had insulated itself from all this, until the economic depression forced the issue. It was to the credit of men like Macauley, who had guided Packard through its years of greatest glory, that the company was willing to take this step into a new era.

The new Packard 120, named for its wheelbase, was announced on January 6, 1935, by headline singer Lawrence Tibbet, on his top billed national radio show. A few days later, when the car appeared "in the flesh" at the 35th annual National Automobile Show in New York,

Another of the great Packard Queens, the Packard V-12 Victoria convertible was made in 1939, the last year of the great Twelves. (Photo courtesy of Henry Ford Museum)

it was the sensation of the show, attracting jam-packed audiences.

Here was the chance for the middle class professional man, the small town doctor, lawyer, grocer or drug store owner to own what had been only a dream until now—a Packard.

Prices started at less than a thousand dollars — $980 for a business coupe — with the top of the line, a touring sedan, going for $1,095.

Even more sensational, considering that the country was still in the grip of a murderous depression, was what began to happen at Packard dealerships around the country. Orders poured in at such a rate that 10,000 of the new Packard 120's were sold even before delivery began.

Success of the new project was immediate and dramatic. In 1933 and 1934, Packard had sold less than 10,000 automobiles per year, including all models. In 1935, with the new 120 coming off the assembly lines, production and sales shot up above the 30,000 mark. In 1936 the Packard plant produced, and salesmen sold, 55,000 of the new 120's.

The full measure of this success can be seen by the fact that Packard was still making three other lines of cars under the old production methods: the Packard Eight, the Super Eight, and the stately Twelve. Total production of the traditional Packards reached only 5,985 in the 1936 model year, and it required 2,500

Packard workers, operating in the traditional methods, to produce the 5,985 cars. Across the street, in the new mass production plant, an almost equal work force of 2,600 men was producing almost 10 times as many of the new 120's.

Then there was the matter of price. The lowest priced of the traditional Packards in 1936, the 130 hp 14th Series Packard Eight, was selling at prices ranging from $2,385 to $3,400. The Super Eight, the 150 hp model, sold at prices from $2,990 to $4,010. The senior Packards, the big Twelves, cost between $3,820 and $5,050, not counting the custom and semi-custom models. Since it took 10 times as much time and manpower to make one of these cars as the new 120, something was wrong with the arithmetic—especially considering that, while not a classic in any sense, the new 120 (with a 120 hp straight eight engine, a well engineered suspension system, and a solid Packard-styled body) was selling for $1,000.

The Packard 120 was not the car of a man who considered only esthetics, the appeal of a fine motor car built to a standard. But the man on the street—and he was the man who was now saving the Packard Motor Car Co. — could hardly tell the difference between a Packard 120 and a Packard Eight when he saw them parked side by side.

By the fall of 1936, with the sensa-

154

tional Packard 120 well on the way to saving the company, Packard executives took another plunge in the same direction—only deeper. The results were a still smaller Packard, the 110, with a six-cylinder engine and a 115-inch wheelbase. Introduced in the fall of 1936, for the 1937 model year, the new 100 hp machine was the first six to come out of the Packard plants since 1928.

With prices on the new line starting as low as $795, the low-priced motor car bearing the Packard name became a sensational success. Production for the first year shot up to 65,000 units, while another 50,000 of the 120's were coming off the production line.

Although these cars could not compare to the hand-made cars which had created the great Packard name, they were coming off the assembly lines and being sold at a rate Packard executives had never dreamed possible back dur-

ing the fabulously prosperous days of the 1920s.

Of course, profits per car for the cheaper car were much less, but profits they were—and, to Packard stockholders who had seen the red ink in the early 1930s, happy days were here again. Some of the older stockholders might have hated to see the passing of tradition. But such a stockholder could always take his profits from the manufacture of the 120 and 110, and buy himself one of the traditional Packards still being produced in the plant across the street.

He could even buy one of the stately Twelves, queen of them all — until August 8, 1939. On that day, the last of the great Packard Twelves rolled out of the assembly shops.

Only 446 of the classic Twelves were made that last year. Another era had come to an end.

The final decades: 1939-1956

*" **A** s long as there is a man left to own one, there will be a Packard for him."*

These words, written by a prominent auto historian, were published in a national magazine in 1953, only three years before the final Packard disaster.

In the same year, another well known auto columnist wrote, "... the progressive and energetic executives now in office (at Packard) intend to place Packard at the head of the luxury car list or know the reason why. Prospects look favorable for the most remarkable come-back in automotive history."

The truth is, that as these words were being written, the final grave for Packard was already half dug: proof abundant that all the words auto historians write are about as sturdy as the perishable paper they are written upon.

How could disaster strike and slay a great company so fast and so finally?

The story of the final Packard years answers that question. The final chapter of Packard history may have begun on the day in 1939 when production halted on the great, classic V-12.

True, classic status has been granted to a few Packards built after that—a few "top of the line" 180's built in 1940, 1941

and 1942. But the era of the hand-crafted Packards, which sent the company's name to the pinnacle of glory, ended in 1939.

In the depths of the depression, Packard executives had been faced with a "change or die" decision: to enter the mass production market or close down. The phenomenal success of the cheaper mass production lines—first the 120, then the 110 — and the continued vanishing market for luxury cars left Packard executives no room to look backward into the years of glory. The new glory was on the fast-moving assembly lines.

When the 120 was introduced in 1935, Packard built an entirely new mass production plant to turn out the new car. Workers continued to labor in the old plant, turning out a few of the traditional cars, including the great V-12. But when Packard closed down production on the V-12 in 1939, the old plant was converted to operations for the mass assembly system. Robert Turnquist, a leading Packard historian, wrote of this decision, "...Packard would never again regain the prestige it had gained in the first three decades of the century."

As Packard closed its doors on the past, the company came to the 40th annual

1942 Custom Super Clipper. Fall 1939 had marked the first major styling change in many years. By 1942, the sharply delineated edges of the traditional Packard hoods were gone, but the lines were still unmistakably Packard.

Automobile Show with what many critics have called — despite the stigma of mass production — the most beautiful styling in Packard history. The 18th Series cars introduced the first major styling change in many years.

Gone were the sharp edges of the traditional and classic fluted hood contours; replacing them were gentle, rounded edges laced with chrome. Yet it was unmistakably Packard.

The new styling was an instant success, and kept the Packard assembly lines rolling. A total of 98,000 units were sold to eager buyers in 1940, and another 75,855 in 1941. Production was now being slowed, not by the depression, but by the lengthening shadows of the coming global war — a war which was already burning on the horizons in Europe.

The war had not yet directly involved the U.S., but it brought production contracts to Packard, to build giant V-12 engines for the famed PT boats and to produce the equally famed Rolls-Royce Merlin aircraft engine destined to play such a decisive role in World War II. Chief engineer Jesse Vincent and his men demonstrated their genius once more, by simplifying, improving and raising the power of the British-designed engine. Packard built 55,523 of these engines.

In the meantime, Packard took one more great styling fling. Perhaps there was still hope among auto designers that the politicians would manage, as they had promised, to keep America out of the war. The name "Clipper" appeared on the Packard horizon.

Introduced in 1941, to be produced simultaneously with the conventional Packards of the 18th Series styling, the Clipper revealed the most drastic styling changes in Packard history to that moment.

The traditional Packard lines were almost completely gone. The well known grille and hood design had almost disappeared; the grille was narrowed to a shadow of its former shape, and the famed hood fluting was reduced to the disappearing point. The rear of the body no longer contained a sharply delineated trunk, but came nearer resembling the "fastback" of today.

Introduction of the Clipper kicked off a great debate over Packard styling, which would reach its most heated point in the next styling "forward leap" in 1947-1948. The traditionalists have argued that these radical styling changes were tragic and fateful, pointing toward the end. Packard executives at the time argued that they were merely doing what had been forced upon them, to keep up with the rapidly changing trends — and it is true that other car makers at the time were proceeding in the same direction.

There is merit on both sides of the argument. But based on personal taste, the styling introduced with the 18th Series Packards was vastly more beautiful and certainly more in keeping with the Packard tradition than the Clippers of 1941 and the even more "bulbous" designs to come.

Any chance of retaining the traditional Packard styling received still another blow in the midst of the war, when the politicians played a brief but decisive role in the Packard drama. The Russians, both before and after the 1917

Revolution which brought the Communists to power, had been enamored of the Packards. Many a Packard — including many of the original Twin Sixes — had found its way into the land of the Czars.

The Russians let it be known during World War II that they admired the 18th and 19th Series Packards, and President Franklin D. Roosevelt apparently decided it would help political negotiations with the Communists if he offered them the dies for the beautiful cars. Packard executives were persuaded to send the dies to Russia for a nominal fee and thus, when the war ended, it was the Russians who continued making the beautiful Packards while the Packard plant in Detroit was left with nothing but the Clipper dies. Until new styling could be developed and new dies made, Packard was stuck with the Clipper design alone.

This really should not have been fateful. To a degree, the changing times would probably demand some styling changes anyway. New dies would have to be made. Besides, Packard's future looked rosy.

• First, there was the healthy financial picture. War-time production of aircraft, marine and truck engines had left Packard in its healthiest financial condition since the fabulous 1920s. The company was debt free, and had a bulging bank account of dollars and assets.

• Second, with pre-war cars largely worn out and pockets of citizens bulging with unspent war-time earnings, the U.S. now possessed the most fabulous seller's market for automobiles of all time. Millions of buyers were begging for new cars. Most of them were willing to pay premiums—even bribes—to get a new car. How could any company, owning an auto production plant, possibly lose?

Gremlins crept into this rosy picture: first, in the form of steel shortages. The giant auto makers, such as GM, Ford and Chrysler, in a sense almost owned their sources of supply. Packard, as an independent, was more vulnerable.

Three of Packard's pre-war suppliers changed hands or became involved in mergers which left Packard forced to fight for supplies in the open market at a time when, like the auto buyers themselves, everyone was fighting for short supplies. Packard ended up paying almost black market prices to get enough steel to start auto production.

The shortage was so acute that after the government gave the go-ahead for civilian auto production in 1945, Packard was able to produce only 2,722 units between October 19 and the year's end.

At the beginning of 1946 the situation became even more acute. Steel supplies were so miserly that Packard was held to a total of nine days' production during the entire first quarter. Only 42,102 units were made during the entire calendar year, despite the fact that the public was clamoring to buy every car the makers could produce. Even in 1947, Packard was able to get only enough supplies to make 55,477 units.

So great was the demand that Packard could easily have sold several times these figures — if the material with which to build them had been available. The Packard plants had demonstrated, between 1935 and 1942, that greater numbers could be produced. Thus, in spite of the dream situation of a seller's market where demand never seemed to end, Packard operated in the red during the first post-war years. It was a tragedy that would cost dearly later.

Of course, all the first post-war Packards were of the Clipper design. But the matter of styling was, at this point, of no importance. Buyers were willing to purchase anything that rolled on wheels. All the car makers were doing the same thing —selling cars which were nothing more than slightly revamped 1942 models — while they fought to increase production rather than change styles.

Behind the scenes in all the auto plants, production men were the heroes of the day — and stylists were at work against the day when the market would become saturated and buyers would once again want something that looked new. Studebaker made it first, with a highly modernistic design in 1946. A few other makers offered new models in 1947.

There is no way of knowing what the effect might have been if Packard had not sold the pre-war non-Clipper dies to Russia, and had built some of these models after the war, instead of the Clippers. Having the dies would not have solved the steel shortage.

But when the time came to introduce the first new Packard model, there was one design on the shelf: the Packard Phantom. This prototype model had been built in 1941 under the direction of Edward Macauley, the son of the former Packard president, who had been brought in as vice president in charge of design.

When Packard executives decided to introduce their first post-war new design, it was the Macauley Phantom that was given the nod, with some changes.

The original Phantom, which had created a sensation at the auto shows, had a front end design in which the traditional Packard grille lines were recognizable only by a single bar in the center of the hood to suggest the car's identity. Aside from this, the car might well have been a Buick. When the 22nd Series Packard finally appeared, the traditionalists had rescued a bit more of the Packard image by increasing the size of the grille and restoring some of the Packard shape.

The public was given a glimpse of the new Packard in a convertible version produced on a limited basis late in 1947. The regular line of cars—the sedans based on the same style lines — came later, in time for the 1948 season. These models, with minor styling changes, were produced from the model years 1948 through 1950. They were the cars, and

this was the styling, which created a tempest of controversy in the Packard teapot.

The body was wide, bulbous and round. Many critics referred to it as the "inverted bathtub." Packard purists showed no hesitation in spitting out the word "ugly." This was the car, the critics said, which lost Packard its battle for survival.

Introduced at a time when the seller's market was coming to an end, it should have been a model that would excite the buyer and send him reaching for his checkbook. This, the critics said, was not the car to do it.

On the positive side, it must be said that the 22nd Series Packards, when they appeared, were hailed as a styling breakthrough, and won world-wide styling awards. It must also be said that if the Packard designers had made a mistake, they were not alone: a number of competitive models, notably Lincoln, had the same bulbous, bathtub design.

Also on the positive side, Packards of this period were among the most dependable and reliable, from a mechanical standpoint, of all Packards ever produced. Few major changes in engine, transmission or chassis design had been made since the early 1930s, and if any model engine or chassis ever had a chance to have all the bugs worked out, this design—with the coiled spring suspension up front, and the proven flat-

1953 Packard convertible. The next major step in Packard styling, introduced in 1951 and continued through 1954, was more of a compromise. Recognizable Packard hood fluting and grille lines were back. Many said these were the most handsome of the postwar Packards.

head, straight eight engine—was it.

The biggest mechanical innovation introduced at this time was the Packard Ultramatic transmission, which appeared on May 2, 1949, following the trend to automatic shifts. This in itself was a Packard achievement of no small proportions. Only four companies at this time possessed the technological expertise to produce automatics on a successful basis. Two of them were the giants, General Motors and Chrysler. The third was Borg-Warner, the biggest of the transmission specialty firms. The fourth was Packard—the only independent auto maker on the exclusive list.

Furthermore, many auto experts still insist that the Packard Ultramatic, with direct clutch lock-up for economy, engine braking and heat reduction, was the best of the automatics on the market until 1954. It failed then only because the giant, high-torque V-8 engine with which it was coupled in 1955 placed too heavy a burden on the up-shift mechanism when heavy-footed drivers demanded the ultimate in "drag-off."

In the meantime, styling once more became a major factor. Late in 1950, Packard introduced the 24th Series cars, representing a completely restyled body. This time, it was a compromise between tradition and the future.

The Packard engineers topped it off by installing two short auxiliary torsion bars at the rear, hitched to the overall suspension system and also to an electrical control box which automatically leveled the car when the load at the rear exceeded the load at the front.

The magic seemed to work for one more year. The Packard with the new engine, new syspension system, and new styling brought sales back up to 68,770 for 1955. But then, with dramatic suddenness, disaster arrived.

Sales in 1956 dropped to the lowest level in four decades—only 13,193 cars. The first 5,400 units had to be impounded and repaired, at a terrific loss, because of a faulty axle flange.

The Packard Ultramatic transmission began to fail when the more than 400 pounds of torque from the big engines were applied by a new generation of drivers living in the age of performance consciousness. They demanded that all big engines deliver, on the "scratch-off." The Caribbean engine had 310 horses.

Even the great new engine developed a few bugs, with soft valve lifters sometimes showing up.

The final ignominy was that the sensational new torsion suspension system began developing bugs in the load leveler. The electrical leveling switch underneath the car was not properly protected from the weather.

These were the kind of failures Packard had never known before: engineering and construction failures. Were quality controls inadequate? Had Packard put the new engine and suspension system on the market too quickly, without working the bugs out? It would seem so.

It is impossible to say how much of the disaster might have been averted if these bugs had not shown up. Other factors were at work, too.

Nance and the management team had felt that Packard must move into a wider field in order to stay in the race with the Big Three. Thus, a merger with Studebaker was brought about. The merger, which went into effect on October 1, 1954, was designed not only to move the combined companies into the low price field, and give better coverage from top to bottom, but also to give better service and dealer coverage. In many smaller towns Packard had no dealers, but Studebaker did.

This logic may have been an error, too, for small Studebaker service shops were not equipped — and did not have properly trained men — to service a car like the Packard. In the end, it was the customer who suffered.

Perhaps the worst factor in the merger was that before the marriage, Studebaker was in worse financial condition than Packard. In that first period, Packard funds were used to shore up Studebaker. These were funds Packard badly needed in its own fight for survival. But the blame cannot all be laid to Studebaker, for Packard management had also wanted the merger and what — they thought—Studebaker had to offer.

On top of all these troubles, Packard had spent a vast sum on a multi-million dollar ultra-modern engine plant at Utica, Michigan, largely on the basis of sales of

1954 Packard Caribbean convertible

engines and transmissions to American Motors. Then American developed its own V-8 engine, and Packard lost this market.

Government contracts might have saved Packard, as they bolstered many another company. But someone discovered a slight "conflict of interest" involving a Packard executive, and Packard was barred from such help.

With all these disasters piling up and money draining away, Nance pulled off one final "coup" which many said was his final mistake. He obtained funds to shore up Packard by arranging a "management contract" with Curtis-Wright.

It has been said that Curtis-Wright, from the beginning, wanted the Packard contract only to use Studebaker-Packard as a tax loss write-off, and that no real effort was made to save Packard.

When the facts are considered, this statement seems logical. While Packard had been experiencing some bad years, it also had its good years. Even 1955 was an operation "in the black." For a company with such a history as Packard — going back 56 years — why would the order to close down come so quickly, after only one disastrous year?

In any case, when the Packard crisis became acute in 1956, it was clear that Curtis-Wright management, under Roy Hurley, had no stomach for a prolonged fight. The order to close shop in the Packard plants and dispose of the property came swiftly—on August 15, 1956. It was the end of a great company and a great story that began in Warren, Ohio, on November 6, 1899.

The remainder of the story is almost a postscript. Hurried arrangements were made in 1957 to keep the Packard name alive by placing it on a Studebaker which had been revamped with a bit of trim. But nobody, least of all the buying public, was fooled by the move. Only 5,543 of these "Packards" were made.

The fraud should have been dropped, but for reasons known only to the management, it was tried one more time. In 1958, only 1,745 of the so-called Packards were produced.

Most Packard lovers refuse to recognize as a Packard any automobile made after August 15, 1956. It's been said that Packard never died, it was murdered. Perhaps this judgement is a bit too harsh. But the question remains: how could a company in good financial health as late as 1953 meet disaster so fast and so finally in one tragic year?

Many factors led to Packard failure:

• The millions of dollars in profits lost by the shortage of steel during the seller's market.
• The controversial body styling.
• The possible continuance of body styles for too long a time.
• The millions spent on an engine plant that could never be fully used.
• The merger with Studebaker, which drained away needed funds.
• The unexpected mechanical and engineering bugs which were unknown in the days of Packard greatness.
• The final lack of will on the part of Curtis-Wright to fight to save the company when the chips were down.

In any case, it happened. It is history now. Packard is gone, except for the thousands of Packard automobiles, restored and unrestored, in the hands of old car lovers throughout the country. Perhaps no other marque is quite so popular among car collectors, the men and women who cherish the memory of the great Packard years: the indestructible classics of the 1920s and the 1930s; the earlier memories of the fabulous Twin Sixes; or even further back than that, when a man named James Ward Packard became distressed at the quality of automobiles then being offered for sale, and determined to build a better one.

(Editor's note: Our thanks to Packard Automobile Classics, Inc., for material and assistance in the preparation of this chapter.)

VI
STEARNS-KNIGHT

The beginning of greatness: 1896-1905

It was probably the most powerful and fastest American stock car of its era. Ralph Stein, the famed motor car writer, said it flatly: "the most potent car of its time."

Imagine, within the 1907 to 1910 period, a stock car with a motor that could slam out 100 horsepower and propel the machine at 100 miles per hour. True, the six-cylinder engine was a monster, with 800 cubic inches, but still....

Such performance would not be reached by standard American stock cars, on a routine basis, for many years—perhaps not until the late 1950s and early 1960s.

This car, it was said, was more of a sports car than a stock car, the forerunner of something like the fabulous Chevrolet Corvette of a much later era. Even the famed Stutz Bearcat and the Mercer Raceabout, both much more widely renowned cars in their time—and now — could not match the performance of the "brute": the Stearns 45-90 of the 1907-1910 period.

Never heard of it? You have plenty of company. The Stearns 45-90 has been one of the best kept secrets of American motor car history, especially for a car with such fantastic credentials.

It might be hard to prove the thing ever existed if Harrah's famed collection out in Reno, Nevada, hadn't managed to corral one example: the last 45-90 known to exist. On the few occasions when this well-restored machine has been taken out for a "run" in recent years, it has delivered a bit of a shock—if not the shivers—to drivers and passengers privileged to make the ride.

Ralph Stein, one of those who has taken a ride in it, nudged the driver to slow down when he saw the speedometer needle touching the 90 mark, and the mighty engine still reaching for more.

It would be in 1901 when Frank Stearns would build the biggest single-cylinder motor car engine on the U.S. market. With a bore of 6½ inches and a stroke of 7½ inches, the machine had a whopping displacement of 230 cubic inches from one cylinder.

The machine was blasting up hills as if they didn't exist.

A car built in 1908 wasn't supposed to be doing things like that—behaving like a modern sports car.

One reason the big 45-90 was so obscure was that the man who built them, Frank B. Stearns, wanted it that way — and because so few of them were made. Nobody knows for certain exactly how many were built, but it was probably no more than 200 at most.

Most Stearns enthusiasts who have studied the available record believe that Frank Stearns really didn't want to make the machine at all. Company advertising always downplayed the 45-90 and featured instead the peppy four-cylinder 30-60 model which Stearns thought was car enough for his time. The truth was that the 30-60 was going to make a lot of history of its own, maybe even more than its big brother.

As the speculative story goes, most of the prestige auto makers of the day were coming out with smoother, more powerful six-cylinder engines. The carriage trade wanted them, the voices of authority said. So it was probably James Gilman (Pete) Sterling, Stearns' chief engineer, who persuaded his boss that the F.B. Stearns Co. needed a six.

When Sterling got the reluctant go-ahead to make the six, he turned it into a sensation — or, at least, it would have been, if it had been properly advertised, promoted and sent out to do battle with the competition.

It is interesting to speculate on what might have happened if Stearns and his company had prepared the car for racing, and had mounted a well-organized racing effort with the 45-90.

But Frank Stearns had been seriously injured in a car crash, a collision with a horse and wagon. A cousin, whom he had hired as a factory test driver, was killed in another crash while driving at high speed. Perhaps it was understandable that Stearns did not want his company involved in the hoopla of motor car racing, and was reluctant to push the 45-90.

Thus, much like the people running the Pierce-Arrow Co. at that time, Frank Stearns was simply interested in making the highest quality passenger car possible. The unspoken suggestion remained that racing was, perhaps, just a bit on the vulgar side.

If the high quality Stearns cars just happened to perform to the envy of the competition, well, so be it. If individual owners, or dealers, saw fit to take their cars to the races, again, so be it. It certainly did no damage to the reputation of the company, or the car, if the Stearns machines started flicking their heels at the competition in hill climbs and races — and they did.

In fact, in the period shortly after the 30-60 and the 45-90 Stearns machines were placed on the market, their performances were so spectacular they would win hill climbs, endurance runs and races all over the country.

- A Stearns was the first motor car to climb Pikes Peak under its own power. It did it carrying seven passengers.
- A Stearns claimed three world speed records in 1907, including a stock car record of 41 2/5 seconds for a mile at Atlantic City.

- A Stearns, in August, 1910, set a new world record for the 24-hour run, shattering the old record by 57 miles. All this and more—much more.

There would come a time when the F.B. Stearns Co. would, in a sense, change direction and gamble all the company's reputation and resources on a somewhat controversial type of motor car engine, the sleeve valve type.

But here again, under the brilliant direction of Pete Sterling, and with utter devotion to the highest craftsmanship, the company would carry the sleeve valve engine to the highest peaks of performance, quality and perfection ever reached by an American manufacturer. It was not because others didn't try. Before the sleeve valve chapter of American motor car history ended, a whole covey of car makers made the try, led by the famed Willys-Knight.

But the Stearns company was forever out front, leading the way in engineering, innovation, quality and performance. The commitment remained until economic conditions in the country — more than failure of the car — brought the end. And that end came in a time when the F.B. Stearns Co. had on the market an incredibly smooth, quiet, powerful and fast straight eight sleeve valve machine, the only sleeve valve straight eight ever made in America. It was a machine which, in its final form, produced a claimed 112 brake horsepower and ran at speeds of up to 105 mph. They were dealer guaranteed to 102 mph.

The incredible Stearns story began when a 14-year-old boy from Cleveland, Ohio, got stars in his eyes when he visited the World's Fair of 1893. There he saw the crude, early day internal combustion engines and examples of the first attempts at making self-propelled vehicles—mostly foreign machines.

As Frank Ballou Stearns remembered it, years later: "My father was not impressed with the gas driven vehicles, and impressed upon me the fact that gas engines were far from what they should be."

That fatherly "impression" could be interpreted two ways. The first was, simply, "They are no good. Forget about them." The second, focusing on "what they should be," could be taken as a challenge—a big challenge to make them better. The elder F.M. Stearns may never have intended that way, but that was the way it was going to be.

For the moment, the budding young genius had to stay in school. The stars in his eyes, instead of fading, became more intense by the day.

After two more years of high school and through his freshman year at the Case School of Applied Science, it persisted. "My desire to build and operate a motor-driven vehicle became so strong, I decided to quit school and start the manufacture of motor driven vehicles, with the ultimate aim of making it my life's work." This, at age 17—the audacity of youth.

Even so, young Frank Stearns probably would never have been able to pull it off if it had not been for a fortunate set of circumstances. First, he was lucky enough to be born to wealthy parents. F.M. Stearns had operated a stone quarry at nearby Berea, and had accumulated what has been described as a "comfortable fortune." Second, the elder Stearns had been somewhat generous with an allowance to his son Frank, enabling the thrifty youth to save some money. Third, the young man made his decision to become a college "dropout" at a time when his father was on an extended trip to Florida.

Imagine the surprise of the elder Stearns when he returned home to find that his son had not only quit school, but had blown his savings on enough machinery to equip a small machine shop in the basememt of the family home. There it was, rattling away from the power of a two-horsepower steam engine.

It doesn't take much imagination to hear the explosion of fatherly wrath. Even Frank himself would confess to it, describing the argument as "forcible and at some length."

But, he said, "I finally convinced my father that since I had a strong mechanical bent, and since he had retired from business, I might as well take up the development of a practical motor car."

It was typical Frank Stearns to add, as an afterthought, "as nobody knew anything about motor cars at that time, my chances were as good as anybody's." All this from a 17-year-old in the year 1896.

Apparently, things moved pretty fast after that. Stearns said that by the fall of that year, his first self-propelled motor car went chugging down the driveway.

Actually, young Stearns' first engine design was a bit on the super-ambitious side, considering the time in history. It was nothing less than a four-cylinder engine — at a time when Henry Ford and nearly all other would-be motor car "inventors" were struggling with crude one-cylinder machines.

In fact, the four-cylinder design did turn out to be a bit too ambitious, even for the audacious youth. With the primitive carburetion and ignition systems available at that time, he was unable to get the four cylinders to fire smoothly or evenly.

This was one time when a fatherly suggestion was accepted by young Frank. The father proposed that, for the time being at least, his son should stick to the simpler one-cylinder engine. Frank accepted that advice.

This explains why the first "Stearns" motor car was a single-cylinder machine with a hefty 4 x 6 bore and stroke. Big engines with huge displacements would become almost a Stearns trademark, as if Frank Stearns felt a constant subconscious urge to over-build, to make certain he always had enough size and power, so that his engines would deliver all the "oomph" a man needed. This power and size mania—if, indeed, it was that — resulted in Stearns' building the biggest motor car engines of their type in the U.S.

In the first one-cylinder Stearns, as the young inventor himself described it, the engine valves were operated by an eccentric and the spark was "hit or miss." This meant, simply, that he was using the system commonly used on almost all one-cylinder engines at that time. The engine fired only when load demand or idling dropped engine revolutions below a certain point. The drive to the rear wheels was by chain, also a common practice of the day.

The machine performed well enough that father Stearns advanced another $1,000 to expand the little machine shop and move it to the horse barn at the rear lot behind the house.

It should be remembered that 1896 was also the year in which Henry Ford completed and tested his first one-cylinder "quadricycle." It would be another seven years — 1903 — before he would actually get the Ford Motor Co. established and begin selling the first Model A, a two-cylinder machine. The year 1903 would also be the first for Cadillac, coming onto the market with a one-cylinder machine. By that time, Stearns had been selling successful machines for five years, and had his first successful four-cylinder engine under development.

By the winter of 1898 Stearns had his experimental machines working well enough to begin offering them for sale. The first sale was to Frank Hilt, of Dayton, Ohio. By 1900 young Stearns had built and sold some 50 machines. With his office mostly "in his hat," as the cliche goes, he wasn't even sure himself as to the exact number.

During this period, Stearns actually had partners. While engaged in the development of his first motor cars, he had become aware of two brothers, Ralph and Raymond Owens, who were also tinkering with self-propelled motor vehicles. After meeting and discussing the projects, the three agreed to pool resources. It was under the name F.B. Stearns and Co., which included the Owens brothers, that the first series of one-cylinder Stearns machines were built and marketed.

The first Stearns cars offered for sale were powered by a single-cylinder, eight horsepower, two-cycle engine, 4 x 6. It may have been the Owens brothers who influenced Stearns to use the two-cycle engine.

In any case, for reasons which have not been recorded, by 1900 the Owens brothers pulled out of the enterprise to go their own way. Shortly after that, the project became known as the F.B. Stearns Co.

After that, Frank Stearns didn't have to answer to anybody because he owned every nut, bolt, wrench and lathe in his little factory. By 1901, when he placed a new model on the market, Stearns had switched to the more conventional four-cycle engine, although it was still a one-cylinder.

Ah, but what a cylinder. The new, enlarged machine had a 6¼-inch bore and a 7¼-inch stroke. It was said to be the biggest one-cylinder motor car engine on the market. Imagine: 230 cubic inches from a single cylinder.

For an engine with such a huge cylinder, it had a modest horsepower rating of 10. But Frank Stearns and his company would always be noted for conservative horsepower ratings, so it might be safe to say it whipped out a bit more.

On the 1901 machine the engine hung under the chassis, also a more or less standard practice for the day. The new Stearns also very nearly scored a major "first" by featuring a steering wheel instead of the then-conventional tiller. Packard and Winton managed to beat Stearns to this feature by only a few months.

The next big event for the Stearns enterprise came when the project was considered successful enough to move from the tiny horse barn to a small, single-storied shop on Euclid Avenue in Cleveland. This site would eventually be expanded to contain a multi-storied plant covering six acres.

The year 1901 was also momentous for Frank Stearns because it was the year in which he married Mabelle Wilson, the daughter of another prominent Cleveland family. Her father, Captain Thomas Wilson, had pioneered iron boat shipping on the Great Lakes, and was also a successful banker. With wealth on both sides of the family, Frank Stearns would never have to worry about paying the rent or selling stock to expand the firm.

In 1901 a Stearns machine took part in the New York to Buffalo endurance run on September 9-11. Despite terrible road conditions, the Stearns was running perfectly, among the leaders, when in the midst of the run — at Rochester — word arrived of the assassination of President William McKinley. Out of respect for the fallen president, the run was halted.

By 1902 the tiny Stearns company was able to announce another major engineering development: a new, two-cylinder opposed engine, 5 x 6, lifting the horsepower all the way to 20. It was available with a touring body. The single-cylinder machine was also still available, either with the tonneau (removable

By 1905 the Stearns had grown into a very large machine, with a four-cylinder engine rated at 40 hp. (Photo courtesy Arthur W. Aseltine)

rear seat) or phaeton body. Stearns was now confident enough about what he was doing to advertise that his car was no longer an experiment but "A Reliable Motor Car"—and it was.

In 1902 the company was reorganized and incorporated with a capitalization of $200,000. It was young Stearns, now aged 23, who became president, general manager, and treasurer. His father, although retired from his own business, was well enough impressed by what his "dropout" son was doing to join the enterprise as vice president and secretary.

Perhaps the most significant "happening" for Stearns in 1902, as far as the future success of the company was concerned, came when a young engineer named James Gilman Sterling joined the firm as chief engineer. Known simply as "Pete," Sterling would, in time, earn the reputation as one of the most brilliant automotive engineers in the profession.

By 1903 the Sterling influence was beginning to be felt, as the Stearns company claimed 25 horsepower for a motor now grown to 5 ¾ x 6¼, a whopping 324 cid. (Most motor publications reported 24 hp, but company ads claimed 25.) The car was bigger now, running on a 98-inch wheelbase, with a three-speed

planetary transmission, a claimed speed of 40 mph, and a selling price of $3,000. The body was a large European type. The new car also sported a front hood, or "bonnet," that would soon become virtually standard on all motor cars.

On the two-cylinder Stearns, however, the new bonnet was mostly a styling feature since the engine remained hung under the frame, midway, with only the radiator and an extra water tank housed under the hood. The extra water reserve was to enable the machine to go 200 miles without stopping for water.

The Stearns made a bit of history in 1903 when one of the machines was entered in what was billed as the first race for a Stearns—and won.

It took place on "home ground," the Glenville track near Cleveland, in a race sponsored by the Cleveland Automobile Club on September 3-4.

A reporter for *The Horseless Age* wrote, in describing the events, "Perhaps the most popular wins of the day were those of the Stearns machine—first because it was the first attempt of the Stearns company to win glory on the race track and then because the machine, being of local manufacture, stirred the local patriotism of the visitors; in addition one of the races was quite close."

In the second race of the program a

Stearns, driven by William H. Wright, was entered in a handicap race for members of the Cleveland Automobile Club. Conditions were that all cars had to carry four passengers and "full road equipment," with handicaps assigned by car weight. Since the Stearns was the heaviest car in the race, at 3,000 pounds, it was forced to start last, a full minute behind the front cars in a five-mile race.

The Stearns caught up with and passed the other cars in the third mile, and won going away with a time of 8:28, or approximately 35.5 mph — not bad for a two-cylinder machine made in 1903 and carrying four adult passengers.

Later, in a 10-mile handicap race in which the famed Barney Oldfield drove a 40 hp Winton Pup, the Stearns won again, but Oldfield claimed mechanical troubles. Later in the same program, W.C. Schroeder, with a stripped-down Stearns, challenged Oldfield to a one-mile sprint race. The Stearns managed to stay neck and neck with the heavier, more powerful Winton. At the ¼-mile point, it was even ahead — but Oldfield, in one of his famed finish dash performances, managed to beat the Stearns to the wire by three feet. It was the kind of a finish that brought the crowd to its feet.

It was one of the few occasions when the Stearns company more or less sponsored the racing machines. It was a taste of glory, but there was more to come.

In 1904 Stearns and his new engineer, Sterling, announced what was, in effect, a dream come true for young Stearns. His first attempt at designing an engine had been with an ambitious four-cylinder machine he had not quite been able to perfect. But now, with the help of the brilliant Sterling, Stearns had his four-cylinder motor — and a good one, this time.

The cylinders were cast in pairs, and the crankcase was aluminum. Original announcements said it was a 32-36 hp powerplant, but in later company specifications it was always referred to as a 34 hp engine, weighing in at 4⅜ x 5¼. With 316 cid, it was the biggest four-cylinder engine in the U.S.

Previous Stearns machines had ridden on wooden frames, reinforced by steel. The new four-cylinder machine rode on an all-steel frame. The car had been stretched all the way to 111 inches, weighed 2,600 pounds, and sold for $4,000. The Stearns motor car was growing up.

One of the mechanical mysteries of the Stearns motor cars of this period was that the engines rotated counter-clockwise. No surviving record of the company gives any indication as to why it was done this way but, one thing for certain, it made cranking difficult for right-handed men and women. As the engines grew into monsters, this backward rotation was one of the few features Stearns owners had to complain about.

In any case, it was in August, 1904, when Stearns returned to the Glenville track, the scene of its triumphs in 1903. This time a Stearns, running in a handicap race for "stripped touring cars" at five miles, won the race with a time of 6:19, or 47 mph.

The Stearns was not only growing up, it was becoming faster.

For 1905, although the size and mechanical specifications of the Stearns remained the same as in 1904, Sterling and his crew were able to work a few refinements into the motor which allowed a claim of 40 hp. The Sterling magic was beginning to work.

The glory years: 1906-1910

A new name had begun to muscle its way into the American racing picture. The period was 1907 to 1910. It was a time when the unwritten cardinal rule of American motordom decreed that supremacy in racing, and competition, was the road to success in making motor cars.

The new car was the Stearns, the product of a small, virtually unknown company in Cleveland, Ohio. Although few people beyond the boundaries of Cleveland had paid any heed when the name was first introduced in the 1896-1900 period, the motor car world was now jolted to attention as the new challenger began flipping its heels at its competitors. In the process of doing so, it was also setting a few world records.

In 1907 the F.B. Stearns Co introduced the model 45-90, with the biggest and most powerful motor car engine

This Stearns 30-60 was the first car to conquer Pike's Peak under its own power. It managed the feat on Sept. 6, 1907.

in the country—a six, displacing a staggering 800 cubic inches. The machine was promptly taken to Ventnor Beach in Atlantic City, N.J., where it set a proclaimed world record for stock cars in the straight-away mile with a speed of 87 miles per hour, or a mile in 41⅖ seconds.

Most American motor cars at this time were chugging around at 15 to 20 miles per hour. In its final form, the 45-90 would prove that it could churn out 100 horsepower and do 100 mph. There was hardly a road, or a track, where one could safely run a motor car at such speeds at that time.

When the machine started showing up at hill climbs, another favorite for proving the supremacy of a make of motor car, it began winning every event in sight. If a Stearns 45-90 showed up at a hill climb, the other drivers might just as well pack up and head home.

Most students of Stearns history have more or less agreed that Frank Stearns never really wanted to make the six. He believed that four cylinders were enough.

Again, one must keep things within the

context of time. A major portion of the motor car industry back then was still producing one and two-cylinder machines. The four-cylinder engine was just coming into prominence, and was considered the "in" thing. Only a very few makers—such as Pierce-Arrow, Thomas, Ford and Franklin — had been making noises in the six-cylinder field. These machines were generally considered freaks.

But Stearns had hired a brilliant young engineer, Pete Sterling, in 1902. Sterling was a man with bold new ideas for the future, and it was he who persuaded Stearns to give the go-ahead to develop the big six.

There probably were other factors, too. We remember, Stearns had been severely injured in a high-speed crash in 1905; a young cousin was killed in another crash. Like other manufacturers, when faced with such tragedy, Stearns more or less turned thumbs down on company support for racing and speed competition.

Any glory won by Stearns machines after that was due to dealers and private owners who entered races with no company support.

And then came one of the strangest factors of all, the 30-60 story.

Stearns had introduced his first four-cylinder engine for sale in 1904, a 4⅜ x 5¼, for 316 cubic inches. It was rated at 36 hp. By 1905 that engine had been improved and rated at 40 hp.

For 1906, the engine was stretched to 4⅞8, with 439 cubic inches and a rating of 40-45 hp. In the 1907 model year Stearns introduced the machine which was, in a sense, to become the "Cinderella" car of the entire Stearns story.

To produce this "wonder car," the engineers stretched the size of the big four still farther: all the way to 5⅜ x 5⅞, for a whopping 533 cubic inches. It was the biggest stock four-cylinder engine being made in America at the time. This, in itself, should have been — and was — an attention grabber.

The new machine was called the Model 30-60, for its horsepower rating. The double number requires an explanation. Stearns, Sterling and their men had come up with what, for its day, was a unique carburetor that was almost prophetic in pointinng the way to the future, when knowledgeable men would talk about "two barrels," "four barrels," etc.

The Stearns men described their new carburetor as being "of the double jet type, practically two carburetors with but one reservoir or float chamber."

Pictures of the carburetor and descriptions published in the motoring journals of the day made it clear that the new carburetor really had two throats, each fed by its own main jet. When traveling at low or idling speeds, only one throat (or venturi) was in play. Air was sucked in past the jet through a spring-loaded valve which yielded to the slightest suction.

It was only when the driver opened the throttle past a certain middle position to grab for more speed, or more power for a steep hill, that a lever would open a second valve. This valve allowed intake suction from the engine to enter throat (venturi) number two and then, in turn, lift open a second spring-loaded valve to allow air to come in from the bottom, past jet number two. A third jet was simply an idler jet, to allow a bit of air to enter throat number one for idling.

Stearns ad men claimed you could run the car down the street at idling speed, using perhaps three horsepower. When you opened the throttle far enough to get full use of throat number one, your engine was shoving out 30 hp — all a man needed for normal driving, they said. Only by stomping the throttle all the way to the floor, with both throats roaring at full blast, did you get 60 hp.

Perhaps Stearns and his men did not realize what they had on their hands when they took the new 30-60 out for its first test drive. With that whopping four-cylinder engine and the new dual throat carburetor, they probably should have been prepared for it. The 30-60 would go out to do battle on the race-tracks and hills of America, and bring most of the glory to the Stearns name in the next three years.

It was not done with the backing of the parent company. Dealers and private owners did it because the new machine was simply too hot to be kept secret.

A look at the record for 1907 presents a sensational picture for the new upstart. At Brighton Beach, one of the big time circular tracks of its day, a Stearns 30-60 driven by Guy Vaughn ran away with three races in which it was entered, including the five-mile Atlantic Sweepstakes, which it won with a time of 5:11. At the Latonia track in Cincinnati, a 30-60 Stearns driven by A.V. Stegman claimed a new world record for the 25-mile distance for fully equipped touring cars, with a time of 29.30.

In Sacramento, a fully equipped Stearns touring car claimed another world record for a five-mile race, with a winning time of 5:19. At Atlantic City, Guy Vaughn won eight of the 10 races he entered. The only car that beat him was another Stearns—a "Big Daddy" 45-90 driven by F.W. Leland.

At Point Breeze in Philadelphia, the Stearns driven by Vaughn won every race in which it was eligible, defeating a 60 hp French car and a 60 hp German car. At Harlem track in Chicago, a Stearns won two more races.

It was also in this first year, 1907, that the new 30-60 began winning hill climbs wherever it went — at places like Fort

This 1908 Stearns 30-60 is fitted with the toy tonneau body. The car's incredible power made it a formidable competitor on any track.

Pierce Hill, New York; Stucky Hill, Ohio; and Wilkes-Barre, Pennsylvania. In most of the hill climbs, the Stearns was out in front by as much as 11 to 17 seconds.

But the most sensational hill climb that year involved Pikes Peak in Colorado. Here there was no half mile or even mile climb to the top of the hometown favorite "steep hill," as in most hill climbs. Here was a 14,110-foot mountain whose peak could be reached only by a tortuous trail more than 12 miles long which had, until now, defied all challenges by a motor car.

On September 6, 1907, a Stearns 30-60 not only became the first motor car to climb the entire distance under its own power, but it carried seven passengers. Could a Stearns earn any brighter laurels than this?

In 1908, it was virtually a repeat. For example: in the 1908 Long Island Motor Club's road race, Stearns cars took all four first places in the four-cylinder class. In the six-cylinder class, the 45-90 took top honors by beating such cars as the famed Thomas—considered one of the toughest and fastest cars of its day — plus an Acme, a Hotchskiss, a Mora and one of the new six-cylinder Fords.

In 1909 Stearns cars, especially the 30-60, once again took more than their share of honors in races and hill climbs.

In 1910, after a new series of wins, a Stearns 30-60 driven by Al Pool and Cyrus Patschke claimed one of the most prestigious world records of all: the most miles covered in a 24-hour run at Brighton Beach (New York). The sturdy Stearns covered 1,253 miles in the 24-hour grind, or 57 miles more than the record set the previous year by a Lozier.

One of the leading motor journals of the day, *The Automobile,* pulled no punches in terming the new record "the most marked exhibition of consistent running ever seen in this country."

What the Brighton Beach run proved, if proof were still needed, was that the Stearns motor cars were not only fast, but tough and durable. A 24-hour grind was the kind of thing a manufacturer shied away from unless it had the utmost confidence in the toughness and durability of the machine it was making—or, if not the manufacturer, the dealer or owner.

Why didn't the big 45-90 — purportedly the fastest and most powerful motor car made in the U.S. — win more honors for the Stearns name? Why was it the smaller 30-60 that copped so many of the big honors, including the Pikes Peak climb and the Brighton Beach 24-hour run?

The answer involves several factors, some factual and some based on conjecture. First, there was the fact that Frank Stearns apparently had built the big 45-90 reluctantly. He did not actively promote it, always downplayed it in Stearns ads, and certainly never gave it the backing needed to mount a successful racing program. Beyond that, with so few of the big machines made and most of them probably supplied in ornate limousine or landaulet bodies, few owners were willing to strip them or risk their appearance in races.

The 45-90 was a luxury car, pure and simple, selling at prices ranging from $6,250 to $7,600 in the 1909-1910 period. These prices were head-on in the upper class, with Pierce-Arrow, Packard and Peerless. It was not a race car.

Much the same could be said for the 30-60, but here the old "horsepower-to-weight" ratio came into play. The smaller Stearns had just about the biggest four-cylinder engine in the U.S., and even the company boasted that the top horsepower rating of 60 was conservative. It was, indeed, a healthy hunk of motor; equipped with that superb double throat carburetor, it was a "go" machine.

Since the car was selling for prices at least a couple of thousand dollars below the big 45-90, and was sold in far greater numbers, owners and dealers were probably less reluctant to strip and prepare a 30-60 for battle.

Although there is no evidence to prove it, the 30-60 may have been one of those rare machines where everything turned out just right: balance, engineering, weight, the harmony of iron and steel, all coupled to one of the most powerful, flexible and willing engines ever installed in a motor car up to that time. Several critical drivers, given a chance to drive one of the Stearns 30-60's in restored form many years later, would say, "Gee, this thing takes off like a modern day sports car."

Stearns dealers and owners knew it in the 1907-1910 period. The competition was learning.

For years, Stearns fans have asked, "Which one was better and which was faster—the 30-60 or the monstrous 45-90?"

In 1965, the late Bill Harrah, owner of the fabulous Harrah Collection of old cars and of the only Stearns 45-90 known to exist, agreed to race it against an equally well restored 30-60 with Ben Mozzetti at the wheel. "Big Daddy" proved on this occasion that it could easily outrun the 30-60, as it did on a few occasions back in the 1907-1910 period. But, as the rec-

ord clearly shows, with a skilled driver at the wheel, in the blood and guts competition of real racing, it was the 30-60 which set the blood to tingling in the showdowns.

There is one published record of the Jamaica, Long Island, speed trials on April 27, 1909, which seems to indicate that both a 30-60 and a 45-90 ran in the "equipped" stock car runs, and that the 30-60 set better times than the larger car. The exact circumstances which made this possible are unknown.

What was happening during this period in the area of Stearns passenger cars — the street machines? After all, this is what automobile manufacturing is all about, with sales to the public paying the bills.

First, it must be remembered that Stearns never built a special racer. If any Stearns won a race, a private individual could buy a duplicate from a Stearns dealer.

For 1906 Stearns had upped the size of the four-cylinder engine, and had introduced the first version of the two-stage carburetor, resulting in the 40-45 hp rating. Three Hess-Bright ball bearings were used on the crankshaft. Cylinders were still cast in pairs.

Back in 1905, the Stearns had been the first American car to use a four-speed transmission. This feature continued into the 1906, 1907 and later models. The wheelbase on the 1906 models remained at 118 inches, and the final drive remained by chain, although the industry had begun its swing to shaft drive. Stearns ad men pointed out how much easier a chain drive was to repair in the field, when expert mechanics were not available.

In 1906 the Stearns 40-45 was available as a touring, a toy tonneau (the model that could be converted from a four-passenger touring to a roadster in minutes), a pullman touring (with a semi-hard top) and a limousine. The toy tonneau was the model usually used for racing, by removing the rear seat.

Stearns was advertising cast-aluminum bodies to reduce weight. This had been a Pierce-Arrow feature of the time. The use of aluminum made it possible to hold down the weight of a car with touring body to 2,800 pounds. Was this, pos-

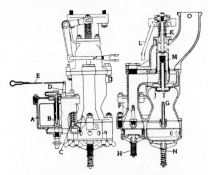

Schematic illustrates the intricacies of the Stearns two-barrel carburetor, which enable the 30-60 to develop 30 hp for normal street operation and, by opening the throttle and kicking in the second barrel, to deliver 60 hp for climbing that steep hill or shooting past neighbor Jones in his new "Whooshmobile."

sibly, another factor in the nimble performance of the Stearns machines in racing?

Front tires were 36 x 4, and rear were 36 x 4½. Prices on the 30-60 ranged from $4,000 for the standard touring to $5,200 for the limousine. Styling, especially on the closed body types, was ornate and luxurious, even if somewhat high-topped and "stilted" to a modern viewer.

Searching for a unique method of making the Stearns motor cars easily identifiable amid the vast array of offerings available at that time, Stearns stylists came up with a white line running around the edge of the radiator shell. It was the "distinctive" feature on the Stearns from that time on, and was heavily promoted in the ads: "When you see the white line you know it is a Stearns."

Following Frank Stearns' mania for quality, 44 ball and roller anti-friction bearings were used on the car. Company ads claimed that at least 2,000 man hours were expended in the construction, assembly and testing of every Stearns made. Ad men further boasted that the new Stearns was the fulfillment of "the prophecy of ultimate supremacy of the American motor car."

Then came 1907, the year of the big jump—the appearance of the famed 30-60 and, a few months later, the 45-90.

The wheelbase on the 30-60 was 120 inches; on the 45-90, 128 inches (it would eventually go to 130). By way of comparison, the wheelbase of the big-

gest Packard model that year was 122. Perhaps the only car with a longer wheelbase at that time was the Pierce-Arrow, at 135, which led its proponents to boast that the Pierce Great Arrow was America's biggest motor car. In length and weight, perhaps it was, but the Stearns had by far the biggest and most powerful engine, rated at from 90 to 100 hp, compared to 60 to 65 hp ratings for Pierce.

The 45-90 used the same bore and stroke, plus the same block, pistons and connecting rods as the 30-60; the difference being made by adding an extra block in the two-cylinder block configuration, plus a longer crankshaft. This latter item, conforming to the Stearns mania for quality—only the best—was machined from a solid billet of steel. There was no more expensive way to make a crankshaft.

The Stearns plant was expanded by another 10,000 feet in 1907, and the April, 1907, issue of *The Automobile* noted that Stearns had ordered a number of special gear-cutting machines made in Germany because the type and quality he demanded was not available in the U.S. It was more proof that Stearns and his top engineer, Sterling, would never settle for anything less than the best.

"America has not produced a rival to the Stearns," the ad men boasted.

For 1908 the 30-60 and 45-90 models were continued with few changes, the biggest being the switch to double ignition. The front of the 30-60 frame got a drop of 2½ inches for better roadability. The 45-90 got this change the next year. Specifications listed improvements in the transmission, the steering and the carburetor. Basically, however, the famed double throat carburetor remained.

Then came 1909, with the big news from the Stearns plant that the company would now market a smaller, lower-priced car, obviously in an attempt to capture a larger share of the market. But Stearns ad men didn't advertise it that way. It was, they said, targeted at the car buyer who was "intent upon securing the utmost in modern car construction, yet not desiring the wonderful power of our larger cars."

The new, smaller machine, for the first

time in Stearns history, had a four-cylinder monobloc engine, 4½ x 4⅝ — very nearly square, but still a good-sized engine at 294 cubic inches. Using the old standard double throat carburetor, the power designation on the new machine was 15-30.

Also new on the smaller Stearns was shaft drive to the rear wheels, a feature advertised as optional equipment on the 30-60. It was standard on the 15-30, which also carried the transmission on the rear axle, this time a three-speed as compared to the famed four-speeds of the bigger cars.

The new car rode on a 116-inch wheelbase, and was available in the familiar toy tonneau (four-passenger, except when switched to roadster form), the five-passenger regular touring, a limousine, and a landaulet. Colors were Stearns red, blue, maroon, gray or green. Prices on the new, smaller cars ranged from $3,200 for the five-passenger touring to $4,600 for the limousine or landaulet. With such prices, it was impossible to suggest it was a cheap car. It wasn't — in price or in quality.

Now that a smaller machine was in the Stearns showrooms, it was time to phase out the big 45-90 which, in a sense, had been an orphan from the beginning. The big machine was listed in the catalogs for the last time in 1910. Indications are that few of them were made or sold that year.

Brilliant as the concept may have been, and powerful as the machine was, it had its drawbacks. With the engine turning counter-clockwise, a feature Stearns never attempted to explain, it took a very strong man to crank it even with compression release features. For a woman, it was nearly impossible. (This was before starters had been invented.) And where were the roads on which to use all that power and speed?

For 1910 the 30-60 and the 15-30 would continue with minor changes, and the company announced that Stearns cars would no longer be designated by model year.

The Stearns ad writers, obviously with the approval of Frank B. Stearns, began to suggest that, with the latest Stearns machine, a millennium — perfection — had been reached. "The time has come," the ads declared, "when Stearns represents about the best we ever can hope for. For 13 years we have constantly added perfections. But we are now pretty close to the limit."

It was strange language to come from the maker of any motor car, especially one which planned to continue building cars.

A similar incident involved Ransom E. Olds, one of the most famed of the early day motor car pioneers, who created both the Oldsmobile and the Reo. He believed his great Reo the Fifth was the perfect car, and went so far as to call it his "Farewell Car."

The Stearns ad men had not gone quite that far, but there it was. Was it some kind of a smokescreen, to assure prospective Stearns buyers of the quality of the cars being offered — while the company and its engineers planned one of the most radical changes in motor making in American history?

The sleeve valve engine returns to America: 1909-1915

I t had to be one of the major events in the history of the American motor car: bringing the sleeve valve engine to the U.S.

Perhaps it is more correct to say it was brought "back home" to the U.S., for it was originally an American invention.

It was an important moment. Before the sleeve valve chapter of motor car history ended, there were more than a dozen American manufacturers involved, with thousands upon thousands of the machines running successfully on the streets and highways of the country.

Into this picture, the F.B. Stearns Co. is assigned top honors for two reasons:
• Stearns was the first maker to bring the exotic and "different" engine back to the U.S.
• It is a virtually undisputed fact that Stearns made the most powerful, the best performing, and the most highly crafted sleeve valve engines in the country.

They were, perhaps, the equal of any

in the world, although this means matching Stearns against such European makers as Daimler, of England; Mercedes, of Germany; and Minerva, of Belgium. Such a tall claim becomes even taller when one finds in today's world the owner of a 1913 six-cylinder Stearns-Knight willing to match the performance of his machine against nothing less than the mighty and legendary Duesenberg J—a story which will be told later.

The sleeve valve story is an old one, told and retold, but most often in context with Willys-Knight history. This is, perhaps, understandable when one considers that the Willys-Overland Co. made more sleeve valve engines than any other maker, and probably had them on the market longer than any other American make. In addition, John North Willys was a flamboyant character who knew how to capitalize, publicity-wise, on what he was doing. So did the engine's inventor, Charles Y. Knight.

This is not to say that Willys-Knight engines were not good ones. They were, with a long and honorable record for service and reliability. But the Stearns-Knight was, in a sense, almost a breed apart, with quality and performance unmatched by any other American sleeve valve engine.

And, again, it was Stearns who brought the sleeve valve engine back to America. The concept had originally been the brainchild of Charles Knight, a newspaperman, salesman, tinkerer and inventor with roots in places like Salem, Indiana, Chicago and Milwaukee.

Unimpressed with the noisy and trouble-prone poppet valves used on the early day internal combustion engines, but impressed with the smoothness and efficiency of the sliding valves on steam engines, Knight set about to apply the sliding valve to internal combustion engines.

After several years of experimenting around 1903 and 1904, he came up with an engine in which the piston was surrounded by a sleeve — eventually, two sleeves—with slotted ports. The sleeves were geared to slide up and down, open-

The first sleeve-valve-powered motor car made in the U.S, the Stearns-Knight Four, was introduced in June, 1911, for the 1912 model year. Although it was rated at only 28 hp, it produced an eye popping 61 hp on the test stands.

173

ing and closing ports at the proper instant to admit the mixture of air and gasoline, and to exhaust the burned vapors after combustion. It represented quite a departure from the normal valve practice.

After he had "perfected" the sleeve valve engine — and impressed with the quiet manner in which his engines operated — he dubbed them the Silent-Knights. Then, with the backing of a wealthy man named L.B. Kilbourne, Knight made a few of the Silent-Knights and sold them, around the 1905-1907 period.

But Knight never really wanted to be a manufacturing mogul. Instead, he tried to sell the concept, the design, to already established auto makers. When this part of his dream didn't jell in America, and after receiving an inquiry from the Daimler Motor Co., of Coventry, England, Knight packed up one of his Knight-powered cars and took off for England.

Thus begins the strange story of the prophet of sleeve valves, who was unable to establish enough honor in his own land to make them a success, but obtained results abroad. In a short time the roster of European car makers producing sleeve valve engines included the most prestigious names of all: Daimler, Belgium's Minerva, Germany's Mercedes, and Panhard et Levassor, of France. All were makers of the great, ornate limousines in which rode the royalty of Europe, including the Czar of Russia.

Daimler, as the first to use it, adopted the strange engine only after a lot of soul searching and extensive testing.

The engine not only withstood the most grueling tests the Daimler engineers could dream up, but passed them with flying colors. The tests were conducted under the auspices of the Royal Automobile Club of Great Britain to make certain nobody could accuse Daimler of cheating. Then Daimler challenged any other motor maker to match its results. Nobody did. In the end, it was sleeve valve powered cars which began winning prestigious endurance tests in Europe.

Perhaps the features that did the most to sell the Europeans were silence and the marvelous characteristic sleeve valve engines had of improving with age and hot running. The utter silence of the engines was important, considering the clientele. Kings and queens didn't like a lot of clatter with their transportation.

In the poppet valve engines of that day, even the best of steels did not prevent valve springs from weakening with heat, or valves from warping and choking up with carbon — all robbing the engine of efficiency. Here was a strange import from America that seemed to thrive on heat and long hours of running.

The carbon, instead of gunking things up, seemed to improve the sealing of compression. You put one of the sleeve valve engines on a dynamometer and, after running it 50 hours or so, the horsepower needle began climbing instead of dropping.

Many old time car lovers laugh when they hear stories about the sleeve valvers. Sleeve valve engines, they suggest, are something on the freaky side from long, long ago. They're duds, they say, weak sisters with little "oomph."

It is true that, as the years passed, spring steel improved, new valve alloys became available, and more efficient designs came along, allowing the poppet valve engines to catch up with the sleevers. But in the period from around 1909 to 1915, perhaps even as late as 1920, the sleeve valve engines may well have been the best and most efficient motor car engines made.

Perhaps the biggest drawback at that time was the added time and cost of making them. They were simply too expensive for low-priced cars.

Daimler continued to make sleeve valve engineered motor cars as late as 1935 — and Minerva, as late as 1939 — long after the poppet valve engines supposedly had knocked the sleeve valve engines out of the picture.

Sleeve valve powered tanks broke the Hindenburg line in World War I. In 1915 a Mercedes-Knight placed fifth in the famed Indianapolis 500, despite the fact that it had the smallest engine of any car finishing in the top 10. The winner, a Peugeot, had a 448 cid engine, compared to the 251 inches in the Knight.

It was in 1909 that the Stearns company sent its brilliant chief engineer, Pete Sterling, to England to check on the Daimler success story. The impetus for

The new six-cylinder sleeve valve entry from Stearns was a phenomenal machine in terms of performance. This stately seven-passenger touring car is shown as it appeared in the company's 1913 catalog.

the trip obviously came from the fact that Daimler had just won the famed Dewar trophy for the most significant contribution to the development of the motor car for that year.

Daimler won the trophy by putting two of its sleeve valve engines to the most grueling tests a man could devise, on the test stands and on the racetrack at Brooklands, proving that the engines improved after hours of running. They challenged anyone, including Rolls-Royce, to match the performance—but nobody could.

Sterling's grandson, another "Pete," remembers that it was the Association of Licensed Automobile Manufacturers (ALAM) which financed Sterling's trip. The younger Sterling said his grandfather immediately met Knight, the inventor, who had moved to England to be near the scene of his brilliant success. Sterling was a guest in the Knight home, and Knight personally escorted Sterling to the Daimler plant to meet the engineers, see the engine at work, and inspect the assembly lines.

It would be interesting to speculate on what was going on in Sterling's mind at this point. He had, behind him, a brilliant record as the designer and builder of some of the best and most powerful motor cars in America. The 45-90 and the 30-60, combined, had been a spectacular coup. Now he was contemplating moving into a completely new field of motor car engine design.

He simply had to make the right decision for he, and his company, had everything to lose if the sleeve valve engine turned out to be a flop. On the other hand, the test results he saw at Daimler, the

quiet, masterful performance of the cars he tested, were so convincing he couldn't lose. If Daimler could do it, he could do it.

Sterling came home with at least one complete Daimler automobile and several of the Daimler engines, his suitcases stuffed with blueprints, and four licenses from Knight for manufacturers in the U.S. to make the sleeve valve engines. Knight had been willing to grant more licenses but, under pressure from the already licensed European makers, he cut the number to four. Sterling had been entrusted with the licenses as a representative of the ALAM.

One thing was certain: Stearns would get license No. 1. Other early licensees were the Columbia Motor Car Co., of Hartford, Connecticut (Columbia-Knight); the Dayton Motor Co., of Dayton, Ohio (Stoddard-Knight, which later became the Edwards-Knight); and the Atlas Motor Car Co., of Springfield, Massachusetts (Atlas-Knight). Knight had stipulated that his name must be connected to each make of car using his engine design.

Even with the Daimler engines as patterns, plus the blueprints, Sterling did his own designing and testing. He started by taking the beautiful and sweet running little four-cylinder 15-30 Stearns engine, tuning it to the highest peak possible, and incorporating every engineering improvement available under the "state of the art" in 1910. He then used this engine as the comparison model against which he would match the new sleeve valve engine he was about to produce.

The results on the 15-30 engine were spectacular enough. The engine had always been rated at 15 and 30 horsepower under the old, reliable Stearns dual carburetor system. Of course, Stearns ratings had always been conservative, so maybe the little engine could be credited with 35 hp in its original form. After the Sterling "soup up" job, they were able to squeeze 51.3 brake horsepower out of the little engine. The results may have been so astounding as to give Sterling second thoughts about his sleeve valve project. But he had started, and he would complete the test.

He now designed and built the prototype for the new Stearns-Knight engine. The 15-30 four-cylinder poppet valve engine had been a 4 ½ x 4⅝, which measured 294 cubic inches. The prototype sleeve valver checked in at 4¼ x 5½ — with a smaller bore but a longer stroke, adding up to a slightly larger engine at 312 cid.

The results are interesting. Although the engines were not exactly the same size, a comparison can be made by using a bit of simple math. The 15-30 came up with a maximum of 51.3 hp at 2,140 rpm. The sleeve valve engine, when put on the dynamometer, shoved the horsepower needle all the way to 64.1 at 2,290 rpm.

By applying a bit of basic math, we come up with .173 horsepower per cubic inch for the 15-30 poppet valve engine, and .205 horsepower per cubic inch for the sleeve valver.

The torque curve showed even more interesting results. The poppet valve engine churned out its highest torque—165 pounds — at 600 rpm. The sleeve valve engine produced that much torque at speeds as low as 480 rpm, then went on to push it up to 185 pounds at 1,200 rpm. Even more significant, the torque curve on the sleeve valve engine remained above the 160-pound mark all the way to the 1,800 rpm range, while the poppet valve engine's torque, at this speed, had dropped to 138. Obviously, the new sleeve valve job was a work horse, a real puller, uphill or on the flat, and at all normal driving speeds.

With the new Stearns-Knight prototype engine running flawlessly on the test stands, Sterling was ready to drop it into a modified 15-30 chassis. When he climbed behind the wheel and began his first test drive, his smile began to grow.

He told his test drivers to drive the new engine to death. They tried, and couldn't. He had another winner.

On June 20, 1911, Sterling invited a reporter for *The Horseless Age,* a leading motor magazine of the day, for a demonstration drive. The engine ran so quietly, the reporter said, "at from 6 to 40 miles per hour one could neither distinguish a sound from the motor nor perceptibly feel it."

The car would accelerate easily up to 60 miles per hour, he wrote, with the engine turning at 2,100 rpm. A hill climb, the reporter added, "showed the motor to be able to run at exceedingly low speed under full load." On an acceleration test, he said, "the car went from zero to 49 miles per hour in 40 seconds."

The first production machines came off the assembly lines in July, 1911. Sterling proudly invited five passengers to share and witness the first long distance trip— from Cumberland, Maryland, to Cleveland — for a car powered by the new generation of sleeve valve engines. They made the trip from sunrise to sunset, stopping only for fuel. There were no service stations, and the roads were on the rough side. The new history of sleeve valve engines in America had begun.

Now it was time to pull out all stops in production of the new machine. Orders were pouring in by the hundreds. Stearns felt so confident of success that he leased the production facilities of the old Royal Tourist plant to expand production.

The Stearns had always been a low production machine, committed to quality rather than quantity. But in the first year of production for the new sleeve valve engine, production climbed to 875 —doubling that of the previous year.

A bit of description may be in order. For his new engine, Sterling had abandoned the old Stearns practice of using only ball bearings for main engine crankshaft mounts. Instead, he went to a five main configuration, using the best bronze-backed bearings available. Oiling was by pressure pump except to the connecting rods, which grabbed their oil by dipper, the dipper troughs being adjustable to allow changes for engine load and speed, and to prevent excessive oil consumption. The engine drew its air through boxed beams inside the engine for heating, a feature so important in that day of poor quality gasoline.

The clutch was a multiple disc dry type, with alternate discs of steel and asbestos fabric. The clutch was so smooth that one dealer allowed his picture to be taken as he closed the lid on his expensive gold watch by running the wheel of a Stearns against it — without crushing the watch. The drive was by a sturdy, yoked torque tube to the rear axle, where the differential and transmission were encased in the same housing.

Later day practices would rule out such construction, on the grounds that it placed too much unsprung weight on the axle, but in that day the design was used successfully on several cars, including the famed Stutz Bearcat.

Always fearful of multi-piece, riveted rear axle housings, Sterling was not satisfied until he could come up with a means of forging a one-piece housing. The rear axles were the floating type. Brakes, on the rear, were of the internal expanding type in a day when most cars used external contracting, a type more exposed to dirt.

The new sleeve valve Stearns-Knight was available in the famed toy tonneau, a roadster, a touring and a landaulet. Prices ranged from $3,500 for the roadster to $4,900 for the landaulet. These prices were $300 more than the previous year's models, and probably reflected the additional cost of making the sleeve valve engines. Adding $300 to the price of the cheaper cars of the day — a Model T Ford, for example—would have been prohibitive.

It was probably inevitable that Stearns would continue production of the highly successful 30-60, with the old poppet valve design, for at least a year after the introduction of the smaller sleeve valve

The unusual landaulet body style was offered in both four- and six-cylinder models in the Stearns-Knight line for 1913. This is a six-cylinder version.

engine (which was intended to succeed the 15-30).

Was it insurance against a possible failure of the sleeve valve to capture a buying audience? That's a thought, of course. One could always fall back on a tried and true design. But from another standpoint, it would have strained the facilities of the Stearns plant to introduce two sleeve valve engines simultaneously.

It was equally inevitable that, once the Knight-engined car had "caught on," a bigger Knight-engined car would be on the boards.

It was. Sterling, always a lover of hefty, muscular engines, was coming up with a six-cylinder sleeve valve engine — another first for America.

The bore would remain the same as the four, at 4¼, but Sterling stretched the stroke a bit, to 5¾, which meant that the new engine displaced a hefty 489 cubic inches. It was not quite as big as the hotshot 30-60 had been, at 533 — but almost. The longer stroke meant higher compression and more power, made possible by use of an electric self-starter.

Some old timers may be surprised to hear that the new Stearns-Knight six had a counterbalanced crankshaft. It was a feature Hudson would tout as a "first" in 1916. But the feature made the new six even smoother, and more powerful.

After the engine had been completed and put on the test stands, it became apparent Pete Sterling had come up with another "eye-popper" with power and performance, a la sleeve.

His earlier sensation, the lively 30-60 that won a world record for a 24-hour run, had been given a top horsepower rating of 60. Considering the usual conservative rating that was traditional at Stearns, it is likely the true power was nearer 70.

Even with 44 fewer cubic inches in size, the new sleeve valve six—officially rated at 43⅓ hp on the old license system — quickly shoved the horsepower needle all the way to 70 at speeds as low as 1,200, and all the way to 100 at 2,300 rpm. Even the monster 45-90, with its whopping 800 cubic inches, hadn't been able to top that. The torque on the new six was more impressive: 280 pounds at 1,200 rpm and remaining above the 250-

pound range all the way to 1,800 rpm. Who could match this, inch for inch?

Another Stearns-Sterling sensation had been born.

Once again it was, strangely, without the hoopla one might have expected to accompany an engine with such exciting performance — especially since Stearns, and other sleeve valve engine makers, were fighting so hard at the time for recognition.

One searches the old motoring journals of the day almost in vain for anything that boasted of the performance prowess of this machine, even in the company's ads.

The ads spoke of the Six's remarkable durability, reliability and quality. There were testimonial letters, such as the one from Dan H. Wesson, of the famed Smith & Wesson arms maker, who told of driving one of the 1913 sixes 137,000 miles in five seasons and liking it so well he was going to put a new body on it.

In a speech made in 1923, Henry H. Hower, once with the Stearns company but later a newspaper automotive editor, said, in speaking of the Stearns Six of the 1913-1915 era, "They had one of the finest engines ever put into an automobile by anybody, anywhere."

But when it came to sheer performance, it almost seemed as if it had to remain for a much later generation — present day restorers lucky enough to own one of the few remaining examples — to really "discover" the 1913-1915 Stearns-Knight Six.

In 1984 Arthur W. Aseltine, of Forbestown, California, the owner of the only 1913 Stearns-Knight Six known to exist, said: "I will be glad to match the power of my 1913 Stearns-Knight Six, with its 490 cubic inch engine, any day with any Duesenberg J. My 1913 Stearns-Knight goes up the hill above my home in high gear, and without downshifting, faster than the late model generation of V-8 muscle cars. It even amazes my son, who had a 485 hp Corvette-powered Chevrolet El Camino. At speeds above, say, 50 miles per hour, the more modern high-speed engines would, of course, have the advantage."

One might be tempted to suggest that there is just a bit of wishful thinking in a statement as bold as that, but there it is.

And, whether true or not, when a mature man like Aseltine — engineer by profession and car restorer by avocation —makes a statement that bold, it cannot fail to arouse wonder at what type of black magic Sterling had been able to come up with in 1913.

Another American first— a sleeve valve V-8: 1915-1922

A nd then America had its first sleeve valve V-8. It was a Stearns, of course — or, more appropriately, a Stearns-Knight.

The new sleeve valve engine for the Stearns-Knight was developed in 1915 and introduced to the public at the auto shows in January, 1916.

There would be only one other sleeve valve V-8, a Willys-Knight, which appeared on the market a year later.

The new sleeve valve V-8 for Stearns was a product of the times. Cadillac, under the direction of the brilliant Henry Leland, had pioneered America's first production V-8 engine around the 1914-1915 period. This engine set off a flurry of activity from the competition.

Suddenly, it seemed, nearly every motor car maker which considered itself in the middle or upper-price range wanted a V-8. Before the flurry of V-8 activity would subside, perhaps a dozen or more makers were loudly touting their own version of the V-8. Among them were Apperson, Chevrolet, Cole, Cunningham, Daniels, King, Lafayette, Lincoln, Mitchell, Oldsmobile and Scripps-Booth. All of the new V-8's were standard poppet valve types, except for the Stearns-Knight and the Willys-Knight engines.

Of them all, only Cadillac and Lincoln (which was a latecomer to the scene) would remain with the V-8's for the long haul.

This is a picture of Frank B. Stearns and is believed to have been taken shortly after his retirement as president. He was only 37 years old.

It was, perhaps, inevitable that Frank Stearns and Pete Sterling, who considered themselves among the top makers of quality motor cars, should find themselves compelled to join the parade—or, in a sense, to lead it, since they would be tackling a new concept in V-8's. Adapting sleeve valves to a V-8 engine wouldn't be easy.

Instead of shuddering at the engineering problems involved, Sterling and his men in the Stearns engineering department simply did it. When it was completed, they were willing to claim it was a good one. Hundreds of Stearns customers would drive the machine and agree.

The new, history-making machine weighed in with a 3¼ bore and 5-inch stroke, with a very respectable 332 cubic inches and a taxable horsepower of 33.8. The brake horsepower is a bit of a mystery.

For reasons which Stearns-Knight researchers have been unable to discover, the F.B. Stearns Co. apparently never published the brake horsepower on the new V-8. Arthur W. Aseltine — who, in 1984, probably had the best collection of Stearns/Stearns-Knight literature in the country and had been researching the make for years—had been unable to find it.

It is a bit strange when one considers that, from the very beginning, even in the early one-cylinder days, Stearns, and later Sterling, had always been eager to boast of the power of their magnificent engines. The great 45-90 engine, for example, had produced 100 hp as early as 1907. There was a long and loud boast about the horsepower ratings of the first sleeve valve engines, when they were produced in the 1911-1912 period. Then there was the magnificent 1913 Stearns-Knight Six, for which a dynamometer reading of 100 bhp had been claimed, even though it was a much smaller engine than the famed 45-90.

Why, suddenly, was there silence about the brake horsepower of the new V-8 engines? Was it, perhaps, because the new V-8—for the first time in Stearns history — had come up with a power rating so disappointing one didn't want to talk about it?

Probably not. More likely is the theory of Aseltine, who guessed that it was more because Stearns and Sterling had come somewhat under the spell of Rolls-Royce and Daimler, and perhaps were coming to think of themselves as makers of cars in the Rolls-Royce class—but for America.

In England and on the Continent, Rolls and Daimler had enjoyed the reputation of "the elite" when it came to the making of luxury motor cars: never mind the price. These makers, especially Rolls-Royce, had come to consider it a bit on the vulgar side to advertise, or even discuss, such things as brake horsepower. There would be no horsepower race for them.

An association by Stearns with Rolls and Daimler would be a bit more than incidental. It was the Daimler plant in England that Pete Sterling had visited while studying the possibility of making sleeve valve engined cars in America. He had brought several of the Daimler sleeve valve engines home to the Stearns plant to serve as models. The Stearns-Knight sleeve valve engines were born from that association.

Now there was also a connection with Rolls-Royce.

When World War I began in 1914, the European Allies suddenly found themselves short on manufacturing facilities for making the truck engines, aircraft engines, and other machinery of war so necessary to support the giant effort. In casting about for help, they had only one place to go: the new, lusty and growing giant of an industrial complex developing in America. When Rolls was given the job of building aircraft engines—but was unable to build enough of them—they joined the trek for help to the U.S.

Being Rolls-Royce, they had to search out a plant capable of meeting their incredible standards for precision and quality. Is it surprising that they selected the Stearns plant?

Stearns now had a connection with both Rolls and Daimler. If Rolls and Daimler considered it a bit on the vulgar side to talk about power in relation to motor car engines, perhaps the F.B. Stearns Co., makers of fine motor cars in the U.S., also adopted such a principle.

But the question remains and, to satisfy one's curiosity, it is possible to indulge once again in a bit of simple math. The results may not be as good as a dynamometer test, but....

An earlier math computation came up with a reading of .205 horsepower per cubic inch on the first Stearns-Knight sleeve valve engine in 1911. It had been considered an "eye-popper." Using the same formula on the super-hot Stearns-Knight Six for 1913 provides almost identical results: .204 horsepower per cubic inch.

By reversing that calculation, and assuming that the new V-8 engine had the same efficiency rating as the earlier engines (.205), then applying that figure to the 332 cubic inches of the new V-8, the answer is 68.6 hp.

It is possible to assume that the state of the art in motor car engine making had progressed a bit over the years, which might make the rating even a bit higher. Another "plus" is the fact—as it has so often been touted—that the V-8 engine configuration is a plus factor when it comes to power and efficiency. The new V-8 Stearns-Knight may well have churned out 75 to 80 hp, perhaps even more. (The first Cadillac, incidentally, had 314 cubic inches and a published rating of 60 hp.)

It is known that the new engine performed well enough to obtain the approval of Stearns and Sterling, neither of whom would have approved a dud. The Stearns ad writers were willing to say, in the sales brochures, "This eight imparts a smooth and unusual quantity of power."

The ad writers also pointed out that the new engine had a counterbalanced crankshaft — a feature pioneered by Stearns in 1913—and "It permits higher engine speed with mechanical safety, which means greater power and flexibility."

The new V-8 Stearns-Knight rode on a 123-inch wheelbase, weighed 3,600 pounds in touring body form, and was also available in a seven-passenger touring, a four-passenger roadster, a four-passenger landaulet, a four-passenger coupe, a seven-passenger limousine, and a landaulet brougham. The machines, incidentally, used 12-volt electrical systems. Prices ranged from $2,050 to $3,400.

By way of comparison, the only other sleeve valve V-8 to be made in the U.S. was the Willys-Knight of 1917 and 1918. It had a 3⅜ x 4 engine, weighed 3,550 pounds, and rode on a 125-inch wheelbase. Prices began at $2,000. A specifications chart published by MoTor in 1942, many years later, showed a bhp rating of 65. This chart did not list the Stearns-Knight.

Actually, in introducing the Stearns-Knight V-8, we have jumped ahead of our story a bit. It had been in the fall of 1914, for the 1915 model year, that the Stearns company had introduced a new model which seemed to head the company in a new direction—into a lower-priced field, with a smaller car.

The new Light Four (L-4) had been put on the market with an even smaller four-

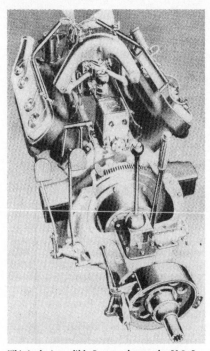

This is the incredible Stearns sleeve valve V-8. It had a bore and stroke of 3¼x5 inches. No horsepower ratings were claimed. A 12-volt electrical system was standard.

cylinder engine than the original sleeve valve four introduced in 1911. The earlier version was still in production, along with the mighty six introduced in 1913. The L-4 had a 3¾ x 5⅝ engine, with 249 cubic inches, compared to 312 for the earlier four. It used the 12-volt electrical system which would remain a standard Stearns-Knight feature until 1927.

The wheelbase on the L-4 was 119 inches, and the machine was available in a five-passenger touring, a cabriolet and a limousine. Prices ranged from $1,750 for the touring to $2,250 for the cabriolet and $2,750 for the limousine. By comparison, the other two Stearns models being offered at that time had prices ranging from $3,750 to $6,200.

Was the F.B. Stearns Co. attempting to enter the low-priced field? That suggestion will hardly float: the Model T Ford, at that time, was selling for less than $500. Stearns cars were never cheap.

Frank Stearns put it another way.

• First, he said, the company had been developing the new, smaller model for three years. That would mean it had been at least in the planning stage when the first sleeve valve engine had been introduced.

• Then, he said, "For a long time we have recognized the growing demand for a car that would appeal to that class of citizen whom we would call Mr. Substantial Citizen. This type of man, we believe, will always be a steady buyer of a legitimate high grade automobile at a moderate price."

Stearns wasn't even thinking about trying to compete with Henry Ford.

The Stearns company had been prospering mightily. The company was able to declare a 25 percent dividend in 1912, and another 18 percent the following year. Profits dropped somewhat in the next few years, mostly because they were being spent for expansion of manufacturing facilities. In simple terms, the company was growing.

In June, 1917, the company announced plans to spend $500,000 on further plant expansion.

The F.B. Stearns Co. at this time had reached its highest peak in production and sales, with approximately 3,000 cars made and sold in 1916 and 4,000 in 1917. But a new element entered the picture: World War I.

In 1917 the U.S. finally became involved in the war, which had been raging in Europe for three years. With the U.S. in the fray, the government imposed restrictions on steel and other materials needed for the war effort—the production of guns, tanks and airplanes.

Stearns had already become involved in the making of aircraft engines for Rolls-Royce. Obviously, there would be fewer Stearns-Knights for 1918—a drop all the way to 1,450 machines.

For 1918 the wheelbase of the L-4 was stretched to 125 inches, while the V-8 remained at 123. Bodies on both cars were restyled. The war was bringing higher costs for labor and other materials, which were reflected in the price of the cars. Prices on the Light Four now started at $1,785, running up to $3,350; on the V-8, prices ranged from $2,575 to $3,875. The earlier four had been dropped after the introduction of the L-4, and the big six had been dropped when the V-8 appeared.

Production of passenger cars was slow in recovering in 1919, with steel and other vital materials still in short supply even though the war had ended in November of 1918. Stearns Knight produced only 1,256 cars in 1919 and, strangely enough, only 56 of them were V-8's. Perhaps the materials available were being allocated to the smaller, easier to build car.

In the meantime, aside from all the influence the war was having on the Stearns picture, a new kind of crisis was brewing. Frank B. Stearns, the man who had given birth to the dream of making fine motor cars, and nursed it into being, was gravely ill.

Family members reported that pneumonia struck in the spring of 1917, and he nearly died. This was in the days before antibiotics, and pneumonia was, more often than not, fatal. Even when Stearns finally began to recover, his recovery was so slow — dragging over months—that he was unable to fulfill his duties as president of the company. He decided to resign from the presidency but, for the time, remained as chairman of the board and retained his financial holdings.

Exact details of his slow recovery are not known, but Stearns must have been ill indeed to decide, at age 37 and at the peak of his career, to give up what he had so proudly accomplished. The decision to give up the presidency of "his" company, the post he had held for 20 years, could only have been forced upon him.

Stearns would eventually recover and would live a relatively long life, but he never returned to active management or participation in the operation of the company.

An indication of just how far Stearns had brought the company can be seen from a news item which appeared in *Automobile Topics* for May 12, 1917, just about the time he became ill.

The company had been reorganized and capitalized at $200,000 in 1902. Later, that capital stock had been increased to $240,000. In May of 1917, capital stock was suddenly increased to $2,000,000. Of this amount:

- $550,000 was issued as a stock dividend to present stockholders, which meant much of it went to Stearns and his family.
- Another $200,000 was purchased by present stockholders—again, partly by Stearns.
- $500,000 was sold to new investors.
- About $500,000 of the stock remained unissued.

The exact details of what was taking place behind the scenes in this financial picture have not been uncovered, but it can easily be seen that the "new investors" and whoever, in the future, would control the unissued stock could just about control the F.B. Stearns Co. This would be important, in view of what was about to happen.

The *Automobile Topics* news story also reported that the volume of business for the company in 1917 was running at the rate of $5,000,000 per year. Add it all up: the new capitalization, with a large block of unissued stock; the all-time high in the production and sale of cars; the record rate of cash volume; the illness of the man who had created it all —there was a ripe financial plum for the person who could get his hands on it.

Something similar had happened to Harry C. Stutz, the maker of the famous Stutz machines that included the Bearcat, and at about the same time.

The details of what took place at Stearns remain hidden, but it is obvious that, with the prolonged illness of Frank B. Stearns, someone was looking for a manager to take his place. In the early fall of 1917, L.M. Sanford, who had been manager of the European branch of General Motors (in London) since 1911, was named general manager of the F.B. Stearns Co. It is believed that he was a Stearns appointee, making it possible for Stearns to resign — which he did, in September.

But the man who took over as president that same month was George W. Booker, described in the motoring press of the day as a banker "representing other financial interests." Booker had also been a Stearns dealer in St. Louis.

Roy York, who had been with Stearns since 1903 and had been vice president since 1905, was suddenly out. He was replaced by William McGuire. Edwin McEwen, who had been secretary-treasurer since 1909, was replaced by Martin L. Henschen.

Guy Vaughn, the man who had won races and set world records for Stearns and had become first a test driver and later sales manager, also left.

Then McGuire, who had barely warmed the seat of his vice president's chair, departed.

To top it all off, Sanford, the man who had been brought all the way from London to take the general manager's post, left in November. The experienced auto manufacturer lasted only two months.

Years later, members of the Stearns family remembered it as a house cleaning by Booker in order to place his own people in charge. It was an old, old story in the history of American industry — the story of a company carefully nursed to greatness and health, then taken over by bankers and men of finance.

The nearest thing to an explanation of why Sanford left so quickly may be found in a news item in *Automobile Topics* for November 17, 1917. It said, of the incident, "It was not an economic situation to have two such capable men (Booker and Sanford) in the home office, consequently Sanford felt justified in relinquishing the business to the control of Booker." Note the word "control."

Whatever was happening behind the scenes, apparently it was enough to convince Stearns—as he recovered from his long illness — that he was no longer an effective part of the company that bore his name and which he had labored so hard to build. The following year, in May, 1918, he sold his interest in the company and severed all connections with it. The surgery was complete — or almost. The magnificent engineering and production team, headed by Pete Sterling, was still on the job, but their days were numbered, too.

In any case, it soon became apparent that the new management had little interest in the development of new engines, cars or models — at least, for the present.

They had taken over a company which, over the years, had laboriously built a reputation for making fine cars. The period during World War I, and the first years thereafter, were years of a seller's market in which cars were scarce and buyers were plentiful.

The new managers, after 1919,

dropped the proud V-8 and concentrated on the production and sale of a single model: the small, four-cylinder L-4. Because of the seller's market, they could take this risk and get by with it, ringing the cash register.

According to serial numbers assigned, the company made and sold 3,849 cars in 1920 and 3,046 in 1921 — near record numbers for the relatively small company. Then the bottom dropped out. In 1922, as the post-war boom suddenly ended and a small but sharp economic recession took charge, the seller's market very quickly flipped to a buyer's market. Obviously, buyers were tired of purchasing the same unglamorous four-cylinder model, year after year. Serial numbers indicate that only 693 Stearns-Knight cars were made in 1922. Even bankers interested only in milking as much money as possible, coasting free on a past reputation, now had to recognize that they could not travel forever on a single, out-of-date model.

Pete Sterling and his crew of engineers were gone. In April, 1920, Sterling had resigned from the F.B. Stearns Co. Almost the entire engineering and production staff left with him. Sterling announced publicly that he was resigning to go into the business of making his own motor car.

It would be powered by a sleeve valve engine, for he was recognized as the master of this type of engine. Most of the men who had left with him would form the nucleus of the new Sterling-Knight production project.

But it was a dream that would not jell. When Sterling resigned, the motoring press said he already had his new organization in place, with adequate machine shop facilities, and that "production will begin shortly."

But a year later, on April 21, 1921, *Automotive Industries* reported that the new Sterling-Knight Car Co. had built three prototypes and that "production will begin immediately."

There was more silence until April 6, 1922, when an announcement was made that the new Sterling company had purchased the Accurate Machine Co. for $1,000,000 and that production would "begin shortly."

The next announcement bore a Warren, Ohio, dateline. On May 31, 1923, it was reported that the company — now called the Sterling-Knight Co. of Warren —had purchased the Supreme Motor Co., also of Warren, and would shortly begin production of a six-cylinder machine of Sterling's design.

Something had gone wrong. The Sterling-Knight eventually appeared and a few hundred were made, but by early 1925 the dream had evaporated. The car and the company were gone.

Things were not going well for Stearns and Stearns-Knight either. When the bottom dropped out of the motor car market in 1922, it quickly became apparent that from somewhere — and somehow — someone would have to come up with new ideas, new engineering, and new models if the F.B. Stearns Co. was to be kept alive.

Laying the groundwork for the greatest car of them all: 1922-1927

S tearns-Knight was the king of motor cars in America in 1928. In power, performance, and perhaps even speed, it was the number one production motor car in the country. Strangely enough, it was powered by a straight eight sleeve valve engine, the only such engine ever produced in America.

If this comes as a shock to some old car fans, so be it. But there it was, a standard production motor car rated at 112 horsepower (the National Red Book said 120), and capable of speeds up to 110 miles per hour.

This was in 1928 — but it may also have been true for 1927, and very nearly so in 1929. This was decades before the years of the hot overhead valve V-8's of the 1950s and 1960s.

It is all the more unbelievable when, in the minds of so many old car fans, it has almost become engraved in stone that the sleeve valve engine was a freak and a dud. How could a sleeve valve engine outperform the Packard Custom Eight of that period? Or the Cadillac and Lincoln V-8's? Or the famed Pierce-Arrow, which that year had an enormous twin valve six of 414 cubic inches, rated at 100 horsepower? (Pierce-Arrow would not have a straight eight until 1929.)

The horsepower rating on the magnificent Packard for that year was 106. Lincoln and Cadillac, both V-8's,

were rated at 90. The Stearns-Knight engine had 385 cubic inches, the same as Packard and Lincoln. Cadillac had 341.

If we were to rate the engines by horsepower per cubic inch, the Stearns-Knight straight eight would come up with .290. The Packard would come closest, with .275, while Cadillac was at .263 and Lincoln at .233.

The mighty Stearns-Knight sleeve valve engine was built to such exacting standards of precision, quality and design that it became more or less routine for them to run 100,000, 200,000 or even 300,000 miles with no major engine repairs — at a time when many motor cars had to have a valve grind job every 10,000 miles. The Stearns-Knight didn't have valves, in the usual sense of the word. It had only the ported sleeves.

Perhaps it is not so surprising, after all, when we remember that Stearns had built the most powerful and fastest motor car in the country as early as 1907 — stock car, that is. It also was Stearns that produced the eye-popping 100 hp six-cylinder sleeve valve engine in 1913.

True, both of the earlier record breakers had been much larger engines. The 1907 machine had weighed in with a whopping 800 cubic inches; the 1913 machine had boasted 490.

In describing the greatest car of them all, we've jumped ahead of our story. The F.B. Stearns Co. had been in somewhat of the doldrums along about 1922.

Frank B. Stearns, the man who had created it all, had been forced by ill health to give up the presidency and, a short time later, to sell his interest in the company. In April, 1920, Pete Sterling, the brilliant chief engineer, had also left.

Large in size and stature, this five-passenger standard sedan limousine is a Stearns F-6-85 of 1927.

The company, under the presidency of George W. Booker, a banker, had more or less been coasting on past performance, milking what profits it could from a year-after-year production of a single four-cylinder model Stearns-Knight. It was possible because of a war-created seller's market.

But in 1922 the seller's market disappeared, and a short but sharp economic depression kicked the bottom out of the auto market. Something had to be done if the company and the car with the great reputation were to be saved.

The company did it by placing on the market, for the first time since 1915, a new six-cylinder motor car with updated styling and, of course, a sleeve valve engine.

The new engine checked in at 3⅜ x 5, for a respectable 268 cid and 68 hp — not spectacular, but a large improvement over the nine-year-old L-4, which had originally been designed as a smaller, lower-priced companion car to earlier sixes and a V-8 of the 1916-1919 period.

The new S-6, introduced in July, 1922, for the 1923 model year, rode on a 130-inch wheelbase, compared to 125 for the L-4, which continued in production. The new six weighed from 3,600 pounds (for the roadster and coupe) to 4,000 pounds (for the seven-passenger limousine and town car). Prices on the S-6 ran from $2,700 to $3,700, with prices on the L-4 beginning at $2,250. Four-wheel hydraulic brakes and wire wheels were offered at extra cost.

The available record does not show who designed the new six, or who was chief engineer at the time. When Sterling left in 1920, he had taken all the top engineering and production personnel with him.

Several students of the Stearns-Knight story have speculated that the new six was a Sterling design worked up before he left. It is further speculated that part of the reason for Sterling's departure may have been the foot dragging by management in putting the new engine into production.

If the new six was being counted on to help save the fortunes of the company, it did—at least to an extent—succeed. Production for 1923, after a disastrous dip to less than 700 units in 1922, managed to top 2,000, with 1,723 of the machines being the new six. Production of the four barely topped the 300 mark. It should have been clear by now that buyers wanted something new.

If the Stearns-Knight model picture had been on the sparse side before 1923, with that single model on tap, it was about to become a bit on the confusing side. For the 1924 sales season, production on the four-cylinder machine—now known as the B-4 (Big Four)—continued, despite the poor sales record of four-cylinder machines for the past several years. The engine, at 3¾ x 5⅝, remained virtually unchanged, but the chassis and body were updated and restyled.

The wheelbase, which had been 125, was reduced to 119, and an Eaton axle

185

A sporty looking but still huge roadster with rumble seat was in the F-6-85 line for 1927.

replaced the more expensive Stearns-designed axle previously used. Prices were reduced to the area of $1,595 to $2,095 for six body styles that ranged from a roadster to a five-passenger coupe brougham. But sales of this less expensive model dropped to just over 100 units for 1925 and to less than 80 for 1926.

Meanwhile, the engineering staff was busy with another six — this time, a smaller engine with a 3¼-inch bore and 5-inch stroke. This new engine would be introduced in a new car, to be known as the C-6-75, in October, 1924, for the 1925 model year. The new six, strangely enough, had the same cubic inch displacement as the four — 249 inches — but was rated at only 55 hp.

By using simple math, it is possible to calculate horsepower per cubic inch. When Stearns-Knight produced its first sleeve valve engine in 1911, the results were considered sensational when the engine churned out .205 horsepower per inch; the best Pete Sterling and his men had been able to squeeze out of their poppet valve engine was .173.

By the early 1920s the old standby four, which had been designed by Sterling for 1915, weighed in at 3¾ x 5⅝ and 249 cubic inches, and was rated at 64 hp. This translates into .257 per inch. Efficiency was still improving.

The larger S-6, believed to be a Sterling design, but only introduced in 1922, came up with .246 hp per inch. It was not quite as good as the four, but very close. When the formula is applied to the new, smaller six apparently designed by a post-Sterling engineering crew, however, the horsepower per inch shows a slip backward to .221.

In any case, the new six would ride on a 121-inch wheelbase and was available in six body styles, including a sports coupe. It sold for prices ranging from $1,875 to $2,475. It cost a bit more than the B-4, but would outsell the four by nearly 1,250 units to 100. It all meant that, instead of the single model the company had relied on in the years before 1922, there were now three model lines in the Stearns-Knight stable: the B-4, the S-6, and the C-6-75. Or was it three and a half model lines?

When production had started on the so-called 1925 models in the latter half of 1924, the larger S-6 had been continued with the 3⅜ x 5 engine, rated at 66 hp. But just before the New York auto show in January, 1925, the size of this engine had been upped. The cylinders were bored out to 3½, bringing the cubic inches up to 278 and the horsepower rating to 70.

In the midst of all this juggling of models and engines, a new element was about to enter the picture. The ownership of the company was about to change once more.

This time the big name in the picture was John North Willys, who had been making a big splash in the automotive world with sleeve valve engines of his own. Willys had started later in the sleeve valve field but, with the resources of the

The Stearns-Knight factory in Cleveland, OH, is shown the way it looked in the mid-twenties.

giant Willys-Overland Co. behind him, he had been able to hold prices lower and adapt the new engine design to, more or less, mass production.

The Willys-Knight sleeve valve engined cars being made by the Willys-Overland Co. were good cars. Thousands of them turned in excellent performance and endurance records on the streets and highways of America for many years. But they had never quite matched the quality and luxury of the Stearns-Knight or, possibly, its performance. The standards for precision and quality workmanship at Stearns had always been the ultimate.

Even after Frank Stearns had retired from the company, the luxury image lingered on—despite the ill-fated commitment to a single model by the post-Stearns management. It was this image of quality and luxury that Willys wanted to add to his stable of sleeve valve powered motor cars. In the low-priced field, he would continue making Overlands and Whippets.

In any case, in December, 1925, an announcement appeared that Willys and his backers had acquired the 250,000 outstanding shares of the F.B. Stearns Co. for $2,500,000. It was a takeover. A few days later, Willys also announced a new management team at Stearns, to replace George Booker and company.

The new president, the announcement said, would be H.J. Leonard, formerly with the Stephens Motor Co. John T. Trumble, formerly an engineer with General Motors, would take over as chief engineer. O.T. Lawson, also an experienced automobile man, would become manager of production.

The new management, and Willys, stated that:

• The F.B. Stearns Co. would retain its identity as a separate corporation.
• The present manufacturing facilities would be kept intact.
• Production policies would be unchanged.

If the commitment to quality was renewed under the new chief engineer, it was because John North Willys wanted it that way.

One of the first major actions of the new management was to drop production on the old four-cylinder machine which had been on the assembly lines since 1915. The small Model C-6 was retained through the 1926 model year but then it, too, was dropped. The new engineering staff would be designing its own new models. The company could well afford to drop the Model C anyway, in view of its somewhat disappointing performance.

In September, 1926, the first new model under the new management was announced: the Model D, series 6-85.

Actually, the engine from the larger sleeve valve six, the Model S-6-95, which was upgraded in January of 1925, would be updated and retained for the new model, at least for the time being. Engine improvements were on the way, but there had not been enough time to complete them.

Perhaps the most unusual feature on

the new car was a worm drive rear axle as standard equipment. This permitted a substantial drop in overall height, and vastly improved roadability — especially on what had been somewhat top-heavy sedans. The worm drive was a feature rarely seen on American motor cars, with Stutz and Cunningham the notable exceptions. Stearns-Knight had offered it as optional equipment as early as 1914.

The new Stearns-Knight had semi-elliptic springs. Replacing the cantilevers and brakes were four-wheel mechanicals, the hydraulic option being dropped. The wheelbase was stretched to 137 inches. There were longer, lower bodies in 10 styles ranging from a two-passenger roadster, at $3,250, to a seven-passenger limousine, at $3,750. There was a new Tillotson carburetor, air cleaner and oil filter, probably because Willys owned Tillotson. A Myers magazine chassis oiler, similar to the famed Bijur system, was used.

But hectic work was continuing on more improvements. After 432 of the new models had been made, and in time for the 1927 auto show, the engine was redesigned to incorporate seven main bearings — a must on a modern luxury machine. In mid-model year, the 12-volt electrical system was changed to six volts, an industry trend.

Although the size of the engine had been kept the same, at 3½ x 5, internal refinements in combustion, breathing and other components enabled the company to advertise the engine at 82 hp. This upped the horsepower per cubic inch rating to .284, the highest for a Stearns-Knight engine to that date. It was obvious that the new engineering staff, which now included W.E. England, was learning some of the old Pete Sterling magic.

Drivers who took the wheel of the big new machine glowed with satisfaction at the smooth power under their control. They pronounced it a worthy car, in the true sense of the word, to carry the Stearns-Knight banner. The machine was said to be capable of speeds above 80. It was in this form that the new machine, now known as the Model F-6-85, would be retained in production into 1928.

The greatest car of them all — the sleeve valve straight eight: 1927-1929

*T**he Stearns company had experienced many breakthroughs in engine design over the years, but there was still more to come — including the biggest Stearns-Knight bombshell of them all: the first and only straight eight sleeve valve engine ever to be made in America.***

A straight eight engine, of itself, was not new. Duesenberg had introduced a straight eight for 1922. Packard had unveiled its great straight eight in 1923, for the 1924 model year. Gardner, Hupmobile, Jordan, Kissel and Locomobile were among the manufacturers who followed the trend around 1925. The Stutz had been ready for 1926. Others were on the way.

It was becoming a major trend, with each maker of cars above the middle-price class feeling compelled to join the parade. If Stearns-Knight intended to keep its reputation as a maker of fine motor cars, an eight would be a necessity. And, since Stearns was committed to the sleeve valve principle, the new eight would have to be a sleeve valve.

Pete Sterling may have been the man who pioneered the sleeve valve engine in America, and who had brought it to its highest peak of perfection in his time. But it was now obvious that the new engineering staff at Stearns had not only absorbed all the sleeve valve lore Sterling had been able to incorporate into his engines, but to add a bit more. Otherwise, would it have been possible to create a sleeve valve straight eight destined to be, in its time, the king of American motordom?

With a renewed commitment to quality design and production, the new engine incorporated nine main bearings. Instead of a single eccentric shaft (the camshaft on a sleeve valve engine) to operate the sleeves, the new eight had two eccentrics, one on each side of the crankshaft. They were driven by silent chain.

By using a new alloy of "semi-steel," the engineers were able to come up with

much thinner, and lighter, sleeves. Then, using the latest techniques in precision manufacturing, tolerances and clearances were reduced to nearly the ultimate limits—as low as .00025 inches, or even .00005. This was extremely important in the performance, silence, durability and oil consumption on an engine of such design.

The huge crankshaft was drilled for pressure oil feed to its entire length, including tubular connecting rods for pressure lubrication to the wrist pins. The engine had a new Skinner oil rectifier, a new harmonic balancer, and an improved hot spot intake manifold for better combustion. The ultra-precision fitting also made it possible to reduce the number of oil rings on the cylinder heads. Only a sleeve valve engine would create such a concern.

The compression ratio was given as 5 to 1, the first time this term was used in connection with Stearns-Knight cars. It was near the peak for the motor car industry, and at least partly made possible by the perfect spherical shape of the combustion chambers, another plus for sleeve valve design since there was no clutter of valve ports, or valves, in the combustion area. Old time car lovers may recall the fanfare raised by Walter P. Chrysler when, in 1924, he produced what would be called the first modern high compression engine—with a 4.7 to 1 ratio.

In any case, the new Stearns-Knight eight, when first introduced in January, 1927, as the Model G-8-85, was rated at 100 hp. For 1928, that would be jumped to 112 (or 120).

If the rating of 112 hp is accepted as the valid one, and the horsepower per cubic inch is applied to the new Stearns-Knight straight eight, the result is .290 —once again, the highest rating ever for a sleeve valve engine or, for that matter, nearly any motor car engine in 1928.

There it was: the epitome, the greatest of the sleeve valve engines in America. It would be surpassed only, perhaps, by a great Daimler sleeve valve V-12 that was introduced nearly at the same time, with a rating of 180 hp. It was not only the most powerful sleeve valve engine ever developed in the world, but perhaps was also more powerful than poppet valve engines in its time.

If there were still those who doubted that a sleeve valve engine could ever match the performance of conventional engines, they now had their answer.

The new eight rode on the same chassis as the big six, at 137 inches. In hindsight, it is probably safe to speculate that Stearns-Knight engineers already had the eight-cylinder machine in mind — and under development—at the time the big six was placed in the 137-inch chassis.

The eight was only slightly heavier than the six, starting at 4,448 pounds for the two-passenger roadster and going to 5,102 pounds for the seven-passenger limousine. The same body styles with the six-cylinder engine weighed 4,250 to 4,777 pounds.

Prices ranged from $3,950 to $5,250 for the eight, and $3,250 to $3,950 for the six. To handle the higher horsepower and torque, a double-plate Long clutch was used on the eight; a single-plate Borg and Beck was used on the six.

For 1928 a longer chassis, at 145 inches, was available for the seven-passenger models, but production of the 137-inch chassis also continued for the five-passenger models. The shorter car was designated as the Model H, Deluxe 8-90, while the longer chassis was the Model J, Deluxe 8-90.

Stearns-Knight ad writers were willing to boast, without shame, of the great eight's life expectancy as the new 8-90 came into being. The car, one ad said, "possesses a length of life out of all proportion to the popular conception of what a motor car can have."

Another ad writer said, of the motor

itself, "The greatest of all motors."

Still another ad boasted: "The De Luxe Stearns-Knight holds such a marked margin over contemporaneous cars in magnificent power, surpassing quietness, effortless control and alluring comfort, that the standards this car creates are not to be comprehended until the car is actually seen and driven in person."

If one needed a slogan, how about "For those who appreciate supreme achievement"?

This was the machine that remained in production from 1927 through 1929. The 1929 models continued to be known as the Model J-8-90 and the H-8-90.

One more major development was coming at Stearns-Knight: a smaller, updated and improved six-cylinder engine, at 3⅜ x 4¾, with 255 cubic inches and a rating of 70 hp at 3,200 rpm. It is interesting to note that the peak rpm figure was creeping up, disproving a widely held belief that sleeve valve engines did not lend themselves to high rpm. In fact Voisin, in France, had been making sleeve valve engines which turned more than 4,000 rpm as early as 1921.

Beyond this, the new engine, together with its new chassis, marked the first major cooperative production effort between Willys-Knight and Stearns-Knight. The engine and chassis would, in fact, be produced in the Willys-Knight plants, and be used by Willys-Knight as its model 66-A, beginning in 1927. However, the bodies for the Stearns-Knight Model M (126-inch wheelbase) and Model N (134-inch wheelbase) would be Stearns-Knight coachwork. The design of the engine and chassis would be to Stearns-Knight specifications.

Except for the wheelbase length, the two models were identical. They were designed to fill the niche in a slightly lower-priced field and, if possible, to capture more of the market. These models sold for prices ranging from $2,195 for a cabriolet-roadster to $2,645 for a seven-passenger limousine. The latter, of course, was on the longer wheelbase.

These models were introduced in May, 1928, and continued in 1929.

Despite the fact that these were Stearns-Knight's greatest years in the production of its greatest motor cars, the company was in financial trouble. It was the old story of great motor cars of the 1920s and 1930s. The big shake-out in the motor car industry did not begin in the great depression. It began in the prosperous 1920s.

In hindsight, the major reason is easy to see. The industry was producing too many different makes of cars in a proliferation of models that could only be confusing. Some 50 different companies produced as many makes of cars. Competition, especially in the middle and higher price brackets, was murderous. In the midst of all this, the confused buyer longed for familiar names and familiar cars.

In this jungle, a small company such as Stearns, no matter how high the quality of its cars, would find it difficult to operate—if for no other reason than that it was nearly impossible to maintain proper sales and service facilities on anything near a national scale.

Despite the glorious cars offered, only 877 Stearns-Knight machines were produced in 1927. In 1928, the great year of glory for the sleeve valve straight eight, production dropped again—to around 816.

In 1929, the last year of prosperity before the big crash, production rose somewhat. But the accumulation of costs from the development of the new cars, coupled with lack of sales, brought trouble to the doors of the F.B. Stearns Co. The stock market crash in the fall of that year was the final blow.

John North Willys had the good luck of selling his stock in the summer of 1929, just months before the crash. It might be suggested that he knew about the shaky condition of the company, and got out just in time. Perhaps he did, but the official reason was that President Herbert Hoover had appointed him ambassador to Poland, and he was severing his connections with the auto industry.

It was the combination of the Willys sell-out, the dismal sales picture and, finally, the stock market crash in the fall of 1929 that spelled the end for Stearns and Stearns-Knight. On December 20, 1929, the assembly lines came to a halt. Ten days later, on December 30, stockholders were summoned to a meeting

This '29 Stearns was John N. Willys' personal car. Willys departed the Stearns organization just in the nick of time, shortly before the final curtain fell on the luxury car maker. (Photo courtesy Arthur W. Aseltine)

where they heard the sad news. After hearing a detailed description of the financial condition of the company, they voted to cease operation.

What the stockholders probably did not know was that the company had been in financial trouble, and barely able to survive from year to year, for quite some time — at least as early as 1925, when Willys took over. The troubles may have begun as early as 1922, as a result of the bank management's policies of milking profits with little thought for the future.

H.J. Leonard, the last president, confessed it quite bluntly in a statement to the press on that fateful day, December 30.

He said: "The management took charge of the company January 1, 1926, at a time, although it was not known for some months, when the company was practically bankrupt. The inventory was unbalanced, written up beyond its real value, and its product scattered throughout the country in the hands of dissatisfied dealers. Large sums were owed to the banks and the company was involved in considerable litigation.

"We hoped," Leonard added, "for a complete financial reorganization or consolidation with a strong automobile company which could absorb our product, but these efforts have been frustrated by business conditions, including the recent slump in the stock market."

Some observers of motor car history have been quick to suggest that one of the causes contributing to the failure of such companies as Stearns was the freak nature of the sleeve valve engine.

But this simply could not have been true, except possibly from a cost standpoint. It did cost a good deal more to manufacture the sleeve valve engines and, beyond that, the manufacturers were required to pay hefty royalties to inventor Charles Y. Knight. But for performance, power and durability, the sleeve valve engines had produced plenty of evidence, over the years, to show they could not only match the performance of the poppet valve engines, but surpass it.

George M. Hower, an engineer who had worked with Pete Sterling, put it this way in a statement published in *The Scientific American:* "Curves that have been made, as a result of scientifically conducted power determinations, have demonstrated conclusively that the Knight type motor gives more power for a given piston displacement than any other form."

In addition, the longer a sleeve valve engine ran, the stronger it ran — while the poppet valve engine grew weaker. True, as steel for producing valves and springs improved over the years, the poppet valve engine overcame some of these weaknesses. But one can always ask, "What if development on the sleeve valve engines had also continued?" They, too, were growing stronger, year by year.

Perhaps, because of the cost factor, the sleeve valve engine could never have been a factor in the low-price field. The engine itself might cost as much as a Model T Ford.

The concept of the sleeve valve engine as a freak can never stand up when

The man who founded the F.B. Stearns Co. and steered the small auto maker to a record of greatness in its early years. This photo was taken in Stearn's later years, after his retirement. He died in 1955. (Photo courtesy Arthur W. Aseltine)

one considers that, at one time or another, some 50 car manufacturers have used it. Some of them, such as Voisin, of France, set world speed records — and remember the little sleeve valve Mercedes which made such a good showing in the Indy 500? In their days of glory, in such places as Britain, Germany and Belgium, the sleeve valve motor cars found great favor among royalty, the rich, or anybody who could afford one.

In any case, the end had come to Stearns which, while a small company, had produced some of the finest, most durable, most powerful and fastest motor cars ever built in the U.S.

Frank B. Stearns, the man who had started it all as a starry-eyed college "dropout," the man who had seen his project flourish for a time under his direction but had to give it up because of illness, certainly must have felt pain at seeing the Stearns-Knight name removed from the roster.

When it happened, he had recovered his health and was working with a small crew of men in a private workshop, experimenting with diesel engines. In the mid-1930s he had developed a giant 24-cylinder (two V-12's locked together) diesel which performed so well the Navy contracted to use it. In his later years, he retired to putter in his garden. He died in 1955.

In acknowledging the painful truth, it must, perhaps, be admitted that the Stearns, and the Stearns-Knight, never quite acquired that mystic aura of greatness which had hovered for a time over a few other American motor cars — Packard, Cadillac and Pierce-Arrow, to name a few. The list has always been a brief one.

Part of the reason may be that Stearns had never been able to obtain nationwide distribution and, thus, national renown. In fact, while Frank Stearns had been in control, he had never wished to make a mass production car. But with its area of distribution thus limited, Stearns could not penetrate that tiny, mystic circle.

Even most of them which did make it did not survive. Pierce-Arrow disappeared in the 1930s, Packard in the 1950s. Cadillac has survived but, some observers say, no longer commands the respect it once did. Is it now Mercedes which has inherited the mantle?

At any rate, the Stearns and Stearns-Knight motor cars were simply too good and too important to be so utterly ignored as they have been by many historians of the American automobile industry. It is a motor car which truly deserves more attention than it has received, either in its time or in ours.

Stearns/Stearns-Knight, for at least a moment in history—perhaps two or even three moments—was the king of American motor cars!

Author's note: The generous assistance of Arthur W. Aseltine, of Forbestown, California, must be acknowledged. Aseltine, an engineer by profession, not only owned a small fleet of Stearns-Knights, but also possessed one of the country's best collections of Stearns literature. A walking encyclopedia of Stearns lore, Aseltine freely shared his knowledge and his collection. Perhaps his greatest contribution to this chapter was something intangible: his quiet insistence, over the years, that this was a story that needed to be told.

VII
DOBLE

The story of Abner Doble and his magnificent steam cars

If the dreams of a mechanical genius named Abner Doble had been of internal combustion, rather than steam, he probably would have come up with a Duesenberg—perhaps even a finer machine than the mighty Duesenberg J, which would be saying quite a lot.

As it was, since his dreams moved in an aura of steam, Doble produced a classic symphony of power, precision, performance and efficiency, the like of which has seldom, if ever, been duplicated. His symphony was set to the incredible score of almost complete silence, except for the singing of tires and the whistle of the wind as the superb giant Dobles cruised the highways at 90, 100, or more miles per hour at a time when most of the finest gasoline engines being made were struggling to do 70 or 80.

When it came to climbing hills with almost ridiculous ease—hills which defeated the best of the gasoline machines—the magnificent Dobles, when developed to their ultimate peak of perfection, seemed to laugh with scorn at the entire automobile industry.

Long before the age of the Hydramatics, the Ultramatics, the Dynaflows, the Torqueflites and other automatic transmissions, the Doble had something far better—that mysterious ingredient called steam, an element that handed you, on a silver platter, maximum torque at zero rpm's.

When you speak of 1,000 pounds of torque at zero rpm's, or something near that at 10 rpm's, or 500, you are talking about a brand of black magic that the biggest high-efficiency Cadillac, Lin-

This 1930 Doble roadster was one of the last steamers to be made.

coln or Imperial engines of the 1970s could not match.

In fact, when you try to tell the story of Abner Doble and his magic steam flying carpets, you have to stretch the credible so far it is almost impossible for the average mind, nourished on a diet of piston and crankshaft internal combustion lore, to consider that you are telling the truth.

But the truth will have it that Abner Doble not only matched the precision and perfection of that old "master of precision," Henry Leland, but also boggled the minds of the best engineers in the "old country" homes of fine machinery, France, Germany and England.

Some of these men simply refused to believe what they were told until they had taken a Doble machine apart, bit by bit, had measured and tested the fine jewel-like parts and had seen the machines perform miracles of acceleration and speed.

Until recently, automobile manufacturers choked and gagged when asked to provide warranties on their machines which would cover perhaps a year in time and 12,000 miles in travel. But Abner Doble, in a time when it was common to overhaul internal combustion engines at 10,000 miles, guaranteed his engines for 100,000 miles.

Then why, if the Doble was all that great, are we not all rolling on steam today—a la Doble?

One of the most obvious reasons is that Doble steamers were extremely expensive for a mass market, plus the fact that Doble was primarily an engineer, a designer and maker of fine steam cars. If he had had a man like Walter P. Chrysler or Alfred P. Sloan, Jr., to run the business end and to leave Doble in peace to design and make the cars, we might indeed be riding in Doble steamers instead of the highly inefficient, gasoline gobbling internal combustion engines we are saddled with.

For the sad truth is, that at several critical points in his career, Abner Doble was slammed to the floor by some cruel blows that stymied his plans for production and forced him to start over again. The fact that this man had the courage to continue trying, and that he accomplished as much as he did, is a part of the incredible saga of Abner Doble.

Looking back on it now, it would seem that when Abner Doble was born, in San Francisco, California, in 1895 — a year when the infant automobile industry was struggling into being — he was a child bred and born for the career he was to follow.

His grandfather, also named Abner Doble, had set up a forging shop in San Francisco as early as 1850, when the "Great Gold Rush" was on. The business that was passed on to W.A. Doble, Abner's father, had grown far beyond the simple forge for making picks and shovels. It had become a proper manufacturing plant, making sophisticated tools.

By the time young Abner, together with his three brothers, appeared on the scene, the Doble firm had merged with another company and was engaged in business far beyond the borders of California.

W.A. Doble believed in the work ethic, for boys as well as men. At the age of eight, Abner was already at a workbench in the family business, after school, serving a part-time apprenticeship and learning to use tools properly.

Young Abner apparently had a passion for doing things with his hands, with tools. He not only learned how to make things, he enjoyed it. He also had a mania for precision, learned from a father who preached, "The best is not good enough."

Young Doble's obsession with the idea of steam propulsion came early. By the time he was in high school, he had built his first steam car.

In this early effort, which was not a glowing success, he used salvaged parts from other steam cars. But he did design his own engine and the fact that he had acquired the skill and engineering ability to do this, while still a child, pointed to the direction his career was going.

Using steam to drive a self-propelled vehicle was not new. During those early years of the automobile, there were times when steam cars outnumbered gasoline or electric cars. Steamers came years before the internal combustion engine appeared.

The trouble was that steam had several decided drawbacks when it came to powering vehicles. One of the biggest was the long and complicated proce-

DOBLE SEVEN PASSENGER TOURING CAR

Only 22 moving parts were used in the Doble Steam Car, of which eleven are in the engine. No clutch or driveshaft were used.

dure for getting up a head of steam from a cold start. It meant building a fire — ranging from a coal or wood fire, under a boiler, to use of complicated oil or kerosene burners which had to be coaxed into operation—before you had enough steam to drive.

Then there was the problem of water consumption, which made it risky to venture far from a water supply. Each of these primitive machines came equipped with bucket, hose and pump, and it was no novel sight to see a steam motorist stopped on a bridge or creek bank, dipping his bucket or pumping to obtain a few gallons of water.

There was the considerable problem of lubrication and rust control, where the engineer had to combat the old edict that oil and water — or steam — do not mix. Finally, there was the problem of freeze-ups in cold weather.

Abner Doble decisively whipped every one of these problems except the last.

His father sent him for engineering training to the Massachusetts Institute of Technology — then, as now, one of the foremost schools in the U.S. But Abner's thinking often ranged far ahead of what MIT had to offer.

While still in his first year at MIT, he set up a machine shop in nearby Waltham to work on some of his ideas. Most of these ideas concerned steam, for Doble was convinced that the power source of the future was steam, despite the booming success of the internal com-

bustion engines he could see all around him.

It was inevitable, since the Stanley steamer was being produced in Massachusetts (at Newton), that Doble would make at least one trek to that seat of steam power to discuss his ideas for recondensation of steam to conserve water and provide faster starting.

Doble found that the Stanley brothers were not only slightly contemptuous of his youth—he was only 16—and his ideas, but they considered that they were already making and selling the most successful steam motor car in America. Why would anyone demand an instant start from steam, considering all the other advantages?

Doble went back to his workbench in Waltham and decided to make his own machine to prove his theories. He was not the least deterred by the fact that Stanley machines had set speed and performance records that impressed the entire motoring world.

One of the characteristics of the early steam cars was the puff-puff spurts of steam coming from the exhaust. Doble decided that this steam, puffing out into the air, was not only a waste of good steam but of water as well. The Stanleys had fashioned a condenser of sorts for their machine, but it had by no means solved the problem of re-use of steam or water.

Doble, with the help of his younger brother, John, succeeded in making a steam automobile which had no exhaust. He designed a condenser so efficient that, at one stroke, it eliminated the exhaust feature of the steamer. Most important, with the escaping steam bottled up, reheated and re-used, Doble had solved one of the biggest bugaboos of the steamer: its hoggish use of water. Doble could travel hundreds of miles without refilling his water tank.

With his new steam car—which he labeled his Model A — finished and running smoothly, Abner Doble decided to do a bit of "nose tweaking" at the Stanley brothers. He drove his machine back and forth in front of the Stanley plant until the brothers, bursting with curiosity, came running out.

As the Stanleys examined the machine, noting its absence of exhaust and its smooth running, they were willing to treat young Doble with a bit more respect. Within a few years the Stanley brothers incorporated a steam condenser in their own cars, although it never worked as well as the Doble condenser and was bothered with sludge problems which Doble had solved.

From this time forward, Doble's improvements in steam engines came so fast that all steam engineers, including the Stanley brothers, were left far behind.

Young Doble and his helpers made five Model A steamers, selling four of them and keeping the fifth for experimental work. By 1914, at the age of 19, Doble had left MIT and incorporated the Abner Doble Motor Vehicle Manufacturing Company, at Waltham, Massachusetts, for the purpose of manufacturing new, improved Model B steam automobiles.

It was quite an audacious move for a youngster not yet old enough to vote.

Specifications on a steamer, including the early Doble machines, may be a bit confusing to car bugs reared on standard bore and stroke, cubic inch displacement, and brake horsepower specifications. Take horsepower, for example.

In the early days of the internal combustion engine, the horsepower figure was based on the bore size and had little actual relationship to how much power the engine produced. Steamers were rated on the size or capacity of their boilers, rather than on actual power.

The early Doble boilers, used on the

Model A and B, by size and capacity were rated at 25 horsepower. Abner Doble, however, had increased the efficiency of his boilers so greatly that tests showed he was producing an actual 75 horsepower out of a 25 hp boiler.

Doble's engine was a double acting, single expansion design, mounted directly on the rear axle, with a bore and stroke of 4 x 6. Since the drive was direct, with full torque from rpm zero, when you were going 60 miles per hour the engine was only turning 560 rpm's —merely a "fast idle" for ordinary internal combustion engines such as a Buick, Cadillac or Lincoln.

But the amazing thing was that Doble's car would "scratch off" from a standing start to 60 mph in 15 seconds, with a top speed of 75 mph. Talk about "hot rods." In 1914, there was nothing on the road that could match this acceleration.

The Doble car had only a 10-gallon fuel tank — kerosene — and was said to get from 15 to 20 miles per gallon of fuel. The water tank held 25 gallons and, with the efficient recondensing system designed by Doble, this amount of water would last 500 to 1,000 miles.

Doble hatched ideas and improvements faster than he could translate them into iron, steel and brass. Quickly on the heels of his Model B came the Model C, with greater improvements. Instead of a long stroke and smaller bore, he reversed the principle, using a five-inch bore and a four-inch stroke. But the biggest advance was a new "uniflow" steam flow system.

The accepted practice in most steam engines was to inject the steam—through an intake valve—at the beginning of the power stroke, allowing the hot, expanding steam to push the piston down. The piston then pushed the "used" steam out through the exhaust valve on the upward stroke. The steamer operated much on the order of a two-cycle internal combustion engine, with a two-stroke principle.

Doble thought that this actually reversed the flow of steam on each stroke, causing a loss of power and heat, and requiring much more condensation.

Doble's uniflow steam engine drew the fresh steam into the cylinder with an in-

The two-cylinder engine used in the Doble power plant was very simple—containing only eleven moving parts. Doble introduced the "uniflow" principle in which the exhaust value (common to other steam engines) was eliminated. It was unnecessary to use superheated steam, thus requiring less internal lubrication.

take valve, as before. He tossed away the exhaust valve, allowing the used steam to escape through a port as the piston neared the bottom of the stroke. This kept the steam flowing more or less in one direction, for less heat loss, less condensation and less loss of power.

Perhaps the most amazing feature of the new Doble steam engine was his system of lubrication: the introduction of oil into the water and cylinders themselves. This was considered impossible, as it contradicted the old adage that oil and water do not mix.

The generally accepted principle was to allow the water—or steam—to provide what lubrication it could of the cylinders and valves, while the engine was in motion. Then, to prevent rust while in storage, the cylinder was "blown" clean after use. To provide lubrication to moving parts not in direct contact with the steam, a heavy cylinder oil was used.

Doble simply mixed a light engine oil with water, or steam. He discovered that hot water—or steam—would mix with oil by more or less emulsifying the oil, especially when kept hot and in movement or agitation. Agitation was provided by the motion of the engine parts themselves and by the jogging and jolting of the vehicle as you drove. It was much the same principle used to homogenize milk, forcing the fatty cream to stay in suspension in the "skim" part of the milk.

In any case, it worked. The oil even provided a thin film of lubrication, not only on the inside walls of the cylinders but on the inside of the boiler tubes, largely eliminating corrosion and scaling. The film of oil, under heat, was so thin it did not prevent the heat transfer

so necessary to the operation of a steam engine.

Through his efficient condensing system, Doble was saving his steam exhaust, using the same water and steam over and over. With the introduction of his lubrication system, he was recovering the oil and using it over and over again. His oil consumption was less than a pint per 1,000 miles, a rate that many modern internal combustion engines can scarcely match.

Although Doble's biggest and best ideas were still to come, 1916 saw one of the biggest of them all: the fast start feature.

To increase the thermal efficiency of his boiler, Doble provided an extremely large area exposed to heat—576 tubes, giving 150 square feet of heating surface, on a capacity of only eight gallons of water. The tubes were tested to stand 5,000 pounds of pressure for safety. But, like all steam car makers, Doble had been saddled with the old Bunsen type burner for heat, which could drive an early morning driver to drink or profanity before getting up a head of usable steam.

Doble's new system used almost the same type of electrical ignition that sparked the spark plugs of an ordinary automobile. A Sirocco type blower, blowing air through a throat much like a carburetor throat, picked up and vaporized the fuel just as on an orthodox carburetor. He then provided the ignition, or firing, with a buzzer spark generated through a high tension coil.

It may sound complicated, but it worked. As far as the driver of the steam car was concerned, the system was amazingly simple. You simply turned the ignition switch. This set the fan in motion and provided the buzzer spark. Your fire was going immediately, with a roaring flame and super heat.

With 150 square feet of water-filled tubing exposed to the flame, it was only a minute or two before the steam pressure gauge hand would start climbing. The process took no longer than for the driver of an internal combustion motor car to crank his engine or start it with an early starter system, with a good deal of "goosing" from the hand choke, then warm up the engine and take off.

Doble designed his new electric ignition system to be automatic, thermostatically controlled. When steam pressure in the boiler reached a working pressure of 1,200 psi, the thermostat cut off the fan and the spark. As pressure dropped, it came on again. For normal cruising this was a great economy feature, with the flame burning only intermittently.

Doble had, with one stroke, wiped out one of the biggest advantages gasoline internal combustion engine makers had been able to boast of up to now.

Beyond that, he offered many other advantages over the sputtering, noisy and temperamental gasoline engines. First, almost complete silence. Next, full power at zero engine revolutions, from the first stroke of the pistons, without clutch stomping and gear clashing. The Doble had the fastest acceleration of any automobile on the road. It had the torque to climb, fast or slow, the steepest hill. Its fuel economy would match anything except that of the small, economy cars.

At a time when the steam automobile industry was on the verge of disappearing, a victim of its own shortcomings, Doble was able to show the world a machine which promised to challenge the best of the gasoline powered cars.

Abner Doble was ready to enter the marketplace.

When he put his machine into production in 1916, all seemed to go well. Doble had learned, when he built his Model A cars, that to produce cars on an assembly line basis, you needed more than a small machine shop with a few helpers, and the boss doing most of the engineering and high precision machine work himself.

Now, with the need for bigger production facilities and the capital to bring them into being, Doble set out to knock on doors, seeking support and money. His best salesman was the machine he drove and demonstrated, incorporating all those revolutionary new ideas.

He wasn't merely selling an idea—he had a complete machine to prove his claims.

The car did its work well. Doble obtained the backing of C.L. Lewis, who had been president of another motor car company, and $200,000 in capital to produce the new car.

The Doble steam generator offered greater thermal efficiency because of the large area exposed to heat—576 tubes, giving 150 square feet of heating surface. The fuel was completely burned within the generator's aluminum combustion chamber.

The Model C Doble was introduced at the New York automobile show in 1917. In spite of meager advance publicity, the new Doble turned out to be the sensation of the show. It was the machine itself which accomplished this, creating its own publicity by its amazing performance during demonstrations.

The public could hardly believe what it was seeing. Nobody had ever heard of a steam powered machine that started at the flick of an electric switch, and re-used its own water and steam. This machine could outperform the best of the internal combustion powered automobiles.

In a matter of days the headlines about the new Doble machine had reached far beyond the crowds at the New York show, and the mail began pouring in:

• From people who wanted to buy a Doble.
• From dealers who wanted franchises to sell them.
• From those who wanted to invest money in the Doble enterprise.

The mail became so heavy that, after a few days, the post office refused to deliver and Doble had to send trucks to pick up the mail. More than 50,000 letters were received and over 10,000 of the writers said they wished to place an order for a Doble steamer.

A Doble ad, a short time later, boasted that orders had been received for

$20,000,000 worth of steamers, that more than 1,000 dealers were waiting to sell and service the machines, and that demonstrator models would be in the hands of dealers by the spring of 1918.

The Doble-Detroit Steam Motors Company had been organized to produce the car. It seemed that nothing could stop Abner Doble from realizing his dream.

From Detroit to California: the rest of the story

On a day in 1923, a long, sleek automobile smoothly and silently approached the Grand Avenue Hill in San Francisco — a hill with a 27 percent grade that was known widely as "the hill of defeat" for the driver of many a powerful motor car of that day.

But this quiet, sleek car approached the killer grade and — with almost ridiculous ease — glided silently toward the top.

Then something seemed to go wrong. The car came to a sudden stop, halfway up the murderous grade. Had the machine run out of power, as so many other machines had done as they struggled at that slope? This would have been the guess of most bystanders on the street.

But the answer was no. A confident smile still appeared on the face of the driver. This stopping at mid-climb, with the nose of the car pointed upward, was simply a part of the plan to demonstrate the capabilities of the most incredible car in existence. In a moment, with almost impudent silence, the great car eased forward again without strain, and skimmed easily over the top of the hill at 25 mph.

The driver of any other car of that day, even the best of them, would have been accompanied by the roar of a racing engine, the clash of low gears and the belching of smoke from the exhaust — if, indeed, he climbed the hill at all.

And as for stopping and starting again, so silently and smoothly, this was simply beyond the capability of any motor car being made anywhere in the world.

But the automobile which performed this almost impossible feat in 1923 was no ordinary motor car. It was, in fact, the latest creation of Abner Doble, a man who very nearly gave the country a revolution in steam locomotion in the period between 1915 and 1930.

The Doble steam car had been the sensation of the 1917 New York auto show. Then things began to happen which replaced rainbows with storm clouds.

One of the first problems was that the country went to war, World War I. Government agencies refused to allocate steel to the Doble project. Faced with this fact, some of those helping to organize financial backing for the new company began to have second thoughts.

If Doble had been interested merely in making money, he probably could have salvaged the company. During the war it had converted to making high efficiency burners for kerosene-fired furnaces. The new furnace system used the electric-blower system developed by Doble for his cars.

But Doble was interested only in steam cars—and he himself may have contributed to the failure of the Detroit project by the very speed with which his brain kept jumping ahead with one improvement after another in the design of his cars. His mania for perfection sometimes delayed production while precious time passed and the buying public lost interest.

He decided that the uniflow steam engine he had developed was not the best design after all. He also decided that two cylinders in a steam car were not enough to produce the silky smoothness that would compete with the eight and 12-cylinder internal combustion machines already on the market. And he decided his multi-tube, vertical tube boiler was not as good as the monotube boiler.

So Doble decided to switch to a compound type steam engine, to increase his cylinders to four, and to switch to a monotube boiler in which a single coil of cold drawn steel tubing was coiled inside the outer casing of the boiler to expose the greatest possible area to burner heat. In the Doble boiler, the steel tube ended up being 575 feet long.

The monotube boiler was not a Doble invention. It had been used on other early

The DeLuxe Runabout came complete with a "disappearing seat under rear deck."

steam cars. But this design never reached sensational performance until it was exposed to the electric forced-air burner developed by Doble.

In any case, with the Detroit plant converted to making furnace burners, with difficulties in raising sufficient capital to start production of steam cars at war's end, plus the fact that he now planned a completely new design, in 1920 Doble decided to sever connections with the Detroit company and return to California to start over.

The Detroit chapter of the Doble story is a strange one. Various sources quote figures that range from three to 200 Dobles being made during this period. It is known that Abner made the one he used as a demonstrator. A news item in *Automobile Topics,* dated September 16, 1916, stated that five more were under construction. However, in subsequent news stories, production was always "about to begin." At one point it was announced that manufacture was being transferred to Chicago. It appears that very few Dobles were made, and not one is known to exist today. The few Dobles still in existence seem to be from the California phase of Doble history.

When Abner gave up the Detroit and Chicago projects to return to California, he joined with his brothers to organize a shop aimed at designing a new steam car. Abner brought along one Model D

to be used as the basis for the experimental work, but apparently this car was torn to pieces in the process of developing the vastly improved Model E.

The car designed at Doble Steam Motors in San Francisco embodied the changes Abner had been working out in his head—the compound engine design instead of the uniflow, the monotube boiler instead of the vertical tube design, and four cylinders instead of two.

Two of the cylinders were small, high pressure cylinders. The other two were larger, for lower pressure steam exhausted from the high pressure cylinders. All four pistons were on a five-inch stroke.

This arrangement injected steam at pressures of 750 pounds into the high pressure cylinders, then used the exhaust from the high pressure cylinders to obtain additional power through the low pressure cylinders. The valve arrangements of the compound engine injected steam both above and below the piston to create a power stroke on each stroke of the piston. (Published specifications on later Doble engines showed boiler pressures as high as 1,500 pounds.)

This high-low pressure steam cylinder system was not invented by Doble, but it reached a new peak of efficiency when it was used in connection with the unique Doble-developed electric-blower combustion system.

It is difficult to make a direct comparison in horsepower and performance between a steam engine and an internal combustion engine because the differences are so vast. The Doble Model E, with its four cylinders, had a cubic inch displacement of 213 inches and produced 125 bhp at 1,300 rpm's.

In comparison, the Packard Twin Six was a 12-cylinder machine with 424 cid —but rated at only 90 bhp at 2,600 rpm's. The Cadillac V-8's being produced at that time, with 314 cid, were rated at 87 bhp at 2,700 rpm's. The Lincoln V-8's, with 358 cid, were rated at 90 bhp at 2,800 rpm's.

But it was torque where the Doble truly outshone its gasoline powered brothers. It has been said that torque is the true measure of usable power on any engine and, while torque figures were not published with engine specifications in the 1920's, it has since been established that engines like the Packard Twin Six and the Lincoln and Cadillac V-8's were in the 175 to 200 foot-pound range. To make a torque comparison with the Doble, which provided peak torque at zero revolutions, you might note the statistic which gave the Doble 1,000 pounds of torque as it stood poised with a full head of steam, ready for a take-off.

How can you make that comparison when a gasoline internal combustion engine must be revved up and driven through a geared down gear box to produce power and torque? The Doble required no transmission, no clutch and no driveshaft because the engine was mounted at the rear, attached to the rear axle.

What would these performance figures mean if you decided to match a Doble in a "scratch off" or drag race against one of those Packards, Cadillacs or Lincolns? Test drivers for Doble often did that, and the race went like this:

The driver of the Packard, Caddy or Lincoln would rev up his engine, shift into low, hold down the clutch and wait for the go signal. The driver of the Doble would wait quietly, with his foot on the steam valve. At the signal, the Packard driver would slam out his clutch and roar his engine at top speed. The Doble driver would push on his accelerator and glide smoothly away.

At 15 to 20 miles per hour, the Packard driver would shove down on the clutch, jerk his transmission into second, roar the engine again until he got up to 25 or 30 mph and, meantime, stare at the rear end of the Doble disappearing ahead. At that point the Packard driver would repeat the clutch shift and roar procedure to get into high gear, then take off after the Doble in an attempt to catch up.

Which he couldn't do—for, it was said, the Doble could go from zero to 75 mph in 10 seconds and, in chassis form, could reach 108 mph. With the heavy Murphy bodies in place, that performance was reduced but the car would still do between 95 and 100. Meanwhile, top speed of the Packard-Cadillac-Lincoln group would be somewhere around 75, possibly 80. Usually less.

As for water consumption, tests on the new Doble showed that the steam machine, with its closely fitted parts and efficient recondensing system, would go nearly 500 miles on a gallon of water. Although Doble gave no fuel consumption figures, it has been found that the big Dobles would do from eight to 15 miles per gallon on kerosene fuel, depending on speed and operating conditions.

Then there was the matter of the quick starting of the engine on a cold morning. Even on the earlier Detroit Dobles, the electric-blower system had reduced start-up time to as little as one or two minutes. With the Model E, Doble had improved that time. At a 1924 stockholders' meeting, Doble told of a test made under the auspices of the American Automobile Club.

In this test a Model E was left to stand in an unheated garage on a night when the temperature dropped to 32 degrees. Early in the morning the Doble was pushed out of its garage and allowed to stand in the open for another hour and a half. Then the ignition switch was flipped on. In 23 seconds, the boiler had reached operating pressure of 750 pounds steam. In 41 seconds, the driver pushed down on the accelerator and moved off with four passengers.

"It accelerated from 0 to 20 mph in 3.9 seconds and from 0 to 40 miles an hour in 12.5 seconds," Doble told his audience. Try that with a 1923 Packard or

Lincoln — or try it with a later model gasoline powered car.

Meanwhile, the Model E's new four-cylinder engine was as smooth as a 16-cylinder Cadillac, which had not even been built at that time. Why make the comparison with a 16-cylinder engine? With the four pistons on the Doble steamer given a power push on every stroke, both up and down — compared to one power stroke out of four on a four-cycle, internal combustion engine—you truly had the same results as on a 16-cylinder engine.

Up to this time, the makers of the well known steamers had been able to produce a usable product which had one big advantage over internal combustion powered cars. This was zero torque, which eliminated the clutch and transmission, giving super performance at low speed.

But the 1923 Doble managed to match the internal combustion car in almost every aspect, and was far superior in most. It was the first practical substitute for the internal combustion engine.

From its outside appearance the Doble gave hardly a sign that it was different from the gasoline motor car. With its Murphy custom body, the Doble was among the most beautiful cars on the road. Even the hood, which covered the high pressure steam boiler, was of conventional design and might have covered a straight eight engine. The engine, under the floorboard at the rear, was a pancake type that occupied much less room than a conventional engine.

The Doble even appeared to have a radiator, just like its gasoline powered rivals. In a sense it *was* a radiator, for it served as the body of the condenser, converting the exhaust steam back to water for reheating and turning back to steam.

With such a machine, such performance and such handsome coachwork, it would seem that everything was coming up roses for the Doble brothers. The truth was something different. Financial troubles once more were plaguing the Doble enterprise.

When the new enterprise first got under way, the Dobles planned not only to produce the Model E Deluxe, in the luxury car field, but also a smaller, less expensive steam car. To be called the

A radiator shroud reminiscent of an internal combustion engine powered car hides Doble's steam lineage. (Photo courtesy of Henry Ford Museum)

Simplex, it would sell for $2,000. Other plans called for Doble engines to power boats, trucks and industrial machinery.

The company obtained permission to issue stock and made plans for a reinforced concrete production plant at nearby Emeryville. As the sale of stock began, the company, capitalized at $5,000,000, also began a limited production. Abner Doble made his presence felt in the machine shops, in his constant pressure for higher precision standards to match the finest machine work being done anywhere in the world.

Parts for the new Doble steam cars were machined to tolerances as close as one-ten-thousandths of an inch. Determined to produce the best, Doble had a mania for precision. And, by the very nature of its design, a steam engine required precision fit of moving parts — valves, slide rods and packing glands to contain the high pressure steam.

A machine made with such painstaking production methods inevitably became expensive, especially when the bodies mounted on these cars were custom-made Murphy coaches. As the first Dobles came out of the plant, the price on the bare chassis was $6,800. With the Murphy bodies, it ranged from $8,000 to $12,000.

Even with such price tags, the Dobles found a ready market among the wealthy and the notable. Hollywood stars bought them and parked them proudly beside their Packards and Pierce-Arrows. Howard Hughes bought two Dobles and said of his steam cars, "I know them all, but I prefer the Dobles."

But while Abner Doble and his brothers were getting the production plant built, machinery bought and production under way, events were taking place on the financial front which spelled disaster ahead.

Financial troubles struck the Doble enterprise in 1923 and 1924. As the Doble stock went on the market, some of the shares were sold by agents who never turned the proceeds over to the company. The company ended up as the principal defendant in lawsuits from irate stockholders.

Although stock agents and other representatives had been responsible for the alleged frauds, it was Abner Doble, as president of the company, who was held responsible. He was fined $5,000 and sentenced to a term in jail. And, while the jail sentence was eventually set aside, the publicity shattered public confidence in the project. Financial support faded away.

Abner Doble and his brothers were forced to sell property acquired for future expansion, and assets needed to keep the firm going. The brothers traveled about the country trying to drum up new support, citing the magnificent performance of the Model E. But it was all in vain.

During the next few years, Abner managed to keep the company alive by doing repair work and research, at a greatly reduced scale. The results of that research brought forth still another model, with higher steam pressure, more power, and other refinements. A few Model F's, the last of the Doble steamers, were produced in 1929 and 1930.

Most observers believe that, as late as 1929, Abner Doble had a chance to get his car into production. But fate—in the form of the greatest economic depression of the century—was about to strike the entire country.

It was against this bleak background that Doble made his final plea in banks and board rooms to obtain financial backing. But his pleas fell on deaf ears. Healthier and better established companies than his were in the process of going broke.

By 1932 Doble Steam Motors Company was bankrupt. It was taken over by William and George Besler, railroad men, who used the Doble patents and produced steam engines under their own name. Doble type engines produced by the Besler firm powered electric generators, boats and even an experimental airplane.

Abner Doble went to England, where he did engineering work for a company making steam trucks. Later, back in the U.S., he continued to seek out other steam projects. But the dream that had driven him throughout his lifetime — of convincing America that steam was a better way to go—always eluded him.

Among the people who knew steam and steam engineers, the name of Abner Doble always ranked near the top. Some said that he was the greatest steam engineer the country had produced. But when he died of a heart attack in 1961, his passing was hardly noted in the press.

He is survived only by a handful of his "children," the fine Doble machines he built in his lifetime. It is interesting to read the report of a man named Dick Hempel, the owner of a 1925 Model E steamer, as it was published in the *Horseless Carriage Gazette* a few years ago.

"I drive my Doble every day, to the grocery store, to the airport. I drive it on the freeways and boulevards along with modern traffic and have no trouble whatsoever. Have you tried this recently with a 1925 Lincoln, Cadillac, Packard or Duesenberg?"

Hempel wrote with glee of the puzzled motorists who pull up beside him at a stoplight, notice the vintage model of his car and listen for the sound of the engine. When faced with complete silence, their reaction is, "Ah ha, you killed your engine." The grin turns to a gape of astonishment when the light turns green and that "killed" engine pulls the heavy car away in a smooth glide—more often than not, in front of the gaping driver.

Abner Doble, despite his genius and his magnificent accomplishments, did fail to solve one great problem with steam: freeze-up. But it is highly probable that,

if Doble had obtained commercial success and adequate financial backing, he would have solved this problem, too.

It is difficult, even in hindsight, to predict what might have happened:

- If the government had not denied Abner Doble his steel in 1917.
- If there had been no stock manipulation and the Doble project of 1923 had gotten under way.
- If the 1929 stock market crash had not prevented Doble from obtaining backing for his final effort.

Certainly, if these things had not happened, there would have been many more Doble steam cars than the handful of perhaps 50 which actually were made.

The easiest thing to say is that Abner Doble failed. But he succeeded, magnificently, in creating the machines which were the true object of his lifelong devotion—great steam automobiles.

If there was a failure, it was more from lack of support from agencies which could have made other decisions. If Abner Doble had been blessed with a capable manager who could have solved the financial problems and left Doble alone to tinker with his machines, we might indeed be riding in non-polluting, silky smooth, steam powered automobiles today.

Abner Doble would have liked that.

VIII
DORRIS

Mark Twain could have had fun with this story: the story of George Preston Dorris.

It's a chronicle that has, somewhere at its beginning, the rollicking tale of two young self-styled "river rats":

- Who used their mechanical ingenuity to outwit government regulations.
- Who refused to hoist the white flag when they became—unwillingly—pioneer guinea pigs in the effects of an early day gasoline explosion...a blast which flipped them bodily into the Cumberland River.
- Whose spirits weren't dampened, as their britches were, when their "launch" struck a rock and sank.

It is the story of a man who became one of the true pioneers of the American auto industry, a worthy contemporary of men like Henry Ford, Henry Leland, Ransom Olds, Walter Chrysler or the Dodge brothers. He was a man who created engines, automobiles, new inventions; a man devoted first to craftsmanship, ahead of the dollar.

It is a story which must be shared, in part at least, with his elder brother, Duncan R. Dorris, who provided him with the workshop and the indulgence to tinker, and with John L. French, the other half of the river rat team.

It was the brash young George who, as a lad, became entranced at the sight of early Otto engines chomping away in Nashville, tied to their umbilical cords of illuminating gas for fuel. He decided, while yet a stripling, that he would attend Vanderbilt University to study engineering so that he, too, could build an engine. It is likely, even then, that he dreamed of making an engine independent of the gas pipe. But the Vanderbilt career was a short one.

"He quit after one year, when he decided he knew more about engines than his professors did," recalled George's older brother some years later.

George Preston Dorris, one of the true pioneers of the American auto industry, was devoted to craftsmanship, rather than the dollar.

It was around 1890 when Dorris and his boyhood buddy, John French, somehow acquired a coal-burning steam launch as a business venture, hauling excursion parties on the river—until the day when a government steam inspector came around and discovered that the pair were too young to obtain licenses to operate a steamboat on the river.

However, the law specifically spelled out the word "steam," and this was what set wheels to turning in the computer brain of George P. Dorris. "The law doesn't say anything about a gasoline engine," he opined, and hied himself to his workbench and lathe.

"I was running a bicycle shop on Church Street in Nashville at that time," remembered brother Duncan. "George had a lathe in the shop and did all my repair work.

"But he never came to work before noon, because when the shop closed in the evening, he would stay there and work all night on his gasoline engine. So I really only got a half day's work out of him."

It was sometime late in 1891 when George finished his first gasoline engine —a two-cylinder, upright 5 x 5—cranked it up, and installed it in the launch in place of the steam engine.

Needless to say, it was the first gasoline engine ever built in Nashville, and created quite a sensation when it went chugging up and down the Cumberland River. The youthful pair, Dorris and French, were now able to thumb their noses at the steamboat inspector, for laws had not yet been written about gasoline engines.

However, the young engine pioneers soon found out that gasoline fumes in a boat could be as dangerous as an overheated steam boiler, for one day an accumulation of such fumes in the hold went bang.

"It flipped George out of one side of the boat and French out the other side," recalled elder brother Duncan. "But they were not hurt."

The intrepid pair swam back to their boat, repaired the damage and continued to operate it — until the day they struck a rock and the launch sank. Fortunately, the river at this point was not very deep.

"When they hit bottom, they were standing up to their necks in water. The deck canopy was sticking out of water about a foot," remembered Duncan.

Somehow the youngsters managed to raise the boat and get it going once more.

Then came the fateful day in 1895 when George picked up a copy of *Scientific American* and read an account of the first automobile race ever run in the U.S., at Chicago. With his imagination fired in a new direction, George promptly abandoned the boat and decided to build a motor car.

By 1897, after two years of burning more of the midnight oil in the bicycle shop, George P. Dorris had his first automobile running: a high-wheeled, iron-tired, horse buggy type.

Dorris promptly learned his first lessons about swivel axle steering. He scarcely had his new contraption running before it flipped him into a ditch. In fact, on one occasion it flipped him into a ditch when he had his fiancee on board. Although unhurt, she lost her parasol, a fact young George was to hear about for months on end.

"George figured out what was wrong, and drew up a sketch for a steering knuckle system, took it to the foundry and had the parts cast," recalled Duncan. That put a stop to the ditch flipping.

It was a steering lesson almost every

The Dorris 6-80 Seven-Passenger Touring Car. Company sales literature touted this model as ". . . roomy enough to be comfortable, yet not too large to handle easily in close quarters . . . particularly desirable for women drivers."

early auto designer had to learn. After George redesigned the steering assembly, the car ran so well that he was able to make a 60-mile trip to Lebanon, Tennessee, and back—quite a trek for a 19th century machine.

Meanwhile, Dorris' boyhood pal French, of motor boat days, had moved to St. Louis to join a family venture in the piano manufacturing business. It was in St. Louis that French ordered a Winton automobile.

After waiting patiently, month after month, for delivery, he finally sent for George. "Let's build some automobiles," said French. And thus was born one of the real pioneer auto factories of America, the St. Louis Motor Carriage Co., with French as president and Dorris as vice-president and chief engineer.

Dorris sent back to Nashville to have his first auto shipped to St. Louis to use as a pattern for the company's first production.

"The first two cars manufactured in St. Louis by the St. Louis Motor Carriage Co. were practically copies of my first machine," said George Dorris in a brief autobiography written for publication about 1930. The engine was a copy of the river launch engine, except it was a 4 x 5 instead of a 5 x 5.

One of these first two cars was to make history by being, it is claimed, the first gasoline motor car to be sold or driven in the state of Texas. Its new owner was a man of some renown himself, Col. E.H.R. Green of Dallas, son of the famed Hetty Green, reputed to be not only the richest but also the stingiest woman in the world. However, her son didn't share her penchant for penny-pinching and was known as a free spender.

The second car was sold in St. Louis. These two cars were completed and sold in 1899 — the first production of the fledgling company.

By 1900, however, Dorris had developed an entirely new engine, this one a single-cylinder. It had the unique feature, probably the first of its kind, of having the transmission as an integral part of the engine, with the sliding gears running on oil.

It was also about this time, around 1900, when Dorris made and patented two devices which later found their way onto many another American car of the day:

- A locking device which kept a sliding gear transmission from going into more than one gear at once.
- A float feed carburetor, reputed to be the first in America.

The carburetor was put on the market by another pioneer in the auto business, A.L. Dyke, later to become famous for his well-known *Dyke's Automobile Encyclopedia.* Dyke was a close friend of Dorris' and acknowledged that Dorris had played the major part in designing the carburetor.

Dorris told friends he got the idea from seeing the float valve water closet operate in his bathroom. The young auto company also claimed that the St. Louis auto was the first American auto to be equipped with Timken bearings. In fact, H.H. Timken, of the bearing company, was another close friend of Dorris'.

The Dorris family recalled in later years the Sunday afternoon when Timken and Dorris sat on the front porch and Timken tried to talk Dorris into joining the bearing company. "No," replied Dorris. "I have my automobile business to look after."

It was around 1901 when the St. Louis Motor Carriage Co. produced its first truck. Typically enough, it was sold to the Jesse French Piano & Organ Co. to transport pianos. This machine also used the early two-cylinder design engine, but this was a huge 7 x 9 size. The company also produced a bus using this engine.

As early as 1902, still fired by the sprit of racing which had led to the construction of his first automobile, Dorris built his first experimental four-cylinder engine, a giant 5¼ x 6, which was installed in a combination touring-racing machine. Records show that this machine was clocked at 53.73 miles per hour, and won a free-for-all 10-mile race at the St. Louis Fair, running against all comers in American and French autos.

The most famous and most widely sold of the St. Louis cars of this period was the Boston model, introduced in 1902. It used the newly designed single-cylinder engine and had a body somewhat resembling the famed curve dash Oldsmobile. The model was probably named after Boston simply because, at that time, the city had one of the most successful St. Louis dealerships in the country. It was reported to have sold 65 St. Louis machines in 1901.

"This was practically the entire output of the St. Louis Motor Carriage Co. for that season," wrote Dorris in his autobiographical sketch. No wonder he was willing to name his new model for the city.

In 1902 fate struck a cruel blow at the young motor company. French, the company president, took one of the new Boston models to Pittsburgh, Pennsylvania, in an attempt to break into that city's market. It was while on a demonstration run in Pittsburgh that French collided with a streetcar and suffered injuries which brought about his death some six months later.

At first French's successor, Jesse French, Jr., was content to remain in St. Louis and, although production figures are not available among surviving papers owned by the Dorris family, Dorris later recalled that it was one of the flourishing periods of production. But by 1905, in a move intended to reduce production costs, French decided to move the St. Louis Motor Carriage Co. to Peoria, Illinois.

Dorris refused to go. He stayed in St. Louis and, by obtaining financial backing from a wealthy St. Louisian, H.B. Krenning, he established the new company that was finally to bear the name of the inventor and designer of the machines—the Dorris Motor Car Co. Krenning, however, became president of the new firm.

When the new Dorris Co. exhibited its first car in the New York automobile show in 1906, the newest Dorris machine incorporated an engine Dorris had been working on for several years, a four-cylinder "dream engine." The new engine, 4¼ x 5½, was a valve-in-head, valve-in-line motor.

"So far as I know, it was the first motor of this type," said Dorris himself.

This powerful and highly successful engine became the backbone of the Dorris automobile in the years to come, until the first six-cylinder was introduced in 1916. The four was, however, increased slightly in size later, to 4⅜ x 5½.

The first six-cylinder machine, the

Model 1-A-6, although a much larger and more powerful machine, 4 x 5, still had the blocks and heads cast in one piece. It was not until 1919 that the most famous and powerful of all the Dorris production engines appeared on the scene —the 6-80.

It was given this name simply because the engine developed an honest 80 horsepower. This was the first Dorris-designed engine with a detachable cylinder head.

It was during the period of the famed 6-80 that George P. Dorris, Jr., son of the inventor, had his first association with the company—as a test driver.

George, Jr., a highly skilled engineer in his own right, later commented: "I was only 12 years old then and I wasn't supposed to be driving the cars, especially not on the streets. But we took those 6-80 machines, in chassis form, out of the shop and if they wouldn't go 75 miles per hour we'd take them back and they'd work on them until they did."

In 1922 came the show car, the Pasadena. Basically it was a 6-80, but a luxury model with leather upholstery and deluxe trim.

George Fuchs, an old friend of the family in St. Louis, located one of these Pasadena models in California in 1953, and bought it for $75. Carefully restored, it became the show piece of Fuchs' collection of Dorris cars.

Anyone examining one of the Dorris engines that survive today would be forced to agree that the company slogan, "Built up to a standard, not down to a price," was no idle boast. Superb craftsmanship and engineering are in every part. One example is the roller bearings on the overhead rocker arm assembly, with additional rollers on the tappet ends.

Another feature of the Dorris engines for many years, a patented engineering design available as an accessory on other makes of cars, was the famed Dorris Distillator. This gadget was developed during the years when the low grade gasoline available had what was called "heavy ends"—heavy petroleum residue which refused to burn, especially until a motor car was well warmed. The results were that this residue was drawn through the motor, destroying the efficiency of the

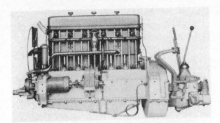

In 1919, the six-cylinder production engine featured a detachable cylinder head which made " . . . the necessity for grinding valves much less frequent."

lubrication and diluting the oil.

Dorris designed an intake manifold with low pockets between the cylinders which trapped the unburned "heavy ends" until the motor became hot enough to vaporize them — to draw them into the cylinders as vapor to be burned.

To demonstrate the distillator, Dorris designed a demonstration model with little drain pipes running from the manifold pockets to little glass vials. As the motor started cold, you could actually see the "heavy ends" collecting in the glass vials and finally being drawn off and burned as the motor warmed. This is an invention that would be of little use today, with our high octane fuels, but in his day it was a highly efficient contribution to the engineering of contemporary automobiles.

Actually the Dorris machine, regardless of its high quality and satisfied owners, was never a great financial success. The exacting, hand-crafted production methods simply made production costs too high. In the later years of the company, it was the Dorris trucks and buses that kept the company going. The passenger car was never mass produced and the most optimistic — perhaps over-optimistic — production report published told of a peak of 1,000 cars in 1922.

Few company records and papers survive today. Those still in existence have authentic production records of the Dorris car for only one year, 1923. Exactly 100 cars were produced.

If serial numbers in *Branham's Automobile Reference Book* for 1922 can be trusted, they show:

• 110 Dorris cars made in 1915
• 180 in 1916, the year the first six-cylinder machine was introduced

• 194 for 1917
• 92 for 1918
• 274 in 1919, the year the 6-80 was introduced
• 396 for 1920.

George, Jr., who was a youth at the time, believed that these production figures were probably correct. He recalled that the Dorris plant, which also manufactured the trucks and buses, employed about 200 workers.

"When Dodge came out in the early 1920s with the die-pressed steel bodies, mass produced at low cost, that spelled the end for small, independent shops like Dorris," said George, Jr.

By 1926 the last Dorris auto had rolled out of the shops; another name forced to the wall by high production costs — and George P. Dorris' unrelenting search for quality.

But when production of the Dorris automobile came to an end, it was far from the end of the long, productive life of George P. Dorris, Sr. He later organized the Dorris Speed Reduction Co., of St. Louis, and continued to produce finely engineered speed reduction equipment. The company was later operated by his son.

Far past the age when most men are doddering on a cane, or creeping about in wheelchairs, George P. Dorris continued the highly active pace of his inventive years. "Grandfather could still go off a 12-foot diving board when he was 80," recalled George III, in 1968.

It was during the six-cylinder years of the Dorris car that Dorris returned to his first love, the river, and obtained for himself a boat. It was the Mississippi River this time, and installed in his boat was one of the big 6-80 engines.

"That was quite a boat," said George, Jr. The family also remembered that when Dorris went out for a cruise with this highly dynamic craft, he was only allowed to take one of the children along.

"Mother knew he was a good enough swimmer to rescue one child if something happened to the boat, but she didn't trust him to rescue two," said George, Jr., who was one of the youngsters who got his share of river thrills on that powerful boat.

Dorris was in his 70s when he found, in California, one of his famous Boston

The Sedan. Each early 6-80 was road-tested to be sure it would go 75 miles per hour.

models of 1902 vintage, bought it and brought it back to St. Louis.

He not only fully restored it but, since he intended to do some driving in it, added a few items like hydraulic brakes, a generator, electric headlights, and late model wheels with modern tires.

When friends chided him about this, saying it would destroy the authenticity of the machine, the elder Dorris retorted, "I'm the man who designed and built this automobile in the first place. If I want to change it, I have a perfect right to do it. It will still be an authentic Dorris model."

Nobody could argue with that. And it was still while he was in his active senior years that he took great pride in driving the perky little machine on trips, just to prove that he made good automobiles in 1902. In 1949, for example, he drove it all the way to the Minnesota Aqua Centennial, a total round trip distance of 1,253 miles — no bad feat for a 1902 model.

In 1951 he took the machine to Texas, on a commemorative run of that date, back in 1899, when it was a Dorris-built and designed machine that became the first automobile to be sold in the Lone Star state. He drove the little one-lunged machine from Dallas to Terrell and back, averaging 30 miles per hour. What better way to prove that Dorris quality?

That "Boston Baby" eventually went to George P. Dorris III, who also did a bit of restoring on his own, on one of the last experimental models made by his grandfather — a 6-80 type engine with an overhead cam cylinder head.

In 1968 Dorris III, admitted that he might make a few improvements on this car, too, but — as a genuine grandson of the man who started the Dorris story — he felt he had a right to do that.

"Grandfather wouldn't mind," he said. "After all, I'm a Dorris too."

This is the Dorris story.

It's the saga of a man who has not always been credited for the great part he played in the creation of the American automobile. Too often, in talking to old car fans, one mentions the name "Dorris" and hears the remark, "Oh, yes, one of those assembly cars."

This is injustice, per se, to the man who built his first gasoline engine in 1890... to the man whose personality was stamped on every Dorris engine ever made... to the man whose engineering genius spoke most loudly in the throb of the big 6-80.

Dorris models

An examination of available records of the Dorris Motor Co. indicates that from the time the company was first formed, in 1905, until the end of production in 1926, the following model designations were used:

1905—Model A
1906—Model B
1907—Model C

1908—Model D
1909-1910—Model E
1911—Model F
1912—Model G
1913—Model H
1914—Model I
1915—1-A-4
1916—1-A-6 (first six-cylinder)
1917—1-B-6
1918—1-C-6
1919 — 6-80 (the first motor with detachable cylinder head)
1919 through 1926—6-80 continued
1922 — Pasadena luxury model introduced.

Dorris racing and competition records

In the early years of American auto manufacturing, many a car won or lost its reputation — often, its very existence — on the basis of races won and record runs. Here is the known record of Dorris races and endurance runs. It includes some records set by St. Louis machines, designed and built by Dorris.

1900— November, record run, New York to Boston without changing gears.

1900— First International Autumn Exhibition and Race Meet, Chicago, Illinois. Second place, grade climbing competition.

1900— Only American car that took Fort Lee Hill, New York, in high gear.

1902— Dorris-designed four-cylinder experimental racer won Free-for-All, 10-mile race, St. Louis Fair.

1903— October 28, Gold Medal winner, three-mile race, Brightwood, Washington, D.C.

1904— June 14, first prize for cars under 1,800 pounds, one-mile stock car race.

1904— November 5, first prize, championship race, Delmar Track, St. Louis.

1909— Won first place, Hermitage Cup Race, Nashville, 50 miles.

1911— August 14-18, won prize, perfect road and technical score, Cross-State Reliability Run, St. Louis Motor Association.

1921— For three consecutive years, Dorris 6-80 won California economy run for cars in its class.

INDEX

Abner Doble Motor Vehicle Manufacturing Co.: *196.*
American Automobile Association: *28-31.*
American Motor Car Co.: *3.*
American Underslung: *3.*
Anderson, Gil: *4, 6-12.*
Atlas Motor Car Co.: *175.*
Bendix, Vincent: *134.*
Booker, George W.: *182-183.*
Boyer, Joe: *56-57.*
Brown, Alexander T.: *86.*
Buehrig, Gordon: *78.*
Bugatti, Ettore: *30.*
Burns, John: *111.*
Chadwick: *58.*
Christopher, George: *153.*
Cobb, John: *76.*
Columbia Motor Car Co.: *175.*
Cooper, Earl: *9-12, 57.*
Cord: *78.*
Cord, E.L.: *68, 71, 78.*
Crawford, Charles S.: *20.*
Curtis-Wright: *160.*
Daimler Motor Co.: *174-175, 180.*
D'Alene, Wilbur: *51-52.*
Dayton Motor Co.: *175.*
DeCausse, Frank: *108.*
DePalma, Ralph: *55, 148.*
DePaolo, Pete: *56-57, 61.*
Die casting: *84, 96.*
Doble
  Depression, effects of: *203.*
  Fast-start features: *197.*
  Monotube boiler: *199-200.*
  Series/models/engines: Model A *196;* Model B *196;* Model C *198;* Model E *201-203;* Simplex *47, 203.*
  World War I, effects of: *199.*
Doble-Detroit Steam Motors Co.: *198-199.*
Doble Steam Motors Co.: *200-203.*
Doman, Carl: *89.*
Dorris
  Distillator: *208-209.*
  Production/sales statistics: *208, 210-211.*
  Racing: *211.*
  Series/models/engines: Boston 208 *210-211;* Bus *209;* Pasadena *208;* Truck *207, 209.*
Dorris, George P., Jr.: *208-209.*
Dorris Motor Car Company: *208.*
Dorris Speed Reduction Co.: *209.*
Duesenberg
  Hydraulic brakes: *64-65, 70.*
  Marine engines: *48-49, 54, 62.*
  Production/sales statistics: *66, 71, 73, 79.*
  Racing: *42, 44-45, 47, 49-62, 74, 76-77.*
  Series/models/engines: Boattail Speedster *79;* Double walking beam engine *53;* Duesenberg-Mason *47-49;* Duesenberg-Maytag *46-47;* Duesenberg-Miller *60;* Model A *62-67;* Model J *34, 67-75, 77, 79-80;* Model SJ *76-77;* Walking beam

engine *46-49, 65.*
  Supercharger: *57-58, 60, 67, 74.*
Duesenberg, August: *42-43, 76-77.*
Duesenberg, Fred: *42-45, 55, 74-75.*
Duesenberg Motor Co.: *52, 66, 68.*
Dyke, A.L.: *207.*
Endicott, Harry: *47.*
Frame, Fred: *59.*
Franklin
  Dyneto system: *104.*
  Production/sales statistics: 87-88, 92, 99-100, 105-106, 109, 112, 115, 118.
  Races: *87, 92-94, 98-102, 106, 113.*
  Series/models/engines: Flying Cloud Six *118;* Model Z *115-116;* 1901 prototype *85-86;* Olympic *116;* Series Four *105;* Series Five *105;* Series Seven *105;* Series Eight *105;* Series Nine *109-110;* Series Ten *109-111;* Series Twelve *115;* Series 13 *115;* Series Fourteen *115;* Series Fifteen *115;* Series Eighteen-B *116-117;* Series Nineteen-A *119;* Six *91-92, 97-99, 104-105, 114-115;* Six-Thirty *105;* "Telephone booth" *99;* Type A *88-89, 91;* Type B *89-91;* Type C *89-91, 95;* Type D *89, 91-92, 95, 104;* Type E *89, 91-92;* Type F *89, 91;* Type G *92-95, 99, 104;* Type H *91-92, 104;* Type K *100;* Type L *100;* Type M *104, 106.*
  Valve-in-valve: *95-96, 102-103.*
Franklin, H.H.: *86-87, 107-108.*
Franklin, H.H. Co.: *22, 86-87, 94-95, 100, 106-107, 115-116, 118-119.*
Gorrell, Edgar S.: *38-39.*
Greuter, Charles R.: *23-25, 29.*
HCS Motor Car Co.: *19.*
Hamlin, Ralph: *100-102, 107-108.*
H.C.S. Specials: *2.*
Hispano-Suiza Boulogne: *32-33.*
"Hot engine" principle: *103-104.*
Hudson Motor Car Co.: *146.*
Indianapolis 500: *1, 5-6, 8-9, 39, 47, 50-52, 56-58, 59-62, 77, 174.*
Jeffery, Thos. B. Co.: *42-45.*
Jenkins, Ab: *76-77.*
Joy, Henry B.: *141, 148.*
Kissel Industries: *138.*
Kissel Kar
  Early prototypes: *123, 125.*
  Racing: *101.*
  Series/models/engines: "All-year" convertible *127-128, 130, 133, 135;* Coach sedan *133;* 8-65 *136;* 8-75 *135;* "50" Touring *122, 124;* Gold Bug Silver Speedster *131, 133-134;* Semi-racer *125;* "Six" *125;* 6-48 *126-127;* 6-55 *132-133, 135;* 6-60 *127;* Staggered Door Sedan *133;* Trucks *130;* Western special *126;* White Eagle Deluxe *136.*
Kissel Motor Car Co.: *123.*
Knight, Charles Y.: *173-175, 191.*
Lawson, O.T.: *187.*
LeMans: *1, 58-59, 61, 33-34, 37-39.*
Leonard, H.J.: *187, 191.*
Lockhart, Frank: *31, 33, 61.*
Loew-Victor Engine Co.: *52-54.*

Macauley, Alvan: *143, 145, 148.*
Marion Motor Car Co.: *4-5.*
Marmon-Nordyke: *22.*
Mason: *44-45.*
Mason, Edward R.: *42-45.*
Mason Motor Car Co.: *44-45.*
Maytag: *47.*
Maytag, Fred L.: *46.*
McKuen, Edwin: *116-117.*
Merlin aircraft: *156.*
Miller, Harry: *60-61.*
Milton, Tommy: *53, 55-56.*
Moscovics, Fred: *2, 22-37.*
Murphy, Jimmy: *55-57, 59-61.*
Murphy, Walter H. Co.: *108.*
National: *101.*
New York Automobile Co.: *83.*
O'Donnell, Eddie: *49-52.*
Ohio Automobile Co.: *140.*
Oldfield, Barney: *8, 11, 50, 166.*
Packard
 Production/sales statistics: *142, 147, 152, 154-157, 159-160.*
 Racing: *141-142.*
 Series/models/engines: Clipper *156-167;* 18th Series *156;* 14th Series *154;* "Gray Wolf" *153;* Model C *143;* Model F *140;* Model K *142-143;* Model L *142;* 110 *155;* 116 *148;* 120 *153-154;* 180 *155;* 1-25 *147-148;* 1-35 *147-148;* Phantom *158;* Single Six *148-149;* Standard Eight *150;* Super Eight *154;* 30 *142-143;* Twelve *144, 152, 155;* 22nd Series *158;* 24th Series *159;* Twin Six *144, 146-149.*
 World War I, effects on: *144, 148.*
 World War II, effects on: *156-157.*
Packard Motor Car Co.: *140-141, 151-152, 155, 159-160.*
Palmer, Herman: *121, 124, 133.*
Patschke, Cyrus: *169.*
PT boats: *156.*
Pool, Al: *169.*
Rickenbacher, Eddie: *12.*
Rowland, W.W. ("Brownie"): *131.*
Ruxton: *138.*
Sanford, L.M.: *182.*
Schmidt, Charles: *141.*
Shoemaker, Glen: *114.*
Silent-Knights: *173-174.*
Silver, Conover T.: *130-131.*
Souders, George: *61.*
St. Louis Motor Carriage Co.: *207.*
Stanley Steamer: *195-196.*
Stearns and Stearns-Knight
 Double jet carburetor: *168.*
 Production/sales statistics: *170, 176, 181-183, 185, 190.*
 Racing: *162, 164-169.*
 Series/models/engines: B-4 *185-186;* C-6-75 *186-187;* D-6-85 *187-188;* 15-30 *171-172;* 45-90 *161-162, 166-172;* 4-cycle one-cylinder *161, 164;* 4-cylinder *165, 168;* 4-cylinder monobloc *172;* 4-cylinder sleeve valve *173-176, 181;* G-8-85 *188-189;* H-8-90 *189-190;* J-8-90 *189-190;* L-4 *180-181, 183, 185;* Model

M *190;* Model N *190;* S-6 *185-186;* 6-cylinder sleeve valve *177-178;* Stearns-Knight Four *173, 176-177;* 30-60 *161, 167-172, 177;* 2-cylinder opposed *164;* V-8 sleeve valve *179-180, 182, 183.*
 World War I, effects of: *180.*
Stearns, Frank B.: *161-164, 169, 179, 181-183, 189, 192.*
Stearns, F.B. Co.: *162, 164-165, 171, 175-176, 181-182, 187, 190-191.*
Sterling, James G.: *162, 165, 174-176, 183.*
Stewart vacuum tank system: *130.*
Stutz
 Challenger engine: *31-32.*
 High performance engine: *24.*
 Hydraulic brakes: *27.*
 Models/series: Bearcat *3, 15-17, 177;* Black Hawk *29, 31-34;* Blackhawks *36;* Bulldog *15-16;* DV-32 *3, 39;* Series A *1;* Series B *15;* Series E *15;* Series R *16;* Speedway six *21, 28;* Super Bearcat *39;* Torpedo Speedster *39;* Vertical Eight Safety *25-26.*
 Production/sales statistics: *17, 35.*
 Racing: *1-2, 6-12, 28-31, 32-34, 37-39, 50.*
Stutz Fire Engine Co.: *19.*
Stutz, Harry C.: *2-5.*
Stutz Motor Car Co.: *5-20, 24.*
Timken, H.H.: *207.*
Tone, Fred I.: *4.*
Trumble, John T.: *187.*
Ultramatic transmission: *159.*
"Uniflow" steam system: *196-198.*
Van Ranst, C.W.: *53.*
Vaughn, Guy: *168, 183.*
Vincent, Jesse G.: *143-145, 151-152.*
Weidley engine: *128.*
Werner, J.F.: *121, 124, 127.*
White Squadron: *8-12.*
White Steamer: *123.*
Wilkinson, John: *82-83, 106-109.*
Williams, Paul: *110.*
Willys, John North: *5, 173, 186-187, 190, 191.*
Willys-Overland Co.: *187.*
Winton, Alexander: *139-142.*